AQA

AS Business
Studies

John Wolinski & Gwen Coates

Philip Allan Updates
Market Place
Deddington
Oxfordshire
OX15 0SE

Orders
Bookpoint Ltd, 130 Milton Park, Abingdon, Oxfordshire, OX14 4SB
tel: 01235 827720
fax: 01235 400454
e-mail: uk.orders@bookpoint.co.uk
Lines are open 9.00 a.m.–5.00 p.m., Monday to Saturday, with a 24-hour message
answering service. You can also order through the Philip Allan Updates website:
www.philipallan.co.uk

© Philip Allan Updates 2004

ISBN-13: 978-0-86003-753-8
ISBN-10: 0-86003-753-3

This textbook has been written specifically to support students studying AQA
Advanced Business Studies. The content has been neither approved nor endorsed
by AQA and remains the sole responsibility of the authors.

All efforts have been made to trace copyright on items used.

All website addresses included in this book are correct at the time of going to press
but may subsequently change.

Design and artwork by Juha Sorsa and Gary Kilpatrick
Printed in Italy

Philip Allan Updates' policy is to use papers that are natural, renewable and
recyclable products and made from wood grown in sustainable forests. The logging
and manufacturing processes are expected to conform to the environmental regulations of the country of origin.

Contents

Module 2 People and Operations Management

People in organisations

Operations management

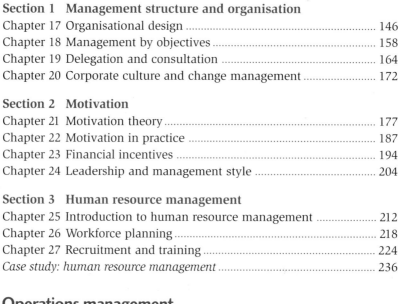

Module 3 External Influences and Objectives and Strategy

External influences

Objectives and strategy

Index

Introduction

This textbook has been written specifically to meet the needs of students taking AQA AS Business Studies. It provides comprehensive coverage of the subject content of the AQA AS specification, module by module, section by section, as it is laid out in the specification document.

Up-to-date examples and illustrations from real-life organisations and situations are used throughout the book in order to help you to recognise the dynamic and changing nature of business studies and its relevance to society.

Course coverage and how to use this book

Terminology

All A-level specifications use the following terms:
- a **module** is a body of learning (i.e. the content of the specification)
- a **unit** is the method of assessment (e.g. an examination or a piece of coursework)

Structure

This book follows the order of the AQA AS Business Studies specification. The specification is divided into three modules, each of which is split into two parts.
- **Module 1:** 'Marketing' is covered in Chapters 1 to 10; 'Accounting and Finance' is covered in Chapters 11 to 16.
- **Module 2:** 'People in Organisations' is covered in Chapters 17 to 27; 'Operations Management' is covered in Chapters 28 to 34.
- **Module 3:** 'External Influences' is covered in Chapters 35 to 44; 'Objectives and Strategy' is covered in Chapters 45 to 51.

For each module, the order of the chapters in this book provides a logical progression of learning, with the later chapters building on the theory and understanding acquired in the earlier chapters. Some questions at the end of chapters also assume an understanding of work in previous chapters.

Module 1
The view of the authors is that it is advisable to follow the order of the specification and commence with Module 1 for two main reasons:

- The 'lower level' skills are tested to a greater extent in this module, making the transition to AS easier.
- It enables you to sit the Unit 1 (BUS1) examination in January of your AS year. This relieves the time pressure facing you in June of your AS year, as all three of the AS Business Studies examinations are scheduled for the same morning or afternoon in the examination timetable.

However, this is not a clear-cut decision and your teacher will decide on the most appropriate sequence of chapters for your learning.

Chapters 45, 47 and 49

Although working through the book from Chapter 1 to Chapter 51 would ensure that the topics in the AS course are developed in a progressive manner, there is one exception to this logic. The second part of Module 3 (Objectives and Strategy) is placed at the end of the course because 'this module section draws together all the other modules' and 'emphasises the interactive nature of the business world'. However, three of the chapters in this section (Chapters 45, 47 and 49) act as a foundation for many other topics within the course by providing the background knowledge needed to understand business activity, the types of business organisation, the legal structure of business units, and the ways in which business organisations set their aims and objectives. For this reason, the authors suggest that you study Chapters 45, 47 and 49 at the beginning of your course. These chapters are shaded in a different colour from the other chapters in the 'Objectives and Strategy' section of Module 3, to highlight the fact that they can be studied out of sequence.

These three chapters each conclude with two practice exercises. If you study these chapters at the beginning of your course, you should only answer the first practice exercise in each chapter at this point. The questions for the second practice exercise in each of these chapters are based on more advanced, integrated issues. You should only attempt to answer these exercises at the end of your AS course. Of course, if you cover these chapters in sequence (i.e. towards the end of your course), then you should answer both sets of practice exercises on completion of the relevant chapter.

Special features

This book contains several special features designed to aid your understanding of the requirements of the AQA AS Business Studies course.

Key terms

These are clear, concise definitions of the main terms needed for the course. In Module 1, every term in the AQA specification is included as a key term to enable you to respond accurately to all of the part (a) questions that require terms to be explained. An accurate understanding of the definitions of key terms will reduce the chances of you producing irrelevant answers in all three modules.

Examiner's voice

Both authors have over 20 years' experience of examining and have used this to provide snippets of advice that will help you to present your ideas effectively and to avoid potential pitfalls. Some of this advice is specific to a particular topic; the remainder is general advice on how you should approach the examinations.

Fact files

Topical examples from the world of business are included at regular intervals in order to help you to develop your application skills by showing how the business ideas you have studied can be applied to real-life situations. The fact files will also help you to increase your awareness of current developments and practices.

Did you know?

These boxes are placed throughout the book; they provide useful insights into the ideas and concepts covered in the AS course and their use in businesses. The comments will help you to improve your understanding of business activities.

What do you think?

On occasions, facts or comments on business activity are presented in the form of a challenge — what do you think? There is often a range of possible solutions to business problems or many differing consequences to an action. These boxes will get you thinking about possible alternative solutions or consequences.

Group exercises

These are included when a part of the specification lends itself to discussion or a cooperative approach to study.

Practice exercises

Over 80 different practice exercises are provided to help you to check your understanding of the topics you have covered within each chapter. Many of these exercises are geared towards testing knowledge, but several are based on relevant articles. You can use the latter type to test your higher level skills, such as evaluation. Although individual questions within a practice exercise may match the style of AQA AS questions, overall the practice exercises do not adopt the AQA examination style — the case studies perform this role.

Case studies

A common problem facing both teachers and students is finding suitable material for examination practice. The examinations are based on the whole of the specification and so, on completion of a particular topic, it is not possible to find a past examination paper that sets a realistic challenge. To fill this gap, over 50 examination-style questions have been included in this book. The heading 'case study' is used wherever the style of the questions is the same as in the AQA AS examinations.

Unit 1

In the Unit 1 examination there are two 30-minute stimulus-response (sometimes known as data-response) questions worth 25 marks each. They are based on stimulus material and cover Marketing and Accounting and Finance. Thus, in Module 1 virtually every chapter concludes with a 30-minute 'case study' question based on the material included in that chapter in the style of the Unit 1 stimulus-response questions.

In addition to this, two 'integrated case studies' are included at the end of both the Marketing and the Accounting and Finance sections. These test the whole of Marketing and Accounting and Finance respectively.

Units 2 and 3

The Unit 2 and Unit 3 examinations are based on a single 2,500–3,000 word pre-issued case study. It would not be appropriate to produce a series of such lengthy case studies at the end of each chapter in Modules 2 and 3 of this book. Instead, where there is sufficient breadth to a chapter (or set of chapters), a 'case study' has been produced that can be read in 5–10 minutes. This material provides the background for a 1-hour set of five questions that reflect the style of questions posed in these two examinations exactly. Thus in 60 minutes it is possible for you to test your understanding under similar conditions to the examination.

In addition to this, to assist you in recognising the requirements of the pre-issued case study, you can simulate the actual examinations by using the two examples of full length pre-issued case studies (and sets of questions) that are included at the end of Modules 2 and 3.

Assessment

The hierarchy of skills

Every mark that is awarded on an AS paper is given for the demonstration of a skill. The following four skills are tested:

- **Knowledge and understanding** — demonstrating knowledge and understanding of the specified content of the course, such as the definition of a business term or the stating of an advantage of a particular method.
- **Application** — relating or applying your knowledge and understanding to a specific organisation or situation. An example might be advising a business to target a particular segment of consumers, based on recognising the most relevant consumers for that organisation.
- **Analysis** — using business theory to develop a line of thought in relation to the solution of a business problem. An example might be showing how improvements in the quality of a product may cause cash-flow problems in the short term but more satisfied customers, and therefore more sales revenue, in the long run.

- **Evaluation** — making a judgement by weighing up the evidence provided, and, possibly, recognising the strength, quality and reliability of the evidence before making a decision.

All questions are marked according to this hierarchy of skills, with knowledge being the easiest, progressing on to evaluation as the most difficult.

- An AS question that requires you to define a term will only reward **knowledge** — do not waste time on showing the importance or application of this concept.
- A question asking you to explain will test **application** — both knowledge and application are needed.
- Questions requiring **analysis** will have marks allocated for knowledge, application and analysis.
- **Evaluation** questions will award marks for all four skills. You cannot evaluate (make a judgement) effectively without showing knowledge, applying it to the situation and then developing the argument (analysing).

To reflect the relative difficulties of these skills, most AS and A2 examinations allow for progression, with AS papers placing more emphasis on the skills of **knowledge** and **understanding** and **application** and A2 papers testing **evaluation** to a much greater extent.

However, despite the natural progression of skills in this hierarchy, in AQA AS Business Studies examinations students tend to find **application** more difficult than **analysis**. They are often able to show their ability to use theory and business logic (analysis), but are less skilled in applying this theory to the business in the stimulus material or case study (application). Always ensure that your answers are linked to the situation in the case study. This will gain you application marks and will also make it easier for you to evaluate, as evaluation marks are gained by assessing the particular situation in the question.

Recognising the skills required

There are two ways in which you can identify the skills that are being tested by any particular question:

- trigger words
- mark allocations

Trigger words

In AQA AS Business Studies examinations specific 'trigger' words are used to show you when you are required to demonstrate analysis or evaluation (this is not the case with the A2 examinations).

Analysis

Only the following trigger words will be used at AS when you are being asked to analyse:

- 'Analyse…'
- 'Examine…'
- 'Explain why…'

It is worth noting that 'explain' on its own means that application is needed.

Evaluation

Only the following trigger words will be used at AS when you are being asked to evaluate:

■ 'Evaluate…'   ■ 'Discuss…'   ■ 'To what extent…'

Knowledge and understanding and application

There are no prescribed trigger words for knowledge and application. The mark allocation for each question is the best guide for this (see below). However, questions testing only knowledge will usually ask you to 'define', 'explain the meaning of the term' or answer a question commencing 'what is meant by'. It is possible that you may be asked to 'state' or 'identify'. Typical application questions will ask you to explain, but there may be a requirement to calculate. The Unit 1 paper guarantees that at least one question (and possibly more) will require you to demonstrate numerical skills.

Mark allocations

In general, the more marks a question is awarded, the more skills it is testing. There is no set pattern for every question, but Tables 1 and 2 show how 'typical' questions on the AS examination papers might be assessed.

Unit 1 examination papers have two questions worth 25 marks each; each question is usually subdivided into parts (a)–(d).

Question	Knowledge	Application	Analysis	Evaluation	Total
			Skills		
(a)	2				2
(b)	2	4			6
(c)	2	3	3		8
(d)	2	2	3	2*	9
Total	8	9	6	2	25

Table 1 Typical mark allocations for a Unit 1 question

*Note that for the Unit 1 (BUS1) examination paper, AQA states that there will be 2 marks awarded for evaluation on question 1 and 3 marks awarded for evaluation on question 2.

Unit 2 and Unit 3 examination papers have five questions worth 50 marks in total.

Question	Knowledge	Application	Analysis	Evaluation	Total
			Skills		
1	3	3			6
2	2	2	4		8
3	3	3	4	5	15
4	3	3			6
5	3	3	4	5	15
Total	14	14	12	10	50

Table 2 Typical mark allocations for a Unit 2 or 3 question

Demonstrating the skills required

Avoid the temptation to show off your knowledge by listing lots of different points. The AQA examinations reward quality, not quantity. As a general rule of thumb, it is best to focus on two or three points and to develop them in depth. Typically, for an evaluation question you should identify two or three relevant ideas, explain their relevance, wherever possible using arguments that are specific to the situation or organisation in the question, and then draw a conclusion/make a decision based on your arguments. If, and only if, time permits, you can add and develop further ideas. In short, you should move up the skills levels from knowledge to application and analysis and on to evaluation as quickly as possible.

The AS examinations

Scheme of assessment

Each module is tested in a separate 1-hour examination.
- Module 1 is tested in Unit 1 (BUS1).
- Module 2 is tested in Unit 2 (BUS2).
- Module 3 is tested in Unit 3 (BUS3).
(This may seem obvious, but it is worth noting that there is a significantly different approach to the A2 papers.)

The marks awarded for each unit are weighted. Because Unit 3 builds on some of the topics covered in Units 1 and 2, it has a higher weighting. The weightings of each paper are detailed in Table 3.

Table 3 Weightings of each AS paper

Unit	Topics	Weighting
BUS1	'Marketing' and 'Accounting and Finance'	30% of the AS
BUS2	'People in Organisations' and 'Operations Management'	30% of the AS
BUS3	'External Influences' and 'Objectives and Strategy'	40% of the AS

BUS1 is designed as an initial foundation paper; BUS2 and BUS3 are designed to be taken at a time when the more challenging skills (notably evaluation) have been developed. Consequently, the marks awarded in BUS1 have a relatively high allocation of marks for knowledge (33% of the total) and a lower allocation of marks for evaluation (only 10% of the total). For both BUS2 and BUS3 examinations, 28% of the marks are awarded for knowledge and 20% are given for evaluation.

The skills demonstrated in all three papers are marked out of 50. Table 4 shows the AQA guidelines for the number of marks awarded for each skill in each of the three papers.

Unit	Skills				Total
	Knowledge	Application	Analysis	Evaluation	
BUS1	16 or 17	16 or 17	12	5	50
BUS2	14	14	12	10	50
BUS3	14	14	12	10	50

Table 4 Marks awarded for each skill at AS

Your 'Quality of Language' is also awarded a mark (a maximum of 2 marks for BUS1 and a maximum of 3 marks for BUS2 and BUS3).

The case studies in this textbook are designed to reflect the AQA exams. Thus all the case studies in Module 1 are designed to have only a small proportion of evaluation questions (10% of the marks), while the case studies in Modules 2 and 3 include a larger proportion of evaluation questions (20% of the marks). Each of the other skills is tested in exactly the same way as a real examination.

Unit 1

The topics covered in Module 1 are tested in Unit 1 (BUS1). This is a 60-minute stimulus-response (sometimes known as 'data-response') examination paper. You will not see the stimulus material or questions before the examination.

The examination will consist of two sets of stimulus material, each about 300 words in length. These may be a written article, graphical or numerical data. Each will be followed by four or five questions based on the material provided. At least one of the articles (and possibly both) will be based on a real-life business or situation.

The aim of the examination is to test the two sections of the specification ('Marketing' and 'Accounting and Finance') equally. However, the specification encourages you to see business studies as an integrated whole and so you are advised not to try to identify a marketing and an accounting and finance question.

The structure of this book means that a series of marketing questions is followed by a series of accounting and finance questions. The actual examinations are unlikely to follow this pattern. If the first set of questions is predominantly about marketing, the second set of questions will be mainly financial. If the first set of questions is evenly divided between the two areas, then the second one will be too.

During your revision you are advised to practise answering actual past papers. AQA AS Business Studies past papers are available (in pdf format) from the AQA website (www.aqa.org.uk). Mark schemes for these examinations can also be downloaded.

Units 2 and 3

The topics covered in Modules 2 and 3 are assessed in a different way. Approximately 8 teaching weeks before the examinations a pre-released

case study of 2,500–3,000 words will be issued to schools and colleges. (Your teachers will decide on the most appropriate time to issue you with this case study.) All the questions on Modules 2 and 3 will be based on this case study.

The style of questions is shown in the sample case studies included throughout Modules 2 and 3 in this book. Although at the time of writing only two series of papers have been sat, the standard pattern to date is:

- two 6-mark questions
- one 8-mark question
- two 15-mark questions

Both examinations (BUS2 and BUS3) are 1 hour in duration.

Unlike some pre-released case studies, you are not allowed to take an annotated copy of the case study into the examination room. Instead, a fresh, 'clean' copy of the case study is issued at the same time as the questions. This means that you can refer to the case study during the examination. However, in a 1-hour examination there is not enough time to read through all of the case study again. Therefore, it is imperative that you have read and understood the case study, in as much detail as possible, before the examination.

The signs from the first two pre-released case studies are that this style of examination works well, but students have found it difficult to apply their theory to the situation in the case study. The authors recommend that you become as familiar as possible with all aspects of the case study before the examination. This will enable you to answer questions without constantly checking back through the case study for reminders. Referring back in the examination should be limited to confirmation of factual details and numerical data. (It would not be feasible or sensible for you to try to remember all of the statistics in a table.)

How to approach the course and examination

Study advice

Keep up to date

This book contains many topical examples for you to use, but business studies is constantly changing. Although a textbook provides you with the theory, reading newspapers and magazines, and using other topical media such as the internet, will help you to keep pace with changes. One thing is guaranteed: the study of business will have changed between the beginning and the end of your AS course and so there is no substitute for keeping an eye on the latest business news.

Build your own business studies dictionary

As you progress through this book, build up your own glossary/dictionary of terms. This will ease your revision and help to ensure that you can define terms clearly. Knowing the exact meaning of terms will also make sure that you write relevantly on the other, non-definition questions.

Read each chapter thoroughly

On completion of each topic, make sure that you have read each page of the relevant chapter and use the questions at the end of each chapter to test yourself. If you adopt this approach for every chapter of the book, then your revision will be just that: revising what you have already learned rather than learning material for the first time.

Complete the practice exercises and case studies

Tackle the practice exercises and case studies at the end of each chapter, even if not asked to do so by your teacher. Completion of the practice exercises will help you to check that you have understood the basic ideas in the chapter. Completion of the case studies will give you useful examination practice and help you to learn what you can achieve in the examination. It will also help you to develop the best approach to answering business studies questions.

Develop your communication and data-handling skills

There is no need to have studied GCSE Business Studies before taking AS; the AQA AS specification assumes that you have no prior understanding of the subject. However, the AS does expect you to have already developed certain skills during your general GCSE programme. These skills are communication and the ability to use, prepare and interpret business data. You should be able to understand and apply averages (the mean, median and mode), prepare and interpret tables, graphs, histograms, bar charts and pie charts, and use index numbers.

Focus on the higher level skills

It is tempting to focus chiefly on the facts when you are revising. Remember, the really high marks are given for the depth of your answers. Include scope for this within your revision so that you are able to earn marks for analysis and evaluation. Try to think of applications of your learning. For example, as people become richer they buy more products, but some firms (those making luxuries) will probably benefit more than those providing necessities.

Read the Chief Examiner's Report

This report will alert you to the strengths and weaknesses shown by previous students and will help you to refine your approach. Along with previous examination papers and mark schemes, these reports are available in pdf format from the AQA website (www.aqa.org.uk).

Examination advice

Advice is provided throughout the book in the examiner's voice boxes. Some of the key points are noted here:

- **Practice makes perfect.** Examination practice will help you to establish the best approach for you to take in the exam itself.
- **Plan the length of your answers.** After allowing for reading time, you will have approximately 1 minute for every mark awarded. Use this as a guideline to the timing of your answers (6 marks = 6 minutes; 10 marks = 10 minutes etc.).
- **Use the trigger words and mark allocations.** Use these to discover the skills that you need to show in each question.
- **Move up the hierarchy of skills as quickly as possible.** Do not spend an excessive amount of time on stating points when analysis and evaluation are required.
- **Read the wording of the question carefully.** Half a minute spent on deciding exactly what is needed by the examiner can save you 10 minutes of wasted effort.
- **Do not be tempted to display unnecessary knowledge.** Be prepared to accept that your favourite topic is not relevant to this examination if there are no questions on it.
- **State the obvious.** Some explanations might seem to be too easy, but they need to be included in your answer. The examiner can only reward what you have written.
- **Leave a space at the end of each answer.** If time permits, you can then add more detail at the end of your answer.

We wish you well in your studies and examinations, and hope that this book helps to provide you with the understanding needed to succeed. Good luck!

Acknowledgements

The authors would like to express their thanks to numerous individuals who have contributed to the completion of this book. Particular gratitude is shown to Philip Cross for the initial idea, unstinting support, good humour and patience. Thanks are also due to Chris Bessant and Catherine Tate, whose suggestions have greatly improved the final version.

John owes a debt of gratitude to Yvonne for her stoicism and tolerance during the writing, and to Lara, Nina, Marje, Joe and Tricia for their support over many years.

Gwen is grateful to John and Jessica, both of whom are always calm, relaxed and supportive, allowing her the time and space to complete this work.

Marketing

"Good companies will meet needs; great companies will create markets."

Philip Kotler

CHAPTER 1

Introduction to marketing and the market

This chapter defines marketing and examines the concept of the market: what it is, how it can be measured and the factors that influence its growth. The difference between quantitative and qualitative market analysis is noted and the technique of market mapping as a form of market analysis is described and its benefits are explained.

> **KEY** TERM
>
> **marketing:** the anticipation and satisfying of customers' wants in a way that delights the consumer and also meets the needs of the organisation.

What is a market?

> **KEY** TERM
>
> **the market:** a place where buyers and sellers come together.

Traditionally, markets were physical places, often in the centre of a community. However, as a result of developments in communication, many markets exist through the postal service, telephone and internet links.

Firms need to recognise the market that they are in. TGI Friday's sees itself as being in the entertainment industry rather than as a 'restaurant'. A similar view is held by McDonald's, which aims to make eating out a social rather than a culinary experience. By redefining their market, these and other companies have seen a rapid increase in 'eating out'. In 2003 over 30% of all food expenditure was on meals provided by restaurants and takeaways, in comparison to less than 20% 15 years ago.

How is a market measured?

> **KEY** TERM
>
> **market size:** the volume of sales of a product (e.g. the number of computers sold) or the value of sales of a product (e.g. the total revenue from computer sales).

Many markets are measured by *volume* because it is easier for people to identify with an item than with a sum of money. For example, in the car market it is easier to picture 2.5 million cars being sold than a value of £30 billion. However, in some markets (e.g. hair care products, dog food and deodorants) there are many different products with huge variations in price. In these cases, it is easier to measure the market in terms of the *value* of goods sold.

Market size can increase as a result of extra sales of goods or persuading customers to pay higher prices. Trainers and other markets with premium brands are good examples of this latter point.

The market size indicates the potential sales for a firm. In a car market worth £30 billion a year, a car manufacturer can earn huge revenue even if it is only small in comparison to its competitors.

KEY TERM

market growth: the percentage change in sales (volume or value) over a period of time.

In Table 1.1 below, it can be seen that the volume of car sales grew by 0.6% between 2002 and 2003. Growth markets offer potential for increased sales, but they also encourage competition. In contrast, in a low-growth market, a dominant company can 'milk' its 'cash cows' to boost its profits.

In 2003 the growth rate of the car market was below the average growth rate in the UK. However, in 2001 and 2002 the rise in market size had been much larger than the markets for most other products. Luxury products are likely to register high growth in periods of general economic growth, but to decline rapidly or stagnate during recessions or periods when people are more cautious.

Manufacturer	Cars sold 2002	Cars sold 2003	% change	Market share 2002 (%)	Market share 2003 (%)
1 Ford	400,808	378,942	−5.46	15.63	14.69
2 Vauxhall	318,633	326,433	2.45	12.43	12.66
3 Renault	194,685	189,427	−2.70	7.59	7.34
4 Peugeot	208,920	184,940	−11.48	8.15	7.17
5 Volkswagen	178,924	178,953	0.02	6.98	6.94
6 Citroën	130,415	117,602	−9.82	5.09	4.56
7 Toyota	104,498	117,531	12.47	4.08	4.56
8 Nissan	100,751	105,798	5.01	3.93	4.1
9 MG Rover	99,108	95,848	−3.29	3.87	3.72
10 BMW	85,567	93,822	9.65	3.34	3.64
Additional information:					
Luxury cars	405,566	442,307	9.06	15.82	17.15
Other cars	2,158,065	2,136,743	−0.99	84.18	82.85
Total market	**2,563,631**	**2,579,050**	**0.60**	**100.0**	**100.0**

Source: The Society of Motor Manufacturers and Traders (SMMT), January 2004.

Table 1.1
Analysis of the UK market for new cars, 2003

Factors influencing market growth

Market growth is largely outside the control of individual firms. However, a business should be aware of the factors that influence growth, so that it can predict future trends and make sure that it is taking advantage of the potential for growth in certain markets (or avoiding the problems faced in declining markets). Key factors are as follows:

- **Economic growth.** If a country's wealth is growing by 3% per annum, then sales are likely to rise in any given market.
- **The nature of the product.** Markets dealing with luxury products, such as jewellery or investments, tend to grow more rapidly when growth is high, but often suffer more severe cutbacks when people are worried about their living standards.
- **Changes in taste.** As lifestyles change, new products become more popular while others decline. This is a factor that firms can influence through good marketing.
- **Social changes.** The way in which people live may influence product sales. A greater tendency to stay at home will assist sales of digital television, while longer working hours have led to fewer people preparing their own meals.
- **Fashion.** Recent television programmes highlighting the delights of home cooking, garden design and do-it-yourself are likely to influence the number of people pursuing those activities. Note how the market for home cooking is being increased by this factor but reduced by the previous influence.

Market share

KEY TERM

market share: the percentage or proportion of the total sales of a product or service achieved by a firm or a specific brand of a product.

Market share is usually measured as a percentage, calculated by the formula:

$$\text{market share} = \frac{\text{sales of one product or brand or company}}{\text{total sales in the market}} \times 100$$

EXAMINER'S VOICE

When defining terms in an examination, you must not repeat the words that are included in the question in your answer. Thus market share is not 'the share of the market owned by a company'. This style of repetition is a common mistake in examinations.

Market share is an excellent measure of a company's success because it compares a firm's sales to those of its competitors. A company's market share can increase only if the company is performing better than some of its rivals.

In 2003 Vodafone's mobile phone connections were increasing in total sales because of market growth, but the company's percentage share of the market was falling because connections to Orange and T-Mobile were increasing more quickly. Firms often aim to be the market leader — that is, the company with the largest share in its market. In mobile phones, Nokia is the market leader for handsets in the UK market, while Vodafone is the market leader for network connections.

In Table 1.1 (see p. 3) it can be seen that Vauxhall sold more cars in 2003 than in 2002 (a growth of 2.45%). As economic growth in the UK during this period was 2.1%, this could be seen to be a marginal success. However, for the car market as a whole there was growth of 0.6%. Thus Vauxhall grew more rapidly than most of its rivals. This is shown by its market share — Vauxhall's share of UK car sales rose from 12.43% in 2002 to 12.66% in 2003.

Analysing the market

KEY TERM

market analysis: the study of market conditions to assist a firm's plans.

Market analysis can be quantitative or qualitative:

- **Quantitative analysis** examines statistical information in order to draw conclusions about the nature of the market (e.g. How much growth is there in a market? Who is the market leader?). Tables 1.1 and 1.2 provide quantitative information on the market for cars in the UK in 2003.
- **Qualitative analysis** considers the reasons why certain actions take place (e.g. Why did luxury car sales grow so rapidly in 2003? Why is the Ford Focus the most popular car in the UK?).

Market mapping

Market mapping is a technique that analyses markets by looking at the features that distinguish different products or firms. In the case of the car market, people may buy cars because they are:

- suitable for family use (e.g. they are large enough to carry a pram or to seat three children)
- cheap to buy and/or run (e.g. replacement parts are cheap, so garage bills should be less)
- environmentally friendly (e.g. they have very efficient consumption of fuel to limit emissions)
- capable of fast speeds (e.g. they accelerate quickly and so appeal to 'boy racers')
- safe and secure (e.g. off-road vehicles protect the passengers in case of an accident)

Model of car	Total sales	Market share (%)
Ford Focus	131,684	5.11
Vauxhall Corsa	108,387	4.20
Vauxhall Astra	96,929	3.76
Ford Fiesta	95,887	3.72
Renault Clio	83,972	3.25
Peugeot 206	82,667	3.21
Renault Mégane	71,660	2.78
Volkswagen Golf	67,226	2.61
BMW 3 Series	65,489	2.53
Ford Mondeo	60,046	2.33

Source: The Society of Motor Manufacturers and Traders (SMMT), January 2004.

Table 1.2
Top ten selling models of car in the UK, 2003

Interestingly, in relation to the last point some people would argue that off-road vehicles can cause more injuries to other road users, but for the person making the decision to buy, this is not such an important consideration. For a similar reason, cigarette companies were unsuccessful when they developed a smokeless cigarette because it was not smokers who disliked cigarette smoke, and so they did not buy the new product.

Features such as those listed above can be 'mapped' in order to identify the extent to which an individual car possesses them. An example, featuring

the market for female clothing, is illustrated in Figure 1.1 (see p. 7). A computer-based model or map could examine any number of factors at the same time, but for convenience it is normal to show the two most important factors in a market map. For the female clothing market, these could be price and fashion. A firm or product at the centre of the map would not be seen to possess either feature significantly. In this market, Karen Millen represents a brand that is considered to be set at a premium price (often a measure of quality) and offers fashionable products. Peacocks provides functional (non-fashionable) clothing that is relatively cheap to buy.

Market mapping has the following benefits:

- It helps firms to identify their closest rivals, in order to plan suitable competitive strategies.
- It helps to identify gaps or niches in the market that it could fill by introducing a new product or image.
- If carried out through market research, it can help a firm to realise the public's view of it as a business/brand.
- It may help a firm that needs to reposition itself in a market (e.g. Skoda).

PRACTICE EXERCISE
Total: 40 marks (40 minutes)

Read the information in Tables 1.1 (see p. 3) and 1.2 (see p. 5) and, using your knowledge of business, answer the questions that follow.

1 How large was the market for new cars in the UK in 2003? *(1 mark)*

2 Which company was the market leader? *(1 mark)*

3 a Between 2002 and 2003 which firm had the largest increase in the number of cars sold? *(2 marks)*
  b Between 2002 and 2003 which firm had the largest percentage increase in its sale of cars? *(1 mark)*

4 How was it possible for Volkswagen to increase sales but suffer from a fall in its market share? *(4 marks)*

5 Explain two possible reasons why the luxury car market grew by over 9.0% at a time when sales of non-luxury cars fell. *(6 marks)*

6 The market leader in the car market was the Ford Focus. Analyse two possible reasons why Ford Focus sales were greater than the sales of other cars. *(6 marks)*

7 In Table 1.1 Volkswagen is shown as the fifth largest car manufacturer. However, Volkswagen is part of a business that also owns Audi, Skoda and Seat (fourteenth, seventeenth and twentieth in the market). Explain why a firm might choose to use different brand names for different cars in this way. *(6 marks)*

8 Why might the use of volume (the number of cars sold) give a misleading impression of the market share of a car manufacturer? *(4 marks)*

9 Evaluate the usefulness of the information in Tables 1.1 and 1.2 to a foreign manufacturer that is considering entering the UK car market. *(9 marks)*

CASE STUDY Market mapping

Market maps are useful to a fashion retailer because they show the position of each firm in relation to the organisation being studied. In some market maps, circles of varying sizes are used to represent the size or market share of each firm in the map.

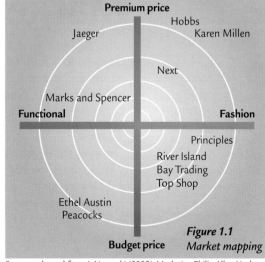

Figure 1.1
Market mapping

Source: adapted from J. Nowacki (2002) *Marketing*, Philip Allan Updates.

Question 1   Total: 25 marks (30 minutes)

a Figure 1.1 shows a market map that uses 'price' and 'fashion' to map different firms in the female clothing market.

   (i)   Suggest **two** different ways in which the car market could be mapped.   *(2 marks)*

   (ii) Justify your choices.   *(6 marks)*

b Analyse the possible reasons why there is a cluster of firms in a similar place in the bottom right-hand quadrant of Figure 1.1.   *(8 marks)*

c Information in Figure 1.1 suggests a gap in the market for functional clothing that is in the middle range of the price levels. Discuss the reasons for and against setting up a business that fills this gap.   *(9 marks)*

Question 2   Total: 25 marks (30 minutes)

a What is meant by the term 'market share'?   *(2 marks)*

b Marks and Spencer has tried to reposition itself in the market in recent years. Explain **two** ways in which it could achieve this aim.   *(6 marks)*

c Analyse the implications for Ethel Austin of its position on the market map.   *(7 marks)*

d Discuss the problems that might face a fashion retailer that tries to reposition itself on the market map.   *(10 marks)*

CHAPTER 2

Market segmentation

Organisations need to identify their potential customers. This chapter looks at the different categories that marketers use to segment their customers. The applications of 'market segmentation' are investigated and the potential problems and limitations of its use are considered.

KEY TERMS

market segmentation: the classification of customers or potential customers into groups or sub-groups (market segments), each of which responds differently to different products or marketing approaches.

segmentation analysis: where a firm uses quantitative and qualitative data or information to try to discover the types of consumer who buy its products and why.

Types of segmentation

A number of different ways of segmenting a market may be identified.

Age

For many products and services, age is a crucial influence on demand, so firms will segment on this basis. Holidays are a classic example: Club 18–30 targets its holidays at a specific age range, while Saga holidays are aimed at people aged over 50 years. Large firms will try to provide a range of products that will reach all ages. A magazine publisher will produce different magazines for teenagers, 20- and 30-somethings, the middle-aged and the elderly.

Gender (sex)

Some products are specifically targeted at males or females. The market for perfume is dominated by females, while attendance at sporting events has been dominated by male customers. However, in both these cases, firms have recognised the potential for growth by targeting the other gender.

Social class

I/A	Professional
II/B	Managerial and technical
IIIN/C1	Skilled: non-manual
IIIM/C2	Skilled: manual
IV/D	Partly skilled
V/E	Unskilled

In general, social class influences purchasing habits because class A will receive more income than class B and so on. However, there are some activities that may appeal to particular social classes regardless of income: for example, purchasers of golf items are more likely than football supporters to be from the middle classes, A, B and C1.

Lifestyle

Lifestyle-based segmentation is becoming more popular as firms can use credit card and loyalty card records to identify the pattern of individuals' expenditure. Family food purchases are classified into categories according to the tendency to buy takeaways, organic food, economy brands, health foods etc. Leisure pursuits are also used to segment customers for marketing purposes.

Geographic

Although regional variations in taste are becoming less significant, there are still major differences in tastes and purchasing behaviour based on geographical features. Rambling, surfing, theatre visits and night-clubbing are all activities that are influenced by the place where someone lives.

Usage/frequency of purchase

Some customers, known as **early adopters**, like to be the first to try new products; in contrast, **followers** are more cautious. Awareness of these customer types will allow a firm to target the right people. Similarly, consumers can be classified according to how often they purchase products. A frequent purchaser will have a different view of a product from an occasional, casual user.

Residential (e.g. ACORN)

ACORN (A Classification Of Residential Neighbourhoods) segments the market according to types of housing. Over 30 different categories of housing are identified by this technique. Families in suburban detached houses are expected to have very different tastes from those living in terraced houses in rural areas. Postcodes can be used to identify these segments, helping firms to target their marketing.

Conclusion

The exact type of segmentation used will depend on the firm or the product. For example, in the case of clothing, gender is important and so is age, especially for children's clothing. Not every type of segmentation will be used by every firm. In general, organisations will identify the market segments that are relevant to their products and services. Products, services, marketing strategies and the marketing mix will then be geared to the targeted segments.

Reasons for segmentation

There are several reasons why companies might use market segmentation:

■ **To increase market share.** An organisation can identify market segments

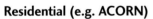

EXAMINER'S VOICE

Market segmentation is becoming much more sophisticated because databases can now provide firms with quite detailed data on consumers. Loyalty cards and credit or debit card transactions also enable firms to identify potential customers more accurately. This has led to an increase in direct mail promotions to customers.

that have not been reached and adapt its products and marketing to reach those segments. For example, Mothercare extended the age range of its products to attract older children and mothers.

- **To assist new product development.** Gaps in market segments can be used to indicate the scope for introducing new products. Originally, software offered with new computers tended to be games. These offers have been extended to appeal to more segments by including Microsoft Office, photographic processing and educational software.
- **To extend products into new markets.** Mobile phones were initially targeted at business users before being extended to teenagers and then whole families.
- **To identify ways of marketing a product.** A company that recognises its customers' characteristics can target its advertising to media used by that market segment. For example, social class A is most likely to read *The Times* whereas social class E has a greater tendency to read the *Star*. Similarly, promotional methods and messages can be modified to suit specific segments — for instance, young people prefer different images from older consumers.

EXAMINER'S VOICE

In questions on market segmentation, identify and focus on the market segments that are relevant to the product/firm in the case study.

Problems with market segmentation

Segmentation analysis may involve the following problems:

- **Difficulty in identifying the most important segments for a product.** Successful segmentation requires market segments to be identifiable, reachable and distinct. In practice, a firm may be unable to categorise its customers. Some segments, such as gender, are easy to identify, but it is more difficult to put consumers of bread, household cleaners and pillows into categories.
- **Knowing how to reach your chosen segment with your marketing.** Lifestyle categories in particular are difficult to identify or locate. What media would you use to attract primary school parents on a national scale?
- **Recognising changes in the segments interested in your product.** Markets are dynamic and firms cannot assume that an existing segment will always stay loyal to a product. Thus firms must constantly research their market segments.
- **Failure to meet the needs of customers not included in your chosen segment.** Emphasis on market segmentation may lead to a firm ignoring other potential customers. This may prevent a firm from attracting the mass market.

DID YOU KNOW?

Sometimes it is important to identify the buyer rather than the consumer when segmenting a market. Surveys show that women buy more male underwear than men. Information such as this can make a big difference to the way in which a product is marketed.

1 Would you know whom to target when it comes to selling make-up to 11- to 14-year-old girls? Is it mum or the youngster, and does the age of the youngster make a difference to who makes the decision?

2 BMRB TGI, a market research organisation, uses a set of lifestyle market segments. One market segment is described as 'sophisticated good lookers'. These are consumers who want to keep up with the latest fashions, consider themselves stylish and like to 'stand out in a crowd'. But where would they want to buy their shoes and which television programme are they most likely to watch? (Answers on p.12.)

(Answers on p.12.)

e EXAMINER'S VOICE

Use the mark allocation as a guide to the length of your answer. After allowing for reading time, all AQA A-level Business Studies papers use the same formula: a mark a minute.

PRACTICE EXERCISE

Total: 50 marks (40 minutes)

1 What is meant by the term 'market segment'? *(3 marks)*

2 Identify a product for which 'age' would be a useful way of segmenting the market. Justify your choice, indicating the specific ages that would be targeted. *(4 marks)*

3 Name four products for which gender would be used to segment the market. *(4 marks)*

4 Explain three benefits of the use of market segmentation for a clothing retailer. *(9 marks)*

5 Examine two problems for a furniture manufacturer when trying to use segmentation analysis. *(6 marks)*

6 Why is 'social class' such a popular method of market segmentation? Support your answer with real-life examples. *(6 marks)*

7 How might market segmentation influence the media (television, radio, newspapers etc.) that a business might use for its advertising? *(5 marks)*

8 In what circumstances is market segmentation unlikely to be helpful to a business? *(6 marks)*

9 How might a supermarket use information from a loyalty/reward card to assist its marketing? *(4 marks)*

10 What is an 'early adopter'? *(3 marks)*

CASE STUDY BMRB TGI lifestage segmentation

The examples of market segments given in this chapter are only illustrations, and different markets will use very different methods. Many industries find it useful to combine 'age' and 'household composition' in order to study the buying habits of consumers.

BMRB TGI, the market research organisation mentioned earlier, segments the population of the UK into 12 'lifestages' as shown in Table 2.1 (see p. 12). The 'lifestage' surveys record other segmentation data, so it is possible to combine the above classifications with data on social class and gender. In this way, 24 or 48 different groups can be identified.

BMRB aims to sell this information to businesses such as insurance companies, car manufacturers and restaurants, that believe it can help them to increase their market share. It reveals major differences in spending patterns (e.g. BMW car buyers are much more likely to be male 'mid-life independents' than any other segment). It also shows their exposure to advertising media (e.g. women who have 'flown the nest' are 2.5 times more likely to be heavy radio listeners than females who fit into the category of 'primary school parents'). Use of the internet is even more varied between different segments.

TGI lifestage group	Description: age and household background	% of population
Fledglings	Aged 15–34, not married and no children, living with own parents	10
Flown the nest	Aged 15–34, not married, do not live with relations	4
Nest builders	Aged 15–34, married, do not live with son/daughter	5
Playschool parents	Live with son/daughter and youngest child is aged 0–4	14
Primary school parents	Live with son/daughter and youngest child is aged 5–9	8
Secondary school parents	Live with son/daughter and youngest child is aged 10–15	8
Mid-life independents	Aged 35–54, not married, do not live with relations	4
Unconstrained couples	Aged 35–54, married, do not live with son/daughter	7
Hotel parents	Aged 35+, live with son/daughter and no child aged 0–15	10
Senior sole decision makers	Aged 55+, not married and live alone	10
Empty nesters	Aged 55+, married and do not live with son/daughter	17
Non-standard families	Individuals who do not fit any other category	3

Table 2.1 *BMRB TGI's 12 lifestages*
Source: www.bmrb-tgi.co.uk

Questions

Total: 25 marks (30 minutes)

1 What is meant by the term 'market share' (line 16)? *(2 marks)*

2 Explain **two** reasons why 'male "mid-life independents"' are more likely to buy BMW cars than any of the other market segments (lines 17–19). *(6 marks)*

3 Analyse **two** ways in which an insurance company might use the information given above in order to improve its sales. *(8 marks)*

4 To what extent would this information be useful to a restaurant? *(9 marks)*

Answers to *Did you know?* questions on p. 11
1 Aged 11: 39% girl, 61% mother; aged 12: 44% girl, 56% mother; aged 13: 59% girl, 41% mother; aged 14: 73% girl, 27% mother.
2 Shoe shops: Dolcis, Ravel and Next; television programme: *Hollyoaks*.

CHAPTER 3

Market research

Firms need to understand their market. The purposes of market research are studied and comparisons made between primary and secondary market research and between quantitative and qualitative data. Other topics that are considered in this chapter are the need for sampling and advice on how to analyse market research information.

> **KEY TERM**
>
> **market research:** the systematic and objective collection, analysis and evaluation of information that is intended to assist the marketing process.

Purposes of market research

Market research is undertaken for descriptive, explanatory, predictive and exploratory reasons.

Descriptive reasons

The collection and analysis of data allows organisations to identify a number of important pieces of information. Examples include:

- **Achieving objectives.** Has the firm achieved its target sales figure or its desired percentage market share?
- **Identifying trends.** Are sales rising or falling? Is the trend stable or unpredictable?
- **Comparisons.** How are the firm's sales performing relative to a competitor? Is its advertising expenditure matching its rivals? Is it appealing to the same market segments?

Explanatory reasons

Market research can help an organisation to investigate why certain things occur. For example:

- Does the weather affect sales? If so, how big is the impact and is it consistent?
- Is the brand name attractive to the targeted consumers?
- What are the main reasons why customers buy the product? How can this information be used in the firm's marketing?
- Why was a promotional campaign unsuccessful?

Predictive reasons

Information can be used to predict trends and find links between sets of data. This will help the firm to predict what will happen in the future. Typical uses include:

- calculating the extent to which advertising influences sales volume

- discovering whether introducing a new flavour affects the sales of existing flavours
- predicting whether a new price will boost sales value
- examining the likely effect of the arrival of a new competitor on profit levels

Exploratory reasons

On occasions, such as when a new product is introduced, there will be no existing information to guide an organisation. In this situation, a business may conduct research into the probable consumer reaction to the product or its marketing. This may help the firm to assess factors such as:

- the probable level of demand
- the most suitable market segments to be targeted
- the ideal price level
- the best ways of promoting the product

Types of market research

Market research is classified in two ways, according to:

- how the data are collected (primary or secondary)
- the content of the data (quantitative or qualitative)

How data are collected

There are two sources of information, primary and secondary.

KEY TERMS

primary market research: the collection of information first-hand for a specific purpose.

secondary market research: the use of information that has already been collected for a different purpose.

Primary market research

Although called 'primary', primary research actually comes second — it should only be used to complete the gaps that cannot be filled by secondary data. Because researchers often need to go out (into the field) to collect primary data, it is frequently called field research.

There are several methods of conducting primary research:

- **Experiment.** An organisation experiments with a particular approach in certain areas or for a certain time. If successful, it then uses this approach nationally or on a more long-term basis. For example, the supermarket chain Safeway (which is now owned by Morrisons) allowed local store managers to decide on the special offers that they made because its experiment showed that different offers worked best in different parts of the country.
- **Observation.** Stores watch customers while they are shopping and gather information on which displays or offers seem to prove the more effective. Although psychologists are employed to offer opinions on customer reactions, the weakness of 'observation' is that it shows what is happening rather than why it is taking place.

- **Focus groups.** A group of consumers is encouraged to discuss their feelings about a product or market. This enables the firm to gather in-depth details of why consumers react in the way that they do and to uncover new ideas on how to market its product or service. However, a single focus group can often cost between £2,000 and £4,000.

- **Surveys.** Consumers are questioned about the product or service. Surveys can take a number of forms, but usually involve the completion of a questionnaire that is designed to collate the characteristics and views of a cross-section of consumers. The main types of survey are:

  - **Personal interviews.** These are conducted face-to-face, with the interviewer filling in the answers given by the interviewee. A wide range of information can be gained because questions can be either closed, where a limited choice of answers is allowed, or open, where the interviewee chooses what to say. Closed questions are easy to collate and compare; open questions are best if *qualitative* information is needed. Another advantage is that any uncertainties can be explained to the interviewee by the interviewer. However, they can be time consuming and the person responding may give false answers to please the interviewer.

  - **Postal surveys.** This method is cheap, allows more specific targeting and avoids the possible bias from a personal survey. However, response rates are low (often less than 2% are returned if no incentive is given) and there is no guarantee that the responses are representative, as people completing them may have a strong opinion (or a lot of spare time). Firms often offer free gifts or competition entries to encourage more replies, thus adding to the expense.

  - **Telephone interviews.** Telephone calls are cheap and can be targeted. They are also used because they 'get entry into the house' — whereas postal surveys are often considered to be 'junk mail', relatively few people will refuse to answer the telephone. However, detailed questions are impossible and the increased use of unpopular telesales (often initially disguised as a survey) has led to customer resentment.

  - **Internet surveys.** Questionnaires on internet sites are cheap to operate and target those most likely to be interested in the product, although they will not tend to help a firm discover why people are *not* buying its product. Response rates are much higher than for postal surveys.

- **Test marketing.** By launching a product in a limited part of a market, usually a geographical area, a firm can discover customer opinions. For example, Northern Foods tested new flavours of muffins in Sainsbury's stores, in order to a compare their popularity with the original flavours. The results of test marketing are a very accurate predictor of future popularity, but fewer firms now employ the technique because it can lead to 'me-too' products (copies) being produced by rivals. Thus test marketing can reduce the time during which a firm benefits from being the only producer.

Sampling and confidence levels

> ### KEY TERMS
>
> **sample:** a group of respondents or factors whose views or behaviour should be representative of the target market as a whole.
> **statistical significance:** the extent to which a statistical conclusion is likely to be true.
> **confidence level:** the degree to which the statistics are a reliable predictor of actual events. A 95% confidence level means that the prediction will be correct 19 times out of 20 (95% of the time).

> ### DID YOU KNOW?
>
> A sample size that is large enough to give the accuracy needed by an organisation is said to be 'statistically significant'.

Primary market research is undertaken by **sampling** the views of a small selection of consumers. The **sample size** measures the number of people or items in the sample. When conducting primary research, a firm needs to balance the need for accuracy against the cost of the survey. Large samples increase reliability but cost more. Small samples decrease costs but are less reliable.

A sample size that is large enough to give 95% confidence in the results (a 95% confidence level) is usually acceptable for a firm. This may not involve huge surveys — often less than 1% of the target market. Opinion polls estimate that they need to survey 2,000 (carefully selected) voters in order to be able to predict, with a 3% margin of error, the voting intentions of 30 million voters. Most businesses will have much smaller target markets and will not require such a high level of accuracy. In some cases, however, such as research into the side-effects of prescription drugs, much higher levels of certainty are needed. An organisation conducting an opinion poll will normally want a higher confidence level than a business conducting market research because its results will be closely scrutinised by the public.

> ### KEY TERMS
>
> **random sample:** a group of respondents in which each member of the target population has an equal chance of being chosen.
> **quota sample:** a group of respondents comprising several different segments, each sharing a common feature (e.g. age, gender). The number of interviewees in each classification is fixed to reflect their percentage in the total target population.

Random sampling can include: choosing a selection of names from a list such as a computer database; a personal surveyor stopping every tenth person who passes; or a telephone survey dialling the second name on each page of the telephone directory. Random sampling is cheap, but it assumes that all consumers are equally important, so it is less useful if the product is targeted at a specific market segment. It can also lead to unexpected bias. One conservatory firm surveyed every tenth house and concluded that there was a high demand for conservatories. However, actual sales proved to be disappointing because the company had not realised that all of the even-numbered houses that it had surveyed had south-facing gardens. The odd-numbered houses were much less likely to buy conservatories because their gardens faced north and so received less sunlight in the summer.

In **quota sampling**, if 20% of the target market are males aged 20–29, then 20% of the people questioned must be males aged 20–29. For example, if 200 people are to be surveyed, then 40 (20%) of them should be males aged 20–29. Once this quota has been reached, no more interviews should be conducted with people in that segment. Quota sampling takes more care and time than random sampling, but it should provide results that are more suited to the firm's needs because the people surveyed match the background of the target customers.

The problems of sampling are as follows:
- Samples may be unrepresentative (e.g. asking the wrong people).
- There may be bias in questions or in the answers that they encourage (e.g. questions such as 'Do you clean your teeth every day?' and 'Do you use deodorant?').
- It may be difficult to locate suitable respondents (e.g. people who listen to a particular radio programme).

> **DID YOU KNOW?**
>
> You should beware of internet, teletext and similar surveys that require people to choose whether they wish to respond. These surveys tend to get responses from people with strong views who may not reflect the vast majority of the population (who may not have strong views on most issues).

FACT FILE

Market research is also used to see if marketing has been successful. Cadbury knows that its sponsorship of *Coronation Street* was successful because its 'before' and 'after' surveys show that people who watch *Coronation Street* now buy more chocolate than they did before the sponsorship began. Similarly, Jacob's Creek's research showed an increase in the value of sales of its wine of 45.8% during a 2-month television advertising campaign.

𝑒 EXAMINER'S VOICE

For those of you who will be taking the AQA coursework option at A2, a popular method of analysing sample data is to apply the 90/30 rule. Questions asked offer five possible answers:

1 Yes, definitely try/buy
2 Yes, very probably try/buy
3 Yes, possibly try/buy
4 Probably not try/buy
5 Definitely not try/buy

The number of respondents to each option is then calculated as a percentage and the following formula

applied: 90% of those who answered 'definitely buy' are included as potential buyers plus 30% of those who answered 'very probably buy'. Anyone answering 'possibly buy', 'probably not buy' or 'definitely not buy' are not counted as potential buyers. Thus if 30% of your sample say they will definitely try, 20% say they will very probably buy, and the remaining 50% are neutral or negative, you are likely to sell to 33% of potential customers:

$$90\% \text{ of } 30\% = 27\%$$
$$+ \ 30\% \text{ of } 20\% = 6\%$$
$$27\% + 6\% = 33\%$$

Secondary market research

Secondary information is found by examining published documents (i.e. through desk research). Firms may be able to save a lot of money by using

data that have already been compiled. As market research is never going to be 100% reliable, it is often more cost effective to accept cheap, reasonably accurate and fairly relevant secondary research than to spend money on primary research. Primary research can then be used to fill any gaps.

Secondary research data can take many forms. Firms will select data that suit their particular purposes. Some key sources are:

- **Government publications.** The Office of National Statistics (ONS) provides information on economic and social trends, so that firms can investigate the implications for their business. Detailed surveys on individual industries are also prepared. The Census of Population provides a detailed survey once every 10 years.
- **Newspapers.** Broadsheet newspapers such as *The Times* and *Guardian* contain articles on specific industries and more general features.
- **Company records.** The company's own records, sales figures, accounts and previous surveys are an easily accessible source and have no cost attached (they are secondary sources because they are not going to be used for their original purpose).
- **Magazines.** Publications such as *The Economist*, *Media Week* and *Grocer Today* can provide helpful data through articles and surveys.
- **Competitors.** Brochures, promotional materials, company reports and investor information can help a firm to study its rivals' actions.
- **Market research organisations.** In addition to conducting primary research, organisations such as Mintel and Dun & Bradstreet produce detailed secondary surveys, the results of which can be purchased by firms.
    - **Loyalty cards.** Cards such as Nectar allow a range of businesses to identify the spending patterns of consumers and target them with relevant promotions.
    - **The internet.** This is a rapidly increasing source of secondary data, but it should be treated with caution as it may lack the reliability of the other sources listed.

Secondary market research offers the following advantages:

- The information is already available, so quick decisions can be taken based upon it.
- It is cheaper than primary research; for some government research and the company's own information, it will be free. Market research organisations usually charge for their general research, but the expenses are shared between different organisations, making the cost cheaper.
- Secondary surveys are often conducted regularly, and so the information obtained is particularly helpful in identifying trends over time.

There are, however, the following disadvantages:

- The information may be dated, and therefore could be misleading.
- It is available to other firms, so it is unlikely to give the organisation any advantages over its competitors.

■ There may be no relevant secondary data to meet the specific needs of the firm.

 EXAMINER'S VOICE

For questions that are based on market research data, it is always worth looking at the quality of the data before drawing firm conclusions:
■ Is there a possible bias in the sample, the questions or the person conducting the survey?
■ Is the sample large enough to be statistically significant? (see p. 16)
■ Is the survey recent and are opinions likely to have changed since it was conducted?

DID YOU KNOW?

The faster the pace of change, the more useful it is to conduct primary research, but the information becomes out-of-date more quickly.

The content of data

The content of information obtained by market research can be quantitative or qualitative.

 TERMS

quantitative market research: the collection of information about the market based on numbers.
qualitative market research: the collection of information about the market based on subjective factors such as opinions and reasons.

Quantitative market research

Quantitative research can answer the following questions: how many, who and how often? For example, to help sell advertising space or sponsorship during *Emmerdale*, Yorkshire Television finds it useful to be able to show that the programme is watched by 10 million viewers, 30% of whom are social class C1, and 82% of whom view every episode. Figures can also be used to show changes in popularity. Quantitative data are excellent for analysis, but they do not explain *why* people act in a particular way.

Qualitative market research

Qualitative research deals with issues such as: why and how? With this information, Yorkshire Television might be able to see why people watch *Emmerdale*: is it the quality of the acting, the stunning scenery or the brilliance of the story lines? An organisation can use this information to plan appropriate strategies. For example, Sky has been able to attract more advertisers to its football programmes through market research showing that football matches were watched by larger groups than other programmes. The normal measure of demand (the number of sets being used) therefore underestimated the number of people actually watching the programme. The disadvantage of using qualitative research is that it is often hard to convert into a statistical format.

Tips on using market research information

When considering the outcome of market research, you should take the following points into account.

DID YOU KNOW?

According to Anita Roddick (The Body Shop): 'Market research is like looking in the rear view mirror — it tells me where I have been rather than where I am going.'

Trends or directions of change in the data

- It is usually safer to project that trends will continue into the future. However, it could be argued that a trend will not continue (e.g. if a market is reaching saturation). Mobile phones, for example, have not continued growing at their initial rate.
- If there is no clear direction of change, is there an obvious cycle? The figures shown may be seasonal. Does the product being discussed support this logic?

Links between different sets of data

- If two sets of data follow the same trend, is one causing the other to change? Increased advertising, for example, should lead to more sales.
- Note that this link might be inverse (negative). Price increases will lead to lower sales.
- If there are no links when logically there could be (e.g. if sales are not rising during an advertising campaign or following a price cut), you can judge (evaluate) that the change is not having the expected effect, or that there may be additional factors affecting sales.

Comparisons

- An increase in the sales of product X may look impressive, but is it a success if the products of other companies are growing faster? Similarly, a decline may show a company that is reasonably efficient if its rivals are declining more noticeably.
- Certain data are always useful for comparison. Examples are inflation and growth rates. Is the firm growing faster than the economy?

Other factors

- There is scope to use your imagination here. A useful approach is to consider the other departments in a business — how would they be affected by the data?
- Look at the company's objectives. Are they being achieved? Should they be modified?
- External influences — what is the state of the market/the economy? Is the government influencing the company's position? Are its competitors changing their marketing?

> **DID YOU KNOW?**
>
> Cause and effect can be confused and lead to incorrect conclusions. Logically, increased advertising will lead to increased sales. However, some companies allocate advertising budgets according to the amount of sales. In this case, the increased sales cause increased advertising, rather than the other way round.

> **e EXAMINER'S VOICE**
>
> Just because market research shows no apparent link between two factors, it does not mean that there is no causal link. The advertising campaign by the local cinema might have failed to increase sales because a rival cinema opened. The advertising might have been successful in preventing a more dramatic fall in customers. For evaluation questions in particular, you should always recognise that other influences are at work, so results may be unpredictable.

PRACTICE EXERCISE

Total: 60 marks (50 minutes)

1 What is the difference between market research that has been collected for 'explanatory' reasons and market research that has been gathered for 'predictive' reasons? *(6 marks)*

2 Distinguish between primary market research and secondary market research. *(4 marks)*

3 Why might secondary research be carried out before primary market research? *(3 marks)*

4 Why might a business use 'observation' as a form of market research? *(3 marks)*

5 Explain two benefits of using personal interviews. *(6 marks)*

6 Describe two problems of using postal surveys. *(6 marks)*

7 What is meant by the term 'test marketing'? *(4 marks)*

8 Explain the meaning of the phrase '95% confidence level'. *(4 marks)*

9 Describe the difference between a 'random' sample and a 'quota' sample. *(4 marks)*

10 Briefly explain two factors that might cause bias in a sample of consumers. *(4 marks)*

11 Identify four different sources of secondary market research. *(4 marks)*

12 Briefly explain two advantages and two disadvantages of secondary market research. *(8 marks)*

13 What is the difference between 'quantitative' and 'qualitative' market research? *(4 marks)*

CASE STUDY 1 Holiday habits

The survey below describes the holiday habits of British people who decide to take holidays abroad.

Year	% of British people taking a winter* holiday abroad	% of British people taking a summer* holiday abroad
1987	5	40
1992	6	38
1997	8	35
2002	10	34

* Winter holiday = between December and February;
summer holiday = between June and August.

***Table 3.1** Holiday habits*

- Beach holidays represent 55% of summer holidays (45% of winter ones). The number of hours of sunshine is the main influence on the choice of resort.
- Short/City breaks are 15% of summer breaks (23% of winter). Shopping facilities and historic buildings

5

are the main reasons for selecting a place to visit.

- Skiing accounts for 2% of summer holidays (9% in
10   the winter).
- Some people take two or more holidays per annum.
- Social classes A and B are 69% more likely to take winter breaks than people from the other social classes.

- Winter holidaymakers are twice as likely to read 15 *The Times* and are 29% more likely to be heavy users of the internet.
- Winter holidaymakers are less likely to watch television, especially ITV1.

Source: *Media Week*, 24 January 2003.

Questions

Total: 25 marks (30 minutes)

1 Briefly explain why social classes A and B are 69% more likely to take winter breaks than other social classes (lines 12–14). *(3 marks)*

2 A tour operator can use different media (newspapers, magazines, television etc.) in which to advertise holidays. Examine the media that might be most effective for advertising winter holidays. *(6 marks)*

3 Analyse how a travel company might use this information to plan the types of holiday that it will offer. *(7 marks)*

4 Discuss how useful this information would be to a UK holiday resort trying to increase its popularity among UK holidaymakers. *(9 marks)*

CASE STUDY 2   A pattern for success at M & S?

Analysts criticised the board of Marks and Spencer for refusing to give details of its plans for the rapid expansion of its food, homeware and financial services sectors. There are fears that rapid expansion may 5 increase costs. After 3 years of declining profit, the company has enjoyed higher profits in 2001/02 and 2002/03.

Using focus groups to gather qualitative market research information, M & S established that its reputation for quality could lead to a successful diver- 10 sification into specialist shops. These would be based on existing strengths such as food and homeware (the latter having proved to be a successful addition to larger M & S stores).

Encouraged by the success of Tesco's move into 15 city-centre convenience stores, M & S decided to open ten 'Simply Food' shops specialising in takeaway foods, offering a total of 1,000 Marks and Spencer food lines. Justin King, Marks and Spencer's food director, commented: 'The Simply Food format was 20 created to take our quality food offering to innovative and more convenient locations for our customers.' Initially, all of these shops were located at railway stations or shopping precincts in the southeast of England. 25

'The trial has been invaluable in allowing us to develop the right product range and to understand the

shopping needs of commuters.' They have been so successful that in the railway stations they are
30 achieving sales per square foot that are four times as high as the shops that previously rented the sites. By 2005 M & S is targeting the nationwide opening of 150 'Simply Food' stores, of which 50 will be railway station locations.
35 In South Wales, primary market research into customer preferences led to the test marketing of a joint loyalty and credit card. Customers were able to collect vouchers to spend in M & S by using their credit cards in M & S or in other places. Positive results led to the national launch of the card in August 2003. 40

Source: adapted from *The Times*, 21 May 2003, and other sources.

Questions
Total: 25 marks (30 minutes)

1 What is meant by the term 'primary market research' (line 35)? *(3 marks)*

2 Explain **one** reason why Marks and Spencer would have used 'qualitative market research' before opening the 'Simply Food' stores. *(4 marks)*

3 Analyse the benefits that Marks and Spencer might have gained from test marketing its credit card before releasing it nationally. *(8 marks)*

4 Discuss the extent to which the success of the 'Simply Food' trial is a guarantee of success for the national launch in 2005. *(10 marks)*

CHAPTER 4

Marketing objectives

This chapter establishes how the marketing objectives of a business are derived from the broader corporate objectives. In showing the process that converts objectives to strategy and tactics, it provides the background to subsequent chapters on marketing strategies and tactics.

A firm's **marketing objectives** are the goals of the marketing function. These must be consistent with the organisation's **corporate objectives**: that is, with the goals of the organisation as a whole. For example, one of Tesco's corporate objectives is to increase market share in the UK grocery market. In order to achieve this objective in 2002/03, Tesco decided to set the following marketing objectives (www.tesco.com):

- introduce price cuts totalling over £1 billion
- broaden the range of products by extending its economy ('value') range and its premium ('finest') range
- introduce new food products
- open convenience stores (Tesco Extra and Tesco Express)

A marketing hierarchy

> **KEY TERMS**
>
> **marketing objectives:** the goals of the marketing function within an organisation.
> **marketing strategies:** long-term or medium-term plans, devised at senior management level, and designed to achieve the firm's marketing objectives.
> **marketing tactics:** short-term marketing measures adopted to meet the needs of a short-term threat or opportunity.

> **ⓔ EXAMINER'S VOICE**
>
> Define your terms at the beginning of your answer. In Unit 1 marks are awarded for correct definitions of the terms used in the questions. This also helps to make your answer relevant.

In order to achieve their marketing objectives, firms use **marketing strategies** and **tactics**. It is therefore possible to place a company's corporate objectives, marketing objectives, marketing strategies and marketing tactics into a hierarchy, as shown in Figure 4.1.

This is not just a one-way process. Feedback from staff involved with organising the company's marketing tactics will be used to advise the directors. Feedback from staff can help the senior managers or shareholders to agree more realistic objectives.

*Figure 4.1 An example of
a marketing hierarchy*

Corporate objectives
These show the main priorities of the organisation, e.g. to improve profitability
by 10% over the next 2 years

Marketing objectives
The marketing department or relevant managers must ensure that the marketing
objectives support the achievement of the corporate objectives, e.g. to increase the
market share of Brand X by 20% over the next 2 years

Marketing strategies
These strategies must assist the targets, e.g. to increase advertising expenditure
on Brand X by 15%

Marketing tactics
Detailed marketing department decisions will also be affected, e.g. the advertisements
must be designed to appeal to the market segments that the firm is targeting

Types of marketing objective

Marketing objectives depend on the aims and priorities of an organisation.
They can be categorised as follows.

Size

Size can be measured by sales or market share. The objective may be
expressed in terms of:

- a specific level of sales volume (e.g. Nestlé trying to maintain Kit Kat's sales
  volume of over 4 million bars every day)
- a percentage rise in sales revenue (e.g. Nokia trying to achieve a 10% rise
  in sales income in 2004)
- a target percentage market share (e.g. Peugeot targeting a 10% market
  share of the UK car market)
- market leadership or a certain position in the market (e.g. Asda overtaking
  Sainsbury's to become the second largest supermarket in the UK)

Market positioning

This is concerned with a company's appeal to particular market segments. For
example:

- rugby league trying to appeal to more females
- Starbucks targeting younger age groups
- Channel 5 bidding for *Robot Wars* in order to attract a new group of viewers
  (11–19-year-old males) who typically do not watch Channel 5

> *e* **EXAMINER'S VOICE**
>
> Marketing objectives
> are not static. They
> change as a business
> develops. They also
> change in response to
> external circumstances.

Innovation/increase in product range

For example:

- Ben & Jerry's introducing unusual flavours and names of ice cream in order to maintain its reputation for individuality
- Vodafone trying to achieve 20% of its sales from third-generation products

Creation of brand loyalty/goodwill

For example:

- McDonald's aiming to maintain the golden arches as the most widely recognised corporate logo in the world
- Specsavers aiming for a set percentage of 'repeat' customers
- Lush being able to set a premium price in comparison to other soap retailers

Security/survival

For example:

- Rover keeping a presence in the UK car market
- Lotto trying to make sure that its overall sales, which fell by 12% in 2002–03, do not fall further

---

GROUP EXERCISE

Hewlett-Packard: converting corporate objectives to marketing objectives

The corporate objectives of the IT company Hewlett-Packard are reproduced below.

Corporate objectives

- Customer loyalty: to provide products of the highest quality and value to customers.
- Profit: to achieve sufficient profit to achieve our other goals and to create value for our shareholders.
- Market leadership: to be number one or two in our chosen fields.
- Growth: to use size and innovation to take smart risks.
- Employee commitment: to value their contribution and help them to gain a sense of achievement from their work.
- Leadership capability: to develop leaders at every level.
- Global citizenship: to be an economic, intellectual and social asset to each country and community.

Source: www.hp.com

Question

Using the five types of marketing objective identified in this chapter, identify suitable marketing objectives to enable Hewlett-Packard to achieve its corporate objectives. Give reasons for your choices.

PRACTICE EXERCISE 1
Total: 20 marks (20 minutes)

1 Place the following in the correct order: marketing strategy, marketing objectives, corporate objectives, marketing tactics. *(4 marks)*

2 What is the difference between a marketing strategy and a marketing tactic? *(4 marks)*

3 What problem might arise if a firm's marketing department ignored its corporate objectives? *(4 marks)*

4 Study Tesco's marketing objectives in the opening paragraph of this chapter. Select any two of Tesco's marketing objectives and show how they will help Tesco to achieve its corporate objective of increasing its market share. *(8 marks)*

PRACTICE EXERCISE 2   Total: 15 marks (15 minutes)

easyCar.com is run in the same way as easyJet. Customers are offered a very basic, low-cost service at a very low price. easyCar.com is an example of how much an organisation's corporate aims can limit its scope for marketing strategies. Its philosophy is based on minimising costs through eliminating unnecessary expenditure. This allows the firm to charge low prices to customers. Marketing costs must also be minimised.

Questions

1 Select two marketing objectives that would be *unsuitable* for easyCar. Explain why you consider them to be unsuitable. *(6 marks)*

2 Select three marketing objectives that would be *suitable* for easyCar. Analyse why you consider them to be suitable. *(9 marks)*

CHAPTER 5

Marketing strategies

In this chapter the main marketing strategies adopted by organisations are considered:

- *The advantages and disadvantages of **niche marketing** are contrasted.*
- *Benefits and problems of **mass marketing** are examined, along with the scope for product differentiation in a mass market.*
- *The **product life cycle** is described and its strategic use examined, with particular emphasis on extension strategies. Problems of prediction and determinism in using the product life cycle are explained and the links between the product life cycle and cash flow and capacity utilisation are described. The role of the Boston matrix in **product portfolio analysis** is studied.*
- *The chapter concludes by showing how **adding value** can be achieved within the marketing function of an organisation.*

KEY TERMS

niche marketing: targeting a product or service at a small segment of a larger market.
mass marketing: aiming a product at all (or most) of the market.
product life cycle: the stages that a product passes through during its lifetime: development, introduction, growth, maturity and decline.
product portfolio: the range of products made by a firm.
adding value: the process of increasing the worth of resources by modifying them.

Niche marketing

A firm needs to decide whether to aim its product at a particular market segment or to appeal to the whole market. Both niche and mass marketing strategies can meet most of a firm's marketing objectives.

One example of a firm pursuing niche marketing is The Bear Factory, a shop that offers custom-made, personalised teddy bears, complete with birth certificates, personal taped messages and customised clothing.

Niche marketing is an attractive proposition for small firms, as there may be little competition in their segment. However, many firms involved in niche marketing are owned by, or divisions of, larger organisations. EMAP, one of the UK's largest magazine publishers, produces mass market publications but even its top sellers, such as *FHM* and *The Garden*, are aimed at specific segments. Niche markets are served more obviously by *Kerrang!*, *Pregnancy & Birth* and *Period Living & Traditional Homes*.

Some niche markets are based on exclusive or high-quality products (e.g. Ferrari) or are located in remote areas, where higher prices can be charged because of the inconvenience for consumers of finding a competitor. But many niche markets focus on lower-priced goods (e.g. Poundstretcher), possibly because larger firms are put off by the low profit margins.

Advantages of niche marketing

- There may be fewer competitors, as large companies are not attracted to a relatively small market. For example, there is only one magazine for orienteering, a minority sport, because the potential readership is too low to interest large firms with high overheads. The lack of competition allows firms to charge a higher price for their products.
- The lack of scope for economies of scale may mean that small firms can compete more effectively in a niche market.
- The limited demand may suit a small firm that would lack the resources to produce on a large scale.
- A firm can adapt its product to meet the specific needs of the niche market, rather than compromise between the needs of many different groups of consumers. This makes the product more attractive and is likely to allow the firm to charge a higher price.
- It can be easier for firms to target customers and promote their products effectively when they are only selling to a certain type of customer.

> **DID YOU KNOW?**
>
> Although more specific targeting is usually an advantage of niche marketing (e.g. *FHM* and *Bliss* magazines have a clear idea of their readership and how to reach them), this is not always the case. The Bear Factory has found it very difficult to reach its customers, who do not fit into the usual market segments. For instance, the firm has been surprised by the number of teenage boys buying bears for their girlfriends — a behaviour pattern not identified in its early research.

Disadvantages of niche marketing

- The small scale of the market limits the chances of high profit. Even if a high price can be charged, the lack of customers will affect the total profit made. In addition, unit costs tend to be higher, again reducing the potential for high profit margins.
- Small firms in niche markets can be vulnerable to changes in demand. Niche markets are specialised, so firms operating in niche markets are not able to spread their risks. For this reason, a decline in interest among consumers may threaten the firm's existence.
- An increase in interest may be enough to attract larger firms into the market. Holland & Barrett identified health foods as a market niche many years ago, but has not grown quickly. This is because, as the demand for health foods increased, the large supermarkets decided to offer many more health foods. In rapidly changing times, it is likely that

firms in niche markets will make high profits only in the short term, unless they can keep reacting quickly to changes.

FACT FILE

Ben & Jerry's ice cream tries to emphasise its reputation for niche marketing by sponsoring, in the firm's own words, 'the world's weirdest championships', in keeping with its 'irreverent personality and quirky approach to life'. Lauren Nola, brand manager, commented on Ben & Jerry's sponsorship of three world championships: bog snorkelling, conkers and toe wrestling. 'We are delighted to lend a hand to each of these wacky events and are looking forward to another season of world record breaking bizarreness.' Ironically, Ben & Jerry's is owned by Unilever, one of the UK's largest companies.   Source: www.benjerry.co.uk

---

Mass marketing

Examples of mass-market goods are petrol and baked beans. Within a mass market there is only limited scope for targeting. For instance, there is little scope to modify petrol to appeal to a niche market, although cars can be modified to run on more environmentally friendly fuel. There are more variations to baked beans, aimed mainly at children, but most baked beans are sold in the mass market.

Advantages of mass marketing

- Large-scale production is possible, which will help to lower costs per unit. This should improve profit margins.
- The sheer volume of customers enables companies to earn huge revenues. The chemicals industry in the UK is worth over £36 billion per annum. There are roughly 500 UK chemical firms with sales turnover in excess of £5 million per year.
- Mass marketing allows firms to use the most expensive (and usually the most effective) marketing. Not only does this help to eliminate smaller rivals, but it can also act as a barrier to entry for new firms. The soap powder industry is dominated by two large firms with huge marketing budgets. For over 50 years this has limited the opportunities for new firms to break into the market, as they cannot afford the advertising budgets required.

- In industries such as pharmaceuticals it is necessary to appeal to large, profitable mass markets in order to be able to fund the research and development costs needed to introduce new products. It is estimated that discovering a new pharmaceutical product and bringing it to the market costs a firm about £400 million.
- Mass marketing increases brand awareness. This not only assists sales of the branded product but can also help to break down consumer resistance to new products.

Disadvantages of mass marketing

- High fixed capital costs are incurred. This will prevent many firms from operating.
- Firms in mass markets are vulnerable to changes in demand. A fall in demand will lead to unused spare capacity, increasing unit costs. As the pace of change accelerates, this is becoming a much greater problem because customers want the latest products.
- It can be difficult to appeal directly to each individual customer because mass-market products must be designed to suit all customers.

Through careful market research, firms in mass markets can reduce these risks, but there is always a danger that demand for their products will fall. Consequently, such firms must continually examine the product life cycles of their products and analyse their product portfolios, in order to ensure that their goods continue to suit the market.

Product differentiation in the mass market

KEY TERM

product differentiation: the degree to which consumers see a particular brand as being different from other brands.

In order to compete in a mass market, a firm needs to make sure that its product is different from competitors' products. If consumers value this difference, it will benefit the firm in two ways:
- increased sales volume
- greater scope for charging a higher price

In a mass market, product differentiation will usually be achieved by using elements of the marketing mix (see Chapters 6–9). Examples include:
- Design, branding and packaging to improve the attractiveness of a product.

FACT FILE

At one time, Quaker Oats manufactured all of the porridge for UK supermarket own labels. Although the contents were identical, consumers still felt more secure buying the Quaker Oats brand, which sold at a higher price. Similarly, General Motors used the Vauxhall brand name in the UK and the Opel brand in Germany to sell identical cars because these brand names were preferred by UK and German customers, respectively.

FACT FILE

Over many years, 'blind taste tests' suggested that consumers preferred Pepsi to Coca-Cola (when they could not see the brand name), but Coca-Cola always sold in higher quantities because people preferred the brand.

- Clever promotional and advertising campaigns to boost image and sales. Are Nike sportswear and trainers of better quality than their competitors, or are they just marketed more effectively?
- Different distribution methods. Avon cosmetics differentiated itself by selling cosmetics directly to the customer; Amazon differentiated itself through internet selling, without the use of a traditional shop outlet.

Many mass-market firms achieve product differentiation through **product proliferation**. This occurs when a variety of products are produced, in order to serve different tastes. In some cases this can mean significantly different products, such as IPC magazines producing *Woman's Own*, *Loaded*, *Ideal Home*, *Uncut* and *NME*. However, the need for mass production in order to cut costs will limit the number of different products that can be offered.

Product life cycle

The product life cycle shows the stages that a product passes through during its lifetime (see Figure 5.1). These stages are:
- development
- introduction
- growth
- maturity
- decline

Stages in the product life cycle

1 Development

During this stage, an organisation will undertake various activities to prepare for the launch of its product. Examples of these activities are given below.
- **Generation of ideas.** For product-led or asset-led products, ideas are likely to come from within the company. This might take the form of research and development, leading to the introduction of a new product (a common approach in the pharmaceutical industry). Alternatively, in industries such as broadcasting, ideas are likely to be generated through brainstorming or suggestions by staff. For market-led products, ideas will normally come

Figure 5.1
The product life cycle

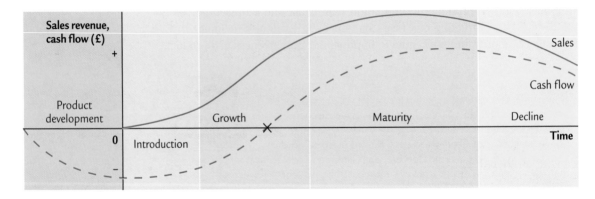

from external market research that will identify the types of new product that customers wish to buy. (Convenience foods are often developed from researching consumer buying habits.)

- **Analysis of ideas.** The next step is to look at the feasibility of the idea, to consider whether it meets the firm's objectives and fits in with its image.
- **Product development.** The working of the product may be tested through a prototype or by simulation on a computer.
- **Test marketing.** The use of test marketing (a small-scale release of the product, usually in a limited area) is helpful as it can avoid heavy losses if a product proves to be unpopular.
- **Launch.** The launch will take place after the firm has made modifications suggested by the previous activities. Over 70% of new products that are launched will fail within 3 years, so firms will want to look very closely at any product before its launch. The vast majority of ideas generated will never reach the launch stage.

As can be seen in Figure 5.1, there is no sales revenue during the development stage and a negative cash flow. Cash is required to fund the research and, if the product is going to be launched, there will be a period of high outflows of cash to purchase equipment, employ staff, conduct research and finance advertisements for the launch.

2 Introduction

This stage starts with the launch and continues during the period in which the product is new to the market. Usually sales pick up slowly at first, as shops are not always keen to stock a new, unknown product, and customers are reluctant to change from their existing brands. Intensive introductory marketing and special offers can lead to increased sales volume as customer awareness grows. However, cash flow continues to be negative during introduction because of high marketing costs and low production levels, which mean high average costs of production. Furthermore, sales revenue might also be low if low prices are used to encourage sales (**penetration pricing**). If the product has a successful introduction, it will pass on to the next stage.

3 Growth

As the product becomes more popular, it enters the growth stage. Retailers are more likely to provide shelf space and brand recognition helps to increase sales. Profitability may be reached as the initial burst of marketing is no longer needed and it becomes cheaper to produce each product.

4 Maturity

During this stage, the firm will hope to make a profit and sales will tend to stabilise. However, they may increase steadily if the product is in an expanding market. For example, sales of garden plants have continued to grow, even though plants such as daffodils have been in the maturity stage for many years.

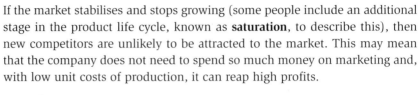

If the market stabilises and stops growing (some people include an additional stage in the product life cycle, known as **saturation**, to describe this), then new competitors are unlikely to be attracted to the market. This may mean that the company does not need to spend so much money on marketing and, with low unit costs of production, it can reap high profits.

5 Decline

Eventually sales of a product will fall. However, some products, such as Kellogg's Cornflakes, have existed for almost a century. Similarly, the major products of each of the three largest UK chocolate manufacturers were launched, respectively, in 1905 (Cadbury's Dairy Milk), 1922 (the Mars Bar) and 1935 (Nestlé's Kit Kat). In more dynamic markets, such as computer games and the pop music industry, product life cycles are measured in weeks. Once a product is in decline, the firm may decide to remove it from its range, to prevent financial losses.

Strategic use of the product life cycle

In theory, a firm should aim to have as many products in 'maturity' as possible, as these are the products that should generate most profit. However, to achieve this in the long run a firm needs to have a policy of **new product development**, so that it has products in the introduction and growth stages which will eventually enter maturity. Consequently, firms attempt to have a balance of products under development and in the introductory and growth stages, financed by the profits generated by their mature products.

The exact strategies used by a firm will depend on the stage of the product life cycle.

Introduction

Pricing strategy is a key element at this stage. Very low prices are an excellent way to persuade consumers to try a product for the first time, but it is usually advisable to make it clear that the low price is being set for a limited period, as all of the goodwill from customers could be lost if there is a sudden price rise later on. For more exclusive products, a high price may be set to show that the product is superior to its rivals. Whatever pricing strategy is employed, promotion and advertising are needed to help customers recognise the product and to increase their awareness of it. The business also needs to put considerable effort into encouraging retailers to provide shelf space for its product. Without this, its other strategies are doomed to failure.

Growth

During growth the firm will adapt its strategies according to its market research results. Possible strategies will include modifying the product, targeting new market segments through different promotions, widening the distribution and changing price.

Maturity

The firm will wish to keep its products in this stage for as long as possible, in order to extend their life. It can do this by using **extension strategies**.

KEY TERM

extension strategies: methods used to lengthen the life cycle of a product by preventing or delaying it from reaching the decline stage of the product life cycle.

The main types of extension strategy are as follows:

- **Attracting new market segments.** Firms may target new groups of consumers or market niches in order to expand sales. Mothercare extended its original baby products to children and expectant mothers.
- **Increasing usage among existing customers.** Kellogg's is promoting its cereal products as items that can be eaten throughout the day, rather than just at breakfast time. This is particularly important as fewer people are eating breakfast.
- **Modifying the product.** Coca-Cola has introduced many variations to its basic product in order to appeal to different consumers.
- **Changing the image.** Lucozade was originally promoted as a drink to help overcome illness; it has been much more successful as an energy drink.
- **Targeting new markets.** This can involve moving beyond the original region or country targeted by the product. Tobacco companies have been very successful in increasing sales in developing countries.
- **Promotions, advertising and price offers.** To maintain consumer interest, new advertisements, prizes, competitions and promotions such as 'buy one get one free' can be introduced.

Decline

If the firm sees a decline in sales for its product as temporary, it should continue to use extension strategies. Once decline is seen as inevitable, however, the firm can 'milk' the product. By cutting advertising expenditure, the firm may be able to achieve high profits for a period of time. Eventually the firm should take the product off the market, but only if it has ceased to be profitable. Most national newspapers are in decline but they can still generate a profit. If their rivals leave the market first, it is even possible that their sales will recover.

Problems of predicting the product life cycle

The product life cycle is of limited use in strategic planning because the exact life span of a product is never known. In industries that experience relatively few changes, the life cycle can be easier to predict, but it is more useful in explaining past events than future trends. The confectionery market is relatively stable, with some products having very long lifetimes. Recent sales figures suggest that the Mars Bar may have entered its decline phase, but this may just be a temporary fall — only time will tell.

It is important to predict life cycles in order to assess whether a product launch is feasible. A record label knows that a record will need to make a profit within months of its launch; a bus company can expect its bus to take much longer to make a profit.

> **DID YOU KNOW?**
>
> Product life cycles are getting shorter. Although the exact lengths are impossible to predict, consumers are constantly striving for new products and are less loyal to brands than in the past. This means that firms need to plan shorter, more intensive promotional campaigns and spend more time on developing new products. Higher prices will be needed to compensate for the higher costs and lower sales figures.

Problems of determinism in the product life cycle

> **KEY TERM**
>
> ▮ **determinism:** the idea that something will occur if you expect it to happen.

Determinism can apply to the product life cycle. If an organisation believes that a product has entered its decline stage, it will be tempted to cut back on promotion and development costs, expecting that these will be wasted. As a consequence, customers may cut back on purchases as they become less aware of the product's existence. Shops may no longer stock the product if they see that the firm has stopped promoting it. Overall these factors will lead to a decline, but the decline has been caused by the firm's actions — it is possible that the original fall in demand might only have been temporary.

Determinism also applies to other stages of the product life cycle. If growth is expected, the firm will spend more on promotions and this additional expenditure on promotion may well achieve the results expected.

Firms can, of course, ignore this deterministic approach. Mars has spent £7.5 million on relaunching the Mars Bar, but if the Mars Bar has reached decline this could prove to be a costly mistake.

> **FACT FILE**
>
> Oxo cubes were introduced in 1910, but in the 1950s they went into an apparently terminal decline. Analysts suggested that the product was too old-fashioned to survive. Rather than accept this advice, Oxo repackaged the product and started to promote it heavily. Product variations and highly successful advertising campaigns have kept Oxo in maturity for a further 50 years. Ironically, one of the main reasons for the repackaging was to save costs — the expensive tin containers, which turned out to be the main cause of consumers' dislike of the product, were replaced by cheaper, paper packaging that presented a more modern image.

The product life cycle and cash flow

> **KEY TERM**
>
> ▮ **cash flow:** the movement of money in and out of an organisation, over a given time period.

Figure 5.1 (see p. 32) shows a typical product life cycle and the pattern of cash flow that arises. The dangers of releasing a new product are clear, as it will take some time before a product starts to generate positive cash flow. The problem is worsened by the fact that many products will incur the costs shown but never reach the introduction or growth stages.

Development

During this stage, research and development costs will be incurred and some market research will be necessary. If it is intended to launch the product, expenditure will be incurred in promoting it just prior to launch and production costs will be high, especially if new equipment is needed to produce the product. No cash inflows will be received at this point.

Introduction

Some cash will be received from sales, but promotion costs will be very high to make the public aware of the product. Price offers may reduce the inflows of cash. Production costs per unit may be high, as the scale of production will be low.

Growth

At this stage it may become possible to cut back on promotion costs, and if growth is good, economies of scale can be achieved. This will mean lower production costs per item. The increased sales revenue should enable the firm finally to achieve a positive cash-flow situation (shown as point X in Figure 5.1).

Maturity

In maturity, the firm will receive the highest inflows of cash from the product, while unit costs of production should be low. Although promotion expenditure may be high, it will be spread over a wider number of products, reducing unit costs.

Decline

In the early stages of decline, a firm may save money by cutting advertising. However, if sales volume falls below a certain level, cash flow may become negative again, particularly because declining products may need price cuts to encourage consumers. A business may be able to anticipate these problems and withdraw a product before this situation arises. Ford replaced the Ford Escort before it reached decline, as it recognised that its new models would attract loyal Ford customers. Allowing the Escort to decline might have led some purchasers to transfer to other manufacturers.

The product life cycle and capacity utilisation

 TERMS

capacity: the maximum amount of output of a product that an organisation can produce in a given time.

capacity utilisation: the actual level of output of a product as a percentage of the maximum level of output that could be achieved.

It is vital for a firm to identify where its products are in their life cycle, and what their likely sales will be in the future, so that they have sufficient capital, labour and land to produce them. The national launch of Cadbury's Wispa was delayed considerably because the company's market research underestimated the product's success and Cadbury did not have the capacity to meet demand. Time was lost setting up a new factory.

However, over-optimism may cause different problems. A huge factory with very low capacity utilisation will incur very high unit costs. A factory working at 50% capacity will incur the same fixed costs as one that is working at 100% capacity, so the fixed costs per item produced will be twice as high. Thus an over-optimistic prediction of future sales may have a big impact on the costs of production (and possibly the success of the product itself).

In multi-product firms, this problem can be relieved by switching between products. If production is subcontracted to other companies, then it may be possible to adjust capacity more quickly.

During maturity and growth, decisions about capacity may be critical to the success of a product. Arsenal Football Club is finding it increasingly difficult to compete with other top clubs financially because it has not increased the capacity of its ground, and so its attendances are lower. However, Huddersfield Town FC got into financial difficulties because it spent a lot of money on developing a ground that it was unable to fill with spectators.

Product portfolio analysis

Very few firms rely on one product. In a multi-product firm, the range of products is its **product portfolio**. For example, at one time Heinz had 57 varieties of products. Most firms plan their marketing strategy in a way that spreads their risk. If one product has low sales, it may be supported by other, more successful products.

A popular method of product portfolio analysis is the Boston matrix (sometimes referred to as the Boston box or Boston grid). This matrix, shown in Figure 5.2, helps a firm to assess the balance of its portfolio of products.

Boston matrix: a tool of product portfolio analysis which classifies products according to the market share of the product and the rate of growth of the market in which the product is sold.

The different types of product identified in the Boston matrix are as follows.

Stars

These are products with a high percentage market share in a high-growth market. They enjoy increasing sales revenue but, because the market is growing, competitors will be encouraged to focus on this market. As a result, stars need a lot of promotional spending and may involve the business in capital expenditure (to increase capacity). Therefore, in the short term, they may cause outflows of cash to exceed inflows. However, usually they will generate profits that can be used to support other products.

Cash cows

These products have a high percentage market share in a low-growth market. Cash cows often exist in established markets that have reached maturity. The low rate of growth discourages new firms from entering the market and so it is possible to spend less on advertising. The name arises from the fact that companies can 'milk' the cash cow in order to support other products. A high proportion of cash cows is ideal for companies seeking high profits, but firms with cash cows will want to develop new products in order to enter fast-growth markets. Prudential Insurance foresaw that the credit card market would grow faster than its core business and used its cash cows, such as standard life assurance policies, to finance the Egg credit card.

Problem children (also known as question marks)

This term applies to goods or services with a low percentage market share in a high-growth market. The name is given because they pose a difficult problem for a firm. By definition they are competing in a competitive market, but as the market is growing there is scope for future sales increases even if the product does not increase its market share. Many new products will be problem children when first released, so it is inevitable that a firm will possess some problem children. These are products that tend to need a lot of market research and promotion in order to succeed. If successful, they may become stars or cash cows.

Dogs

Dogs are goods with a low percentage market share in a low growth market. Firms need to think carefully about retaining such products, as they offer little scope for profit making. In a recession, these products are likely to be withdrawn if they become unprofitable. However, dogs should not be written off too lightly. Cadbury's Whole Nut, for example, could be seen as a dog, as it has only a 1% share of a low-growth market (confectionery). However, this 1% market share represents £40 million of sales per year.

Figure 5.2
The Boston matrix

> **e** EXAMINER'S VOICE
>
> Be careful! The Boston matrix is just a generalisation. Cash cows can lose money and dogs can be very profitable in the right circumstances. Always look critically at business theories; they are usually a guide rather than a scientifically proven fact. You may be asked to evaluate the usefulness of a particular business theory or idea.

Adding value

Adding value is the process of increasing the worth of resources by modifying them. Added value is calculated by the following formula:

added value $=$ sales revenue $-$ the cost of bought-in materials, components and services

The production process is seen to be a major factor in achieving added value. For example, the transformation of various components into a television set adds value, as people place a higher value on the television set than on the bits and pieces used to make it. Similarly, distribution and retailing add value by bringing the product within easier reach of the customer.

Marketing can add value by:
- creating a unique selling point/proposition (USP) — this may be real, such as a different design or different components, or it may be based on image and branding.
- identifying an attractive mix of design, function, image and service.

KEY TERM

unique selling point/proposition (USP): a feature of a product or service that allows it to be differentiated from other products.

If a firm can improve customer awareness and goodwill by making its product different from rival products, it can increase both its sales volume and its price. Loyal customers are also less likely to stop buying the firm's product. Note that the value of an item is the price that people are prepared to pay — branding can improve people's desire for a product and thus add value. Coffee is a classic example of a product that has achieved higher added value through marketing. People will pay much more for coffee than the original ingredients for several reasons:
- Brand names have persuaded customers that certain coffees are superior to others.
- Images created by advertising (e.g. for Gold Blend) attract people who wish to relate to that image.
- Modifications to the blend (decaffeinated, Colombian etc.) can attract specific segments of the market.
- Packaging may enhance the perceived quality of the product.
- Service provided by coffee houses has created a cultural change. Shoppers are prepared to pay much more for a Starbucks coffee because of the attractive environment in which they consume it.
- Greater individuality of blends, as provided by companies such as Costa, have aroused greater interest and have persuaded customers to purchase more coffee at a higher price.

Partially as a result of this marketing activity, coffee is now the UK's second largest commodity market (after oil).

PRACTICE EXERCISE

1 Give three examples of 'niche markets'. *(3 marks)*

2 Why might a magazine publisher target a niche market? *(4 marks)*

3 Is it inevitable that businesses in a niche market will be unable to break into a mass market? *(8 marks)*

4 Briefly explain three benefits of mass marketing. *(6 marks)*

5 What is meant by 'product differentiation'? *(3 marks)*

6 How can a product achieve 'product differentiation'? *(4 marks)*

7 Identify the four stages of the product life cycle that follow the launch date of a new product. *(4 marks)*

8 How does the product life cycle influence a firm's cash flow? *(6 marks)*

9 a Identify the most profitable stage of the product life cycle. *(1 mark)*

   b Why might a business not want all of its products at this stage of the product life cycle? *(4 marks)*

10 Identify four extension strategies and give a real-life example of each one. *(8 marks)*

11 Why is 'determinism' a problem in a firm's management of the product life cycles of its products? *(5 marks)*

12 In marketing terms, what is the difference between a 'star' and a 'dog'? *(4 marks)*

13 Why are some products called 'cash cows'? *(3 marks)*

14 Explain the business significance of the term 'USP'. *(4 marks)*

15 Identify four ways of adding value through marketing and give a real-life example of each one. *(8 marks)*

CASE STUDY 1   The Mars Bar

In the early part of the twenty-first century, sales of Mars Bars began to decline and the product's market share fell to 7.2%. This led to a £7.5 million relaunch in March 2002. Features of the relaunch were:

5 ■ new advertising
■ a modified, slimmer bar with a lighter feel to the inside
■ modernised packaging
■ new in-store promotions
10 ■ a new slogan (strapline): 'pleasure you can't measure'
■ a £250,000 programme of public relations activities

In designing the relaunch, Mars felt that it was vital to keep many of the existing features of the brand in 15 order to retain the loyalty of its traditional customers. The main strategy was to replace its former image (a chocolate to relieve hunger) with one featuring it as an everyday treat. In so doing, it would increase its appeal to the female market — usually the largest 20 chocolate eaters, but only 40% of the consumers of Mars Bars.

Both qualitative and quantitative market research were carried out to identify how changes to the product and its marketing would affect sales. Mars 25 wanted to target the youth market (those aged 16–24)

to a greater extent. Table 5.1 shows the breakdown of Mars' consumers by age.

Age	Proportion of people who eat Mars Bars (%)	Volume of sales by age (%)
45+	37	24
35–44	16	21
25–34	18	17
16–24	14	22
0–15	15	16

Table 5.1 *Consumers of Mars Bars by age group, February 2002*

The public relations campaign was introduced a month ahead of the advertising campaign. Press releases were combined with features in trade magazines and interviews on radio and television. Human interest stories were featured in various media, further increasing awareness. By the time the advertising started, Mars believed that its customers (and its retailers) had achieved a good understanding of the reasons for the relaunch. Mars estimated that the £250,000 spent on public relations produced media coverage that was worth £2.5 million (the equivalent of 100 television advertisements), equating to £10 media coverage for every £1 spent.

In the 6 weeks following the launch, sales of Mars Bars increased by 20% in a confectionery market that showed no change in overall sales, allowing Mars to achieve its highest market share for 6 years.

Sources: various.

Questions

Total: 25 marks (30 minutes)

1 What is meant by the term 'quantitative market research' (lines 23–24)? *(3 marks)*

2 Based on the information above, calculate Mars' market share 6 weeks after the launch. *(4 marks)*

3 Analyse the possible reasons why Mars decided to target the youth market. *(8 marks)*

4 To what extent was the relaunch of the Mars Bar a risky strategy for the business? *(10 marks)*

CASE STUDY 2 Lush Cosmetics

Lush Cosmetics was originally set up in 1978, supplying cosmetics to The Body Shop. However, an ill-fated venture into mail order led to its collapse.

Lush recommenced trading in 1994, producing soaps, shampoos, cosmetics and related products. This time it decided to open its own retail outlets. It has been so successful that, in addition to manufacturing all of its own products, it has set up over 100 stores in the UK alone. Overseas there are over 150 franchises in 30 different countries.

The unique selling point for Lush is its range of products. Each bar of soap, shampoo etc. contains fresh (not synthetic) ingredients, ranging from the predictable (aloe vera, lemon and tea tree oil) to the peculiar (Belgian chocolate, almond shells and marigold petals). In this way, Lush sees itself as operating in a niche market rather than in a mass market. Products are not tested on animals. For its overseas franchises, the products are manufactured locally to guarantee freshness.

Marketing is mostly by word of mouth and through an in-house magazine, which has also been used to re-establish a mail order service. The nature of the ingredients means that the location of a Lush shop can usually be detected by smell from a

considerable distance (depending on the wind direction). This can also help to encourage consumers to visit the shops.

Over 200 products are made, with the range constantly changing according to demand. Unsuccessful products are quickly eliminated and there is constant research aimed at producing new products. The product range is updated every 3 months. Consumers and press reports are used to provide marketing slogans, such as 'Lush is like the AA, pretty vital in a crisis' and 'It's better to bathe in sweets than to eat them'. Interest is also aroused through unusual product names such as 'Honey I Washed the Kids' and 'Sex Bomb'. Staff are encouraged to spot celebrities, and a list of famous names, and their Lush purchases, is regularly updated on the company website.

With product prices ranging from £1.95 per 200 grams for some shampoos to £2.85 for a 30-gram glitter massage bar, Lush is achieving high value added. The ingredients of a glitter massage bar can cost as little as 50p, and bought-in services cost 10p for each bar, on average.

Source: www.lush.co.uk

Question 1
Total: 25 marks (30 minutes)

a What is meant by the term 'unique selling point' (line 11)? *(3 marks)*

b Calculate the 'added value' of a batch of 50 Lush glitter bars. *(4 marks)*

c Analyse the reasons why Lush introduces new products every 3 months. *(8 marks)*

d Evaluate the main factors that allow Lush to add value. *(10 marks)*

Question 2
Total: 25 marks (30 minutes)

a Distinguish between a 'niche market' and a 'mass market' (lines 18–19). *(4 marks)*

b Explain **one** way in which the product life cycle influences Lush's marketing activities. *(5 marks)*

c Analyse **two** reasons why Lush might have decided to open its own shops when it relaunched in 1994. *(7 marks)*

d Discuss the difficulties faced by Lush as a result of its decision to produce a range of 200 different products. *(9 marks)*

CHAPTER 6

The marketing mix: product

ℯ EXAMINER'S VOICE

Chapters 6-9 study the marketing mix. For convenience, each element of the marketing mix is examined in a separate chapter in this book, with questions testing the understanding gained from that chapter. However, the AQA specification states that the marketing mix should be looked at with emphasis on the integrated nature of the mix.

No element of the marketing mix should be treated in isolation from the other elements. Having studied each element in Chapters 6-9, the integrated marketing mix questions after Chapter 9 should be read and attempted. The questions in Chapters 6-9 are presented in the AQA style to help the learning process, but in the examination itself there will not be a whole series of questions devoted to just one element, such as place or promotion. In the examination, the data and the set of questions will cover a broad area, although individual questions might concentrate on just one part of the marketing mix.

*This chapter introduces the idea of the marketing mix: product, price, promotion and place (the **four Ps**). Its main focus is on **product**. The features of a good product are noted and the process of new product development is shown. The concept of branding is explained and the relative merits of focusing on the core product or following a policy of product proliferation are contrasted.*

KEY TERM

▌ **product:** the good or service provided by a business.

The main elements of a successful product are the **design of the product** and **new product development**.

KEY TERMS

▌ **product design:** deciding on the make-up of a product so that it works well, looks good and can be produced economically.
▌ **product development:** when a firm creates a new or improved good or service, for release into an existing market.

Product design

The product must appeal to the consumer. The characteristics of a good product will vary according to the customer and according to the product, but the key features influencing car purchases provide a useful summary:

- **Reliability.** Manufacturers such as Volkswagen have a reputation for reliability that appeals to car buyers.
- **Safety.** Ford introduced a braking system that allowed a car to be steered safely after braking; prior to this invention, cars were less safe when braking.
- **Convenience of use.** All companies make sure that their dashboards are designed for ease of use, with all of the key items within easy reach. The Vauxhall Zafira possesses a variety of seat adjustments to improve flexibility and convenience.
- **Fashion.** Renault is trying to focus attention on the boot of the Mégane, emphasising its uniqueness in order to persuade buyers seeking a fashionable car.
- **Aesthetic qualities.** Ferrari and other sports car manufacturers spend a great deal of time and money on perfecting stylish design.
- **Durability.** Volvo has a reputation for making long-lasting cars. This attracts purchasers looking for a vehicle that will last for many years.
- **Legal requirements.** In recent years, all car manufacturers have been forced to redesign cars in order to improve exhaust emissions, meet stricter safety requirements and become more energy efficient.

To the firm, the key elements are the product's ability to satisfy consumer tastes, its financial viability, its effect on the organisation's reputation and whether the company can produce it without difficulty.

New product development

Every new product will pass through certain stages before it is launched. Each stage is designed to reduce the level of risk, but even after these stages have been completed it is still the case that 90% of new products will not survive. The stages of new product development are described in Chapter 5 (see pp. 32–33). The following example (sourced from www.unilever.co.uk) shows how they were applied to the development of PG Tips Pyramid tea bags.

1 Generation of ideas. Unilever (the owners of PG Tips) wanted to increase the appeal of tea to younger users. The need for the 'ultimate tea bag' design was identified as the key feature.

2 Analysis of ideas. Consumer research was conducted and the product and its packaging were modified as a result. This led to the setting of objectives. The aim of the new product was to achieve consumption levels of 35 million cups a day, with a higher percentage market share of consumers in their twenties. At this point different advertising agencies submitted ideas and one was commissioned to develop a campaign of advertising and promotion. Unilever sales forces were then used to demonstrate the product and its support package (the advertising and promotions) to retailers and wholesalers, to evaluate their views and to try to persuade them of the benefits of stocking the new tea bag.

3 Product development. The specialist machinery needed to make the new style of tea bags was tested and the production line established. Working prototypes were made to support the visit of the sales force to retailers. It was decided not to use test marketing.

4 Launch. The product was launched region by region in a rolling programme, to make sure that the firm had the resources to support the new product (and to minimise wastage of the old square bags).

The product launch took 4 years in total, during which constant research led to numerous changes. Market research is being continued to identify consumer reactions and to inform future strategies and tactics.

Branding

 TERM

> **branding:** the process of differentiating a product or service from its competitors through the name, sign, symbol, design or slogan linked to that product.

Brands can add value to a product and a firm. Consumers are much more likely to buy Coca-Cola than Panda Cola, simply because of the name. When Nestlé bought Rowntree Mackintosh, it paid a sum that was more than double the value of the company's tangible assets (e.g. machinery). In effect, Nestlé paid over £6 billion just to get hold of famous brand names such as Kit Kat and Yorkie.

'Focus on core' versus 'product proliferation'

Views on product strategy vary between companies and over time. Some businesses are noted for their **focus on core products or services**, providing a relatively narrow range of products. Coca-Cola and McDonald's are good examples. Other businesses develop a diverse range of goods and services (**product proliferation**), notable examples being Unilever and Virgin.

Table 6.1 summarises the key reasons for each approach.

In the 1960s and 1970s, business strategies often concentrated on the need for expansion and diversification, mainly so that UK firms could compete with manufacturers from larger markets, such as the USA. However, since the 1980s business thinking has tended to support smaller, more flexible business structures that are able to respond more quickly to consumer tastes. This has led to firms moving from very wide product ranges towards more limited, focused product ranges.

Focus on core	Product proliferation
• Concentration on areas of expertise will lead to greater efficiency, as the firm will benefit from specialisation.	• Increasing the number of products will spread risks and this may help to secure the firm's future.
• The firm is more likely to understand the nature of its core business and is thus more likely to recognise the needs of the market.	• Different products or variations of a product can appeal to different market segments, so this approach will allow a firm to increase sales.
• Each product is likely to be produced on a much larger scale, so the firm will benefit from internal economies of scale.	• Market saturation may mean that a firm can grow only if it diversifies into different areas of activity.
• Consumers will trust a firm's ability to deliver quality if it concentrates on a few carefully selected areas of activity.	• New products may have some connection to existing products and help sales, e.g. a brewer developing soft drinks.
• Directors will be more capable of controlling an organisation with a narrow focus than one that covers many different activities.	• There may be greater scope for expansion in other product areas.
	• Customer tastes may be changing and spreading, e.g. mobile phone companies need to produce a wider range of phones to meet the needs of today's consumers.

Table 6.1 Benefits of different product strategies

FACT FILE

Fat Face started as a business providing printed T-shirts for skiers and snowboarders. Joint owners, Jules Leaver and Tim Slade, realised that in order to sustain turnover throughout the year they would need to produce other products. To satisfy demand in the summer months, they produced T-shirts and fleeces that appealed to sailing and windsurfing enthusiasts. In 15 years, sales turnover has grown to £25 million per annum.   Source: www.fatface.co.uk

The state of the economy also influences the choice between core business and product proliferation. In boom times, firms are anxious to attract as many customers as possible and will therefore broaden their product range. In times of recession, firms seek to cut costs and a reduction in the number of products can be a cost-effective way of achieving this, especially as one product may be 'cannibalising' (taking away) sales from another of the firm's own products.

DID YOU KNOW?

UK consumers spent approximately £230 million on British-style frozen meals in 2002, but this market is falling further behind international-style frozen meals, which exceed £350 million. However, both markets are being challenged by the rise in takeaways and eating out. These constant changes mean that retailers (and the companies that supply them) must keep modifying their product ranges in order to stay competitive.

FACT FILE

The Glastonbury Festival is a good example of a 'service' whose main marketing attempts are focused on its qualities as a 'product'. Whereas other festivals are heavily advertised through the media and promotions, Glastonbury relies on a number of unique attractions:

- its image as a 'lifestyle rather than a big gig'
- its relative lack of corporate sponsorship
- the views and leadership of its organiser, Michael Eavis
- its six-figure support for charities such as WaterAid and Greenpeace
- its tradition and reputation as an institution
- the range of music in its typical line-ups
- its ability to attract acts without incurring the huge fees charged to other organisations

Source: www.glastonburyfestivals.co.uk

e EXAMINER'S VOICE

To evaluate you need to make a judgement. It is good practice to weigh up your arguments at the end of an answer that requires evaluation and make a definite decision, showing the reasons why, on balance, you made this decision.

PRACTICE EXERCISE

Total: 40 marks (35 minutes)

1 Study the list of seven factors described as key features influencing car purchase (see p. 45).

  a Name seven different products, one for which reliability is the most important factor, one where safety is the most important factor, and so on. *(7 marks)*

  b Identify another product where all seven features are important. Justify your choice. *(5 marks)*

2 Analyse two possible reasons why 90% of all new products fail. *(7 marks)*

3 What is meant by the term 'brand'? *(3 marks)*

4 Describe two advantages for a firm that decides to focus on its core business. *(6 marks)*

5 Explain two benefits of 'product proliferation'. *(6 marks)*

6 Look at the fact file on Fat Face (see p. 47) and answer the following questions:

  a State two other examples of firms that produce different goods for different seasons of the year. *(2 marks)*

  b Explain one advantage of this approach. *(4 marks)*

CASE STUDY 1 McDonald's

McDonald's is one of the most famous brands in the world, but its reputation has been based on a very limited range of products. McDonald's now believes that it needs to devote more time to product design 5 and product development in order to boost profitability. The original range is considered to be unhealthy and limited in variety. A key market segment, those in the 15–30 age range, are choosing alternative eating experiences. McDonald's popularity 10 is becoming much more concentrated on younger children and families.

One of McDonald's new tactics is to provide a menu that offers the established favourites (such as the Double Cheeseburger Meal) alongside a constantly changing 15 range of unusual options. The new options will be available for a short period of time, and will then be replaced by another temporary meal offering. These meals will be offered at a slightly higher price than the traditional Big Mac, but lower profit margins are 20 forecast because of higher costs per meal.

McDonald's believes that this tactic will allow it to achieve growth in both sales and profits after a difficult period in 2002, during which 175 restaurants were 25 closed.

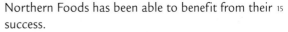
INGRAM

Sources: various.

Questions

Total: 25 marks (30 minutes)

1 What is meant by the term 'product development' (line 5)? *(2 marks)*

2 Briefly explain why McDonald's costs per meal will increase as a result of the changes to its menu that are outlined above. *(6 marks)*

3 Analyse **two** *marketing* benefits to McDonald's of providing a narrow range of products. *(8 marks)*

4 To what extent is broadening its range of products likely to help McDonald's to improve its profit levels? *(9 marks)*

CASE STUDY 2 Northern Foods

Northern Foods is an example of a business that has adopted a policy of product proliferation, but the company has had to reconsider this approach in recent times.

5 Although Northern Foods includes a number of recognised brand names (such as Fox's, Bowyers, Payne's and Dalepak), it is best known as a supplier of 'own-label' brands to supermarkets: 70% of its sales are to five customers — Marks and Spencer, Tesco, 10 Asda, Sainsbury's and Safeway. In this market, Northern Foods is in fierce competition with other manufacturers. However, with the five named retailers accounting for 60% of all UK food sales,

Northern Foods has been able to benefit from their 15 success.

Northern Foods identifies eight core product areas, with thousands of individual products made each day. The eight areas are:

- recipe dishes (e.g. pre-packed Chinese meals) 20
- savoury products (e.g. pork pies)
- speciality bread (e.g. fruited bread, croissants)
- bread-based snacks (e.g. fresh chilled sandwiches)
- cakes and puddings (e.g. supermarket own-label Battenburgs) 25
- dairy products (e.g. yoghurt)
- biscuits (e.g. Fox's Viennese Whirls)
- frozen foods (e.g. Dalepak burgers)

In recent times, Northern Foods' profitability has
30 fallen. Some observers have blamed the company's
product diversification for these problems. Although
Northern Foods is a large business, it is a relatively
small competitor in some of its markets — especially
dairy products, biscuits and frozen foods.

35 In 2002 Northern Foods sold two of its yoghurt
brands (Ski and Munch Bunch) to Nestlé for
£145 million. The company is now considering
whether to sell some of its other brands: Payne's
(chocolates), Batchelors (tinned foods) and Fox's
40 (biscuits, glacier mints and 'XXX' mints) are the
probable candidates.

In 2002/03 the biscuits division recorded sales of
£150 million, but its profits fell by £6 million and its
market share dropped to 13%. Adding value to its
biscuits has been hard to achieve. Overall Northern 45
Foods achieved sales revenue of £1.42 billion and
profits of £106 million.

The biscuits division is currently the least profitable
element of Northern Foods, but the firm is finding it
increasingly difficult to compete in the confectionery 50
market, which is dominated by a few very large firms.
Distribution costs are also higher, as these products
are sold in a wider range of retailers than some of the
core products.

Source: www.northern-foods.co.uk

Questions

Total: 25 marks (30 minutes)

1 What is meant by the term 'adding value' (line 44)? *(2 marks)*

2 a Northern Foods' biscuit sales gave it a 13% market share of the biscuit market in 2002/03.
If McVitie's had a 26% market share, what was McVitie's annual sales income from
biscuits in 2002/03? *(2 marks)*

 b Calculate the total value of sales in the UK biscuit market in 2002/03. *(4 marks)*

3 Examine the main problems that Northern Foods faces in having such a wide range of
products. *(7 marks)*

4 Discuss whether Northern Foods should sell its biscuits division. *(10 marks)*

CHAPTER 7

The marketing mix: price

This chapter focuses on price. It examines:
- **pricing methods:** *cost-plus pricing, contribution pricing and price discrimination*
- **pricing strategies:** *price skimming, penetration pricing, price leader, price taker and predator pricing*
- **pricing tactics:** *loss leaders and psychological pricing*

Pricing methods

Pricing methods are used to calculate the actual price to be charged. There are three principal methods.

KEY TERMS

cost-plus pricing: a method of pricing in which the price set is the average cost of a product plus a sum to ensure a profit.
contribution pricing: a method of pricing in which the price is set to cover average variable costs only, plus a sum to pay towards fixed costs and profit.
price discrimination: a method of pricing in which a firm charges a higher price to some customers, for the same product or service, because they are prepared to pay such a price.

Cost-plus pricing

Here the price set is the average cost plus a sum to ensure a profit. Typically, a clothes retailer will add 100% to the wholesale cost of purchasing a dress, while a pet food manufacturer will add 30% to the manufacturing costs when selling to a supermarket chain. Thus a dress purchased wholesale by a retailer for £40 will be sold to the customer for £80; a tin of cat food that costs 20p to make will be sold for 26p.

In determining what percentage to add to its costs, a firm must remember that it needs both to make profits and to appeal to the market. If the percentage added on is too low, it may mean a lost opportunity to make profit; if it is too high, it will reduce sales. The percentage added on will depend on a number of factors:
- the level of competition
- the price that customers are prepared to pay
- the firm's objectives

EXAMINER'S VOICE

For the AQA AS Business Studies course you need to know the difference between pricing methods, strategies and tactics. There are overlaps between these classifications, but a simple distinction is given in this chapter.

The price charged will also depend on the objectives of the firm. Different businesses may have different objectives, such as maximum profit, maximum sales revenue or a high market share.

Contribution pricing

In contribution pricing, the price is set to cover variable costs only and to contribute to fixed costs/profit. A manufacturer with spare capacity will already have paid the fixed costs for the factory. Any additional production will only incur variable costs (raw materials and labour), so the business may charge a relatively low price. As long as the price is higher than the variable costs, it will make some extra profit. For example, if a hat costs 50p in extra raw materials and £2 in labour costs, then any price over £2.50 will contribute more profit to the firm.

Price discrimination

Price discrimination involves charging a higher price to some customers for the same product or service because they are prepared to pay such a price. Typical examples are train fares and charges for telephone users. Consumers who use peak-time trains or phones are willing to pay the higher price because they value its use so highly at those times (their demand is price inelastic). People who are less desperate to use the service at that time can receive it more cheaply during off-peak periods (their demand is price elastic). The terms **price inelastic** and **price elastic** are explained in detail in Chapter 10 (pp. 77–87).

In practice, price discrimination is much less likely to apply to products than to services. It was tried when the European Union was attempting to reduce its surplus of butter production. Special coupons were printed for people on state benefits, such as pensioners, so that they could get the butter at special low prices, while other customers were expected to pay the higher price. The outcome was that people with coupons bought up huge quantities, selling it on to their friends and families. Some enterprising pensioners even set up improvised car boot sales of butter in the supermarket car park!

This shows that price discrimination only works if the service or product is 'non-transferable', i.e. if it cannot be passed on to someone else. Altogether there are four conditions necessary for the successful operation of price discrimination:

- The service/product is non-transferable.
- The elasticities of demand between users vary — some customers desire the product much more than others, even at high prices.
- It is possible to identify and separate those groups of people — for example, commuters can be identified by the times at which they catch the train.
- There are no close substitutes.

ℯ EXAMINER'S VOICE

Contribution pricing is important when dealing with special order decisions. You will meet this idea in Module 4 of the A2 course.

Pricing strategies

Pricing strategies are adopted over the medium to long term to achieve marketing objectives. There are five main pricing strategies.

price skimming: a strategy in which a high price is set to yield a high profit margin.

penetration pricing: a strategy in which low prices are set to break into a market or to achieve a sudden spurt in market share.

price leadership: a strategy in which a large company (the price leader) sets a market price which smaller firms will tend to follow.

price taking: a strategy in which a small firm follows the price set by a price leader.

predator (or destroyer) pricing: a strategy in which a firm sets very low prices in order to drive other firms out of the market.

Price skimming

In price skimming a high price is set to yield a high profit margin. This price is often used during the introduction of a product, when it appeals to **early adopters** — buyers who want to be among the first to purchase a new product. Such consumers will pay for the status of being an early purchaser.

In the long term, firms use this strategy for products that they hope will 'skim the market'. This means appealing to a more exclusive, up-market type of customer. Chanel, Harrods and Bang & Olufsen are brands that employ this pricing strategy. The objectives in these cases are to maximise value added or profit margins and to establish a prestigious brand name.

Penetration pricing

In effect this is the opposite of price skimming. Low prices are set to break into a market or to achieve a sudden spurt in market share. Many firms use this strategy when a product is first released or to entice new customers. For example, credit card companies often make introductory offers in order to gain new customers and so increase their market share and possibly increase brand awareness.

WHAT DO YOU THINK?

Look for a recently introduced confectionery product or magazine. How much lower is the introductory price than those of its competitors? Have you purchased any new products because the price seemed to be so low?

Price leadership and price taking

In price leadership a large company (the price leader) sets a market price that smaller firms (price takers) tend to follow. Large retailers such as Currys and

DID YOU KNOW?

As society becomes more cash rich (but time poor), firms have recognised more and more opportunities for setting higher prices in this way. In your local shopping centre, look for examples of products that are priced much higher than other, similar products. Why are they able to charge a higher price?

manufacturers such as Ford will influence prices for electrical goods and cars in this way. In some industries, such as petrol, price leadership may be shared among a few major firms. Small firms will usually follow because a lower price could trigger a **price war**, while a higher price will mean that they lose customers. By becoming the established brand leader, a firm can ensure that prices are set at a level that suits it and discourages price competition.

Predator (or destroyer) pricing

In this strategy, a firm sets very low prices in order to drive other firms out of the market. For example, cut-price airline fares have led to some small airlines closing or being taken over by competitors. If predator pricing acts against the consumer interest (by eliminating choice), it can be ruled illegal, but this is often difficult to prove. The sole objective is to reduce the number of competitors in the market.

Pricing tactics

Pricing tactics are adopted in the short term to suit particular situations. There are two main pricing tactics.

KEY TERMS

loss leadership: a tactic in which a firm sets a very low price for its product(s) in order to encourage consumers to buy other products that provide profit for the firm.

psychological pricing: a tactic intended to give the impression of value (e.g. selling a good for £9.99 rather than £10).

Loss leadership

Some firms, such as supermarkets, set very low prices for certain products in order to encourage consumers to buy other, fully priced products. Cheap bread and milk (at the back of the supermarket) will lead customers through the store, during which time they may buy many other products from which a greater profit is made. (In practice, 'loss leaders' are often sold at reduced profit margins rather than at a loss.) Manufacturers use loss leaders too — the main product may be a loss leader, but the accessories can create the profit.

Psychological pricing

Psychological pricing is intended to give an impression of value (e.g. £3.99 instead of £4 or £99 rather than £100). Although a few retailers, such as Marks and Spencer, do not use this approach any more, the frequency of its use suggests that firms believe that it does attract extra customers.

Paintballing is an industry that uses this technique in a slightly different way. The full day fee at the local paintball venue may

be £20. This price encourages customers and provides you with everything that you need to 'destroy' your enemies, including 100 paintballs. However, the average 'paintballer' uses 500 paintballs a day and the additional 400 paintballs needed add between £20 and £28 to the price.

e **EXAMINER'S VOICE**

Application is not just about including the company's name in your answer. If your answer makes as much sense without the company name as it does with it, then it is probable that you are showing the skill of analysis rather than application.

PRACTICE EXERCISE 1   Total: 30 marks (25 minutes)

1 What is meant by the term 'contribution pricing'?   *(3 marks)*

2 Explain two factors that are necessary for price discrimination to be used.   *(6 marks)*

3 The following costs apply to a product: wages 50p, raw materials 60p, other costs 70p.
   a What price would be set if cost-plus pricing were used and a mark-up of 100% were chosen by the business to set the price?   *(3 marks)*
   b Wages rise by 10% and the mark-up is reduced to 80%. Calculate the new price.   *(5 marks)*

4 Explain two reasons why a company might use price skimming and state two real-life examples of this strategy.   *(6 marks)*

5 What is the difference between penetration pricing and predator pricing?   *(4 marks)*

6 What is meant by a 'loss leader'?   *(3 marks)*

PRACTICE EXERCISE 2   Total: 15 marks (15 minutes)

1 If the costs of production per unit are £1.00, calculate the profit at each of the following prices and quantities.

Price	Quantity bought
£1.10	2,000
£1.30	1,500
£1.50	800
£1.70	200

(10 marks)

2 What price will be charged if the main objective is to make maximum profit?   *(1 mark)*

3 What price might be set if the objective is to gain the highest possible market share by volume?   *(2 marks)*

4 What price might be set if the objective is to gain the highest possible market share by value?   *(2 marks)*

CASE STUDY **1**   Shakeaway

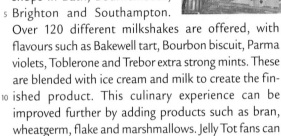

Shakeaway is a retailer specialising in unusual flavours of milkshake. The business runs shops in Bath, Bournemouth,
5 Brighton and Southampton. Over 120 different milkshakes are offered, with flavours such as Bakewell tart, Bourbon biscuit, Parma violets, Toblerone and Trebor extra strong mints. These are blended with ice cream and milk to create the fin-
10 ished product. This culinary experience can be improved further by adding products such as bran, wheatgerm, flake and marshmallows. Jelly Tot fans can choose a Jelly Tots milkshake topped with Jelly Tots.

At present this is a niche market, as other
15 providers of flavoured milkshakes have not ventured far beyond strawberry and chocolate. The business has diversified slightly into hot drinks (including hot milkshakes) and confectionery, but 90% of its sales come from its milkshakes.

The milkshakes are priced at 20 £2.25 (regular) or £3.25 (large). Shakeaway decided on a price skimming policy when it opened its shops. Price skimming policies are popular with new products, but Shakeaway is pleased 25 that it has been able to maintain this pricing strategy for over 4 years. There are worries that it may need to change its strategy in the near future to one that would reduce its profits.

An initial proposal of using psychological pricing to 30 set a price of £1.99 for the regular milkshake was rejected because it was felt that this would reduce profit levels rather than increase them.

The cost of ingredients for a typical, regular milkshake are estimated at 70p, with labour and other 35 costs at 60p per shake.

Sources: various, including www.shakeaway.com

Questions

Total: 25 marks (30 minutes)

1 What is meant by the term 'price skimming' (lines 22–23)?   *(2 marks)*

2 a Calculate the average cost of production of a regular milkshake.   *(2 marks)*
  b Shakeaway uses a cost-plus pricing method. Use your answer to part (a) to calculate the percentage that Shakeaway adds on to the average cost in order to set its price for a regular milkshake.   *(4 marks)*

3 Examine why Shakeaway rejected the idea of psychological pricing (line 30).   *(7 marks)*

4 Discuss possible factors that may lead to Shakeaway being forced to change its strategy of price skimming.   *(10 marks)*

CASE STUDY **2**   The marketing mix at Ryanair

Ryanair is a classic example of a business that uses price as the key element of its marketing mix. However, price cannot work in isolation from the rest of the four Ps. In order to maintain its policy of long-term
5 low prices, Ryanair has needed to look closely at the other three Ps.

Ryanair based itself on the highly successful model

established in the USA by Southwest Airlines, a company that had been operating low-cost flights in the USA since the 1960s. Ryanair's chief executive, 10 Michael O'Leary, attempted to create a low-cost airline by examining every element of Ryanair's activities, in order to cut costs in the way that Southwest Airlines had.

TOPFOTO

Product

O'Leary started by eliminating 'frills' and 'unnecessary' expenditure.

- Travel agents were eliminated, based on the idea that Ryanair's customers would not then be paying towards the costs of their city-centre premises and trained staff.
- Internet bookings were introduced, saving approximately 15% per booking.
- Bookings do not require paperwork at the airport; customers just need to provide a booking reference and their passport.
- Seats are not allocated to passengers; they are taken as passengers board the plane.
- The previous two factors reduce administration costs further, but the main bonus is time savings. The turnaround time on Ryanair planes is 25 minutes on average — half that of BA. This means that the planes are more productive and can make more journeys per day.
- Free meals are not provided — customers must pay for any food they require. Not only does this save costs (especially on staffing and cleaning because passengers eat and drink less), but also it provides an additional source of profit that can be used to keep prices low.

Some examples of Ryanair's cost savings have been less well received by customers. Its customer care department employs six staff (one-tenth of BA's equivalent staff, based on staff per customer) and Ryanair does not offer some facilities that are provided free by other airlines. However, these features reinforce the company's USP.

Place

A key element of Ryanair's strategy is that it only flies to popular destinations, giving it more security of custom. This policy meant that when Ryanair took over Buzz, many of Buzz's flights were removed, where Ryanair considered the destinations to be lacking in popularity.

A major cost saving for Ryanair has arisen from the locations that it has chosen. By using Stansted airport, Ryanair estimates that it saves £3 per customer in comparison to Heathrow. Some of this saving arises from the relatively strong bargaining position of Ryanair. It is vital to Stansted's success as an airport and can therefore negotiate lower charges.

Ryanair also saves money by using secondary rather than 'main' airports in other countries. This means lower costs for Ryanair that can be passed on to customers, softening the blow that the airport is further from the customer's intended destination than they had hoped. In some cases, airports have been so keen to attract Ryanair that they have paid the company to choose that airport. The airport's revenues will increase from retailing activities within the airport as passenger numbers rise.

Promotion

Ryanair keeps advertising to a minimum, relying on newspaper advertisements and posters rather than more expensive television adverts. Simple messages reinforce the philosophy of low cost, low price. As an economy measure, advertising agencies are not used. As a result, there have been some controversial promotions attacking competitors or presenting issues insensitively.

Recognising the benefit of joint activities, Ryanair takes a percentage of any bookings made through its website (typically car hire and hotel bookings). It has also allowed its planes to be used as flying billboards, advertising products such as Kilkenny beer. These ancillary revenues provide 14% of the firm's profits.

Price

Given the vital role of safety in the airline industry, Ryanair has not economised on aircraft — it only uses Boeing 737s. However, shrewd timing of aircraft

purchases (just after the Gulf War and again during and after the Iraq War) to coincide with excess supply has brought Ryanair some bargains. Unconfirmed
95 estimates suggest that some of the Boeing 737s have cost the company less than half the normal £34 million price tag.

Ryanair has adopted the following pricing policies:
- Ryanair's normal pricing is low cost, but based on
100 cost-plus in order to secure some profit. Typically the first 70% of seats are sold on this basis.
- Unlike traditional airlines that sell any remaining empty seats at a low, contribution price (enough to contribute towards fixed costs or profit), Ryanair
105 uses price discrimination. The airline's view is that

anyone seeking to book a flight at the last minute is probably in desperate need and therefore likely to be willing to pay a higher price. Thus the final 30% of the seats are sold at higher prices.
- At times, short-term, very low promotional prices 110 are charged. These could be seen as penetration pricing (to increase market share), but some analysts see them as predator prices, used to drive away competition. In practice, many of these promotional flights are one-way only and so the savings for cus- 115 tomers are less significant than they originally seem (unless the passenger does not want to return).

Source: *The Money Programme*, BBC2, 4 June 2003.

Question 1
Total: 25 marks (30 minutes)

a What is meant by 'cost-plus' pricing (line 100)? *(3 marks)*

b Explain how Ryanair's 'joint activities' have helped it to keep prices low (line 81). *(4 marks)*

c Analyse the benefits to Ryanair of the pricing methods that it has used. *(8 marks)*

d Discuss the potential difficulties faced by Ryanair in trying to maintain its low-price policy in the future. *(10 marks)*

Question 2
Total: 25 marks (30 minutes)

a Explain the meaning of the term 'contribution price' (line 103). *(3 marks)*

b Explain **two** ways in which Ryanair cuts costs in order to keep prices low. *(6 marks)*

c Analyse the possible reasons why Southwest Airlines did not attempt to bring its low-cost approach to Europe before Ryanair used the idea. *(7 marks)*

d Evaluate the reasons why Ryanair charges low prices to early customers and higher prices to people who book flights later, while BA charges higher prices to early customers and lower prices to people who book flights later. *(9 marks)*

CHAPTER 8

The marketing mix: promotion

Promotion refers to the ways in which an organisation attempts to draw consumers' attention to a product. The aims of promotion are explained through the 'AIDA' model. The different methods of promotion (above-the-line and below-the-line) are explained and their relative merits shown. The choice of advertising media is also considered.

KEY TERMS

above-the-line promotion: advertising through media — newspapers, television, radio, the cinema and posters.
below-the-line promotion: all other promotions, such as public relations, merchandising, sponsorship, direct marketing, personal selling and competitions.

Promotions and advertising can be **informative** or **persuasive**. Informative promotions are intended to increase consumer awareness of the product and its features. Persuasive promotions are intended to encourage consumers to purchase the product, usually through messages that emphasise its desirability.

The aims of promotion

Promotions have different purposes. A popular model that is used to demonstrate the different aims of promotion is **AIDA**. This is a mnemonic that stands for Attention, Interest, Desire, Action, and describes the process of a successful marketing campaign.

- **Attention.** The first step in a promotional strategy is to get the attention of the consumer. Attention raising is mainly an attempt to improve awareness of the name and product among the target audience. Typically, advertising at this stage is used to make people aware of the product or service, but it does not attempt to provide them with detailed information.
- **Interest.** Promotional campaigns are usually drip-fed over a period of time, using various forms of media, in order to gain the interest of consumers. After hearing a brand name repeatedly, consumers are more likely to trust it. The intention is to make consumers want to find out more about the product. The choice of media, messages and images will be based on the interests of the target market.

- **Desire.** Having gained the consumer's interest, promotions may change in nature to provide the consumer with more specific reasons for purchasing the product. This will often involve informative advertising, such as giving the technical specifications of a piece of equipment. However, in some markets, desire is fuelled by imagery. In such cases, promotions will be persuasive rather than informative.
- **Action.** The final and crucial step is converting desire on the part of the consumer into the action of purchasing the product. Point-of-sale displays, special offers and competition entries are popular methods of achieving this aim. In the case of goods that are 'impulse buys', promotions within the shop itself are much more likely to be successful.

AIDA should be seen as an integrated whole. A brilliant shop display is unlikely to be successful if earlier stages have been missed and the consumer fails to recognise the item being displayed. Similarly, attention, desire and interest may not convert into action if the product cannot be located in a store.

FACT FILE

Media advertising is popularly seen as the most significant form of promotion, but the AIDA model puts it into perspective. It is unlikely that a consumer's decision to purchase will be based on advertising alone, especially if it is not a printed form of advert. Television, radio and cinema campaigns are usually meant to bring people's *attention* to a product, raising their *interest*. As a general rule, it is the more detailed informative promotions that create *desire* and brochures and merchandising activities that trigger *action*. However, as with so many business issues, there will be many exceptions to this rule.

DID YOU KNOW?

A classic example of a successful 'attention' campaign was the Amy campaign in 1984. A poster of Amy, a young girl, appeared on bus shelters across the country accompanied by the sentence 'I'm Amy and I like slugs and snails.' After a time without any further information the national media picked up on the story, trying to discover who Amy was and what she was meant to be promoting. Eventually, market research revealed that 75% of the UK population had heard of Amy. At this point it was revealed that Amy was promoting the idea of using bus shelters for poster advertising. With 75% awareness achieved, advertising agencies began to recognise the effectiveness of this (previously unpopular) method of advertising. This style of attention or awareness raising is known as a 'teaser campaign' and has been used successfully by organisations such as the government and Orange.

Types of promotion

Above-the-line promotion
Most advertising would be classified as above-the-line promotion. The main media chosen are:

- television
- radio
- cinema
- national newspapers
- posters
- magazines
- internet
- regional newspapers

FACT FILE

Cinema is an excellent medium for reaching the youth market, as the following information shows.

Frequency of cinema visits per annum (aged 15+)	
Never visit	41%
Less than twice a year	15%
2 to 11 times per annum	30%
More than once a month	14%

Those who visit the cinema more than once a month:
- are more likely to be aged 15–24

- tend to be from social classes A and B
- are more likely to drink Stella Artois lager
- are more likely to read the *Independent* or *Guardian*
- are likely to prefer comedies

In comparison to the rest of Europe, people in the UK are not committed cinemagoers. In France and Germany, 20% of adults are regular visitors, although the UK's 14% matches the level of commitment in Spain.

Sources: BMRB; TGI data; *Media Week*, 6 December 2002.

DID YOU KNOW?

Children are an attractive target for promotional activity. Wall's annual pocket money survey showed that in 2001 the average child received £3.19 per week. With earnings from odd jobs at £1.52 a week, and handouts (usually from relatives) at £1.93 a week, this gave spending power of £6.64 per week on average to each child aged 5–16. This means *weekly* spending of £60 million.

Boys spend more on soft drinks, sporting activities and computer games. Sales of ice cream, sweets and chocolate show no significant differences between genders. Girls spend relatively more on magazines, music, stationery, clothing and accessories.

Source: Wall's annual pocket money survey.

INGRAM

EXAMINER'S VOICE

Be aware of the costs of advertising. Relatively few companies can afford television advertising and so they choose media that they can afford and that are appropriate for their situation.

Factors influencing the choice of above-the-line promotion

When deciding what form of above-the-line promotion to choose, a business will consider the following factors:

- **Objectives of the campaign.** If the firm is trying to introduce a new product, it will focus on using media that raise awareness, such as television. If it is aiming to provide information, the internet or newspapers will be more relevant.
- **Costs and budgets.** Small firms will not be able to justify the use of a television campaign because of the expense. For them, local radio or newspapers are a better choice. Media calculate the cost per thousand (CPT) to show how much it costs to get a message to 1,000 consumers. National companies find it much more cost effective to use national newspapers and television, as one advert can reach a very large number of people. The marketing budget allocated to the manager will influence the media that can be used. Ryanair is a large firm, but its relatively low marketing budget prevents it from using television advertising in the way that its rivals do.
- **The target market.** Lord Leverhulme, formerly of Unilever plc, is famously quoted as saying: 'Half of what I spend on promotion is wasted. The trouble is I don't know which half.' Firms will spend more eagerly on a

DID YOU KNOW?

Programmes such as *Coronation Street* and *Emmerdale* gained the nickname of 'soaps' because traditionally they were watched by housewives, who made the decision on which soap powder the family should use. As a result, the advertising slots during these programmes became the most popular times for companies that wanted to advertise their soap.

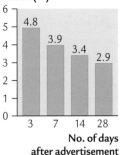

Source: tvWORKS

Figure 8.1
Effect of television advertising on sales

medium that reaches their target market. Channel 4 advertisements have a higher CPT because many of its programmes are targeted towards specific groups of people. For the same reason, magazines and local media can be more effective than national media.

- **The promotional campaign.** Above-the-line methods must be planned along with below-the-line methods to maximise effectiveness. As seen in the AIDA model, above-the-line methods usually introduce a campaign, while below-the-line methods complete the process. However, the effectiveness of sponsorship can be enhanced by having advertisements running at the same time, such as Nationwide Building Society advertisements during an international football match.

- **Legal factors.** Restrictions on the use of media, such as limits on alcohol advertising on television, may encourage firms to use different media. Firms that cannot use television and newspapers use the internet for **viral** (word-of-mouth) advertising, to bypass these restrictions.

A recent research project by tvWORKS, matching advertisements seen on television to purchases of goods by households, revealed the increases in sales shown in Figure 8.1.

Below-the-line promotions

Any promotion not using traditional media is classified as below-the-line. The main types of below-the-line promotion are as follows.

Sales promotions

These are short-term incentives used to persuade consumers to purchase. Popular methods include competitions, free offers, coupons, 'three for the price of two' offers, product placement (featuring a product in a film), credit terms and endorsements by famous personalities. Sales promotions are an excellent way of providing a boost to sales, especially when a product is new to the market or would not have been purchased otherwise. If the consumer enjoys the product, it can mean that a new loyal customer has been gained. Promotional price cuts are often used to persuade consumers to try a product for a short time, in the hope that they will then become loyal customers.

Direct mail and door-to-door drops

Direct mail describes promotions that are sent directly to the customer. It is growing rapidly as a form of promotion. Databases are becoming more detailed, so firms are able to discover an increasing amount about their customers. Organisations such as supermarkets, in particular, have used loyalty cards to get information on buying habits. This has enabled them to target direct-mail offers of certain items to specific consumers. (The 'junk mail' contains less junk because the offers are more likely to interest the person who has been targeted.) Direct telephone and internet links are also used.

Door-to-door drops are promotions that are delivered directly to houses. These are often delivered with the local free newspaper and can be very

cost-effective and targeted. IKEA, for example, delivers its catalogues in August and September, the beginning of the run-up to Christmas. Postcodes that provide the highest sales are identified through sales records, and houses in these postcode areas are targeted to receive the catalogue.

Personal selling

High labour costs have led to a decline in door-to-door selling, but for durable items such as housing, cars and household goods, the role of the individual salesperson is crucial. In these cases, customers may value the expertise or details provided by the salesperson. Personal selling is particularly important in commercial marketing, where a company's sales force will contact other firms that are seen as potential customers.

Sponsorship

Sponsorship means giving financial assistance to an individual, event or organisation. For example, sponsorship of popular football teams can gain companies a lot of publicity. Sponsorship can also be targeted towards a particular audience, as with Carling's sponsoring of the Reading and Leeds pop festivals. Sponsorship can enable organisations that face advertising restrictions to reach customers, and it often improves goodwill when it is seen to be supporting a good cause (e.g. sponsorship of litter bins). It can also give a company access to attractive events such as Wimbledon, performances at the Royal Albert Hall and Grand Prix races. The company can then pass on invitations to customers or suppliers and build goodwill and closer links. However, sponsorship can be unpredictable. An unexpectedly good cup run for a rugby team or a scandal involving the person sponsored can affect the results.

TOPFOTO

FACT FILE

One organisation that struck lucky in sponsorship was T&T, a small soft drinks manufacturer. In 2001 it took a gamble. With a limited marketing budget, it decided to sponsor an untested reality-TV show called *PopStars*. Hear'say may not have survived, but for T&T the venture was a resounding success. Sales rose by 1,300% in that year, with 10 million cans sold while the show ran. Before *PopStars* only 15% of the target population had heard of T&T; after *PopStars* the level of brand awareness reached 62%. Sponsorship also improved the credibility of the brand among 18- to 24-year-olds (the target market).

Source: www.yorkshiretv.com

Merchandising

Attempts to persuade consumers to take action at the 'point of sale' are known as merchandising. Kellogg's tries to persuade retailers to offer more shelf space (e.g. by producing variations of basic cereals); Procter & Gamble has a special team that advises small retailers on the most attractive way to display its products; Tic Tac produces displays that persuade consumers to buy at the point of sale. Both manufacturers and retailers try to maximise sales by using psychological research. To improve shoppers' environment, pleasant

smells (e.g. fresh bread) are distributed around the supermarket and colourful displays of fresh produce are placed near the entrance.

Public relations (PR)

PR involves gaining favourable publicity through the media. The public will recognise that an advert is designed to sell a product, and will therefore be wary of the messages being sent. However, an article in a newspaper that praises a product can raise awareness in a very cost-effective way. If Jeremy Clarkson can be persuaded to test drive the new Porsche on television, it can help Porsche to sell more cars. Newspapers may publish a 'press release' from a business if the story is considered newsworthy, and so firms will often try to find a human interest story connected to their product. Successful PR relies on the reaction of the media to the story being put forward by the firm.

Trade fairs and exhibitions

Although some exhibitions are popular with the general public, most exhibitions and trade fairs are used to target other businesses. They can be used to 'network' (get to know people in other businesses), but more importantly they are used to demonstrate products to potential customers, and to provide detailed information and brochures. At exhibitions, customers can test out and order products, so they can be vital to the success of some firms, especially in industries where new products are being constantly developed.

---

e EXAMINER'S VOICE

Remember that promotion is not just advertising. Advertising is a part of promotion, but there are many other elements. Business organisations will use a wide range of promotional methods in order to raise awareness. Do not underestimate the importance of below-the-line promotions.

FACT FILE

The latest research by TGI shows that users of the internet are likely to be younger than non-users. The age group 20–34 make up 22% of the population but account for over 35% of internet users. In contrast, those over 65 (15% of the population) represent only 9% of internet users. The survey also showed that younger adults were much more likely to watch satellite television. However, pensioners accounted for 22.5% of ITV viewers and 24% of broadsheet newspaper purchasers.

DID YOU KNOW?

Sony Ericsson mobile phones show no distinct variations in the age of users, except for a significant drop over the age of 55 and a huge fall among over-65-year-olds. Heavy users are low watchers of television, but visit the cinema and use the internet. They are more likely to see outdoor advertisements and are more than twice as likely as the average UK resident to have visited the Science Museum in the last year. Other popular activities among Sony Ericsson mobile users are 'visiting Italy', 'going to the Motor Show' and 'taking risks'. How could Sony Ericsson use this information to plan a promotional campaign?

PRACTICE EXERCISE  Total: 50 marks (40 minutes)

1 What is meant by 'below-the-line' promotion? *(3 marks)*

2 What does the mnemonic AIDA stand for? *(4 marks)*

3 What is an 'impulse buy'? *(2 marks)*

4 Explain three factors that an organisation should consider before planning a promotional campaign. *(9 marks)*

5 Which media would you select in order to advertise the following?
 a A job advertisement for a checkout assistant in Woolworths. *(3 marks)*
 b A new CD by a well-known pop star. *(3 marks)*
 c A new model of a car. *(3 marks)*
 In each case justify your choices.

6 Explain the difference between sponsorship and public relations. *(4 marks)*

7 Identify two products that might use exhibitions as a form of promotion. *(2 marks)*

8 What is the difference between promotion and advertising? *(4 marks)*

9 Identify three examples of sales promotion. *(3 marks)*

10 Identify two types of promotion that you believe will increase in the next 5 years. Justify your choices. *(6 marks)*

11 How can a company try to prevent customers from seeing its direct mail as 'junk mail'? *(4 marks)*

CASE STUDY 1 Door-to-door promotions

Marketing budgets of retailers are being diverted from 'above-the-line' promotions to door-to-door methods.

In 2000, Safeway was searching for a USP. It decided to give more freedom to branches to organise
5 their own special offers, in order to suit local demand. According to Carl Nield, head of marketing services, 'The national advertising budget was redirected to a local level, with the majority of spending focused on door-to-door distribution of our weekly deals flyer.'
10 The deals in these flyers vary from store to store, 'to reflect differences and changes in the local competitive situation and any differences in local customer requirements'. The
15 results are astonishing — Safeway has attracted over 1 million new customers since the change.

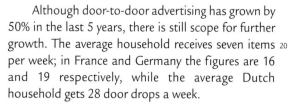

Although door-to-door advertising has grown by 50% in the last 5 years, there is still scope for further growth. The average household receives seven items 20 per week; in France and Germany the figures are 16 and 19 respectively, while the average Dutch household gets 28 door drops a week.

Adam Clark is a director of Brand Connection, an agency that specialises in door-to-door promo- 25 tions. 'Typically we start with heavy outdoor advertising by posters, although television may be used for major campaigns. We then deselect a number of post-codes that do not match our 30 retailers' typical customers. For Waitrose this is typically 30%, but it is a lower percentage for other supermarkets.'

35   In the summer of 2002 Sainsbury's mounted a large campaign, with door drops promoting prizes worth £3 million. This campaign cost £2.5 million, excluding the value of the prizes, and led to a 1% rise in weekly sales (an extra £15 million per week). With 40 profit margins at 7%, this meant an extra £1 million towards profit every week.

  The great attraction of door-to-door promotions is the cost. Direct mail (using the Royal Mail) is much cheaper than most other methods of promotion, with 45 typical costs of £300 per 1,000 letters. Door-to-door deliveries (usually through local newspaper deliveries) cost only £30 per 1,000. With many firms cutting their marketing budgets in recent years, door-to-door promotions and direct mail have increased in popularity. 50

  Market research by BMRB suggests that 79% of people recall the contents of door drops, but the percentage actually purchasing as a result is much lower. According to Colin Keywood, 'Financial services, such as credit card providers, are happy 55 with response rates of 0.1%, while a retailer would expect rates of 2% to 3%.' Because the costs are so low, firms find that they can profit from these methods.

Source: based on an article by Rachel Miller, *Marketing* magazine, 30 January 2003.

Questions

Total: 25 marks (30 minutes)

1 What is meant by the term 'USP' (line 3)?   *(3 marks)*

2 State **two** examples of 'above-the-line' promotions.   *(2 marks)*

3 Based on the figures given for the cost of the campaign and *including* the cost of the prizes, how many weeks would it have taken before a profit was made from Sainsbury's campaign?   *(3 marks)*

4 Analyse the reasons why a business would use television or poster advertising just before the start of a door-to-door marketing campaign.   *(7 marks)*

5 Discuss the advantages and disadvantages of Safeway's decision to redirect its national advertising budget to a local level.   *(10 marks)*

CASE STUDY 2   British Gas seeks public trust

British Gas wants to be trusted. A £50m long-term advertising campaign, fronted by Royle Family actor Ricky Tomlinson with the slogan 'Doing the Right Thing', will hit television and cinema screens, radios, 5 poster sites, newspapers and doormats across the country from today. British Gas has such a wide customer base that it has decided to base its promotional strategy on 'above-the-line' advertising using a wide range of media, with limited use of 'below-the-10 line' promotions.

  But British Gas has to tread carefully as it promotes itself as the consumer's champion. It is only a year since the image of the gas industry was damaged by aggressive and misleading direct selling. British Gas itself was accused of hindering customers who wanted 15 to move to alternative gas suppliers.

  As the market and price leader in the gas industry and a major competitor in the supply of electricity, British Gas is often first in the firing line if there are accusations of high prices. 20

  Despite these issues, British Gas director of marketing and strategy, Nick Smith, insists that: 'This is absolutely the right message for us as we continue to move away from being a gas supplier to a broad provider of home services. We almost always do the 25 right thing for our customers. Of course there are times when we get it wrong but we try to correct things immediately.'

The statistics support Nick Smith's argument.
30 Complaints fell from 0.077 per 1,000 customers in
2002 to 0.066 per 1,000 in 2003, ranking it third best
in the industry. About £400 million has been invested
in customer care improvements, including 5,000
additional engineers to be recruited over the next
35 5 years. British Gas believes that high quality service
will help it in all of its home services. This strategy has
been operated successfully by the AA and Tesco,
whose reputation for their core business has helped
them to enter new markets.
40   British Gas is combining its advertising campaign
with in-house training of staff, to make sure that they
are aware of the messages and promises made in the
advertisements.
    Smith maintains that customer trust is essential if
45 the company is to reduce 'churn' (customers switching
to other suppliers) and boost its marketing objective
of increasing its market share of the various markets in
which it competes (see Table 8.1).

	First half of 2002	First half of 2003
Gas customers	13.0 million	12.8 million
Market share (gas)	65%	63%
Electricity customers	5.6 million	6.0 million
Market share (electricity)	22%	24%
Telephone customers*	371,000	378,000

*These figures do not include the 1.1 million customers of One Tel (also owned by Centrica, the company that owns British Gas).

Table 8.1 *Data on British Gas and its markets*

The 'Doing the Right Thing' campaign will be a risk for British Gas, especially if problems are featured in the 50 media. However, British Gas believes that a successful campaign will make a big difference to its chances of success in its other markets.

Source: adapted from *Marketing* magazine,
9 October 2003.

Questions

Total: 25 marks (30 minutes)

1 What is meant by the term 'marketing objective'? (line 46) *(2 marks)*

2 Study the information in Table 8.1. Using calculations, show that the total market size of the electricity industry (measured by the number of customers) is larger than the total market size of the gas industry. *(6 marks)*

3 Analyse **two** benefits to British Gas of using television advertising in this campaign. *(8 marks)*

4 To what extent does the success of this promotional campaign depend on other, non-marketing, activities within British Gas? *(9 marks)*

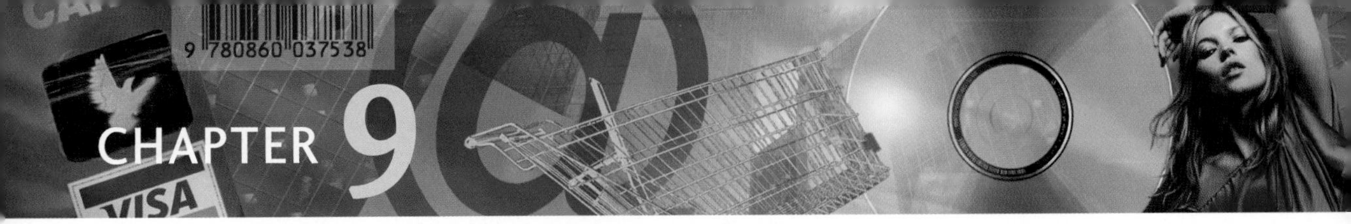

CHAPTER 9

The marketing mix: place

The role of place in the marketing mix is established in this chapter. The alternative distribution channels (and their merits) are contrasted and the key factors influencing the choice of distribution channels are examined. The importance of distribution targets and how these can be achieved is also considered. Other aspects of 'place' or 'distribution' that are examined are the importance of location of the retailer and placement within the point-of-sale.

The distribution channels

KEY TERM

distribution channels: channels or routes through which a product passes in moving from the manufacturer (producer) to the consumer.

Movement of a product from the manufacturer to the consumer in international trade may involve additional agents, but most domestic distribution involves one of three methods, as shown in Figure 9.1.

The job of **producers** or manufacturers is to make the product.

The main task of **wholesalers** is to buy in bulk from the manufacturer (producer) and sell in smaller quantities to the retailer. Their existence can benefit both manufacturers and retailers:

Traditional	Modern	Direct
Producer	Producer	Producer
↓	↓	
Wholesaler		
↓	Retailer	↓
Retailer	↓	
↓		
Consumer	Consumer	Consumer

Figure 9.1
Channels of distribution

- **Wholesalers help producers** by purchasing their stock of finished goods as soon as it is produced, and storing it until consumers want it. This means that producers save on storage costs. By paying immediately, wholesalers can also help the cash flow of producers. This reduces producers' risks — if a product does not sell, it is the wholesaler's problem. Delivery costs are also reduced, as each producer can send a range of products to the wholesaler in one delivery.
- **Retailers can also benefit** from lower delivery costs, as the wholesaler stocks products from lots of different manufacturers and will usually deliver the order. This allows the retailer to compare products and prices in order to get the best deals. Retailers may gain from credit terms being offered by the wholesaler.

Despite these benefits, the role of wholesalers has declined. Wholesalers charge for their services, usually by 'marking up' the price that they paid the producer for the goods in order to cover their costs and make a profit. Large

supermarkets tend to buy directly from the producers in bulk, and receive deliveries either straight from the producer or via their own warehouses. Wholesalers have tried to prevent their decline by supporting the small retailers that still use them. Organisations such as SPAR (the Society for the Protection of the Average Retailer) have helped retailers to get together to share orders, in order to keep prices competitive.

The main roles of the **retailer** are to serve the needs of the customer by providing:

- convenience — a 'place' that is easily accessible to consumers
- advice — knowledge to help the consumer reach the right buying decision
- financial assistance — retailers will often provide credit terms or accept payment in a form that suits the consumer's needs
- after-sales support — for durable products, the quality of the guarantees or after-sales service can be crucial

Where a shop is not necessary to perform these roles, it is possible for a producer to sell directly to the consumer. Catalogues can provide convenience, financial assistance and after-sales support, eliminating the need for the retailer. Screwfix Direct, for example, has used the internet very successfully to sell DIY equipment directly to consumers and tradesmen. Customers do not really want a detailed scrutiny of the product before purchasing it. In the holiday trade, where travel agents add 15% to the costs, direct selling from holiday providers has grown considerably.

 FILE

For some organisations, the internet allows rapid expansion. DV8 is a shoe retailer with six shops in Northern Ireland. Its target market is young, fashion-conscious purchasers. Rather than risk opening in another country, DV8 set up an online shop (voodooshoes.com). This led to accelerated growth, with the company accessing customers from as far away as the USA and Japan.

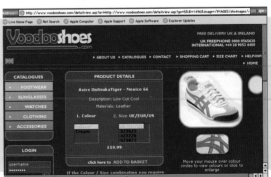

Consumers are the individuals (or businesses) that purchase the finished product for their own use.

Factors influencing the method of distribution

The final choice of distribution channel depends on the following:

- **The size of the retailer.** In general, large retailers will want to bypass the wholesaler, for reasons already given.
- **The type of product.** For a perishable product being sent to a limited number of retailers, it may be desirable to bypass the wholesaler, but for items such as newspapers there is more need for a wholesaler. Delivering 12 different newspapers to each of 100 newsagents would involve $12 \times 100 = 1,200$ journeys. With a wholesaler only $12 + 100 = 112$ journeys are needed.
- **The geography of the market.** In a remote rural area, it is less likely to be cost-effective for a manufacturer (producer) to deliver directly.
- **The complexity of the product.** The product may need direct contact with the producer or an expert retailer.
- **The degree of control desired by the manufacturer (producer).** In order to control quality and protect their reputation, some firms will deliver directly to selected retailers only. For example, Nike and Levi's have prevented retailers such as Tesco from selling their goods.

FACT FILE

Place is an important weapon in the armoury of Zara, the Spanish clothing retailer. Zara controls both the production and retailing of its clothes. In this way it can provide much more flexibility. Half of Zara's clothes are produced within 15 days of design, so Zara's fashion experts can copy a fashion idea and produce it within a very short time.

Store managers are allowed to make their own decisions on stock, so the individual shops can meet local needs. A few copies of each item are distributed directly to each shop and additional orders of those that sell well can be delivered very quickly. This has kept Zara at the forefront of fashion retailing for the general public. In Spain, customers queue up outside stores when a delivery is expected — a phenomenon dubbed as 'Zaramania' by the Spanish press.

Another advantage for Zara has been the impact that its policy has had on customers. Because the whole stock of a shop is likely to be turned over in a few weeks, customers know that they must quickly purchase an item that they admire, as it is unlikely to be there for long. It also means that customers visit the shop more regularly, as totally new styles of clothes are arriving constantly.

The number of outlets

Persuading retailers to stock products is often crucial to success. The more outlets that stock the product, the more sales a firm can generate. For impulse buys, in particular, the number of outlets is vital. Some 37% of mint eaters drive while they eat them. Given the limited space in most garage shops, mint producers see place as very important. If only one mint is stocked, that will be the one purchased, unless the consumer has a very high level of brand loyalty. So persuading the garage to stock your product in preference to a rival's can be vital.

Achieving distribution targets

KEY TERM

distribution targets: objectives given to a firm's staff (usually its sales force) to encourage them to gain as much shelf space in as many outlets as possible.

Firms can take a number of measures in order to reach their distribution targets:

- **Promotional campaigns.** Retailers may be persuaded to stock a product by advertisements in trade magazines. Promotions aimed at consumers may increase demand and so persuade a shopkeeper that he or she needs to stock that product, rather than lose customers.
- **Providing extra facilities or attractive displays.** For example, in the frozen food market manufacturers will provide free freezers in return for agreements to stock the firm's frozen foods. In small stores, the lack of space means that this can also help to exclude rival frozen food manufacturers. Häagen-Dazs achieved its distribution targets by supplying more attractive, upright freezers. These saved floor space and were preferred by customers and retailers.

- **Offering high profit margins to retailers.** Retailers want to use their space as effectively as possible. Supermarkets have been persuaded to devote more space to non-food items because they can make higher profit margins. Tesco outsold all of the UK's bookshops in sales of the latest Harry Potter book — an item that carried a higher profit than its usual stock.
- **Paying generous commission to sales staff.** This will give the sales force the incentive to persuade retailers that they should stock the products.
- **Increasing brand variety.** A firm such as Kellogg's may gain extra shelf space (at the expense of competitors) if it brings out new cereal products. However, if the sales of a product are too low, retailers may decide not to stock it.
- **Investigating alternative outlets.** Distribution targets may be reached by discovering new retailers or ways of selling. Some coffee shops have located within larger stores such as Homebase, while vending machines have become more popular in recent years.

FACT FILE

For impulse buys, place is particularly important. The decline of small convenience stores has threatened sales of impulse purchases. Companies such as Mars have responded by placing vending machines in public places to increase the chances of impulse buying. In the UK, Mars has lost market share to Cadbury and Nestlé. However, through owning Klix and Flavia drinks machines, Mars has obtained more knowledge of the vending market and has used this to its advantage.

In the UK there are over 1 million vending machines, generating sales in excess of £3 billion per annum. The top three chocolate brands sold through vending machines belong to Mars — the Mars Bar, Twix and Snickers. However, vending machines are much more important for sugar-based sweets, with Fruit Pastilles and Starburst leading the way. At a time when confectionery sales are slowing down, vending machine purchases are growing by 9% per annum.

CHAPTER 9 The marketing mix: place

The location of the point of sale

There is a saying in business that the three factors most critical to a firm's success are 'location, location, location'. An important part of 'place' is making sure that you operate in the right location. This involves several elements:

- **Convenience.** Despite their different reputations, product ranges, pricing policies and promotional techniques, supermarkets acknowledge that the convenience of their location to customers is the most important factor.
- **Accessibility.** The further the store is from the town centre, the less likely it is that consumers will find time to visit.
- **Cost of access.** Out-of-town shopping centres which provide free car parking have an advantage over town centre shops in some cases.
- **Reputation.** This is vital for certain goods and services. Doctors in Harley Street and fashion houses in Knightsbridge benefit from their address, both in the volume of sales and in the price charged.

Placement within the point of sale

Sales can be increased by careful placing of products within the point-of-sale outlet. This applies as much to direct selling as it does to shops. For example, supermarkets and greengrocers place brightly coloured, attractive fruit and vegetable displays so that they are visible from outside the store. Impulse buys, such as sweets, are placed by the checkouts to catch people's attention while queuing.

Integrating place and product: the case of the didgeridoo

Where on earth would you get a didgeridoo? Australia would be a good place to start, but where would you find one in the UK?

The didgeridoo (or didjeridu) is a product that is growing in popularity, but retailers need to identify the key features of the didgeridoo that make it an essential item for certain individuals. Recognising the key features that appeal to different consumers will help a business to maximise sales. So what is a didgeridoo to its potential customers, and where would you buy one?

- To some, the didgeridoo is a musical instrument. Musicians will pay in excess of £200 for a didgeridoo that has been correctly crafted from a termite-infested eucalyptus tree — but it will need to pass the 'boing' test to be suitable as a musical instrument. These consumers will naturally seek out a didgeridoo in a music shop, but the limited demand may make it difficult for manufacturers to persuade shops to stock them.
- Other customers see the didgeridoo as a spiritual object or a lifestyle statement, as evidenced by the number of sellers at certain festivals. Ideally, potential sellers should reserve a pitch at festivals such as WOMAD.

- For some buyers, the didgeridoo is an item of ornate decoration, to be artistically placed against a wall. For these customers, craft shops are the best location.
- More socially responsible consumers see the didgeridoo as a way of supporting aboriginal craftsmen and their traditional way of life. These customers are usually targeted by direct mail or internet suppliers.

Place is critical to the marketing of didgeridoos, as there is limited scope for promotion. However, interest is now sufficient to support a magazine, *Didgeridoo*, which is published four times a year.

TOPFOTO

ℯ EXAMINER'S VOICE

Read the wording of the question carefully. It can be tempting to use an answer to a question that you have already practised, but you must resist this temptation if the wording is different. Time spent checking the meaning of the question is time well spent — a few seconds of planning can save you 10 minutes of wasted effort.

GROUP EXERCISE

In order to further your understanding of product placement, visit and examine the following point-of-sale places:

- a food retailer
- a clothing retailer
- a catalogue
- a website offering direct sales to visitors

What conclusions can be drawn about the layout of the places that you visited? Explain why products were located in certain places or displayed in a certain way. What changes to the layout would you recommend and why?

FACT FILE

Claire's Stores is an American multinational with annual sales in excess of $210 million. Although the vast majority of the stores are in the USA, most of the new stores planned are situated in Europe. Sales revenue per square foot (a common measure of success in retailing) averages $340 per square foot overall, but in Europe figures exceed $700 per square foot. This has helped the European stores to achieve higher profit margins than those in the USA.

Source: www.clairestores.com

PRACTICE EXERCISE   Total: 40 marks (40 minutes)

1 Why has the role of the wholesaler declined in recent years? *(6 marks)*

2 Describe three services that a retailer provides for its customers. *(9 marks)*

3 Explain two factors that influence the method of distribution chosen for a product. *(6 marks)*

4 What is meant by the term 'distribution targets'? *(2 marks)*

5 Explain two ways in which a company such as Birds Eye can increase the amount of space that retailers provide for its products. *(6 marks)*

6 Why is the location of a store so important? *(5 marks)*

7 Why do manufacturers of 'impulse buys' see place as an important factor in the marketing mix? *(6 marks)*

CASE STUDY **Distribution at Tesco**

Terry Leahy, chief executive of Tesco, recognises that scope for growth in large-scale groceries in the UK is limited by the level of competition and by government regulations on mergers. This opinion
5 was reinforced by the Competition Commission's refusal to let Tesco bid to take over Safeway in September 2003.

In his 2003 annual review to shareholders, Leahy revealed how distribution channels and place would
10 be used to improve performance:

- 'We have delivered £230 million of efficiency savings by simplifying distribution, and operating more frequent deliveries has reduced delivery and storage costs.'
15 - 'We acquired T&S Stores, a leading convenience retailer. These shops serve local community needs and this increases our share of the convenience retail market from 1% to 5%.'
- 'We will convert 450 T&S shops to Tesco Express stores' — the brand name for Tesco's smaller, 20 localised convenience stores.
- 'Tesco.com is world leading with over 110,000 weekly orders. We will continue to expand internet retailing activities.'
- 'In 6 years we have built up a substantial chain of 25 hypermarkets in over 20 different countries. Our overseas operation now accounts for almost half of our selling space.'

Source: www.tesco.com

Questions

Total: 25 marks (30 minutes)

1 What is meant by the term 'distribution channels' (line 9)? *(2 marks)*

2 On a national scale, convenience store retailing is a declining market in which Tesco has a 5% market share.
   a In the Boston matrix, what name would be given to a product in this category? *(1 mark)*
   b Explain **one** possible reason why Tesco might have decided to enter the convenience retailing market. *(4 marks)*

3 Analyse **two** problems that Tesco might face in its international retailing which are unlikely to cause such difficulties in its UK operations. *(8 marks)*

4 Discuss whether Tesco should continue to expand its internet retailing activities. *(10 marks)*

CASE STUDY

The marketing mix

Although Chapters 6–9 separate the four Ps, in reality the marketing mix is about integrating the four elements in order to achieve the firm's desired objectives. Furthermore, the marketing mix will have been planned as a result of marketing research and will have been designed to fit in with the marketing strategy of the organisation. Below are two sets of questions, based on the Eden Project in Cornwall, which incorporate all four elements of the marketing mix.

CASE STUDY The Eden Project

Product

The Eden Project is set in a former china clay quarry near St Austell in Cornwall. It consists of the world's two largest biomes (dome-shaped greenhouses),
5 which are big enough to contain the Tower of London.

These amazing structures house two distinct sets of plants. The 'warm temperate' biome contains plants from the Mediterranean, South Africa and California,
10 while the larger 'humid tropics' dome features lush vegetation from areas such as the rainforests (and a waterfall that cascades from the top of the 55m high structure).

According to Karen Robinson of the *Sunday Times*:

15   Eden does a superb job of combining a 'visitor attraction' — with an excellent restaurant serving organic local produce and shops that sell garden plants and local crafts — with serious but easily accessible information about its real purpose: to
20   raise environmental awareness about the quality of life at all levels.

The Eden Project website declares: 'The Eden Trust didn't build this place to be a theme park. It must entertain but also encourage action and provide the
25 means for them [people with an interest in the environment] to take action.'

In 2002 it attracted 1.8 million visitors and the organisation is planning a third, 'semi-arid' biome,

additional restaurant space, and educational and conference facilities. Special events are organised 30 onsite to encourage repeat visits.

For many local people, the project is also seen as a way of regenerating the local economy. Eden has created over 1,700 full-time equivalent jobs in the West Country (600 employed directly by the project) 35 and a lot of locals who visit the site view it as a community project. It has also helped to attract more tourists to the area, providing benefits to other businesses, and some of the £90 million funding already spent has been provided by local councils and 40 the EU.

Price

The standard charge is £10 per day. Because of the project's educational focus, full-time students are charged £5 while children aged 5–15 pay £4. Family tickets are £25 and discounts are used to encourage group visits — these make up a significant percentage of visitors. Discounts are available for regular visitors.

Souvenirs, natural and organic products and the restaurant are important revenue earners, with a price skimming policy being adopted for most products offered for sale.

Promotion

Direct mail has been used in the local area and the website is visited by a lot of potential customers. However, the unique nature of the project means that it has interested the media as a story in its own right.

For this reason, public relations (PR) has been used heavily as a cost-effective way of promoting the project. Many national papers have featured the project during its development and since its opening, and Eden has relied a lot on viral (word-of-mouth) advertising as a way of increasing awareness.

Place

Journey times from the UK's main population centres mean that the Eden Project is not in the most convenient location. However, this is set against Cornwall's reputation as a family holiday destination, which means that the project is well placed for people taking holidays in the West Country.

There is little competition in the area, to draw visitors away, especially on less sunny days. For people with a keen interest in plants there are also other attractions, such as the Lost Gardens of Heligan (again featured on television and other national media). These complementary activities encourage visitors to the area.

A disused quarry is not generally seen as an ideal location, but the spectacle of the buildings themselves overcomes this obstacle.

Source: www.edenproject.com.

Question 1

Total: 25 marks (30 minutes)

a What is meant by the term 'price skimming' (lines 51–52)? *(2 marks)*

b Explain **two** reasons why the entrance ticket for a child is less than half the price charged to an adult visitor. *(6 marks)*

c Examine **two** possible benefits to the Eden Project of adding a conference centre. *(8 marks)*

d To what extent was it wise for the Eden Project to have spent only a limited sum on promotions and advertising? *(9 marks)*

Question 2

Total: 25 marks (30 minutes)

a State **one** objective of the Eden Project that is included in the passage. *(2 marks)*

b Explain **two** possible reasons why Cornwall is a good place to locate the Eden Project. *(6 marks)*

c Analyse **two** reasons why the Eden Project is able to use price skimming for the goods sold in its shop. *(8 marks)*

d Discuss the factors that the Eden Project should consider before deciding whether or not to build the third, 'semi-arid' dome. *(9 marks)*

CHAPTER 10

Elasticity of demand

This chapter examines the concept of elasticity of demand.

- *The section on price elasticity of demand shows how it is calculated and the significance of the result for both sales revenue and profit. The factors influencing price elasticity of demand for a particular product are explained.*
- *The section on income elasticity of demand shows how it is calculated and the factors influencing the income elasticity of demand of a product.*
- *The next section shows how elasticity of demand data can be used to analyse an organisation's situation.*
- *The final section examines the difficulties in calculating and using elasticity.*

Types of elasticity

Elasticity of demand measures the responsiveness of a change in the quantity demanded of a good or service to a change in the value of another variable. There are two main elasticities of demand.

> **KEY TERMS**
>
> **price elasticity of demand:** the responsiveness of a change in the quantity demanded of a good or service to a change in *price*.
> **income elasticity of demand:** the responsiveness of a change in the quantity demanded of a good or service to a change in *income*.

The formulae for calculating these two elasticities are as follows:

$$\text{price elasticity of demand} = \frac{\% \text{ change in quantity demanded}}{\% \text{ change in price}}$$

$$\text{income elasticity of demand} = \frac{\% \text{ change in quantity demanded}}{\% \text{ change in income}}$$

Price elasticity of demand

Price elasticity of demand can be elastic, inelastic or unitary:

- **Elastic demand.** If the percentage change in price leads to a greater percentage change in the quantity demanded (ignoring the minus sign), the calculation will yield an answer greater than 1. This indicates that demand is relatively responsive to a change in price.
- **Inelastic demand.** If the percentage change in price leads to a smaller percentage change in the quantity demanded, the calculation will yield an answer less than 1 (ignoring the minus sign). This indicates that demand is relatively unresponsive to a change in price.
- **Unit (or unitary) elasticity.** This name is given to the situation where both percentage changes are the same, giving an answer of (–)1. In theory, the

> **e EXAMINER'S VOICE**
>
> It is worth spending time on this topic. Examiners like it because it can test many skills and usually produces a range of answers. In real life, elasticity is much harder to use because companies cannot change prices without a reaction from competitors — but examinations are not good examples of real life.

DID YOU KNOW?

A fall in price will usually lead to a rise in demand; a rise in price will usually lead to a fall in demand. Thus price elasticity of demand is usually negative. Because it is negative (except in very exceptional circumstances), it is customary to ignore the negative sign. Therefore if you see a figure of 0.5 it means that a 1% rise/fall in price will lead to a 0.5% fall/rise in the quantity demanded.

price change is exactly cancelled out by the change in quantity demanded, so sales revenue stays the same.

Example calculations

Calculation 1: price falls from 25p to 20p, leading to an increase in quantity demanded from 200 to 220 units.

$$\text{\% change in quantity demanded} = \frac{\text{change in quantity demanded}}{\text{original quantity demanded}} \times 100$$

$$= \frac{(220 - 200)}{200} \times 100 = \frac{+20}{200} \times 100 = +10\%$$

$$\text{\% change in price} = \frac{\text{change in price}}{\text{original price}} \times 100$$

$$= \frac{(20 - 25)}{25} \times 100 = \frac{-5}{25} \times 100 = -20\%$$

$$\text{price elasticity of demand} = \frac{+10}{-20} = (-)0.5$$

An elasticity of 0.5 means that demand is *inelastic*.

Calculation 2: price rises from £11 to £13, leading to a decrease in quantity demanded from 76 units to 52 units.

$$\text{\% change in quantity demanded} = \frac{\text{change in quantity demanded}}{\text{original quantity demanded}} \times 100$$

$$= \frac{(52 - 76)}{76} \times 100 = \frac{-24}{76} \times 100 = -31.6\%$$

$$\text{\% change in price} = \frac{\text{change in price}}{\text{original price}} \times 100$$

$$= \frac{(13 - 11)}{11} \times 100 = \frac{+2}{11} \times 100 = +18.2\%$$

$$\text{price elasticity of demand} = \frac{-31.6}{+18.2} = (-)1.7$$

An elasticity of 1.7 means that demand is *elastic*.

> **𝑒** **EXAMINER'S VOICE**
>
> Be wary of using raw data to calculate elasticities, especially in coursework, as the changes in demand will also have been influenced by other factors. In practice, it is impossible to isolate changes in price from other factors that influence demand, although firms will try to estimate its value because of its potential usefulness. In theory, elasticity is based on the assumption that 'nothing else changes' when price (or income) changes. In reality, it is unlikely that a firm such as Tesco will do nothing (or that there will be no changes in external factors) if Asda changes its prices.

Effect of price elasticity of demand on sales revenue and profit

The effect of price elasticity of demand on sales revenue and profit depends on whether demand is elastic, inelastic or unitary.

Inelastic demand

If demand for a good is inelastic, when its price rises the quantity demanded falls by a smaller percentage. This means that the impact of the price increase will outweigh the relatively small percentage change in demand, so sales revenue will increase. For example, a 50% rise in price from £1 to £1.50 leads to a smaller (20%) fall in sales from 100 to 80 units. Price elasticity is –0.4.

Sales revenue increases from (£1 × 100 = £100) to (£1.50 × 80 = £120). Does this mean extra profit? The answer is *yes*. The total costs of producing 80 units will be lower than those of producing 100 units, so costs will fall at the same time as revenue increases. Thus, *a price rise will always increase sales revenue and profit if price elasticity of demand is inelastic*. Similarly, *a price fall will lead to lower sales revenue and profit if price elasticity of demand is inelastic*.

Elastic demand

If demand for a good is elastic, when its price rises the quantity demanded falls by a larger percentage. This means that the impact of the price increase will be outweighed by the relatively large percentage change in demand, so sales revenue will decrease. For example, a 20% rise in price from £1 to £1.20 leads to a larger (50%) fall in sales from 100 to 50 units. Price elasticity is –2.5.

Sales revenue decreases from (£1 × 100 = £100) to (£1.20 × 50 = £60). Does this mean a decrease in profit? The answer is *not necessarily*. It will be cheaper to produce 50 units than 100, so costs will fall as well as income. If costs fall by more than income, profit will still be improved. But if costs fall by a smaller amount, profit will fall. Thus, *a price rise will always decrease sales revenue if price elasticity of demand is elastic, but the effect on profit will depend on cost savings*. The chances of more profit are higher if there is a high profit margin on the good.

In the case of a price fall, the sales revenue of a good with a price elastic demand will always increase. However, the quantity demanded rises and so production costs will rise. Consequently, it is impossible to predict the effect on profits without knowing about the costs of production.

Unitary elasticity

If demand for a good is unitary, sales revenue will be the same whether price rises or falls. A price rise would then be advisable if the business is aiming to increase profit, because this means a lower volume of sales would be required, which would enable production costs to fall. However, the business may not increase price if it has other aims, such as increasing its market share.

The impact of price changes on sales revenue is summarised in Table 10.1.

Table 10.1 Effect of price changes on sales revenue

Price change	Price elasticity of demand (PED)		
	PED > 1 (elastic)	PED = 1 (unitary)	PED < 1 (inelastic)
Price increases	Sales revenue falls	Sales revenue unchanged	Sales revenue rises
Price decreases	Sales revenue rises	Sales revenue unchanged	Sales revenue falls

Factors influencing the price elasticity of demand

The factors influencing the price elasticity of demand are as follows.

Necessity

If a product is essential, consumers will still buy similar quantities even if the price is very high. However, a reduction in price will not tend to encourage buyers to purchase much more, as they will have already satisfied their need at the higher price. The more necessary a product, the more *inelastic* is the demand.

Habit

Some products are habit forming. Typical examples are cigarettes, chocolate, alcohol and watching television. In effect, a habit means that the product or service becomes a necessity to that individual. This means that cigarette manufacturers can increase the price of their product and demand will stay roughly the same. The stronger the habit, the more *inelastic* is the demand for the product.

INGRAM

> **DID YOU KNOW?**
>
> A major reason for the high prices of some habit-forming products (notably petrol, alcohol and cigarettes) is the excise tax charged by the government. The government places heavy taxes on these (inelastic) goods, knowing that people will continue buying them (and so pay taxes). If the government taxed goods with elastic demand, it would not raise as much money.

Availability of substitutes

If there are no alternatives to a product, a consumer is likely to buy a similar quantity if the price changes. However, if there are many alternatives, customers will switch to a close alternative. The impact will also depend on consumer tastes: for example, how close the alternative is seen to be. Some buyers may see beef as a close alternative to pork, but other customers will not see them as substitutes.

The greater the availability of close substitutes, the more *elastic* is the demand, as small price rises will encourage consumers to buy the alternatives. This can be seen in the market for petrol. In remote rural areas or at motorway service stations, prices tend to be higher than they are in big cities, where it is easier to find an alternative supplier. Thus demand at any particular garage is more elastic in cities than it is in the countryside.

In the long term, demand becomes more elastic as consumers search out and switch to alternative products.

Brand loyalty

Firms will attempt to create brand loyalty by various means, such as the quality of the product, advertising and other forms of promotion. In addition to increasing sales volume, the creation of loyal customers will also influence people's reactions to price changes. A consumer who insists on wearing Armani clothing will not be put off by a higher price. The greater the level of brand loyalty, the more *inelastic* is the demand.

The proportion of income spent on a product

Consumers will be less concerned about price rises if a product takes up only a small percentage of their income. For example, a 20% increase in the price of a box of matches will only be 2p or 3p, so the consumer is unlikely to change the number of boxes bought (demand is inelastic). On the other hand, buying a car will use up a lot of income, so consumers will be affected by small percentage changes in price. This factor will make the demand for cars more elastic.

Income of consumers

Rich people are less worried about price rises than poorer individuals. Thus they (as individuals) are going to have more inelastic demand for the products that they buy. David Beckham will pay hundreds of pounds for a haircut, but most consumers would try to find a cheaper alternative if this was the price advertised by their local barber or hairdresser. For this reason, businesses will often target rich consumers. The prices of brands bought predominantly by wealthy consumers can be increased without affecting sales very much, so their demand is *inelastic*. Shops in exclusive areas can often set higher prices because their customers are less conscious of price.

Overall, the elasticity of demand will be determined by a combination of these factors.

DID YOU KNOW?

Firms prefer their products to have price-inelastic demand. A business will not just accept that its products are price elastic or inelastic, but may take steps to change customers' views. How can a firm make its products more inelastic?

Income elasticity of demand

Income elasticity of demand indicates how demand will be affected by changes in income. A 10% increase in income will enable consumers to spend approximately 10% more in total on products, but the change in spending will vary considerably between individual products.

- For **luxury products** the income elasticity of demand will be greater than 1. Expenditure on holidays, for example, tends to increase by a larger

percentage than the change in income as an economy grows richer. Thus holidays in general are *income elastic*.

- For **necessities** there is likely to be a rise in demand that is smaller than the rise in income. This will give an elasticity that is greater than zero, but less than 1. These products are *income inelastic*.
- For some products, such as cheap cuts of meat, demand falls as people experience increases in income and can afford better alternatives. These products have *negative income elasticity* and are known as **inferior goods**.

Calculating income elasticity of demand

$$\text{Income elasticity of demand} = \frac{\% \text{ change in quantity demanded}}{\% \text{ change in income}}$$

Example calculation: income rises by 10%, leading to an increase in the quantity demanded from 250 to 300 units.

$$\% \text{ change in quantity demanded} = \frac{\text{change in quantity demanded}}{\text{original quantity demanded}} \times 100$$

$$\frac{(300 - 250)}{250} \times 100 = \frac{50}{250} \times 100 = +20\%$$

$$\% \text{ change in income} = +10\% \text{ (given in question)}$$

$$\text{Income elasticity of demand} = \frac{+20\%}{+10\%} = +2$$

An elasticity of $+2$ means that demand is income elastic.

Firms cannot control the levels of income in a market, so the main use of income elasticity is to forecast demand.

Example

Firm X produces three products, as shown in Table 10.2.

Table 10.2 Income elasticity of demand

Product	Income elasticity of demand	Current sales (units per annum)
A: luxury	+3.00	1,000
B: necessity	+0.25	4,000
C: inferior good	−0.50	500

Next year consumer incomes in the UK are expected to grow by 4%. What sales levels can be expected for this company's three products?

Product A:

$$\frac{\% \text{ change in quantity demanded}}{\% \text{ change in income } (+4\%)} = \text{income elasticity of demand } (+3)$$

$$\% \text{ change in quantity demanded} = +4\% \times +3 = +12\%$$

$$+12\% \text{ of 1,000 units} = +120 \text{ units.}$$

Therefore sales are forecast to increase from 1,000 to 1,120 units.

Product B:

$$\frac{\text{\% change in quantity demanded}}{\text{\% change in income} \ (+4\%)} = \text{income elasticity of demand} \ (+0.25)$$

% change in quantity demanded = $+4\% \times +0.25 = +1\%$

$+1\%$ of 4,000 units = $+40$ units.

Therefore sales are forecast to increase from 4,000 to 4,040 units.

Product C:

$$\frac{\text{\% change in quantity demanded}}{\text{\% change in income} \ (+4\%)} = \text{income elasticity of demand} \ (-0.5)$$

% change in quantity demanded = $+4\% \times -0.5 = -2\%$

-2% of 500 units = -10 units.

Therefore sales are forecast to decrease from 500 to 490 units.

Inferior goods

The inferior good seems to be doomed to failure. Can you think of three reasons why a firm would continue producing an inferior good? (Answers on p. 85.)

Uses of elasticity of demand data

Elasticity of demand can be used to interpret the market, as the following example shows.

Example

	Product X	Product Y
Price elasticity of demand	(–)4.0	(–)0.3
Income elasticity of demand	–0.6	+2.5

Table 10.3
Elasticity of demand data

The following conclusions about products X and Y might be inferred from the data in Table 10.3.

Conclusions for product X

- Price elasticity of demand is (–)4.0 (very elastic). A change in price leads to a proportionally larger change in quantity demanded. This product is not a necessity and is likely to have many close substitutes.
- Income elasticity of demand is –0.6 (negative). As incomes increase, this product will lose sales. It is an inferior good.
- Product X is probably a cheap, low-quality alternative to other products in a very competitive market, and is likely to be purchased by consumers who cannot afford a better alternative.

Conclusions for product Y

- Price elasticity of demand is (–)0.3 (inelastic). The product is a necessity or has few close substitutes.

- Income elasticity of demand is + 2.5 (high). This product is a luxury, showing a large percentage increase in sales as income rises.
- Product Y probably has few close substitutes and may be habit-forming, or appeals to consumers who can afford higher prices.

Marketing strategies for product X

In the short term:

- Charge a lower price to increase sales revenue, but not if the company is operating on low profit margins.
- Change the product's image because, as the economy grows, the sales of this product will continue to decline and so market share will be lost. However, during a recession the sales would grow.

In the long term:

- Reposition the product in order to appeal to higher income sectors.
- Alternatively, if profit margins are reasonable, the company may keep the product unchanged. It may act as a cash cow, and in periods of fierce competition price cuts should enable the company to generate high sales volumes.

Marketing strategies for product Y

In the short term:

- Increase price as there will be a relatively small fall in demand, creating a rise in sales revenue from a lower level of output.
- Aim for high 'value added' to increase profit margins.

In the long term:

- This product appears to be a cash cow and should be 'milked'.
- Keep the price high.
- Safeguard the product's exclusive image.

Difficulties in calculating and using elasticity of demand

Elasticity of demand can be very unreliable because of the difficulties involved in calculating it. Elasticity of demand calculations assume that 'other things remain equal' while price or income changes. In practice, this does not happen.

The main difficulties in calculating (and using) elasticity of demand are as follows:

- There may have been significant changes in the market, affecting the level of demand independently of price or income. For example:
  — consumer tastes may have changed
  — new competitors may have entered the market or previous competitors may have left the market

 **EXAMINER'S VOICE**

Watch out for the wording of the question. An elastic demand for a product means that a price *cut* leads to an increase in sales revenue (but a price *increase* has the opposite effect).

— technological change may have influenced the market

— the image of the product may have changed

■ Changes in price may provoke a reaction from rival firms which may try to match the change or modify their marketing in response to the change. This reaction may not always be the same. For example, in some markets competitors are more likely to match a rival's cut in price than they are to match a rival's increase in price.

■ Consumers may react differently to increases in price or income than decreases. For example, a decrease in price might not encourage consumers to buy more, but an increase may tempt them to buy from competitors.

■ It may be difficult to use secondary market research to calculate elasticity, as the planned change in price (or expected change in income) may be different from anything experienced in the past.

■ Consumers may be unable to predict how their spending will be affected by price or income changes, and so primary surveys may be unreliable.

Even the company's own actions may reduce the reliability of any calculations. Firms will often promote their price reductions and so brand awareness (and thus the quantity demanded) may increase for this reason rather than because of the price cut.

Answers to inferior goods question on p. 83

Possible reasons:

■ It meets the needs of a market segment (those on low incomes or those not prepared to pay a high price).

■ It helps to provide a balanced portfolio.

■ There may be less competition in this type of market.

■ During recessions, inferior goods may experience rising demand.

■ Inferior goods in one country may have greater potential in other countries.

■ It makes a profit! This is important. Just because sales are declining, it does not mean that a profit cannot be made. A declining market can be a profitable niche (e.g. pipes for smokers).

PRACTICE EXERCISE
Total: 50 marks (45 minutes)

1 What is meant by the term 'price elasticity of demand'? *(4 marks)*

2 State whether each of the following factors will make demand price elastic or price inelastic:

   a It is habit forming.

   b There are many substitutes.

   c It is aimed at a wealthy market segment.

   d Advertising has created brand loyalty.

   e The product is a necessity.

   f It takes up a very small percentage of consumers' incomes. *(6 marks)*

3 Average incomes rise from £20,000 to £21,000 per annum. Sales of playing cards fall from 4 million to 3.9 million per annum.
  a Calculate the income elasticity of demand. *(4 marks)*
  b What name is given to goods with negative income elasticity of demand? *(2 marks)*

4 If demand changes by a greater percentage than the percentage change in price, the price elasticity of demand is said to be .... *(1 mark)*

5 How should a business market a product that has price-inelastic demand and a high income elasticity of demand? *(8 marks)*

6 To what extent can a business influence the price elasticity of demand of one of its products? *(9 marks)*

7 How can a firm increase the income elasticity of demand of a product? *(6 marks)*

8 Discuss the reasons why it would be more difficult for a computer manufacturer to use elasticity of demand than it would for a company marketing pencils. *(10 marks)*

Elasticity in the art market

Drew Thomas studied the sales forecasts for the next 4 years. The art gallery he owned in the wealthiest part of London was expanding rapidly, but he was worried that, if growth carried on at the present
5 rate, there would not be enough room for the original paintings that he displayed.

Drew stocked two types of pictures. Part of his stock was a selection of
10 mass-produced copies of classic pictures such as Sunflowers by Vincent van Gogh. On average these sold for £20 each, but cost him £10 to purchase. Each week he sold 50, but
15 twice a year he had a sale and reduced the price to £15. In these weeks, sales consistently increased to 80 pictures per week. Drew wondered whether he should have these sales more often. These pictures
20 were not framed and were displayed in racks, taking up a minimal amount of space. They provided a steady income, but were not the main part of his business.

The main profit for the gallery came from the original paintings that he sold. The location in an
25 expensive area of London meant that promising young artists were keen to display their works of art at his gallery. Drew had also been the first gallery owner to display the work of a number of (now) successful artists, and in return many of them chose to use his gallery to display their 30 most recent works of art. Of course, Drew did not buy these paintings. He took a commission (15% of the selling price) on any work sold. With many prices in excess of £10,000, 35 this meant that Drew made a nice profit and could afford to expand the gallery if he wished. In order to display the pictures attractively, Drew was determined that he would 40 not put too many pictures in each room. He calculated that the existing gallery would be able to stock 40% more pictures than it currently did. If sales increased by more than 40%, he would need to extend the 45 property.

Drew had calculated that the income elasticity of demand for these paintings was 3.25. Over the next 4 years, government estimates indicated that the average income of consumers would rise by 15%. 50

COREL

Questions

Total: 25 marks (30 minutes)

1 Calculate the price elasticity of demand for the mass-produced pictures (see paragraph 2). *(4 marks)*

2 Should Drew decide to have more frequent sales of these mass-produced pictures? Explain your reasoning. *(6 marks)*

3 Examine whether Drew needs to extend his property within the next 4 years. *(5 marks)*

4 Discuss whether the demand for original works of art by promising artists would be price elastic or price inelastic. *(10 marks)*

INTEGRATED CASE STUDIES

Marketing

The two case studies that follow are based on the whole of the AS Marketing specification. They are intended to reflect the types of data-response question on marketing that may be set in Unit 1 of AQA AS Business Studies.

Case Study 1 is followed by one set of questions. Case Study 2 has two sets of questions; either or both can be used.

e **EXAMINER'S VOICE**

In BUS1 (Unit 1 of the AS course) it is very likely that a data-response question that is mainly about marketing will include financial elements. Similarly, a question based on finance or accounting may include marketing elements. Overall, the BUS1 paper tests marketing and finance equally, but there is unlikely to be a question based totally on marketing (or finance).

CASE STUDY 1 The Exertris interactive exercise bike

On 15 April 2003 Pendle Leisure Centre in Colne, Lancashire, created the UK's first interactive fitness arcade, filled with 25 Exertris interactive bikes, plasma screens, virtual projection, lighting and interactive
5 programming.

The idea is to encourage the local population, particularly the youth market, to try to improve their fitness.

Exertris is a cycle that combines the fitness benefits
10 of an exercise bike with the excitement of interactive games. The energy that the user puts into the cycle directly affects his or her control of the interactive game. Different machines can be connected to provide competition with other users, and settings can be
15 adjusted to provide fair competition between people of different fitness levels.

The cost of a machine means that the target market is the leisure industry rather than individual buyers. Exertris has conducted quantitative primary market
20 research in order to get customers' views. A total of 760 gym members were interviewed, in gyms contain-

ing temporarily installed Exertris machines, with the following conclusions:

- 91% said that their gym should permanently install the Exertris. 25
- 70% said that they would definitely recommend it to a friend.
- 90% 'liked' or 'loved' it.
- 33% said they would consider moving to another gym nearby if it installed Exertris. 30

The survey also involved interviewing 100 gym managers:

- 90% said that it had helped to increase retention levels among members.
- 61% said that it had helped to attract new members. 35
- 81% said it was more popular than other equipment in their gyms.

Sarah Cooper, gym manager at Fitness First in Coventry, says: 'They really are a gym manager's dream. Our members love them, making it easier to 40 stick to their fitness regime, and it means that they visit more regularly.'

Gareth Davies, the inventor of Exertris, argues that the product itself is the key element of the marketing
45 mix. It is reliable, attractive, easy to use, updateable for new programmes and games, durable and compact in size, and it will make people healthy.

In January 2003 Bill Gates, founder of Microsoft, showcased the Exertris at a computing trade fair,
50 and Pendle Leisure's chief executive, Phil Storey, discovered the product at a recent exhibition and conference.

Exertris argues that increased membership in gyms stocking its machines means that the investment pays for itself quickly. 'It also makes gyms more 55 sociable, by giving people something to talk about.'

Source: www.exertris.com

Questions

Total: 25 marks (30 minutes)

1 What is meant by the term 'quantitative primary market research' (lines 19–20)? *(2 marks)*

2 Explain why Exertris interviewed gym users and gym managers in its survey. *(6 marks)*

3 Analyse the reasons for Exertris' use of trade fairs and exhibitions as a way of promoting its exercise bikes. *(8 marks)*

4 Evaluate the relative importance of the product features described by Gareth Davies in contributing to the likely success of the Exertris bike. *(9 marks)*

CASE STUDY 2 New Look

In January 2003, New Look announced new marketing objectives:

- expansion of trading space by 175,000 square feet
- development of a wider product range
5 - expansion of the number of its shops in France

The following marketing strategies were then introduced:

- Project 300 — updating and modernising 300 smaller stores
10 - Project Heartland — relocating larger stores in key cities and major towns, in order to increase the size of the stores to an average of 7,000 square feet
- test marketing in six smaller towns the introduction of medium-sized stores (5,000 square feet), where
15 typically the stores would have been less than 2,000 square feet
- increasing sales of new product types such as footwear and accessories by approximately 50% (in comparison to 10% growth for the core clothing
20 products)

On 30 May 2003, Stephen Sunnocks, the chief executive of New Look, announced record profits for the year 2002/03. In the UK clothing market, the market size (measured by total sales of all firms) was £15 billion (£15,000 million). New Look achieved sales 25 of £643.4 million, giving the company its highest market share ever.

However, Mr Sunnocks also noted that, in the 4 months since the new marketing objectives had been announced, sales had started to decline. 'In volume 30 terms, sales were up by 9%, but the average sale price was down by 10%.'

Mr Sunnocks blamed external factors: 'The rises in taxes seem to be hitting consumers.' 'Changing fashions are also a factor. Last year the big sellers 35 were rugby shirts, gypsy blouses and jeans. But this year it's vests, mini-skirts and three-quarter-length trousers,' he added.

Mr Sunnocks estimated that sales would grow by only 2% in the current financial year. 40

Source: www.newlook.co.uk

Question 1
Total: 25 marks (30 minutes)

a Distinguish between 'marketing objectives' and 'marketing strategies'. *(4 marks)*

b Calculate New Look's market share of the UK women's clothing market in 2002/03. *(3 marks)*

c Analyse two possible reasons for New Look's decision to expand into the French market. *(8 marks)*

d New Look has chosen to open larger stores in big cities rather than opening new stores in small towns that do not have a New Look store. Discuss the relative merits of these two alternative strategies. *(10 marks)*

Question 2
Total: 25 marks (30 minutes)

a What is meant by the term 'market size' (line 24)? *(2 marks)*

b Calculate the apparent price elasticity of demand for New Look's products, based solely on the figures given in lines 31–32. *(3 marks)*

c Briefly explain one problem for New Look of expanding into France. *(4 marks)*

d Analyse the possible implications for New Look of its unexpected fall in sales revenue. *(7 marks)*

e Discuss the merits of New Look's decision to extend its product range into footwear and accessories. *(9 marks)*

Accounting and finance

66 Beware of small
expenses; a small leak
will sink a great ship. 99
Benjamin Franklin

Costs, profit and contribution

This chapter sets out the key concepts used in simple financial calculations. It looks at the basic calculation of profit (revenue minus total costs) and examines the ways in which costs can be classified, distinguishing between fixed and variable costs and direct and indirect costs (overheads). The concepts of 'contribution' and 'contribution per unit' are also explained and their significance for businesses is outlined.

Profit and revenue

 TERMS

profit: the difference between the income of a business and its total costs.
Profit = revenue – total costs
revenue: a measure of the income received from an organisation's activities.
Revenue = total costs + profit

Revenue may also be described by the following terms:
- income
- total revenue
- sales revenue
- sales turnover
- turnover

Profit is a prime objective of most firms. In effect, there are two ways of improving profit:
- increase sales revenue
- decrease costs

A combination of both would be the ideal way of achieving additional profit.

Costs

In marketing, a lot of the focus is on achieving higher sales revenue, without adding too much to costs. However, other functional areas of a business, such as production and administration, can help to achieve rising profits by reducing costs while still providing the same quality of service.

Thus costs are a major factor in determining the overall success of a firm, as measured by its profit. Organisations need to understand their costs if they wish to improve their profit.

Classifying costs

There are two principal reasons for classifying costs:

- **To assess the impact of changes in output on the costs of production.** A firm can compare additional revenue from an increase in output to see if it exceeds the extra costs incurred. Regardless of its current profit level, a firm aiming to make profit should increase output if the extra income exceeds the extra costs of increasing output. Similarly, output should be reduced if cost savings are more than the amount of revenue that has been lost.

- **To calculate the costs of making a particular product in a multi-product company.** It can be difficult to work out whether it is worthwhile making a product. It is easy to calculate the sales income of a product, but many costs (e.g. office rent, canteen facilities) are not specific to any product made by a firm.

INGRAM

Costs and output

A company can use the link between costs and output to calculate the financial *implications* of changing its level of output.

In reality, it is impossible to predict the exact change in each and every cost, so general classifications of costs are used to *estimate* the likely effect of output changes on individual costs. To simplify the calculations, costs are classified in the following way.

KEY TERMS

fixed costs: costs that do not vary directly with output in the short run (e.g. rent).
variable costs: costs that vary directly with output in the short run (e.g. raw materials).
total costs: the sum of fixed costs and variable costs.

If there is an $x\%$ rise in output, it is assumed that:

- fixed costs do not change
- variable costs change by the same percentage as the change in output (a rise of $x\%$ in this case)

EXAMINER'S VOICE

Questions asking for the 'implications' of an action often cause difficulties in examinations. Remember that implications are the effect or consequences of an action, *not* the causes.

This is an oversimplification of what actually happens in real life, but it is helpful to firms because it allows them to make fairly accurate predictions about how costs will change as output changes. In turn, this will assist them in making logical business decisions.

Table 11.1 shows how firms classify the costs they incur into fixed and variable costs. The logic behind these choices is that the costs of items in the first column are not affected by small changes in output. These **fixed costs** will, however, change in the long run if large increases in output are required. The **variable costs**, shown in the second column, do need to change if output changes, even by a small amount.

Table 11.1
Classification of costs by output

Fixed costs	Variable costs
Machinery	Raw materials
Rent and rates	Wages of operatives/
Salaries	direct labour
Administration	Power
Vehicles	
Marketing	
Lighting and heating	

Note that a distinction is made between wages (paid to operatives who make the product) and salaries (paid to staff who are not directly involved in production). Similarly, power to drive the machinery is a variable cost, while office heating and lighting is fixed (not related to output).

Semi-variable costs are costs that combine elements of fixed and variable costs. A worker may be paid a set wage plus a bonus for each item produced. The set wage would be a fixed cost and the bonus a variable cost.

> **ℯ** **EXAMINER'S VOICE**
>
> Do not worry about the merits of individual categories, but accept the logic behind them when carrying out calculations. Analytical skills can then be demonstrated through pointing out the potential flaws in any calculations based on these general classifications.
>
> For example, many offices will employ temporary staff to cover changes in activity levels. Therefore, in practice, administration costs such as salaries will vary with output in the short run.
>
> Similarly, the likelihood of variable costs not increasing by the same percentage as output can be investigated. With economies of scale it is likely that variable costs will rise more slowly than output, but as maximum capacity is approached it can become very costly to increase output just by changing variable factors.

The effect of changes in output on costs

When asked to look at the effect of a change in output on costs, you must assume that variable costs change by the same percentage as output. If output doubles, variable costs will double; if output falls by 10%, variable costs will fall by 10%. In both cases, the fixed costs will stay the same.

For example, let us assume that output is 1,000 units, fixed costs are £5,000 and variable costs are £6,000. Therefore, total costs are £11,000. The fixed costs will not change if output changes. The variable costs of £6,000 will increase, but by how much? To calculate this we need to know the variable cost per unit. If 1,000 units cost £6,000 in variable costs, this is £6 per unit (£6,000 ÷ 1,000 units). If 1 more unit is produced, it will increase variable costs by £6 (to £6,006). If 50 more units are produced, variable costs will increase by £300 (50 × £6) to £6,300 (1050 × £6). Fixed costs will stay at £5,000.

1 What happens to total costs if output doubles from 1,000 units to 2,000 units?

2 What happens to total costs if output falls by 10%? (Answers on p. 100)

℮ EXAMINER'S VOICE

All examiners for AQA use a rule called the 'own figure rule'. This means that if you make a mistake in a calculation, you can only be penalised once. Therefore, it is important to show all of your working. In question 2 above, a student who calculated variable costs as 700 × £6 (instead of 900 × £6) would have reached an incorrect answer (£4,200 instead of £5,400 for variable costs, and thus £9,200 rather than £10,400 for total costs). Typically, this answer (with working) would achieve almost maximum marks, as only one small error has been made. However, an answer of £9,200 without working would have received zero marks because the examiner would not have been able to see that the answer contained only one error.

Table 11.2 shows the link between monthly costs and output for a magazine producer. It illustrates why the magazine producer wants high monthly sales. If only 20,000 magazines are sold, the fixed costs are very high as a percentage of total costs. However, if sales quadruple to 80,000 magazines, total costs increase by less than double (from £70,000 to £130,000) and the fixed costs are a much lower percentage of the total costs.

Units of output (000s)	Fixed costs (£000s)	Variable costs (£000s)	Total costs (£000s)
0	50	0	50
20	50	20	70
40	50	40	90
60	50	60	110
80	50	80	130
100	50	100	150
120	50	120	170

Table 11.2 Monthly costs and output for a magazine producer

Costs and products

Costs are also classified according to whether or not they can be related directly to a particular product.

KEY TERMS

direct costs: costs that can be related directly to a product or service (e.g. raw materials).

indirect costs (or overheads): costs that cannot be related directly to a product or service (e.g. the managing director's salary).

This classification enables a firm to allocate costs to individual products and so calculate the standard cost of making a given product. The firm can then

CHAPTER 11 · Costs, profit and contribution

DID YOU KNOW?

If a company produces only one product, all its fixed costs can be attributed to that product. A multi-product company, on the other hand, needs a system of allocating fixed costs between products, to enable it to calculate the profitability of each product.

control its efficiency by comparing the costs of production of different products. The distinction between direct and indirect costs will also be used in setting budgets for each product.

Contribution

Contribution is an important concept in business studies. It looks at whether an individual product (or activity) is helping the business to make a profit.

All firms need to pay their fixed costs in order to operate. These costs must be covered before a profit can be made.

Contribution ignores these fixed costs. Instead it looks only at the (direct) costs of making the product. If the sales revenue from making the product is greater than the direct costs, the product is contributing towards either paying off the fixed costs or making a profit (if the fixed costs have already been covered).

 KEY TERM

▌ **contribution per unit:** selling price per unit – direct cost per unit

For example, if the direct costs of making a pen are 7p and the pen sells for 18p, the **contribution per unit** is 11p (18p – 7p).

The **total contribution** of a product can be calculated in two ways:
- contribution per unit × no. of units sold
- sales revenue – direct costs

Opportunity cost

The opportunity cost is the next best alternative foregone. This is a vital concept in the business world, as all actions have an alternative. A profitable use of resources should be ignored if there is an alternative that provides a better return. Opportunity cost can be applied to decisions relating to finance, resources and the use of time. For example, the decision by Marks and Spencer to include Café Revive in more of its shops means that it has less shelf space for its clothing and other products.

ℓ EXAMINER'S VOICE

Finance and accounting questions can be quite daunting if you dislike numbers. However, number crunching is not the main skill that is being tested. The high-mark questions on an examination paper are based on evaluation (making a judgement). Numbers tend to give firm conclusions, so it is unlikely that evaluation questions will be based on numerical answers — they are far more likely to ask you to comment on the usefulness of a method or the consequences or causes of a situation.

GROUP EXERCISE

Table 11.3 shows the contributions made by four different 'water features' produced by a firm. The total of £971,000 is a contribution towards fixed costs and profit.

Name of water feature	Price (£) −	Direct costs (£) =	Contribution per unit (£) ×	No. of units sold (000s) =	Total contribution (£000s)
'Cascade'	30	25	5	40	200
'Fountain'	45	22	23	16	368
'Stream'	60	28	32	14	448
'Waterfall'	15	18	(3)	15	(45)

	Sales (£000s) −	Direct costs (£000s) =	Contribution (£000s)
'Cascade'	(30 × 40) 1,200	(25 × 40) 1,000	(5 × 40) 200
'Fountain'	(45 × 16) 720	(22 × 16) 352	(23 × 16) 368
'Stream'	(60 × 14) 840	(28 × 14) 392	(32 × 14) 448
'Waterfall'	(15 × 15) 225	(18 × 15) 270	((3) × 15) (45)
			971

Table 11.3
Contributions made by four different water features

Look at the contributions made by each product.

1 What immediate action should you take to improve profit?

2 Which other product should be investigated to see if its contribution can be improved?

(Answers on p. 100.)

PRACTICE EXERCISE 1 — Total: 6 marks (3 minutes)

Identify three fixed costs and three variable costs from the list below.

- raw materials
- stationery expenditure
- advertising expenditure
- power
- property rent
- wages

ⓔ EXAMINER'S VOICE

When asked to look at the effect of a change in output on costs, you must assume that variable costs change by the same percentage as output. If output doubles, variable costs will double; if output falls by 10%, variable costs will fall by 10%. In both cases, the fixed costs will stay the same.

PRACTICE EXERCISE 2 — Total: 20 marks (20 minutes)

A textile manufacturer sells 400 shirts at a price of £15 each. The costs of producing the 400 shirts are shown in the table.

1 Calculate the profit made from selling 400 shirts. *(4 marks)*

2 The retailers that buy the shirts have said that they will buy 600 shirts if the price is reduced to £13. Calculate the profit made if the textile manufacturer increases output and sales to 600 shirts, with the selling price at £13 per unit. *(6 marks)*

3 Using quantitative and qualitative factors, advise the manufacturer on whether it should charge a price of £13 or £15. *(10 marks)*

Item	Cost (£)
Raw materials	1,600
Marketing costs	120
Power	80
Heating/lighting	60
Property rent	400
Wages	2,220

CHAPTER 11 Costs, profit and contribution

A company makes and sells 100 units each of two products (A and B). The fixed costs and variable costs are shown below.

	Product A	Product B
Fixed costs (£)	200	800
Variable costs (£)	800	200
Total costs (£)	1,000	1,000

1 Calculate the total costs of making:
  a 50 units of product A
  b 50 units of product B *(4 marks)*

2 Calculate the total costs of making:
  a 150 units of product A
  b 150 units of product B *(4 marks)*

3 Briefly explain why the changes in total costs for product A are different from those for product B as output changes. *(3 marks)*

4 Explain the implications that these figures have for a company that is deciding whether to replace its workers with machinery. *(5 marks)*

The table below shows some costs and revenue data at different levels of output.

Output level	Sales revenue	Fixed costs	Variable costs	Total costs	Profit
0	0				
1					
2					
3	75				
4		20			
5					
6			90		

1 What are the total fixed costs? *(2 marks)*

2 What is the selling price of the product? *(2 marks)*

3 What are the variable costs per unit? *(2 marks)*

4 Using the above information, complete the table by filling in the gaps. *(8 marks)*

PRACTICE EXERCISE 5
Total: 15 marks (15 minutes)

The following information applies to a paper manufacturer that produces and sells 1 million reams of paper a week:

indirect costs: £400,000

raw materials: £500,000

wages: £150,000

Assume that there are no other costs.

1 Calculate the costs per unit of a ream of paper. *(2 marks)*

2 Calculate the direct costs per unit of a ream of paper. *(2 marks)*

3 A ream of paper is sold for £1.50. Calculate the total weekly profit made by the firm. *(4 marks)*

4 Calculate the contribution per unit (per ream). *(3 marks)*

5 How much extra profit would be made if 1.1 million reams were made? *(4 marks)*

CASE STUDY Gnomes United

Gnomes United is a small garden centre in Colchester. The owner, Jim Tavare, has successfully increased sales in recent years by widening the range of products and
5 services offered. A total of 70% of the garden centre's revenue comes from the sale of plants and garden tools, but the opening last year of a nearby superstore led to a sharp reduction in sales of these items.
10 Sales of plants have fully recovered, owing to quality problems at the superstore, but sales of garden tools are still low. Market research among his customers has led to Jim realising
15 that the sale of garden tools in his garden centre is important, since customers see them as an essential element of any garden centre. Furthermore, Jim remembers how sales of plants at his cousin Jack's garden centre in Ipswich fell sharply when Jack decided
20 to stop selling garden tools.

Sales records show that relatively few garden tools are bought in the run-up to Christmas.

Last year Jim experimented with selling some Christmas products, such as decorations, as many customers 25 visit the centre once a year to buy their Christmas trees. The restaurant at the garden centre enjoys a boom time in the month before Christmas, and Jim's research shows that about 20% of his 30 customers first came to the garden centre to buy Christmas products and have come back since for other products.

Jim is wondering whether to stock 35 Christmas tree lights this year — an item that he has not previously sold. He has asked 50 customers and they seem to be keen on the idea. Their responses have led him to conclude that he will sell 200 boxes in December. A standard box of 40 lights will sell for £19.99. The lights will cost £13.50 to buy from the supplier, but Jim estimates that he will need to increase the number of part-time hours worked by 4 hours in total, at a rate of £5 per hour. This estimate is based on asking the owners of three 45 other local garden centres.

INGRAM

Questions

Total: 25 marks (30 minutes)

1 Calculate the total contribution made by the Christmas tree lights. *(7 marks)*

2 Calculate the contribution per unit of the Christmas tree lights. *(2 marks)*

3 Analyse **one** reason why it would be difficult to estimate the effect of stocking Christmas tree lights on the number of part-time hours needed. *(6 marks)*

4 Discuss the other factors that Jim should consider before deciding whether to stock the Christmas tree lights. *(10 marks)*

Answers to questions on p. 95

1 variable costs = 2,000 × £6 = £12,000
fixed costs = £5,000
total costs = £17,000

2 variable costs = 900 × £6 = £5,400
fixed costs = £5,000
total costs = £10,400

Note how the total costs have less than doubled in the first case and have fallen by less than 10% in the second case. The fact that fixed costs do not change means that total costs will change by a smaller percentage than the change in output.

Answers to Group Exercise questions on p. 97

1 Stop producing 'Waterfall'. Its contribution is negative, so it is not helping to pay for the fixed costs or make profit. (Alternatively, you might want to experiment with a price above £18, but this could lead to unsold stock.)

2 'Cascade'. It provides almost half of the firm's sales volume but contributes less than 'Fountain' and 'Stream', even though these products sell much lower volumes. (It would be an idea to investigate why these do so well, in order to improve 'Cascade'.)

Breakeven analysis

The concepts explained in Chapter 11 are used to show how firms can conduct breakeven analysis and compile simple breakeven charts in order to calculate or plot the breakeven output and the margin of safety. The assumptions made in simple breakeven analysis are shown and the advantages and disadvantages of breakeven analysis as a business technique are explained.

KEY TERM

breakeven output: the level of output at which total sales revenue is equal to total costs of production.

Assumptions of breakeven analysis

A firm's costs and revenue must be investigated in order to discover the level of output needed to break even. As explained in Chapter 11, costs can be classified as either **fixed** or **variable**.

Fixed costs such as rent must be paid regardless of output. If a firm produces no units of output, it will still have to pay for fixed costs. However, if output increases, it is assumed that these costs will not increase. For example, if fixed costs are £50,000, the firm must pay £50,000 whether it produces zero units, 1 unit, 10 units, 100 units or any other level of output.

Variable costs such as raw materials increase as output increases. It is normal to assume that variable costs stay at the same level per unit produced. Thus if 1 unit costs £5 in variable costs, then 2 units will cost £10, 10 units will cost £50 and so on.

Sales revenue follows a pattern similar to variable costs. If the price is £15, selling 1 unit earns £15, 2 units will earn £30, and 10 units will earn £150.

In practice, costs and revenue do not always behave in a set, predictable way. However, in order to study breakeven, certain assumptions are made.
- The selling price remains the same, regardless of the number of units sold.
- Fixed costs remain the same, regardless of the number of units of output.
- Variable costs vary in direct proportion to output.
- Every unit of output that is produced is sold.

These assumptions mean that objective comparisons can be made between different products or firms.

CHAPTER 12 Breakeven analysis

Calculating breakeven output

Breakeven output can be worked out in three different ways:
- using a table showing revenue and costs over a range of output levels
- using a formula to calculate the breakeven quantity
- using a graph showing revenue and costs over a range of output levels

Using a table

Table 12.1 Deducing breakeven output

Units of output (000s)	Sales revenue (£000s)	Fixed costs (£000s)	Variable costs (£000s)	Total costs (£000s)	Profit (£000s)
0	0	50	0	50	(50)
1	15	50	5	55	(40)
2	30	50	10	60	(30)
3	45	50	15	65	(20)
4	60	50	20	70	(10)
5	75	50	25	75	0
6	90	50	30	80	10
7	105	50	35	85	20
8	120	50	40	90	30
9	135	50	45	95	40
10	150	50	50	100	50
11	165	50	55	105	60
12	180	50	60	110	70

e EXAMINER'S VOICE

Keep a close eye on the units of measurement being used, as it is easy to make a mistake in examinations. A quick glance at Table 12.1 will tell you that the breakeven output is '5'. However, the unit of measure is '000s' (thousands). Therefore '5' means 5,000 units. Similarly, the '70' in the bottom right-hand corner of the table means that when 12,000 units are produced the firm earns a profit of £70,000.

In Table 12.1 it can be seen that the breakeven output is 5,000 units. At this level of output, sales revenue is equal to total costs and profit is zero. Below 5,000 units the firm makes a loss. Above 5,000 units the firm makes a profit.

Using a formula

For each additional (marginal) item that the company produces, its extra revenue will equal the price of the item, but it will incur more costs (the direct costs only, such as raw materials and wages of operatives). As stated in Chapter 11:

contribution per unit = selling price per unit – direct cost per unit

This shows the amount of money that each unit provides (contributes) towards paying off the fixed costs (or creating a profit, once the fixed costs have been met). Thus a product with a selling price of £12 and direct costs of £7 will contribute £5 per unit (£12 – £7), while a product with a price of £60 and direct costs of £22 will contribute £38 per unit.

total contribution = contribution per unit × number of units sold

In the latter example above, 100 units would provide a contribution of £3,800 (£38 × 100) towards fixed costs and profit.

If each unit contributes £38 towards fixed costs and fixed costs were only £38, then only 1 unit would need to be produced in order to break even. If fixed costs were £76, then 2 units would be needed to break even (2 × £38).

From this we can see that the formula for calculating breakeven output is as follows:

$$\text{breakeven output} = \frac{\text{fixed costs } (£)}{\text{contribution per unit } (£)}$$

Using the data in Table 12.1, the price is £15 and direct costs are £5 per unit, giving a contribution of £10 for every unit sold. At £10 per unit, 5,000 units would need to be sold in order to pay the fixed costs of £50,000, so 5,000 units is the breakeven output.

$$\text{breakeven output} = \frac{£50,000}{£15 - £5} = 5,000 \text{ units}$$

Note how the £ signs at the top and bottom of the equation have cancelled each other out. The answer is 5,000 units, *not* £5,000.

Using a graph

Sales revenue can be plotted against units of output. The gradient of the line will be steeper for a higher price than a lower price. Figure 12.1 shows the sales revenue at different levels of output for a product with a selling price of £15 per unit.

In order to produce goods or services, a company must purchase fixed assets. The **fixed costs** incurred must be paid, regardless of the actual units of output produced.

Fixed costs of £50,000 are shown in Figure 12.2.

Variable costs will vary directly with output. At zero output, no variable costs will be incurred. Each unit produced will require additional inputs of variable factors (primarily raw materials and direct labour). In this example, variable costs are £5 per unit. This would be plotted as shown in Figure 12.3.

By adding fixed costs and variable costs the **total costs** of production at different levels of output can be calculated. The total cost line is plotted in Figure 12.4.

It can be seen that costs are incurred even if no units are sold (because fixed costs are paid in anticipation that units will be sold). Therefore, low levels of sales are unlikely to produce a profit.

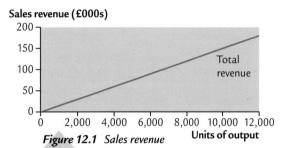

Figure 12.1 *Sales revenue*

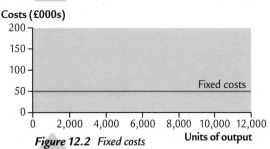

Figure 12.2 *Fixed costs*

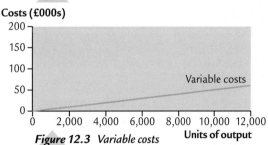

Figure 12.3 *Variable costs*

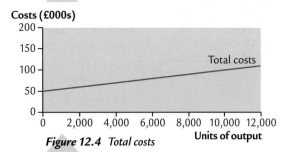

Figure 12.4 *Total costs*

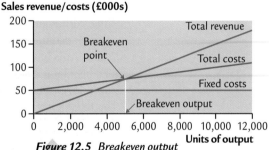

Figure 12.5 *Breakeven output*

As sales (and output) increase, the fixed costs become less of a burden as the fixed cost per unit (the average fixed cost) falls.

Combining the sales revenue and cost lines enables the breakeven point to be determined, marked with an arrow in Figure 12.5. The output required to break even is 5,000 units, at which level the sales revenue and costs are both equal to £75,000.

The **margin of safety** is the difference between the actual output and the breakeven output. If actual output is 9,500 units, the margin of safety is 4,500 units (9,500 – 5,000). Table 12.1 (see p. 102) shows potential output of 12,000 units. If this was the level of output, the margin of safety would be 7,000 units (12,000 – 5,000).

EXAMINER'S VOICE

In a 1-hour examination there is not enough time to ask students to complete a breakeven chart. However, you may be asked to insert a line or two, or work out the breakeven output or profit at a given output. Therefore it is worth spending time constructing these diagrams for homework or revision.

Other financial tasks, such as a completed cash flow or budget, are also too time consuming. Again, a question may ask you to fill in a gap or to explain the significance of the figures given. Do they show a problem? How could matters be improved?

Advantages of breakeven analysis

The use of breakeven analysis offers firms a number of advantages:

- The main benefit is that a breakeven chart can show the different levels of profit arising from the various levels of output and sales that might be achieved. This means that a business can predict its profit levels if it knows the number of units that it is going to sell. Knowing its future profit levels can help a business to plan its future objectives and strategies.
- A new firm can use breakeven analysis to calculate how long it will take to reach the level of output needed to make a profit. This will help it to assess whether the business is viable or not. New firms often suffer from cash-flow problems, so it is useful for them to know when they can expect to reach a profit level.
- The calculations are quick and easy to complete, thus saving businesses time. Although they can be criticised for possible inaccuracy, they give firms a quick estimate before they decide to go ahead.
- Many firms have a target to earn a certain level of profit. Breakeven analysis can be adapted to discover at which point a company can reach a particular profit level. This involves investigating the contribution needed to pay both the fixed costs and the target profit figure. For example, using figures from the previous section on 'Calculating breakeven output' (see p. 102), if the

target profit were £30,000 the calculation would be the same as the break-even formula with £30,000 added to the fixed costs.

$$\text{target profit output} = \frac{\text{fixed costs (£)} + \text{target profit (£)}}{\text{contribution per unit (£)}}$$

$$= \frac{£50,000 + £30,000}{£10} = \frac{£80,000}{£10} = 8,000 \text{ units}$$

Disadvantages of breakeven analysis

Breakeven analysis has the following problems:

- The information may be unreliable. Breakeven charts are based on forecasts. It is very difficult to predict the number of customers who will buy the firm's products, even with careful market research. Similarly, actual production costs can change, especially if there is a shortage of raw materials or a breakdown of equipment.
- Sales are unlikely to be exactly the same as output. If too much output is produced, the actual costs may be relatively high compared to those predicted.
- In practice, the selling price may change as more is purchased/sold. Demand theory indicates that, as price increases, the demand will decrease (very significantly if demand is elastic). In this respect, breakeven analysis is not very accurate, although many firms aim to set a fixed price for their products.
- Fixed costs, in practice, may not stay the same as output changes. For small changes in output there should be no problems, but large increases may mean that the firm has to purchase new equipment.
- The analysis assumes that variable costs per unit are always the same, ignoring factors such as **economies of scale**. In practice, variable costs per unit will decline for larger firms, as they can benefit from advantages such as bulk buying. It is also possible that costs per unit will rise if communication problems (or other **diseconomies of scale**) cause inefficiency.

---

e EXAMINER'S VOICE

In the AQA specification for AS Accounting and Finance, most topics use predictions or estimates. Breakeven analysis, cash-flow forecasting and the setting of budgets are all based on estimates for the future, rather than actual data.

Long-term sources of finance are also usually chosen on the basis of what a company expects to happen in the future. Therefore, a useful line of argument is to look at the reliability of these predictions. A well-established business in a stable market is much more likely to be able to predict accurately than a new business in a changing market.

The people making the prediction are also important. Are they experienced? Are they carrying out research or just estimating? Are they trying to prove a case (in which case there may be a bias)?

The following information applies to a product:

    units of output: 500
    total variable costs: £3,000
    fixed costs: £1,200
    selling price: £11 per item

1 Calculate the contribution per unit. *(4 marks)*

2 Calculate the breakeven quantity. *(5 marks)*

3 How much profit is made if all 500 units are sold? *(4 marks)*

4 What is the margin of safety if 500 units are sold? *(2 marks)*

5 Calculate the breakeven quantity if the variable costs rise to £7 per unit and the fixed costs increase to £1,400. *(5 marks)*

The following details apply to a product:

    sales volume: capacity = 250,000 units
    selling price: £30 per unit
    cost information:
      rent: £250,000 per annum
      wages: £5.50 per unit
      salaries: £670,000 per annum
      raw materials: £11.00 per unit
      administration: £520,000 per annum
      power: £1.50 per unit

1 Calculate the breakeven output. *(5 marks)*

2 Plot the following lines on a graph:
    a sales revenue
    b fixed costs
    c variable costs
    d total costs *(10 marks)*

3 Mark the breakeven point and show the breakeven output. *(2 marks)*

4 Calculate and show the margin of safety, assuming that the company works at full capacity. *(3 marks)*

Rocking horses

Chris Mass produces wooden rocking horses in a barn on his farm in Oxfordshire. The farm itself has been running at a loss in recent years and Chris has managed to survive only by renting out a converted barn to holidaymakers seeking a base for visiting the Cotswolds. He has also made money by charging some local organisations to use a large woodland area on the farm for motocross and mountain biking.

Chris has been seeking to diversify into other activities, and has also developed another area of woodland for pheasant shooting. Many local farmers have sold off land in order to survive, but Mass Farm has been in Chris's family since the Domesday survey and his top priority is to avoid selling any land.

During the winter (December to February inclusive) there is a quiet period on the farm and in the past Chris has always had to reduce his staff by two or three employees. It had always been easy to find new workers for the spring and summer, but in recent years he has found it difficult to recruit good workers for such a short time. He has partly overcome this by employing two of his workers (skilled wood craftsmen who had been made redundant by a local furniture company) to concentrate on making rocking horses for a national chain of toy shops.

The workers' skills were discovered by accident. A storm had led to the felling of a number of trees on the farm, and during a lunch break Chris found some of the workers carving shapes in the fallen trees.

On average the rocking horses sell for £385 each, and Chris's workers can produce 30 horses between them during the 3-month period. Chris's daughter then decorates and varnishes the horses to increase their individuality. During the 3 months the two craftsmen carving the horses work for a total of 990 hours at a rate of £8 per hour. Chris pays his daughter £50 per horse for decorating and varnishing. The other costs involved are as follows:

wood: £40 per horse
equipment hire: £80 per month
heating, lighting etc.: £140 per quarter
decorations and varnish: £11 per horse
administration costs: £300 per quarter

Questions

1 Calculate the fixed costs per quarter (3 months).
(Be cautious: not all the costs are shown per quarter.)   *(4 marks)*

2 Calculate the variable costs per horse.   *(4 marks)*

3 On a piece of graph paper, complete the breakeven chart showing: sales revenue, fixed costs, variable costs and total costs.   *(8 marks)*

4 Mark the breakeven point and show the breakeven output.   *(2 marks)*

5 Calculate the breakeven point using the formula.   *(4 marks)*

6 Calculate and show the margin of safety.   *(3 marks)*

7 Calculate the *loss* that is made from selling 30 rocking horses.   *(5 marks)*

8 Discuss the possible ways that Chris might be able to change this loss into a profit.   *(10 marks)*

9 Discuss the reasons why Chris may be prepared to make rocking horses even though the organisation fails to break even.   *(10 marks)*

CASE STUDY 1 The Glastonbury fence

In 2001 the Glastonbury Festival was cancelled because of safety concerns. In 2000 the festival had broken the terms of its licence with the local council because thousands of gatecrashers had expanded the
5 numbers attending the festival. A licence had been granted for 80,000 spectators, and the gatecrashers had led to an estimated 90,000 people attending the festival.

The local population has mixed feelings about the
10 festival. Some locals complain that they are 'invaded' by festival goers, but many would hate to see the festival die because of its enormous economic benefits. The organisers use local suppliers and workers as much as possible, and local traders earn
15 revenue from the visitors.

Michael Eavis, who has hosted the music festival for more than 30 years, said:

This is our last chance to keep the numbers under control. If people come without tickets, it puts the
20 whole of the festival's future in jeopardy. Glastonbury is hugely important, not just for the music scene and the people who love it, but because it's so well known that it puts Britain on the map. The gatecrashers also reduce the profit and we cannot continue doing the
25 work we do for charities without our profits.

Festivals such as Glastonbury are characterised by very high fixed costs in comparison to variable costs, so their profits are vulnerable if the numbers attending fall or if people avoid payment.

The local police agreed that they would not object 30 to the festival if more security and safety measures were introduced. The main feature would be a security fence costing £1 million. In addition, extra security guards and other security measures would be needed at a cost of £2,000 for each additional 1,000 festival 35 goers. These measures would allow the festival to increase the number of tickets available from 80,000 to 100,000 at a price of £97 per head for the weekend.

Some festival organisers believed that the festival should go ahead only if the security measures helped 40 to increase the number of paying customers enough to cover the cost of the fence and reach breakeven. The low level of variable costs suggested that there would be a very high contribution per unit for each extra customer. 45

The festival organisers were also considering whether they should increase charges to stall holders, such as those providing food and drink. The rents charged in previous years were based on a maximum attendance of 80,000 — although some stall holders 50 argue that they bought the rights to a stall because they expected gatecrashers to swell the numbers.

Source: adapted from Glastonbury Festival website (www.glastonburyfestivals.co.uk) and an article in the *Guardian* by Tania Branigan, 22 January 2002.

Questions   Total: 25 marks (30 minutes)

1 What is meant by the term 'profit' (line 24)? *(2 marks)*

2 How many extra customers are needed (above the original limit of 80,000) in order for the security measures to break even? *(5 marks)*

3 How much extra profit will be made as a result of the fence (and other security measures) if the festival sells 100,000 tickets? *(3 marks)*

4 Analyse why a music festival such as Glastonbury would have high fixed costs, relative to its variable costs. *(6 marks)*

5 Discuss the usefulness of breakeven analysis as a method of deciding whether to build the fence. *(9 marks)*

CHAPTER 13

Cash-flow management

Cash-flow management is vital in all businesses; even profitable firms can be vulnerable if they fail to manage their cash-flow properly. This chapter looks at cash-flow forecasting: the purposes of a cash-flow forecast, how a cash-flow forecast is constructed and the perils of cash-flow forecasting. The causes of cash-flow problems are established in order to scrutinise the different approaches to improving a firm's cash flow: factoring, sale and leaseback, and improved working capital control. The chapter concludes by showing the vital distinction between cash flow and profit.

COREL

KEY TERMS

cash flow: the amounts of money flowing into and out of a business over a period of time.

net cash flow: the sum of cash inflows to an organisation minus the sum of cash outflows over a period of time.

cash inflows: receipts of cash, typically arising from sales of items, payments by debtors, loans received, rent charged, sale of assets and interest received.

cash outflows: payments of cash, typically arising from the purchase of items, payments to creditors, loans repaid or given, rental payments, purchase of assets and interest payments.

Cash-flow forecasting

KEY TERM

cash-flow forecasting: the process of estimating the expected cash inflows and cash outflows over a period of time. Cash flow is often seasonal, so it is advisable to forecast for a period of 1 year.

Cash-flow forecasts have the following functions:

- **To identify potential cash-flow problems in advance.** The forecast can detect if current plans are going to lead the firm into a situation in which it cannot meet payments. This could be a lack of funds at the end of a month to pay the wage bill or a shortage of cash when a tax bill is due.
- **To guide the firm towards appropriate action.** Once a potential problem has been identified, action can be taken to overcome the difficulty. The problem may be solved by a change of plans, such as not extending the office accommodation, if this was one of the decisions that led to the predicted cash shortage.

EXAMINER'S VOICE

Avoid bullet points in the examination. They encourage brief explanations rather than detailed analysis.

- **To make sure that there is sufficient cash available to pay suppliers and creditors and to make other payments.** By studying the cash-flow forecast, the organisation can plan inflows of cash in time to make payments that might have been difficult to meet. Usually this will mean arranging financial help such as a bank overdraft for a temporary cash shortage or a long-term loan for equipment purchase.
- **To provide evidence in support of a request for financial assistance (e.g. asking a bank for an overdraft).** The cash-flow forecast should show the bank manager why help is needed, but it must also indicate how the overdraft can be repaid. An overdraft is intended to cover short-term problems, so the forecast must show that, eventually, the firm will be able to pay back the overdraft.
- **To avoid the possibility of the company being forced out of business (into liquidation) because of a forthcoming shortage of money.** It is estimated that as many as 30% of all companies that liquidate fail because they cannot get hold of cash, rather than because they are unprofitable. Profitable companies must check that they have cash, rather than having all their profit tied up in stock or buildings.

- **To identify the possibility of holding too much cash.** This probably means that a firm has less machinery and stock than it could possess, which gives the firm less production and stock to sell, so it makes less profit. Although this is perhaps less of a problem than a cash shortage, it is not wise for a firm to have too much cash.

Constructing a cash-flow forecast

The details of cash-flow forecasts will vary according to the type of business. However, the key items in constructing a cash-flow forecast are as follows:
- **Cash inflows.** This item usually contains details of income from sales. The timing of the entry depends on when the cash is received, so although cash sales are shown on the date that the sale is expected, goods that are expected to be sold on 60 days' credit terms in February will be shown as forecast cash receipts in April. Other cash inflows may be for items such as rent received, borrowings and sale of assets.

- **Cash outflows.** Many items of expenditure could be included here. Raw materials, wages, rent and bills for utilities such as electricity will all need to be forecast.
- **Net cash flow.** Cash inflows minus cash outflows will show the monthly situation and help the business to foresee months in which cash shortages may occur.
- **Opening balance and closing balance.** A company that starts a year with a cash surplus may be able to survive months with negative net cash flows. The final elements in constructing a cash-flow forecast are to show the opening cash and closing cash balances. The formula for closing balance is:

closing cash balance = opening cash balance + net cash flow

A simplified cash-flow forecast is set out in Table 13.1.

	January	February	March	April	May	June
Opening balance	0	300	(220)	1,060	440	70
Sales income	2,000	3,600	5,000	3,300	3,750	5,000
Borrowings	6,000	0	0	0	0	0
Total inflows	8,000	3,600	5,000	3,300	3,750	5,000
Materials	4,000	1,500	1,100	1,150	1,500	1,800
Wages	2,200	2,200	2,200	2,200	2,200	2,200
Other costs	1,500	420	420	570	420	420
Total outflows	7,700	4,120	3,720	3,920	4,120	4,420
Net monthly balance	300	(520)	1,280	(620)	(370)	580
Closing balance	300	(220)	1,060	440	70	650

Table 13.1
Cash-flow forecast (£), January–June 2005

Perils of cash-flow forecasting

Cash-flow forecasts are an attempt to predict the future — not an easy task. Potential problems that may cause inaccuracy in a cash-flow forecast include:
- **Changes in the economy.** Changes in economic growth or unemployment levels might mean that consumers have less (or more) spending power. If unemployment is higher than expected, sales of most goods will be less than predicted. Changes in inflation may affect both costs and sales revenue.
- **Changes in consumer tastes.** In a dynamic environment, customers often change their opinions. This happens in all markets but is a major peril in fashion and technologically advanced markets.
- **Inaccurate market research.** The research might target the wrong group of consumers, there might be interviewer bias in the questions or the sample might be too small. All of these factors could lead to an incorrect sales forecast.
- **Competition.** New competitors may enter the market or a rival may be aiming to increase its market share. Their actions cannot be predicted but will affect the firm's level of success. (It is also possible that unsuccessful

competitors will mean that the firm's predicted sales are lower than its eventual sales.)

- **Uncertainty.** Estimates of costs for new firms or major projects are often incorrect. New firms may overestimate costs, as they may discover cheaper suppliers once the business starts.

Causes of cash-flow problems

Firms may encounter cash-flow problems for a variety of reasons:

- **Seasonal demand.** The demand for some products and services is seasonal, and companies incur costs in producing in advance of the peak season for sales. This will cause a significant, but predictable, cash-flow problem. Because it is predictable, it is easy to persuade suppliers to provide credit or to negotiate a bank overdraft.
- **Overtrading.** Firms may become too confident and expand rapidly without organising sufficient long-term funds. This puts a strain on working capital.
- **Over-investment in fixed assets.** Firms may invest in fixed assets in order to grow, but leave themselves with inadequate cash for day-to-day payments.
- **Credit sales.** The marketing department will want to give credit to customers, to encourage them to buy, but this can lead to a lack of cash in the organisation if sales are not leading to immediate receipts of cash.
- **Poor stock management.** Organisations might hold excessive stock levels, using up cash that could have been used for other purposes.
- **Unforeseen change.** Cash-flow difficulties might also arise from internal changes (e.g. machinery breakdown) or external factors (e.g. a change in government legislation). These could be attributed to management errors or poor planning but may just be bad luck.
- **Losses or low profits.** Although cash flow and profits are very different, the two are linked. A business whose sales revenue is less than its expenditure will usually (but not always) have less cash than one that is making a healthy profit. Furthermore, creditors and investors will be less likely to put money into a business that is not expected to make a profit in the future. Unless a loss-making business can show how it will become profitable in the future, it will find it difficult to overcome cash-flow problems.

 FACT FILE

It is not just small or new businesses that face cash-flow difficulties. Vodafone spent £6 billion on a licence allowing it to introduce 'third generation' mobile phones and, even with its other activities, it has suffered from cash-flow problems. Massive expenditure on items such as cabling, in readiness for digital communications, has led to NTL and Telewest experiencing even greater problems. NTL is an example of a loss-making business with cash-flow problems that has survived because it has been able to persuade creditors that it will succeed in the long run. Creditors agreed to take shares in NTL instead of demanding repayment of their loans.

Ways of improving cash flow

Factoring (debt factoring)

KEY TERM

factoring: when a factoring company (usually a bank) buys the right to collect the money from the credit sales of an organisation.

The factoring company usually pays the firm 80% of its sales immediately and approximately 15% on receipt of the debt. The firm therefore loses some revenue (about 5%, depending on the length of time and current interest rates), which is the factoring company's charge for its service. The main benefits of factoring to a firm are as follows:

- **Improved cash flow in the short term.** This may save expenses such as overdraft interest charges, and in extreme cases the immediate receipt of cash may keep the business alive by allowing it to pay its own debts on time.
- **Lower administration costs.** Collecting and chasing up debts can be a costly and time-consuming process. The factoring company specialises in this and it is possible that it will be collecting other debts from a particular firm.
- **Reduced risk of bad debts.** The factoring company takes this risk instead of the original firm. However, it does reserve the right to refuse to factor a debt if it considers it to be risky. For this reason, firms such as Comet and Currys (which use factoring companies such as HFC and GE Capital) will contact the factoring company before giving credit to a customer. The factoring companies will have lists of customers who may be a high risk.

Although factoring involves costs, many large retailers take advantage of this service because large factoring companies can carry out the process of debt collection more cheaply, and pass on their cost savings to the retailer.

Sale and leaseback

Assets that are owned by the firm can be sold to raise cash and then rented back so that the company can still use them for an agreed period of time. This will overcome the cash-flow problem, but on the assumption that the new owner expects to make a profit from the asset, it means that in the long run the firm will pay more in rent than it receives. It will also reduce the value of the firm's assets that can be used as security against future loans, if needed.

Another problem is that the business may eventually lose the use of the asset when the lease ends. However, an advantage to the firm is that it can be more flexible, as new, more efficient assets can be leased.

Improved working capital control

KEY TERM

working capital: the day-to-day finance used in a business, consisting of assets (e.g. cash, stock and debtors) minus liabilities (e.g. creditors and overdrafts).

To stay solvent, a firm must manage its working capital. Working capital management involves careful control of the firm's main current assets (**cash**, **debtors** and **stock**) to make sure that there is enough to pay creditors and make other immediate payments.

Cash management

If a firm is short of cash, it has two main options:

- **Agree an overdraft with the bank.** This requires a cash-flow forecast (one that indicates that the cash-flow problem is not going to be permanent) and the firm will need to pay interest on the amount overdrawn.
- **Set aside a contingency fund** to allow the company to meet unexpected payments or cope with lost income. In industries subject to more rapid change, a higher contingency fund should be kept.

Debt management

Debtors are customers who owe a business money. The first decision to make is whether customers should be given credit. If all sales are for cash, the company will have no debtors but more cash, and this should relieve any cash-flow problems. However, there is a conflict here between the desire for sales and profit and the desire for liquidity and cash. Giving customers credit facilities will encourage them to buy the products (hence helping profit in the long run) but will add to cash-flow problems in the short run, as materials and wages will have to be paid even though no cash has been received from sales.

The company must evaluate the benefits of an increase in sales and profit potential against the risks of late or non-payment. This judgement will depend on factors such as the policy of rival companies and customer expectations. For example, customers expect to be offered credit for purchases such as furniture and computers, but not for magazines and confectionery.

If it is decided that credit will be given to customers, the company must control its debtors to ensure prompt payment. The main methods are:

- obtaining a credit rating, which will testify to the customer's ability to pay and so minimise the risk of non-payment
- controlling product quality, as a satisfied customer is less likely to delay or dispute payment
- scrutinising the offer of credit, to ensure that its costs do not exceed the profits gained from offering it
- managing credit control, to gain prompt payment from customers

Stock management

Traditionally, companies tended to keep high levels of stocks of both raw materials and finished goods, to guarantee continuation of production and immediate supply to customers. However, many firms now operate **just-in-time** systems that involve low stock levels in order to minimise storage costs (see Chapter 34). Such systems rely on efficient suppliers and require them to suffer penalties if deliveries are late. Just-in-time companies can operate with lower levels of working capital than other organisations, thus improving their cash-flow situation.

Different departments will view the problem from varying perspectives. From the finance department's perspective, stock should be kept to a minimum because a higher stock level means a lower holding of cash. However, the marketing department will want stocks of finished products to be readily available in order to meet customer demand. The production department will need stocks of raw materials in order to make the products. Again, the company must weigh up the relative merits of these different views.

Low stock levels reduce storage space, and the chances of damage, deterioration and obsolescence. High stock levels allow companies to benefit from bulk-buying discounts and to minimise the risk of lost sales and goodwill through failing to meet customer needs.

Other ways of improving cash flow

A firm can also improve its cash flow in the following ways:

- The sale of fixed assets can raise a considerable sum of money, but it is a fundamental principle of business that a firm should not sell fixed assets to improve liquidity, as the fixed assets enable it to produce the goods and services that create its profit. The exceptions to this rule are when the assets are no longer required (e.g. surplus land) or when the cash-flow situation is threatening the survival of the organisation.
- The firm could diversify the product portfolio to create a range that sells throughout the year. For example, Wall's sales of sausages in winter may be balanced by its ice-cream sales in the summer.
- Improved decision-making procedures, planning, monitoring and control, and more thorough market research and intelligence, will help the firm to anticipate changes.
- A contingency fund should be set aside to allow the company to meet unexpected payments or cope with lost income.

The distinction between cash and profit

Profit is calculated by subtracting expenditure from revenue. It is easy to think that a profitable firm will be cash rich, but this is not necessarily true. Profitable firms may be short of cash for the following reasons:

- If the firm has built up its stock levels, its wealth will lie in assets rather than cash. These stocks may not be saleable in the short term.
- If the firm's sales are on credit, its wealth will be in debtors rather than cash. The firm may have agreed with its debtors that they need not pay for a given time period. Although this helps marketing, it may damage cash flow.

> ### EXAMINER'S VOICE
>
> When asked to suggest methods of improving cash flow it is vital to focus on ways of getting hold of cash quickly (e.g. a bank overdraft or sale and leaseback). Suggestions based on increasing profits (e.g. marketing campaigns) invariably worsen cash flow in the short term and so should be avoided.

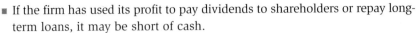
- If the firm has used its profit to pay dividends to shareholders or repay long-term loans, it may be short of cash.
- If the company has purchased fixed assets, this will have involved a large outflow of cash, but in the accounts the 'cost' of these fixed assets is spread over a number of years. Thus in the year in which the fixed assets are purchased, the recorded 'costs' will be much lower than the actual loss of cash, leading to a potential crisis. (In practice, major purchases of fixed assets are often supported by loans that are repaid in future years.)

In the long term, a business must make profit in order to survive. A firm that continually records losses will find it difficult to acquire cash, as sales revenue will be lower than expenditure, and creditors and investors will be reluctant to give the firm credit or loans or buy shares.

However, even profitable businesses may face difficulties if they do not plan their cash flow carefully. For example, a firm purchasing assets may expect to make profit from these assets in the future, but cash payments for the assets could lead to the firm being unable to pay suppliers or workers. This could lead to **liquidation**, with the firm being forced to close and sell its assets in order to make these cash payments.

KEY TERM

liquidity: the ability to convert an asset into cash without loss or delay.

The most liquid asset that a business can possess is cash. The working capital of a business (current assets minus current liabilities) provides an indication of the firm's scope to pay its short-term debts, as it includes the most liquid assets. All firms, however profitable, must manage their cash and their working capital (which includes those items that can be converted into cash most easily) to guarantee their survival. Thus *in the short term, a business must manage its cash flow in order to remain liquid.*

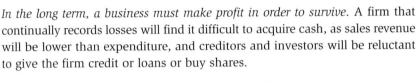

PRACTICE EXERCISE 1   Total: 40 marks (35 minutes)

1 Identify four different sources of cash inflow.   *(4 marks)*

2 Complete the formula below:

.... = cash inflow − ....   *(4 marks)*

3 Why should an organisation prepare a cash-flow forecast?   *(6 marks)*

4 Explain two difficulties that a firm would have when trying to predict its cash flow.   *(6 marks)*

5 Identify three different causes of cash-flow problems and, for each cause, explain how the business could try to limit the impact of the problem.   *(12 marks)*

6 What is the difference between 'cash' and 'profit'?   *(5 marks)*

7 What is meant by the term 'liquidity'?   *(3 marks)*

Fun for Kids Ltd

Siu Wan decided to set up Fun for Kids because she had found it difficult to find a safe place for her young children to play.

Banknotes plc had been a small, but very profitable banknote producer, but a merger with a US security printer had led to the closure of the factory. The premises were ideal for Siu's idea. The landscaped grounds were a highly suitable outdoor play area and she could not believe that there were air-conditioned warehouses until she visited the site. Luckily some friends were also excited about the idea and agreed to put a lot of money into the business.

Fun for Kids was set up on 14 January 2004, with enough capital to purchase the lease and convert the warehouse and grounds into an exciting and colourful play park, with rides and attractions ideally suited to young children. By the end of April, the work had been completed, in time for the grand opening on 1 May 2004.

Siu was pleased to see that Fun for Kids still had an opening balance in the bank account of £9,250 on 1 May.

	May	June	July	August	September	October	November	December
Opening balance								
Cash sales								
Credit sales								
Total inflows								
Wages								
Maintenance and administration								
Electricity, gas etc.								
Marketing								
Rent								
Total outflows								
Net monthly balance								
Closing balance								

Table 13.2   Cash-flow forecast for Fun for Kids Ltd, May to December 2004

Fun for Kids agreed an annual rental of £60,000 per annum, being paid in two equal instalments in June and December. Siu estimates monthly costs as follows:

- Wages are expected to be £5,000 per month in the autumn and winter (September to February); £5,500 in March, April and May; and £8,000 in June, July and August.
- Maintenance is expected to cost £200 per month. Administration is forecast at £3,800 per month.
- Electricity, gas and other costs are due in March, June, September and December. Siu estimates that these costs will be £2,500 per quarter.
- Siu is targeting a major £7,500 marketing campaign

in the opening month (May). The main target market is local families, but Siu hopes to attract tourists in July and August, and is planning expenditure of £2,000 per month in June and July. In August and from September onwards marketing is expected to cost £300 per month.

- Cash sales are expected to be £15,000 per month, except for July (£25,000) and August (£30,000).
- Credit sales will be accepted for 'party' bookings. These will be £2,500 per month, but payment to the firm will take place exactly 1 month after the sales were recorded, so no money will be earned from these sales in May.

Questions

1 Complete the cash-flow forecast (Table 13.2 on p. 117) on a separate sheet of paper, using the template shown. *(12 marks)*

2 Explain two ways in which Fun for Kids Ltd might improve its cash flow. *(6 marks)*

3 Analyse two arguments that Siu could use to persuade a bank manager to provide a bank overdraft where necessary. *(8 marks)*

4 Evaluate the main reasons why this cash-flow forecast may be inaccurate. *(9 marks)*

CASE STUDY VKP Limited

VKP Ltd is a private limited company that sells computer software. The case is based on a real firm whose name has been changed.

Background information

5 - The majority of VKP's sales are internet software; it also sells some CDs.
- Skilful design of the VKP website means that people using an internet search engine to find a certain type of software will usually find VKP listed on the
10 first page of the search engine's list.
- VKP buys the software and uses cost-plus pricing, adding a variable percentage to the purchase cost.
- Customers (mainly businesses) pay VKP for the licensing rights to use the software. Credit terms
15 are not offered to customers.

- The manufacturers of the software supplied to VKP give 30 days' credit to VKP (although this was not given in its first year of trading). As supply is via the internet, VKP does not need to keep any stock. Orders to suppliers can be made directly on the day 20 that a customer orders software, as the product is sent via the internet.
- VAT is included in the price charged to the customer. VKP forwards the VAT that it has collected to the government (Customs and Excise) at the end of 25 each quarter (i.e. the end of March, June, September and December).
- 'Drawings' (see Table 13.3) are payments made to the owners of the business for the work that they have done.

	Jan.	Feb.	Mar.	Apr.	May	Jun.	Jul.	Aug.	Sep.	Oct.	Nov.	Dec.
Opening balance	0	10	56	33	51	77	50	29	19	68	74	100
Cash inflow (sales)	90	118	118	118	118	118	79	54	135	118	118	90
Purchases	64	64	84	84	84	84	84		38	96	84	84
Wages and drawings	4	4	4	4	4	4	4	4	4	4	4	4
Administrative costs	12	4	4	12	4	4	12	4	4	12	4	4
VAT payments to government	0	0	49	0	0	53	0	0	40	0	0	49
Cash outflows	80	72	141	100	92	145	100	64	86	112	92	141
Net inflow/(outflow)	10	46	(23)	18	26	(27)	(21)	(10)	49	6	26	(51)
Closing balance	10	56	33	51	77	50	29	19	68	74	100	

Table 13.3 Cash-flow forecast for VKP Ltd: year 2005 (£000s)

Questions

Total: 25 marks (30 minutes)

1 What is meant by the term 'cash outflow'? *(2 marks)*

2 Sales income (including VAT) is the only 'cash inflow' on VKP's cash-flow forecast (Table 13.3). Identify **two** other items that could be included under the heading 'cash inflows' in a cash-flow forecast. *(2 marks)*

3 Calculate:
   a VKP's predicted 'purchases' in August. *(2 marks)*
   b VKP's closing balance in December. *(2 marks)*

4 Analyse **two** reasons why VKP does not experience cash-flow problems for most of the year. *(8 marks)*

5 At present VKP does not offer credit terms to its customers. Discuss the possible implications for VKP of a decision to offer credit terms to its customers. *(9 marks)*

Sources of finance

All organisations need to be able to access funds in order to continue to operate. This chapter describes the main sources of finance available to a business, showing the distinction between internal and external sources of finance. The relative merits of each source are compared. The same sources of finance are also classified according to the length of time for which they are acquired (long-term, medium-term and short-term) and the reasons for this alternative categorisation are explained.

Internal sources of finance

Trading (retained) profit

KEY TERMS

trading profit: the difference between the income received from an organisation's normal activities and the expenditure it incurs in operating.
retained profit: that part of a firm's profit that is reinvested in the business rather than distributed to shareholders.

Trading profit is a good indicator of the success of a firm, but more importantly it allows the organisation to use the surplus (profit) for future activities. The owners of a business (the shareholders in limited companies) expect a share of the profit as a dividend, but the remaining profit can be retained and used by the business. Although shareholders may be tempted to award themselves high dividends at the annual general meeting (AGM) — a problem at Sainsbury's in recent years — it is usual for the vast majority of profits to be retained in the business. If this source of finance is used well, the company will succeed and then the shareholders will gain because the share price will rise.

This is a cheap and flexible form of finance, which can be used for a long-term project such as a new factory or as revenue expenditure to pay daily bills. It is an attractive source for managers because there are no interest charges. Its main cost is the **opportunity cost**: the next best alternative foregone, such as earning interest in a bank.

In the interests of the business, trading profit should be retained for a specific purpose, such as research and development, and is usually used as a *long-term or medium-term source of finance*. However, it can be used in the short term if a cash-flow problem occurs.

Working capital

 TERM

> **working capital:** the day-to-day finance used in a business, consisting of assets (e.g. cash, stock and debtors) minus liabilities (e.g. creditors and overdrafts).

Working capital consists mainly of cash, stock and debtors (people who owe the business money), but the short-term payments that a business has to make to its suppliers and other organisations to which it owes money must be deducted from this.

If an organisation plans and controls its cash flow well (see pp. 113–15), its working capital will be strong. Chasing up debtors efficiently, keeping a close eye on stock levels and controlling cash flow will all help the firm to pay day-to-day expenses and are therefore vital ways of raising *short-term finance*.

Sale of assets

 TERM

> **asset:** any item owned by the firm.

Selling assets such as a building will allow a business to fund other ventures. A firm will usually sell fixed assets for the following reasons:

- The firm is in difficulties and needs cash as a *short-term source of finance* in order to survive a cash-flow crisis. In the long term, however, selling assets is going to lower the firm's profitability.
- The firm no longer needs the asset (it may be diversifying into other activities). This means that the firm uses the funds as a *long-term or medium-term source of finance* in order to expand other, more profitable parts of the business.
- It has found a more profitable business venture, so it needs funds to develop that venture.

> **DID YOU KNOW?**
>
> One of the largest factoring companies (GE Capital) used this method of finance. Originally known as General Electric, the company's management predicted that financial services would become more profitable than electrical products. So it sold some assets that were not creating profit and, along with some retained profit, it had sufficient funds to set up a division that concentrated on financial services such as factoring. GE Capital now has assets worth more than $425 billion.

 EXAMINER'S VOICE

Be aware of the difference between 'sale of an asset' and 'sale and leaseback'. Selling an asset is sensible if the asset is no longer needed (or if the price offered lets the firm move on to more profitable ventures). Sale and leaseback is used if the asset is still needed but the firm wants an immediate injection of cash. The sale gives the firm immediate cash, but the leaseback means that the firm pays regular sums to rent or lease the asset in the future.

External sources of finance

Ordinary share capital

 TERM

> **ordinary share capital:** money given to a company by shareholders in return for a share certificate that gives them part ownership of the company and entitles them to a share of the profits.

Ordinary shares are known as **risk capital** or equity capital. Ordinary shareholders receive no promises from a company. If the business is successful, each shareholder receives a dividend (a share of the profits). A shareholder owning 1% of a company's ordinary shares receives 1% of the profit that is given to shareholders (and gets 1% of the votes at the annual general meeting). The shareholders themselves decide at the AGM what dividend will be paid, but there is no guaranteed level of dividend. In profitable years, a very high dividend may be paid, but creditors must be paid first and sometimes the future of the firm could depend on profits being retained in the business to finance capital expenditure. In these circumstances, no dividend may be paid at all.

Ordinary share capital appeals to investors who are prepared to take a risk in return for (usually) higher rewards. If a business goes into liquidation and ceases to exist because it cannot pay its debts, money invested by shareholders will only be returned to them if every debt has been paid in full. On the other hand, because profitable companies can borrow at low interest rates, shareholders can get very high returns when things go well.

Ordinary shares are often known as **permanent capital**, as the business will always have shareholders who own these shares. (There are rules that allow a business to buy back some of its shares, but businesses can only do this in a limited way.) For this reason, ordinary share capital is used as a *long-term source of finance*, to set up the firm in the first place or for major expansion plans that cannot be financed from other sources. For expansion plans, companies will often use a **rights issue**, where the new shares are sold to existing shareholders. This reduces the administrative costs that are an element of issuing ordinary share capital, as the new shares are often sold in proportion to the existing number of shares (e.g. one share for every five already owned).

FACT FILE

The Stock Exchange deals mainly in second-hand shares. When shares are first issued they are sold directly to the original shareholders by the company (helped by a specialist bank known as an issuing house). If a shareholder no longer wants the shares, he or she can use the stock market to sell them. The company itself is not involved, but will just change its records so that the dividend is paid to the new owner. The price of shares at the Stock Exchange does not affect a firm directly, because it has already received the original value. However, if a company wants to issue more shares, it may be able to sell them at the current stock market price, and so a high share price helps a company to raise more money in a cost-effective way.

Venture capital

 TERM

> **venture capital:** venture capital is finance that is provided to small or medium-sized firms that seek growth but may be considered as risky by typical share buyers or other lenders.

Venture capital commonly involves sums of between £50,000 and £100,000, which are provided by individuals (often known as **business angels**) or merchant banks. It can take the form of loans or payment in return for share capital (or a mixture of the two). Venture capitalists take a risk, but small/medium high-risk companies can produce excellent returns.

Venture capital is used to fund expansion plans, so it is a *long-term source of finance*, although in rapidly changing industries it can be offered as a *medium-term loan*.

Loan capital

 TERM

> **loan capital:** money received by an organisation in return for the organisation's agreement to pay interest during the period of the loan and to repay the loan within an agreed time.

Providers of loan capital are known as **creditors**. They charge interest on the loan and must be paid before any dividends are received by shareholders. Similarly, if a business liquidates (closes down), the money raised from the sale of its assets must be paid in full to creditors before any payment is made to the shareholders. Three kinds of loan capital are described below.

Debentures

KEY TERM

> **debenture:** a long-term loan made to a business at an agreed fixed percentage rate of interest and repayable on a stated date.

Traditionally, debentures were issued for 25 years, but the pace of change in the business world means that firms expect to be able to repay even very large loans much more quickly, so shorter periods are more common. The current rate of interest is another factor. With interest rates (at the time of writing) at their lowest for half a century, firms are finding long-term debentures very attractive because the interest rate is fixed.

Organisations need to be aware of the repayment date of the debentures to avoid a catastrophe in 25 years' time. Often a business will buy back its own debentures at an earlier date, to avoid the need for a large cash sum on a particular date in the future.

Debentures are a *long-term source of finance*.

Bank loans

> **KEY TERM**
>
> **bank loan:** a sum of money provided to a firm or an individual by a bank for a specific, agreed purpose.

DID YOU KNOW?

Banks take security, usually in the form of property (known as **collateral**), so that they can eliminate the risk of a loan not being repaid. If the loan is not repaid, they can sell the property and collect the sum that is owed to them.

The terms of a bank loan usually specify the purpose, the interest rates and repayment dates. The business receiving the loan is required to provide a form of security, such as the deeds to a property, and will repay the loan and interest on a regular basis over an agreed period of time. Bank loans tend to have fixed rates of interest, but this is not always the case and flexible rates are possible. All banks have a base interest rate, and the rate actually charged will be a set percentage above this base rate, depending on how much of a risk the bank is taking. New and small firms usually pay higher rates of interest than larger organisations.

Bank loans are very useful because they can be set for any length of time, to suit the needs of the firm. They are normally used as a *long-term or medium-term source of finance*.

Bank overdrafts

> **KEY TERM**
>
> **bank overdraft:** when a bank allows an individual or organisation to overspend its current account in the bank up to an agreed (overdraft) limit and for a stated time period.

Overdrafts are widely used and flexible, and can overcome the cash-flow problems suffered by businesses whose sales are seasonal or which need to buy materials in advance of a large order. The rate of interest is nearly always variable and only charged daily on the amount by which the account is overdrawn. As with a bank loan, the interest rate depends on the level of risk posed by the account holder. Security is not usually required, so interest rates tend to be higher.

Although the terms of most overdrafts allow banks to demand immediate repayment, this is rare. In practice, overdraft agreements are often renewed and are treated as a reliable source of finance. A bank manager will get to know the nature of a customer's finances and will be able to recognise times when an overdraft is required.

Bank overdrafts are mainly used to ease cash-flow problems, sometimes being needed for just a few days to fund a major payment, so they are a *short-term source of finance*.

Internal or external sources?

When deciding whether to use internal or external sources, a business will weigh up the following factors:

- **The amount required.** The larger the sum, the less likely it is that a business will be able to generate enough finance from internal sources. Larger sums therefore often mean that external finance is needed. In practice, lenders want to see that the receiver of a loan is also taking a risk, so large loans may depend on a combination of internal and external finance.
- **The company's profit levels.** A very profitable firm will have its own money and may not need external help, although banks and other lenders will be happy to lend it money. Ironically, unprofitable firms are those most likely to need external finance but least likely to be able to receive it.
- **The level of risk.** If an enterprise is viewed as risky, firms will find it harder to attract external finance, although venture capital may be a possibility. High-risk activities, especially among small firms, therefore tend to rely more on internal sources.
- **Views of the owners.** Shareholders or owners may be reluctant to lose control of a firm, so they may reject shares and venture capital, for reasons of control rather than on financial grounds. Many small firms value their independence and will not want 'outsiders' to be a part of the decision-making process. Even if they are only providing a loan, some venture capitalists insist on having a say in how the business is run; some owners will value these opinions and want venture capital support, but others will take the opposite view.

The length of time

When considering sources of finance, the most critical factor is the length of time for which the finance is needed. Finance is used to fund:

- **Capital expenditure.** This is spending on items that can be used time and time again (fixed assets). It may take a long time before these items generate enough revenue to pay for themselves, so a *long-term source of finance* is ideal.
- **Revenue expenditure.** This is spending on current, day-to-day costs such as the purchase of raw materials and payment of wages. Such expenditure provides a quick return, so the company should rely on a *short- or medium-term source of finance.*

Table 14.1 classifies the main sources of finance in terms of the *usual* time period.

	Long-term finance	Medium-term finance	Short-term finance
Internal sources	Trading (retained) profit	Trading (retained) profit	Trading (retained) profit Working capital
	Sale of assets	Sale of assets	
External sources	Ordinary share capital Venture capital Debentures	Venture capital	
	Bank loan	Bank loan	
			Bank overdraft

Table 14.1 Classification of sources of finance by time period

CHAPTER **14** Sources of finance

The flexibility of some sources means that a case could be argued for including some sources under more headings, such as asset sales as a short-term source.

> ### *e* EXAMINER'S VOICE
>
> Sources of finance are a popular way of testing analysis and evaluation in the examination. Each source of finance has its own benefits and problems, so analysing the reasons for choosing a particular source (or evaluating/judging the best source or sources) is a good test of a student's understanding of a business's finances. Always look for clues in the background information on the company and its situation. The owners may want to keep control or may lack security for a loan, so certain sources may not be possible.

PRACTICE EXERCISE   Total: 50 marks (40 minutes)

1 What is the difference between 'sale of assets' and 'sale and leaseback'?   *(4 marks)*

2 Explain the difference between internal finance and external finance.   *(4 marks)*

3 Explain two benefits of using retained profit as a source of income.   *(6 marks)*

4 Identify three sources of short-term finance.   *(3 marks)*

5 What is venture capital?   *(3 marks)*

6 Describe the main differences between a bank loan and a bank overdraft.   *(6 marks)*

7 Distinguish between ordinary share capital and debentures.   *(6 marks)*

8 Explain two reasons why a firm might decide to use internal finance rather than external finance.   *(6 marks)*

9 Identify four sources of long-term finance.   *(4 marks)*

10 Explain one reason why a firm should choose a short-term source of finance.   *(4 marks)*

11 Explain one disadvantage of using ordinary share capital as a source of finance.   *(4 marks)*

CASE STUDY **1** A golden opportunity

James van der Beek was the youngest of seven children. Initially, James worked in the family business as a goldsmith and became highly skilled in making gold jewellery and ornaments.

5   James intended to set up his own business using his savings and some venture capital, but could not raise enough money. When the family heard of his attempt they offered their support. His father and uncle provided the ordinary share capital in return for 70% of the shares, with James given 30% as an 10 incentive. A private limited company was set up with James as chief executive and his girlfriend, Katie Holmes, established as company secretary.

The business grew quickly and 7 years later James

15 was employing ten goldsmiths. James was based in Leeds but planned to expand into retailing elsewhere. The business had made high levels of profit, but these had been retained in the business and used to expand the premises in which the jewellery was made.
20 There was also always a lot of money tied up in stocks of finished jewellery and work-in-progress (partly finished pieces).

James's goldsmiths had produced a number of unusual items of jewellery, at the request of clients,
25 and these speciality pieces were becoming a much larger part of the business. Some basic market research informed James that there was a gap in the retail market for unusual pieces of jewellery, but the main customer base was in London, and a store in Regent Street would be needed. A goldsmith with an 30 unusual range of products would be successful there, according to James's research.

James and Katie prepared a cash-flow forecast for the London store for the next eight quarters, based on them receiving £900,000 from external sources of 35 finance in the opening quarter (see Table 14.2).

James and Katie studied the forecast. 'If this works out, we could be opening another new store in 2007!' exclaimed Katie. 'And we can do it through internal finance,' added James. 40

	2005 Quarter 1	2005 Quarter 2	2005 Quarter 3	2005 Quarter 4	2006 Quarter 1	2006 Quarter 2	2006 Quarter 3	2006 Quarter 4
Opening balance	20	100	(20)	(40)	320	280	175	235
Source of finance	900	0	0	0	0	0	0	0
Sales income	100	150	350	600	200	200	500	800
Cash inflows	1,000	150	350	600	200	200	500	800
Wages	65	65	65	65	65	65	65	65
Cost of stock	750	100	200	70	70	135	270	80
Rent	75	75	75	75	75	75	75	75
Admin. etc.	30	30	30	30	30	30	30	30
Cash outflows	920	270	370	240	240	305	440	250
Net cash flow	80	(120)	(20)	360	(40)	(105)	60	550
Closing balance	100	(20)	(40)	320	280	175	235	785

Table 14.2 Cash-flow forecast for the Regent Street store (£000s)

Questions

Total: 25 marks (30 minutes)

1 Explain the meaning of the term 'venture capital' (line 6). *(2 marks)*

2 If the cash-flow forecast is correct, the business will need short-term finance. During which time period will this be necessary? *(2 marks)*

3 Explain **one** reason why a bank overdraft would help James's business. *(4 marks)*

4 James is planning to use internal sources of finance to open a further store in 2007. Analyse **two** problems of using internal sources to finance this plan. *(8 marks)*

5 Discuss the most suitable way of raising the £900,000 finance needed to open the shop in London. *(9 marks)*

CASE STUDY 2 NTL chief goes to pave the way for $600 million cash call

NTL is preparing to ask investors to support a $600 million (£374 million) issue of ordinary share capital, following yesterday's resignation of its founder and chief executive, Barclay Knapp.

5 NTL needs the money to pay off an expensive $500 million loan. This borrowing, which ensured NTL's survival in January 2003 after it had been threatened with liquidation, carries an interest rate of 19%.

10 Mr Knapp turned NTL into the UK's biggest cable company through a string of acquisitions of other firms. He also started buying European companies, but the cost of these deals, and the sheer expense of digging up roads and laying cables, left the company 15 with debts that it could not repay.

NTL was forced to ask its lenders to forego $10.6 billion of debt and to accept shares instead. In effect, this gave control of NTL to these lenders.

The outgoing chief executive, however, defended his record. He said: 'What we got right was that we 20 created a company offering three key services — television, telephone and broadband — for customers day in, day out.'

NTL's decision to raise fresh finance has been driven by a surge in its share price. In early 2002 the 25 share price fell as low as $5. When share dealing was allowed to recommence in January 2003, the share price was $17.70. Yesterday the share price closed at $42.20, valuing the company's shares at $2.11 billion.

Source: adapted from an article by Dan Sabbagh in *The Times*, 13 August 2003.

Questions

Total: 25 marks (30 minutes)

1 What is meant by the term 'ordinary share capital' (lines 2–3)? *(2 marks)*

2 Calculate the annual interest payments on the loan provided by shareholders (paragraph 2). *(2 marks)*

3 'NTL was forced to ask its lenders to forego $10.6 billion of debt and to accept shares instead. In effect, this gave control of NTL to these lenders' (lines 16–18). Explain why this action gave control of NTL to its former lenders. *(4 marks)*

4 Analyse ways in which NTL might have avoided some of its financial problems. *(8 marks)*

5 'NTL is preparing to ask investors to support a $600 million (£374 million) issue of ordinary share capital' (lines 1–3). Evaluate the reasons for this issue of more ordinary shares. *(9 marks)*

Budgeting

The fundamental aspects of this topic are:
- *the meaning of the term 'budget'*
- *the purpose of a budget*
- *benefits and drawbacks of using budgets*
- *interpreting variances between the budget forecasts and the actual results*

KEY TERMS

budget: an agreed plan establishing, in numerical or financial terms, the policy to be pursued and the anticipated outcomes of that policy.

management accounting: the production and use of financial and accounting information for internal purposes of planning, review and control. It is based on predictions of what will happen and analysis of the actual outcomes in comparison to the original plans.

Budgets are usually stated in terms of financial targets, relating to money allocated to support the organisation of a particular function, but they also include targets for revenue and output or sales volume. Budget holders will try to exceed targets for revenue budgets, whereas for cost budgets (expenditure budgets), of course, the aim is to stay within the planned target. For large-scale construction projects, such as building a new factory, a capital budget will be allocated. This will only exist for the period it takes to complete the project.

The role of a budget

Budgets serve a number of purposes:
- **To ensure that a business does not overspend.** Careful control of budgets will make sure that a firm's finances do not worsen unexpectedly, as a result of a failure to limit spending to agreed levels.
- **To establish priorities.** A budget is a plan for the future. Allocating a large budget to an activity can indicate the level of importance attached to a particular policy or division. Currently the mobile network '3' (mostly owned by Hutchison Telecom, the company that originally set up Orange) is allocating a much larger budget to third-generation mobile phones than to other networks because it believes them to be vitally important for its future development.
- **To encourage delegation and responsibility.** Budgets allow local or junior managers to become budget holders and make decisions on spending in areas of a business in which they are more knowledgeable than senior managers. This improves the quality of the decisions and acts as a motivator for the budget holder.

- **To assign responsibility.** The budget holder is the person who is directly responsible for any success or failure. This makes it much easier to trace mistakes or recognise to whom credit should be given. Budget control can be included in the appraisal of a manager's work.
- **To improve efficiency.** Businesses will monitor and review budgets and be able to establish standards and investigate the causes of any successes and failures. They can use this information to improve future decisions. The discipline of working to a limited budget encourages managers to seek more efficient methods.

Problems of setting budgets

Setting budgets involves a number of potential pitfalls:

- **Managers may not know enough about the division or department.** In this case they will find it difficult to plan a reasonable budget. This problem is particularly acute for new firms or new ventures.
- **There may be unforeseen changes.** Predicting the future is always difficult and unforeseen changes will undermine the budgeting process.
- **The level of inflation (price rises) is not easy to predict.** Businesses tend to use the average inflation rate, but some prices can change by much greater levels. Farmers have been hit by falling prices, but property prices have gone up by more than most other prices.
- **Budgets may be imposed.** A key principle of budgeting is that the budget holder should be involved in setting the budget level. Unfortunately, budgets are often set by senior managers, who may show a misunderstanding of the needs of a certain area and be seen to be unfair, causing resentment and lower morale. On the other hand, a budget determined solely by the manager responsible may ignore potential scope for efficiency gains and fail to take account of developments outside that area of the business. Ideally, both managers should find the time to discuss the budget fully, but this does not always happen.
- **Setting a budget can be time consuming.** It may not be worth devoting too much time to agreeing budgets if only marginal improvements are made.

Benefits of using budgets

A firm stands to benefit in several ways from the use of budgets:

- **They provide direction and coordination.** Budgets ensure that spending is geared towards the aims of the business rather than those of the individual, and they can ensure a united approach within an organisation. If budgets are given only to purposes that match the aims of the business, it will be easier for the workforce to understand the fairness of the allocations or targets.
- **They motivate staff.** According to Mayo and Herzberg, teams and individuals are encouraged by the responsibility and the recognition gained from meeting budget targets. Companies may link rewards to the achievement of targets in a budget, thus providing a further source of motivation.

- **They improve efficiency.** By monitoring and reviewing budgets, the firm will be able to establish standards and investigate the causes of any successes and failures. It can then use this information to improve future decisions. The discipline of working to a limited budget encourages managers to seek more efficient methods.
- **They assess forecasting ability.** Although changes cannot always be foreseen, businesses that can predict the future have significant advantages. Budgeting encourages careful evaluation of future possibilities and realistic planning.

Drawbacks in using budgets

There are, however, a number of disadvantages of using budgets:
- **They are difficult to monitor fairly.** Senior managers will be less aware of detailed expenditure and costs, so they may rely on the honesty of the budget holder in explaining any differences and identifying any problems.
- **Allocations may be incorrect.** Budgeting is based on predictions of future events. In all areas of business there will be unforeseen changes, so the budget allocation will not always be right. A cost budget that is insufficient will demotivate staff. Moreover, it will be difficult to develop the business if there is insufficient money for essential activities. Similarly, an excessively high revenue budget may demoralise a manager who cannot achieve it. On the other hand, a low revenue budget could cause complacency.
- **Savings may be sought that are not in the interests of the firm.** For example, to keep within a budget, a buyer may purchase cheaper materials that will lower the quality of the product. In so doing, the buyer may cause consumer discontent and thereby affect the holders of revenue budgets in particular. Sometimes decisions to save money and keep within a budget in the short term (such as by making cuts in new product development or reducing staff levels) can have disastrous long-term effects.
- **Changes may not be allowed for when a budget is reviewed.** External factors outside the control of the organisation may affect budget holders' ability to keep to their plan. The airline industry has needed to lower its revenue budgets because of terrorist activities; high oil prices have affected firms' heating budgets. Sometimes internal changes, such as a reorganisation, can lead to increased costs or savings that were not originally included in the budget. These changes must be allowed for in any review of the budget.

Features of a good budget

The problems outlined above can be reduced by **flexible budgeting**, which allows amendments in response to changes in circumstances. However, flexible systems reduce the effectiveness of budgets as a means of control, and can lead to inefficiencies if close scrutiny is lost.

A good budget should:
- be consistent with the aims of the business
- be based on the opinions of as many people as possible
- set challenging but realistic targets
- be monitored at regular intervals, allowing for changes in the business and its environment

Zero budgeting

KEY TERM

zero budgeting: a system of setting budgets where managers must justify all of the money allocated to them, in order to ensure that allocations are not excessive.

Advantages of zero budgeting
- It encourages budget holders to plan thoroughly and carefully.
- It identifies changes in needs in an organisation. This avoids declining areas accumulating high budgets and possibly preventing the expansion of newer, more profitable areas of the business.
- It can save money by enabling the business to cut costs where managers are unable to justify their spending.

Disadvantages of zero budgeting
- It can be very time consuming, as detailed planning is needed. The time spent on planning may cost more than the budget savings.
- It may lead to high allocations for those managers who are skilled at presenting their case, rather than those who need the highest allocations.

Interpreting variances

An important aspect of budgeting is monitoring and reviewing the actual outcomes in comparison to the budgeted figure (the target). Differences between budgeted and actual figures are known as **variances**.

KEY TERMS

favourable variance: when costs are lower than expected or revenue is higher than expected.

adverse (unfavourable) variance: when costs are higher than expected or revenue is lower than expected.

After calculating variances the budget holder will interpret their meaning. Adverse variances may show *inefficiency*, where the business has made mistakes. They may also show that *external influences*, such as changes in the market, have made it more difficult for a firm to meet its targets. The opposite will apply for favourable variances.

Example
Table 15.1 shows the variances in the revenue and costs of a fictitious company, Sceptre Paints, a division of HBH Chemicals.

DID YOU KNOW?

Some analysts maintain that changes in the market are not a valid reason for a manager failing to keep within budget. These analysts argue that forecasting market changes is a business skill and should have been allowed for in the original budget.

EXAMINER'S VOICE

An adverse variance may not be the manager's fault. It could be due to an unrealistic budget or an unpredictable external factor.

	Budgeted revenue/cost (£m)	Actual revenue/cost (£m)	Variance (£m)
Sales of emulsion paint	480	495	+15 (favourable)
Sales of gloss paint	220	206	−14 (adverse)
Total sales	700	701	+1 (favourable)
Raw material purchases	50	56	−6 (adverse)
Tins and packaging	14	14	0
Manufacturing costs	88	75	+13 (favourable)
Wages and salaries	240	251	−11 (adverse)
Administration	96	100	−4 (adverse)
Marketing	42	33	+9 (favourable)
Distribution and warehousing	31	26	+5 (favourable)
Other costs	27	27	0
Total costs	588	582	+6 (favourable)
Profit/loss	112	119	+7 (favourable)

Table 15.1
Budget variances for Sceptre Paints

EXAMINER'S VOICE

For variance analysis it is customary to use + for favourable variances and – for adverse variances. Thus a favourable, positive variance would be shown when:
- Actual revenue is greater than budgeted revenue.
- Actual costs are below the budgeted costs.

Similarly, adverse (or negative) variances would be shown when:
- Actual revenue is less than budgeted revenue.
- Actual costs are above budgeted costs.

It is usually safer to think in terms of favourable or adverse (unfavourable) variances, as these are the terms used for AQA AS Business Studies.

According to the table, sales show a favourable variance of £1 million and costs show a £6 million favourable variance, so overall there is a favourable variance on profit of £7 million. These variances can be interpreted as follows:
- Sales show little difference; it is cost savings that have caused most of the favourable variance. The biggest saving has been in manufacturing costs. The business may have automated its production line or improved efficiency in some way.
- Marketing has kept within budget. Although this is a favourable variance, it may have unfavourable results if it leads to low sales. However, the sales figures do not seem to show a problem, despite a fall in sales of gloss paint.
- Distribution and warehousing expenditure is below budget too. Has the firm delivered in larger batches? Are warehousing costs lower because of lower stock levels? The policies in this part of the business have made significant savings.
- Although the overall variance is positive, Sceptre Paints should look closely at raw material costs, wages and salaries, and administration, as these are over-budget. There may be a valid reason, such as the use of better-quality materials, but the variances may show unnecessary spending in these areas.

CHAPTER 15 Budgeting

 **EXAMINER'S VOICE**

For evaluation questions, move up the skills levels as quickly as possible.

- Finally, Sceptre will want to look at the sales revenue to see if the reasons for the good performance of emulsion paints can be applied to gloss paints.

The interpretations of the variances given above are merely suggestions. In practice, a budget holder should be aware of possible variances and so will be in a reasonable position to explain why they have happened.

PRACTICE EXERCISE 1   Total: 50 marks (40 minutes)

1 What is meant by the term 'management accounting'? *(4 marks)*

2 Explain three reasons why a firm sets budgets. *(9 marks)*

3 Explain three difficulties that a firm might have when trying to plan a budget. *(9 marks)*

4 What are the implications for a business when it sets an expenditure budget (cost budget) that is insufficient to meet the needs of the budget holder? *(6 marks)*

5 Describe how budgets are set in a 'zero budgeting' system. *(4 marks)*

6 Explain one advantage and one disadvantage of zero budgeting. *(6 marks)*

7 What is a revenue budget? *(3 marks)*

8 What is meant by the term 'variance'? *(3 marks)*

9 Explain two reasons why an adverse variance might not be a sign of poor management by the budget holder. *(6 marks)*

PRACTICE EXERCISE 2   Total: 30 marks (30 minutes)

Refer back to the budget variances for Sceptre Paints, shown in Table 15.1 on p. 133. Use the information in the table to answer the following questions.

Questions

1 Select five headings from the Sceptre Paints budget and compile a report to the chief executive of HBH Chemicals suggesting reasons for the variances shown. *(20 marks)*

2 Assume that each line of the Sceptre Paints budget is the responsibility of a different manager. Choose two of these managers and analyse the implications of the variances shown for the two managers whom you have selected. *(10 marks)*

CASE STUDY   Budgeting the Eden Project

The Eden Project is an illustration of a large-scale capital project that has managed to be completed without an excessive adverse variance from the projected budget. Many large-scale building projects exceed their budgets by considerable sums. The Channel Tunnel and the Millennium Dome are both examples of projects that actually cost more than twice the sum originally estimated.

In contrast, operating budgets (estimates of sales revenue and plans for day-to-day spending on running the business) tend to be much more accurate. Firms find this type of budget much easier to estimate, although ironically the Eden Project's operating budget for its first year was less accurate than its capital budget. With visitor numbers much higher than expected, the actual sales revenue was 2.5 times the budgeted figure and the £9 million wage bill was more than double the £4 million budgeted figure.

Table 15.2 summarises the main budget headings for the construction of the Eden Project.

Originally, the Eden Project was to be funded by grants from the Millennium Commission (50%), the European Union and various regional organisations, and by loans. When it was realised that there would be an 'over-spend' on the original budget, the

Millennium Commission agreed to increase its grant from £37 million to £43 million. The site was opened to visitors before the final completion and visitor numbers were so high (160% higher than the 'best case' prediction) that the Eden Project found it easy to raise the remaining £6 million needed to pay the actual costs.

Construction work began in October 1998, in a disused china clay quarry the size of 35 football pitches. However, there were problems that had not been anticipated, as nobody had ever undertaken such a project before. Matters were complicated by 43 million gallons of water raining into the quarry in the first 3 months, forcing the builders to halt construction for 3 months. Fortunately, specialist help from consultants overcame these problems and the project was completed on schedule in March 2001.

Source: Eden project website (www.edenproject.com).

	Budgeted cost (£m)	Actual cost (£m)
Purchase of site and car parks	10.0	10.0
Reshaping the ground	5.0	8.0
Construction of greenhouses (biomes)	20.0	25.0
Soil and plants, including nursery	6.0	5.5
Buildings and exhibits	19.0	19.0
Services to keep it running	6.0	7.0
Design, engineering, legal advice etc.	6.0	9.0
Wages and training prior to opening	2.0	2.5
Total	74.0	86.0

Table 15.2 *Eden Project: budgeted and actual costs of construction*

Questions

Total: 25 marks (30 minutes)

1 What is meant by the term 'budget' (line 4)? *(2 marks)*

2 a Identify one favourable variance from Table 15.2. *(1 mark)*
  b Calculate the variance between the total budget and the total actual costs as a percentage of the budgeted cost. *(3 marks)*

3 Explain one reason why firms find it easier to estimate revenue budgets than capital budgets. *(4 marks)*

4 Analyse **two** factors that led to the actual expenditure for setting up the Eden Project exceeding the budgeted figure. *(6 marks)*

5 To what extent did the Eden Project benefit from the time spent on its budgeting? *(9 marks)*

CHAPTER 16

Cost centres and profit centres

This chapter looks at the difference between cost centres and profit centres. It investigates the reasons why they are formed, the processes involved in establishing them and the disadvantages that may arise from their use.

KEY TERMS

cost centre: an identifiable part of an organisation (e.g. a department, a product or a branch) for which costs can be calculated.

profit centre: an identifiable part of an organisation (e.g. a department, a product or a branch) for which costs *and revenue (and thus profit)* can be calculated.

Examples of cost centres are personnel and IT services departments. It is possible to calculate the costs of these activities, but they do not directly create revenue for the business and they do not charge other departments for their services.

Examples of profit centres are a branch of a retail chain and a particular product within a firm. The sales revenue is easy to calculate and it is possible (but not always easy) to calculate the costs of running that branch or making that product.

In both cost and profit centres, it is necessary to identify a person who is responsible for controlling the finances of the centre.

Reasons for cost and profit centres

Organisations use cost and profit centres in order to benefit from delegating power over budgets to managers of the cost/profit centres.

- **They allow a more focused study of a firm's finances.** In the absence of cost or profit centres, a business may be unaware that certain activities are losing money or are acting inefficiently, especially if the firm is making a profit overall. Once identified, areas of weakness can be changed. Using a profit centre approach, the Japanese clothes retailer Uniqlo was able to see that its losses were mainly caused by its shops outside London, so it closed down those stores.
- **Benchmarking can take place.** The most efficient cost and profit centres can show how efficiency may be improved. Branches that have discovered better ways of increasing sales or saving costs can then help other branches to make profit. This improves the efficiency of the firm.

DID YOU KNOW?

A profit centre is not necessarily an activity that makes money. An inefficient profit centre may lose money and in some cases, such as loss leaders, the target may be to make a small financial loss in order to gain marketing benefits.

- **Responsibility for a profit/cost centre may help to motivate the individual responsible.** Centres may therefore be deliberately created in order to give more staff some level of responsibility. If a more motivated workforce is created, productivity should be improved. Mayo's and Herzberg's theories of motivation agree that responsibility motivates people.
- **Finances may be run more efficiently.** By placing responsibility with the person actually involved in the activity, the firm's finances may be run more efficiently than would be the case if a more remote, senior manager controlled it. Zara lets its shop managers decide what clothes to stock because they know what local customers want more than Zara's senior managers.

Setting up cost and profit centres

For a firm to set up cost and profit centres, it must be possible to:
- split the business into separate sections or centres (departments, branches, products etc.)
- identify the person responsible for that centre or section
- identify which costs and revenues relate to that centre or section

If these criteria are met, the business can set up an account for each cost or profit centre and keep track of its performance. The person responsible for the cost or profit centre will meet with his or her line manager to:
- agree the target level of costs (or profit)
- agree the costs and revenues that will be included in the budget
- make any amendments needed, once operating
- review and monitor the success (or failure) of the cost or profit centre against its targets

A department, branch or product must pay towards the business's overall fixed costs, so it is normal for a percentage of these to be 'charged' to each profit centre or cost centre. Alternatively, the profit target for a profit centre will be higher to help the firm cover these costs.

Disadvantages of cost and profit centres

Cost and profit centres have the following disadvantages:
- **Allocating costs.** In practice, it may be difficult to allocate costs to a particular division or centre. For example, in a manufacturing company where machinery is used to process a number of different products, it is not easy to calculate the manufacturing costs of each product. Firms usually have a system for allocating fixed costs to different products, but the amount allocated to each product is hard to judge.
- **Demotivation.** Cost and profit centres may add to the pressure and stress imposed on staff who may have technical skills that do not include financial management. It may thus demotivate certain staff who want to use their technical ability rather than financial skills, or who simply do not have

enough time to cope with the extra work needed. Research has shown that cost and profit centres often fail to improve efficiency because the budget manager lacks the necessary financial skills.

- **Setting targets.** For specialist areas the senior managers of the business may lack the detailed knowledge needed to recognise whether a cost or profit centre is being run effectively or ineffectively. Targets may be too easy or too hard.

- **Diseconomies.** Delegating finances to small divisions may lessen efficiency because the benefits of large scale are lost. If too much financial responsibility is delegated, there may be many profit and cost centre managers all carrying out similar tasks, such as buying materials, on a small, inefficient scale.

- **External changes.** Businesses must be very careful when using cost centres and profit centres to assess the efficiency of the manager responsible for that centre. External factors may make it more difficult (or more easy) for the targets to be reached. If a competitor opens a new shop in the next street, then it is likely to make it much harder for a branch acting as a profit centre to reach the target that it was set. On the other hand, the closure of a rival firm may make it very easy for profit targets to be reached. It is possible that a person in head office may be unaware of these changes and so draw the wrong conclusions from the finances of a profit centre. The matter is complicated by the fact that the way in which the profit centre was run may have been an influence on the competitor's decision. A very efficient shop may force a rival to close down.

> **ℯ EXAMINER'S VOICE**
>
> The idea of cost and profit centres is closely linked to the 'People' element of the AS course. Cost and profit centres give managers more freedom and allow senior managers to delegate responsibility to junior staff. These policies help to motivate staff. It is worth looking at this part of the specification again after you have studied organisational structure and motivation theory to see how it fits into those ideas.

PRACTICE EXERCISE

Total: 20 marks (20 minutes)

1 What is the difference between a cost centre and a profit centre? *(4 marks)*

2 Briefly explain two possible reasons for setting up a profit centre. *(6 marks)*

3 Why might it be easier for a retailer than a manufacturer to use profit centres? *(4 marks)*

4 Multi-product companies such as Walkers and Vauxhall often use individual products as profit centres. Explain two difficulties in organising products as profit centres. *(6 marks)*

CASE STUDY Shakespeare's bookshop

After 3 years of trading, Will and Ann's bookshop had at last shown an overall profit.

Originally, three divisions had been set up, each operating as a cost centre or profit centre. These
5 divisions were: Supplies, Book Sales, and Newspapers and Magazines.

'Supplies' were Will's responsibility. He purchased the book stock and his knowledge of the book trade helped him to locate the cheapest suppliers of books.
10 The shop concentrated on new books, but there was an expanding range of second-hand books. Will enjoyed the challenge of finding first editions, but purchasing these books often led to Will exceeding his budget. Ann had mixed feelings — it meant that the
15 finances were hard to control, but it did help her to reach her sales targets.

'Book Sales' were Ann's area of responsibility. Her job was to manage the shop and arrange the stock attractively, to gain maximum sales. Book sales had
20 exceeded their target in every one of the 36 months of trading, even last February when the River Avon had flooded, forcing the shop to close for 2 weeks.

Suzannah, the couple's daughter, organised 'Newspapers and Magazines'. She decided on the
25 numbers and titles of the newspapers and magazines, and had complete control of the area at the front of the shop. Will and Ann were happy if this division achieved breakeven. In their opinion, its role was to attract people into the shop — once inside, many
30 people also purchased books, particularly the tourists visiting the town.

Hamit, Suzannah's twin brother, joined the business a year after it started. There was a lot of unused space in the bookshop and Hamit's idea of a fourth division,
35 'The Coffee Bar', seemed like a good idea at the time. Will and Ann set Hamit a profit target that included a payment towards the building's rent. Hamit objected because this charge was not included in Suzannah's target. Will agreed that Hamit's profit target should
40 not include a payment towards the building's rent

because this charge was not included in the profit target for Suzannah's 'Newspapers and Magazines' division. Will believed that the coffee bar improved the atmosphere and encouraged shoppers to stay longer and buy more. Ann disagreed, pointing out that 45 there was now less space to sell books. As usual, Ann won the argument.

Will had just bought a large stock of books from a shop that had closed down and Ann was aware that there was no longer enough space in their bookshop. 50 This was going to be a difficult problem to solve, but Ann had suggested the closure of the coffee bar, to free space for more books.

Over tea the family sat down to consider the issues.
- 'The number of customers has increased since the 55 opening of the coffee bar,' argued Hamit.
- Ann unexpectedly sided with Hamit. 'A study of the firm's CCTV footage shows that shoppers using the coffee bar do buy more books.'
- 'Unfortunately, some read the magazines and then 60 leave them in the coffee bar without paying for them,' Suzannah added. 'This makes it more difficult for my division to pay its way.'
- Will delivered what he considered to be the clinching argument: 'The coffee bar is not making money, 65

even though the business as a whole makes a profit. On the basis of our policy to run each division as a cost centre or profit centre, I propose that we vote to close the coffee bar. All in favour raise their right
70 hands.'

- Will and Ann raised their hands and, after an agonising pause, Suzannah slowly raised hers too.
- 'You cannot make a decision like this on the basis of cost or profit centres!' shouted Hamit, as he stormed out of the room. 75

Questions

Total: 25 marks (30 minutes)

1 Taking in turn each of the four divisions mentioned in the passage, indicate whether they should be operated as *either* a cost centre *or* a profit centre. *(4 marks)*

2 Briefly explain **one** important step that Will and Ann should have taken in setting up a profit centre within the business. *(4 marks)*

3 Analyse **two** possible benefits of setting up cost or profit centres to a business such as Shakespeare's bookshop. *(8 marks)*

4 To what extent do you agree with Hamit's view that the use of cost or profit centres is not an appropriate way to decide whether to close the coffee shop? *(9 marks)*

Accounting and finance

CASE STUDY 1 Is Sir Peter losing control of his Sainsbury's trolley?

Things are closing in on Sir Peter Davis and his efforts to turn round Sainsbury's, the once-mighty super-market chain.

The Economist magazine has concluded: 'Sir Peter
5 Davis is failing to save Sainsbury's, perhaps because it is in terminal decline.'

There is much in this argument. For several years Sainsbury's has been losing market share, despite having invested an amazing £2 billion on projects such
10 as new warehousing and revamping its stores. There is little sign of sales improving. While Tesco and Asda are ferociously competitive on price, Sainsbury's refuses to lower itself, seeking to win customers on 'quality'.

Cost savings of £210 million on overheads have
15 been delivered, but profits do not seem to have improved as a result and they are still lower than rivals such as Tesco. In the financial year ending in March 2003, Sainsbury's £695 million profit was only 3.75% of its sales revenue, way off Tesco's 6% figure.
20 The biggest issue among investors and analysts is the company's cash-flow and dividend policy. Net debt is likely to reach a staggering £1.9 billion in 2004,

so no wonder some are querying the wisdom of total dividends to shareholders of £300 million. In essence, the dividend is being paid out of bank borrowings, 25 and that is not a pretty sight for any company.

The reason for the dividend policy is, of course, the Sainsbury family, which still holds 37% of the shares. They are said to remain totally supportive of Sir Peter and his strategy, recently supporting a move to give 30 Sir Peter more shares to keep him motivated.

Source: adapted from an article by William Lewis in the *Sunday Times*, 29 June 2003.

Questions
Total: 25 marks (30 minutes)

1 What is meant by the term 'overheads' (line 14)? *(2 marks)*

2 Calculate Sainsbury's sales revenue for the financial year ended March 2003. *(3 marks)*

3 Explain **one** possible reason why cost savings of £210 million have not improved
Sainsbury's profit levels (lines 14–17). *(5 marks)*

4 Analyse the implications of Sainsbury's cash-flow and dividend policy for the company. *(6 marks)*

5 Sainsbury's needed to raise £2 billion for projects such as new warehousing and
revamping its stores (lines 9–10). Discuss the sources of finance that Sainsbury's might
have chosen in order to raise this £2 billion. *(9 marks)*

Although Module 1 tests marketing and finance through two 30-minute questions, there is no guarantee that one question will be entirely about marketing or completely focused on finance. It is quite common for one or more parts of a (mainly) finance question to be about marketing, or vice versa.

So far in this textbook, questions have concentrated solely on marketing or finance, so that they test the material that has just been studied. The case study that follows is included to show how a mix of finance and marketing may occur. The questions are predominantly about accounting and finance, but there are some marketing questions too.

The case contains two separate sets of questions, taking 60 minutes to complete in total. However, because of the extensive reading required it is suggested that 35 minutes should be allocated if only one question is attempted.

Please note that, because there are sufficient data to set two complete exam-style questions, this case study is more demanding than typical AQA BUS1 papers.

CASE STUDY 2 (extension exercise) The Hallé Orchestra tunes up its finances

Five years ago, the Hallé Concert Society was struggling with a £1.3 million a year deficit. The hole in its finances was not only threatening its funding from the Arts Council — its main source of income —
5 but also endangering the very existence of the world-famous Hallé Orchestra.

Today the Hallé plays to a different tune. It breaks even on a £6 million income. The Hallé may be a not-for-profit organisation, with no ordinary share capital,
10 but to remain in the black it has to stick to strict business principles. 'We are very commercially minded,' says chief executive John Summers, 'but we have two bottom lines: the financial and the public benefit.'
15 That's where a problem arises. The best sources of income are from popular classics that advertisement makers use. But an orchestra whose global reputation means that it can easily fill the great concert halls of cities like Vienna also has to perform less popular
20 pieces to retain its artistic integrity.

The Hallé has a complex income structure. Over half of its £6 million annual income comes from an Arts Council grant (£1.7 million) and ticket sales (£1.4 million). The remaining £2.9 million comes from
25 a mixture of sales, trust income and grants.

To overcome the orchestra's original cash-flow problems, a local appeal raised £2 million to eliminate its debts. Spending was cut by 15%, sales growth of

10% per annum was targeted, and the orchestra size was reduced from 98 to 80. These measures helped 30 the orchestra to break even.

The orchestra gives 140 concerts a year, mainly in Manchester, but also in Nottingham and Sheffield. It also makes guest appearances in other parts of Britain and there are some self-financing overseas tours. 35

The main costs are salaries (£2.5 million) and charges for hiring halls for concerts and rehearsals. A further £1.5 million is spent on guest soloists and conductors.

Hall hire costs are a particular issue for the Hallé 40 Orchestra. In 1996 the orchestra moved from Manchester's Free Trade Hall (its home ever since its first concert in 1858) to the city's new Bridgewater Hall. In addition to obtaining new, modern premises,

the Hallé is given first pick of dates for its concerts. In return the Hallé is contracted to use the venue for 128 days a year — 68 for concerts (at £4,700 a time) and 60 for rehearsals, which at £3,500 a time is far dearer than other suitable halls. John Summers considers the concert fee to be very reasonable, but for rehearsals 'other halls are half that price', with £1,750 being a more usual charge. It is estimated that other costs are £3,000 per performance, but with salaried musicians most of the orchestra's costs are fixed costs.

The average concert attracts 1,000 ticket holders at a typical price of £17. Each customer also spends an average of £2 on programmes and merchandise. This is four times as much as the cost, so these sales produce a healthy surplus for each concert.

The concerts held outside Manchester provide a surplus for the orchestra because it is paid a fixed fee, but Manchester concerts are something of a risk. With an experienced orchestra, only one rehearsal is needed for each performance. The hiring of the Bridgewater Hall for performances and rehearsals might be seen as a variable cost, but Summers believes that it could be viewed as a fixed cost. 'Holding more concerts is not the answer to our financial challenges. If we did any more performances, we would saturate the market and exhaust the members of the orchestra.'

'The future lies in other forms of income. The Hallé has formed a record company and will be recording CDs at a cost of £10,000 each for recording.' Production of the disc itself costs £1.10 per CD, and postage and other costs are £2 per CD. The Hallé spends £3,000 on marketing the CDs to potential buyers. The Hallé Record Company will operate as a profit centre within the Hallé Concert Society.

'We have a sophisticated database,' explains Summers. 'With local competition from the BBC Philharmonic Orchestra in Manchester and the Liverpool Philharmonic we need a strong regional customer base.' A problem for the orchestra is that the public does not see significant differentiation between the different orchestras. The Hallé runs a series of concerts aimed at different market segments, based mainly on musical taste — pop music, classics, film scores etc. 'Our database also tells us how price sensitive our customers are. Some of our series are very price sensitive,' claims Summers (the price elasticity of demand is very elastic). For other styles of performance, demand is much more inelastic.

The Hallé is trying to gain sponsorship from local organisations — an aspect of business that it has not yet explored fully. Sponsorship from a local company with a strong global brand, such as Sharp Electronics, is the initial aim.

According to Summers, the Hallé faces three main challenges:

- maximising income while retaining artistic integrity
- avoiding a loss
- reducing dependence on grant funding

Source: adapted from a report by Philip Smith for the *Sunday Times* Enterprise Network, 29 June 2003.

Question 1

Total: 25 marks (30 minutes)

a Identify **two** marketing objectives mentioned in the article. *(2 marks)*

b The orchestra receives £9.99 for each CD that it sells. Calculate the number of CDs that it needs to sell in order to break even (see lines 71–78). *(5 marks)*

c Analyse **two** problems that the Hallé Orchestra might experience in finding sources of finance. *(8 marks)*

d Discuss the main factors that the Hallé Orchestra should consider when deciding whether to renew its contract with the Bridgewater Hall. *(10 marks)*

Question 2

Total: 25 marks (30 minutes)

a What is meant by the term 'profit centre' (line 78)? *(2 marks)*

b Explain the meaning of the term 'fixed cost' (line 67). *(2 marks)*

c Using the figures in paragraph 9 (lines 55–59), complete the following budget for a performance at the Bridgewater Hall.

Item	Income/expenditure (£)
Ticket sales	
Income from programmes and merchandise	
Total budgeted income	
Hire of hall for performance	4,700
Hire of hall for one rehearsal	3,500
Other costs	3,000
Costs of programmes and merchandise	
Total budgeted expenditure	

(4 marks)

d Analyse the factors that might have caused the demand for tickets for some performances to be very price elastic. *(8 marks)*

e Discuss the reasons why the orchestra focused on cost savings rather than attempting to increase income in its efforts to improve its financial position. *(9 marks)*

People in organisations

"It all comes down to people. Nothing else even comes close."

Richard Branson

CHAPTER 17

Organisational design

This chapter looks at the theory behind the management structure and organisational design of business. It shows how and why organisation charts are compiled and examines organisational hierarchies and the span of control and the links between them. Key concepts such as delayering, accountability and responsibility are explained. The chapter also provides comparisons between functional management and matrix management and between centralisation and decentralisation.

Organisation charts and organisational hierarchies

KEY TERMS

organisation chart: a diagram showing the lines of authority and layers of hierarchy in an organisation.
organisational hierarchy: the vertical division of authority and accountability in an organisation.
layers of hierarchy: the number of different supervisory and management levels between the shop-floor and the chief executive within an organisation.

An organisation's structure is usually illustrated by means of an **organisation chart**, which shows the connection between people within an organisation. The **organisational hierarchy** refers to the levels of authority and accountability in the organisation. Each line linking two different levels of the management hierarchy represents a relationship where instructions are passed downwards and reports and feedback are passed upwards within the organisation. Because lines are used to show the link between an employee and his or her supervisor or manager, it is customary to describe the person immediately above someone in the organisation chart as their **line manager**. Thus in Figure 17.1 supervisor B's line manager is the production manager for product A. This reporting system from the top of the hierarchy down to the bottom is called the **chain of command**. A formal hierarchy, such as that illustrated in Figure 17.1, has a clear vertical chain of command.

Organisation charts show the design of the organisation, including the chain of command, how different functions and divisions fit together, who is answerable to whom, the span of control in each division and the official channels of communication.

Figure 17.1 is a traditional structure which divides an organisation up into functional areas, including marketing, production, human resource management and finance. Within each function there are a number of layers

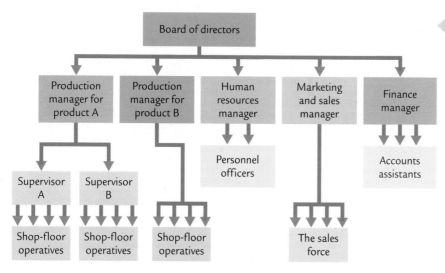

Figure 17.1 Traditional organisation chart

of hierarchy. For example, the marketing function has two levels, whereas the production function for product A has three levels.

Span of control

KEY TERM

span of control: the number of subordinates whom a manager is required to supervise directly.

If a manager has many subordinates answerable to him or her, the span of control is said to be wide. If, on the other hand, a manager has relatively few subordinates answerable to him or her, the span of control is said to be narrow. Normally the greater the degree of similarity in what a group of workers do, the wider the span of control can be. This explains why there is a narrow span of control at more senior levels of management, but shop-floor supervisors have wider spans of control. In Figure 17.1 the span of control for senior managers is narrower than for the shop-floor supervisors.

Relationship between span of control and levels of hierarchy

Traditionally, organisations have tended to have very tall hierarchical structures, i.e. many layers of management, each with a narrow span of control. More recently, hierarchies have become flatter, meaning that the number of layers of management has been reduced and each manager has a wider span of control (see Figure 17.2 on p. 148). Table 17.1 (see p. 148) contrasts the features of a flat organisational structure with wide spans of control with the features of a tall organisational structure with narrow spans of control.

DID YOU KNOW?

Some theorists suggest that the span of control should be between 3 and 6; others suggest between 6 and 12. However, such generalisations are unhelpful, since they ignore the characteristics of the group which is being supervised.

DID YOU KNOW?

The average number of levels of hierarchy between chief executives and the lowest level of managers with profit-related responsibilities is 3.2.

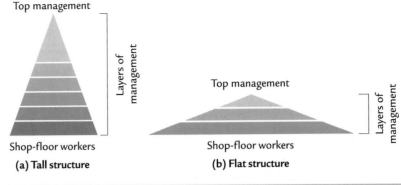

Figure 17.2 Tall and flat
hierarchical structures

Features of tall structures with narrow spans of control	Features of flat structures with wide spans of control
<ul><li>There may be more promotional opportunities because the career ladder has more rungs on it. However, more layers mean more staff, which in turn means higher company overheads.</li><li>Less delegation might mean less stress, but it could lead to low morale and a lack of commitment.</li><li>Narrow spans allow tight control to be kept of the organisation, which might be beneficial if factors such as quality, safety or security are crucial and where any mistake will have very serious consequences.</li><li>Important detail or information may be lost in reporting up through the levels of the hierarchy and the chain of command. An undesirable gap may emerge between what management intended and what actually happens.</li><li>A longer chain of command means that it takes longer for decisions to be made and implemented.</li></ul>	<ul><li>Individual managers may have less time for each subordinate and must therefore delegate effectively.</li><li>More delegation means that staff are given greater responsibility, which might mean more opportunity to use their ability. But staff may become overstretched, which may in turn cause stress.</li><li>Fewer layers of hierarchy between the bottom and the top of the organisation may mean that vertical communication improves.</li><li>Together with the reduction in overhead costs, this should mean greater efficiency within the organisation.</li></ul>

Table 17.1 Tall versus flat
organisational hierarchies
and narrow versus wide
spans of control

Delayering

 KEY TERM

delayering: the removal of one or more layers of hierarchy from the management structure of an organisation.

In a dynamic environment, businesses need to be able to respond quickly and effectively to changes. A very tall management structure is unlikely to be as responsive as a flatter structure. Many organisations have realised that the way to ensure they respond swiftly to change is to flatten or shorten their management structure by **delayering** — removing layers from the hierarchy. This leads to a flatter hierarchical structure with a wider span of control.

The advantages and disadvantages of delayering are similar to those for a flat hierarchical structure with a wide span of control (see Table 17.1). However, delayering is often done in order to cut costs by making people redundant. A real problem with this kind of delayering is that the organisation loses many of its very experienced managers and thus what is sometimes called its

e **EXAMINER'S VOICE**

To help you analyse issues, think about the advantages and disadvantages of different structures and try to see how these link with the strengths and weaknesses of the business being studied.

'corporate memory'. This means the knowledge of its history, past events, situations and contacts — much of which can be extremely valuable in dealing with the present.

Functional management versus matrix management

Functional management

 KEY TERM

functional management: the traditional management structure consisting of a different department for each of the main functions of the business (e.g. marketing, production, finance and personnel).

The traditional functional management structure was illustrated in Figure 17.1 (see p. 147). This structure could be adapted and used for businesses that organise themselves according to geographical regions or product brands. Figure 17.3 shows some organisational charts based on brands and regions.

(a) Based on geographical region

Figure 17.3
Functional organisation charts based on geographical region and product brands

(b) Based on product brands

All of these functional organisations are based on a hierarchy in which each department operates separately under the leadership of those above it. Coordination between the different functions, geographical regions or product brands must occur at the top, as each division in effect operates as a separate organisation. This is therefore a relatively inflexible type of structure.

Matrix management

KEY TERM

matrix management: a flexible management structure in which tasks are managed in a way that cuts across traditional departmental boundaries.

Matrix management tends to be used alongside a functional management structure, not instead of it. Employees involved in a project team will report to the team leader on issues linked to the project, but will also be answerable to their departmental manager for their other roles. An example of matrix management is a new product development team that includes an engineer, a marketing manager, a designer and an accountant, as shown in Table 17.2. In higher education, business schools are often organised on matrix management lines. For example, the staff who contribute to teaching on a BA in Business Management or an HND in Business will be coordinated by specific course tutors, but will also belong to their own specialist academic divisions, where they will have a line manager (see Table 17.3).

Table 17.2 *New product development team: matrix management*

	Engineering department	Marketing department	Design department	Finance department
New product team manager	*The new product team manager takes staff from each of the above departments to form the new product development team*			

Table 17.3 *A university business school*

	Academic divisions					
Degree courses	Accounting and finance	Economics	HRM	Marketing	Operations management	Strategy
BA in Business Management	*Course tutors take staff from each of the above divisions to form the course lecturing team*					
HND in Business	*Course tutors take staff from each of the above divisions to form the course lecturing team*					

Advantages of matrix management

- It ensures that projects are better coordinated.
- It gives people in different departments the opportunity to use their abilities and share their knowledge.
- This in turn prevents a single view — for example, about costs — dominating the decision-making process.
- It may lead to greater motivation.
- It allows for the possibility of synergy.

Disadvantages of matrix management

- It means that each team member can end up with two bosses — their departmental boss and the project leader.
- Since there is usually little coordination between departmental heads and project leaders, individuals may suffer if both bosses make heavy demands on them and insist on their particular concerns taking priority.
- For this reason, the lines of accountability may be unclear.

DID YOU KNOW?

Synergy occurs when the whole is greater than the sum of its parts, i.e. when more advantages occur as a result of experts from different departments working together rather than working separately.

***e* EXAMINER'S VOICE**

Think about the implications of changes in organisational structure for management and workers, communication, efficiency, morale and costs.

FACT FILE

The Phileas Fogg brand, part of the large United Biscuits (UB) group, was relaunched in 2002. This required a new approach to marketing and innovation. To facilitate these changes, patterns of working were changed. Individuals responsible for new product development were put into what the company called 'cross-functional teams'. These were teams of workers with a range of different but relevant specialisms, including specialists in market research, production, design and financial management. Such an approach is very similar to the matrix management approach explained above. The result of this change was that new products were developed and introduced in record time.

Accountability and responsibility

KEY TERM

accountability: the extent to which a named individual is held responsible for the success or failure of a particular policy, project or piece of work.

When a company's management structure is clear, as shown by its organisation chart, staff should know what authority has been given to them and by whom. According to Herzberg, achievement and recognition of that achievement will produce **motivation**. Recognition of achievement is more likely if the lines of accountability are clear. On the other hand, if mistakes are made, it is essential to know how they came about, in order to correct them. This can be identified more easily if the lines of accountability are clear.

In some instances, clear lines of accountability can be seen as a threat that deters managers from taking decisions in case they turn out badly. This in turn may make them overcautious, to the detriment of the business.

Although authority is delegated lower down the hierarchy, responsibility should remain with the senior management, since it is they who are ultimately responsible for the organisation's strategy and for the appointment of the staff involved. There have been occasions, however, when chief executives have refused to accept responsibility for actions taken by their subordinates or when, because of the nature of the organisation, it was very difficult to identify where responsibility and accountability lay. The rail accidents that

TOPFOTO

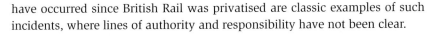
have occurred since British Rail was privatised are classic examples of such incidents, where lines of authority and responsibility have not been clear.

Centralisation versus decentralisation

On the one hand, organisations desire stability, uniformity and centralised control. However, they also recognise the differences in regional characteristics, customers and products, and the fact that individuals tend to identify more readily with smaller work groups than with the whole organisation and desire more authority and involvement in decision making. How these considerations are balanced influences whether an organisation has a centralised or a decentralised structure.

 KEY TERMS

centralisation and decentralisation: the degree to which authority is delegated within an organisation. A centralised structure has a greater degree of central control, while a decentralised structure involves a greater degree of delegated authority to the regions or to subordinates.

Centralised structures

Organisations that keep their decision-making power firmly at the top of the hierarchy, rather than delegating decisions to local levels or lower down the hierarchy, have a centralised decision-making structure. Retail organisations such as supermarkets have traditionally had very centralised structures, where all decisions about the layout of the store, the range of stock held, pricing policies etc. are made centrally. Burger King and other fast-food chains are other examples of organisations with centralised structures. You can recognise this because the meal, service and décor are exactly the same regardless of which branch you enter.

Advantages of centralisation

- It allows consistent policies on, say, marketing and production to be applied throughout an organisation, which in turn means greater control and standardisation of procedures.
- Decisions can be made quickly without the need to consult with all branches or sections.
- Customers may prefer the fact that every branch of a retail business is identical, meaning that they know exactly what to expect.
- It enables tight financial control, the efficient use of resources and lower overheads.
- The corporate view can be clearly emphasised.
- The business has strong centralised leadership in times of crisis.

Disadvantages of centralisation

- Those who might be the most informed about an issue have little input into the decision-making process. For example, the manager of a local supermarket may have far better knowledge about customers' needs than head office.

- The lack of decision-making powers on the part of managers in the local branches may adversely affect their motivation and morale.
- It can lead to inflexibility and inappropriate decisions at local level. It may also lengthen and delay the whole decision-making process.

Decentralised structures

A decentralised structure is where the power and authority to make decisions is delegated from head office to management in the local branches or lower down the hierarchy of a business. This delegation should be backed up by financial resources. Decentralisation involves less uniformity in how things are done, as decisions are likely to be made in relation to local circumstances and opportunities. Safeway for example, has, increasingly devolved decision-making powers to its local branch managers, which means that each branch is slightly different in relation to the stock it provides and the promotions it introduces.

Advantages of decentralisation
- It can empower local managers, encouraging them to be more innovative, thus improving their job satisfaction and commitment.
- Their local knowledge may have beneficial effects on sales if, for example, promotions are targeted more accurately.
- It reduces the volume of day-to-day communication between head office and local branches.
- Senior managers should have more time to consider long-term strategy rather than day-to-day issues. Hence they should be able to react more quickly to opportunities and threats in the external environment.
- Flexibility and speed should improve as an organisation becomes more responsive to changing customer demands.
- All these changes should enhance motivation and in turn improve performance and reduce labour turnover.

Disadvantages of decentralisation
- Customers may not like the reduction in uniformity, especially if they are able to compare branches unfavourably.
- By focusing on local issues, local managers may not see the big picture and hence may miss an opportunity or trend that would have been picked up more effectively in a centralised structure.

Conclusion

The structure of an organisation will be influenced by many factors:
- **The size of the organisation.** The larger the organisation, the more complex its structure is likely to be and the more layers of hierarchy, divisions or departments it is likely to have.
- **The nature of the organisation.** The firm's structure will depend on whether it is in the manufacturing or service sector, national or multinational, single product or multi-product, and on whether it is in an area where tight control, safety or security issues are paramount.

> **DID YOU KNOW?**
> Decentralisation is often associated with simultaneously delayering (or down-sizing), where the number of employees is reduced as a result of a fall in demand for its products.

> **DID YOU KNOW?**
> In a survey of 450 large and medium-sized European companies, well over half had decentralised decision-making structures. The leadership style at the top will tend to be more democratic in a decentralised company.

- **The culture and attitudes of senior management.** The structure will be affected by whether the management style is autocratic and controlling, or democratic and participative.
- **The skill and experience of its workforce.** The nature of the workforce — whether the majority of workers do low-skilled, repetitive jobs or whether they are highly skilled, each doing very different jobs — will also influence a firm's organisational structure.

> **ℯ EXAMINER'S VOICE**
>
> Check that you understand these concepts:
> - wide versus narrow spans of control
> - tall versus flat hierarchies
> - functional versus matrix management
> - centralised versus decentralised decision making
>
> Always remember to apply your knowledge. Think about the particular business you are being asked about, and relate your knowledge to that business — don't just trot out textbook knowledge without giving it context. For example, if you are considering a small, family-run private limited company, your answers about organisational structure will be very different from if you are analysing a large multinational plc.

GROUP EXERCISE

Have a go at drawing the organisation chart for your school, college or workplace. Ask your tutor or supervisor for further information that you might need. Consider whether it has a tall or a flat structure and whether the span of control at different levels of the hierarchy is narrow or wide. Think of these issues in relation to how the organisation is run and whether this is the most effective structure.

PRACTICE EXERCISE 1   Total: 50 marks (45 minutes)

1 Explain what an organisation chart shows. *(5 marks)*

2 What is meant by the chain of command? *(3 marks)*

3 Explain the terms 'hierarchy' and 'span of control' and the relationship between them. *(6 marks)*

4 Describe two implications for a business of having a flat organisational structure with a wide span of control. *(6 marks)*

5 Explain two implications for a business of having a tall organisational structure with a narrow span of control. *(6 marks)*

6 Define the term 'delayering' and explain two possible reasons for delayering an organisation. *(6 marks)*

7 Distinguish between a functional management structure and a matrix management structure. *(4 marks)*

8 Distinguish between centralised organisational structures and decentralised organisational structures.

(4 marks)

9 Distinguish between authority and responsibility.

(4 marks)

10 Explain two factors that might influence the structure of an organisation.

(6 marks)

PRACTICE EXERCISE 2   Total: 25 marks (30 minutes)

United Biscuits

In early 2001, United Biscuits (UB) changed its organisational structure from a geographical to a
5 category structure, supported by common shared services that work across the biscuits and snacks categories. This has given the business greater alignment and common purpose and direction.

10 Previously, the structure was based on three separate divisions with total responsibility for all activities in the UK, France and Benelux respectively. (Benelux is a name used to describe a combination of Belgium, the Netherlands and Luxembourg.) In
15 contrast, the new structure is based on individual products, with managers responsible for a particular product across the whole of western Europe.

As a starting point, UB rationalised its commercial and corporate business premises, moving from three
20 offices to a single cost-efficient head office in Hayes, Middlesex, as well as reorganising its regional offices in France and Benelux.

This is a company with enormous growth potential. Introducing the new structure has helped to release
25 that potential. UB is concentrating on creating an organisational structure that will allow it to grow.

The first phase of this work aims to release £65 million costs from across the business by the end

of 2002, to be reinvested in marketing and technological innovation. This 30 will be achieved in part through centralising service functions, restructuring sites across the UK and Europe, and rationalising manufac- 35 turing capacity.

One of the most visible examples of the change came last September when the management of UB was brought under one roof with the biscuit and snacks business. The new headquarters, based in 40 Hayes, has become a physical expression of the 'one company, one vision' that UB encourages.

Centralising various human resource services has led to increased efficiencies within the group. This process was made possible by the organisational 45 change introduced, moving from a geographical to a category structure. The company now has centralised buying, finance, information technology and human resource management services, avoiding the duplication that existed when each geographical part of the 50 business had its own services and systems.

This activity to date has released £30 million. This puts UB in a strong position to compete in this market and achieve its growth targets.

Source: adapted from United Biscuits' Annual Review, 2003.

Questions

1 What is meant by the term 'organisational structure' (line 3)?

(3 marks)

2 How might the change in United Biscuits' organisational structure release millions of pounds to be spent elsewhere?

(5 marks)

3 Excluding cost savings, explain one other advantage of changing the structure from a geographical base to a product base. *(4 marks)*

4 Why might centralisation help the 'one company, one vision' strategy (lines 41–42)? *(5 marks)*

5 Analyse two possible disadvantages that might arise from the policy of centralisation at United Biscuits. *(8 marks)*

CASE STUDY High Class Furnishings

High Class Furnishings makes furniture for two very different markets. Its original products, made in its Rugeley factory, are high-priced, handcrafted, traditional furniture, often individually designed to the customer's specifications. In its Uttoxeter factory, which opened 3 years ago, it makes flat-packed furniture for the lower-priced end of the market. Its head office is based at the Rugeley site. It has the organisation chart shown in Figure 17.4.

At present, High Class Furnishings has a fairly traditional organisational structure, broadly based on functional divisions. Although both product ranges are successful, it has had some problems in coordinating the activities of all departments and is considering a change in structure, to one where its divisions are based on operational lines. One of the suggestions is that the two product ranges should form two separate divisions, with their own marketing, personnel and financial functions. This would allow for a more decentralised approach to decision making not only within the production area, but also in relation to the marketing of the two products, staffing and financial issues. However, the production director is worried that such a change will adversely affect the current clear lines of accountability and responsibility.

The directors are also concerned because there has been a lack of innovation (new products or methods) and development of the firm's products. Customers are becoming dissatisfied by the limited choice of furniture offered by the firm. The marketing director has proposed that a system of matrix management would help to improve innovation.

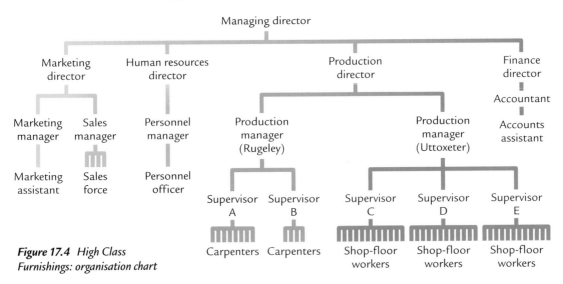

***Figure 17.4** High Class Furnishings: organisation chart*

Questions

Total: 50 marks (60 minutes)

1 Explain the usefulness of an organisation chart to High Class Furnishings. *(5 marks)*

2 a What is the span of control of supervisor C in the Uttoxeter factory? *(1 mark)*

  b Is there an ideal span of control? Analyse your answer in relation to the spans of control of the directors and of the production supervisors at High Class Furnishings. *(8 marks)*

3 Discuss the production director's view that a change in structure might 'adversely affect the current clear lines of accountability and responsibility'. *(15 marks)*

4 Explain how matrix management could help High Class Furnishings to improve the development of its product range. *(6 marks)*

5 To what extent might it benefit the company to move towards a more decentralised organisational structure? *(15 marks)*

Management by objectives

Peter Drucker's theory of management by objectives is the focus of this chapter which begins by distinguishing between an organisation's mission statement, aims and objectives. It then shows how a business can translate these ideas into specific objectives for individual workers. Finally the advantages and disadvantages of management by objectives are assessed.

Aims and objectives

It is important to distinguish between an organisation's mission, aims and objectives. Figure 18.1 presents a hierarchy indicating the order in which they might be set and how they influence each other.

Mission statements

KEY TERM

mission statement: a qualitative statement of an organisation's aims, describing the general purpose of the organisation.

A mission statement is intended to motivate employees and those within the firm as well as convincing customers and suppliers and those outside the firm of its sincerity and commitment.

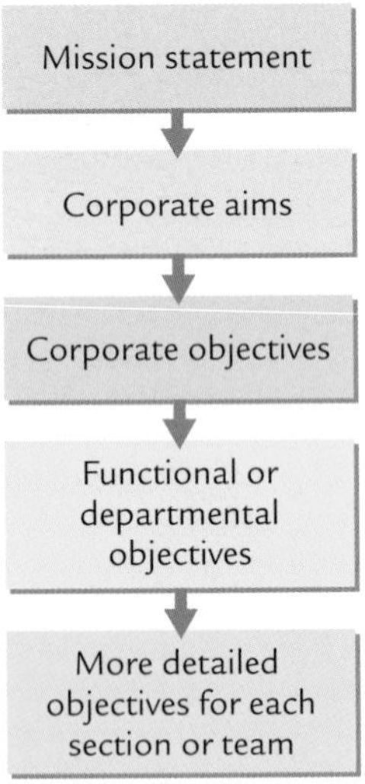

Corporate aims

KEY TERM

corporate aims: the long-term intentions of a business.

Corporate aims should provide a sense of common purpose that directs and stimulates an organisation. In essence, an aim is a long-term plan from which company objectives are derived. Aims determine the way in which the organisation will develop and are usually expressed qualitatively rather than in numerical terms. They provide a collective view, which can build team spirit and encourage commitment.

DID YOU KNOW?

A 'goal' is another term for objective. The term 'targets' is usually used for narrow, very specifically focused objectives, often at the level of department, team or even individual.

Figure 18.1
The hierarchy of mission, aims and objectives

Mission statement → Corporate aims → Corporate objectives → Functional or departmental objectives → More detailed objectives for each section or team

DID YOU KNOW?

Some companies use the terms 'aims' and 'mission' interchangeably, and others refer to their 'vision' or 'core purpose' or 'values'.

EXAMINER'S VOICE

Remember that mission statements can sometimes be more about public relations (PR) than meaningful statements of an organisation's actual aims.

Objectives

 TERM

objectives: targets that must be achieved in order to realise the stated aims of an organisation, department or individual team.

Objectives tend to be medium to long term and set in order to coordinate business activity and give a sense of direction to an individual manager, a department or the whole organisation. Objectives guide the actions of employees step by step.

More specifically, corporate objectives are the goals or objectives of the whole enterprise. These should be based on the firm's mission or aims. Corporate objectives govern the targets for each division or department of the business. They provide a mechanism for ensuring that authority can be delegated without loss of coordination.

To be effective, objectives should be **SMART** — that is, they should be:

- Specific — clearly and easily defined
- Measurable — quantifiable, for example to increase market share from 15 to 20% within the next 2 years
- Agreed — managers and subordinates are involved in setting the targets
- Realistic — achievable and not in conflict with other objectives
- Time bound — based upon an explicit timescale, for example to open 20 new stores within the next year

Peter Drucker and management by objectives

Peter Drucker published his book *The Practice of Management* in 1955. In this book, Drucker presented his theory of management by objectives. This emphasised the importance of objectives as a tool to assist managers in accomplishing their tasks.

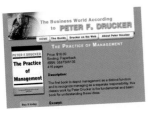

Drucker's view was that, for a business to be successful, the activities of all members of management and the workforce should be geared towards a common goal. This meant that they should each be given objectives or targets that together would help to achieve the firm's corporate objectives.

Drucker suggested that managers should consult with workers on the setting of objectives or targets and that workers should provide feedback to their superiors on:

- what their (and their superior's) objectives should be
- what needed to be done to achieve these objectives
- what could be done by managers to aid workers in achieving their objectives
- what should be done in the future

> **EXAMINER'S VOICE**
>
> Use the SMART criteria when considering business objectives in your case studies. Try to think about the sort of problems a business might face if objectives are not SMART.

> **DID YOU KNOW?**
>
> Some texts suggest an alternative explanation of SMART. They state that the 'A' stands for 'achievable' and the 'R' for 'relevant'.

Figure 18.2 Workers' input to management by objectives

Thus, workers' input to the process of management by objectives is shown in Figure 18.2.

Drucker realised that the most important aspect of actually implementing management by objectives was delegation of responsibility: that is, passing authority down the hierarchy (see Chapter 19). He felt that for management by objectives to work properly, managers and workers should be allowed to control their own performance. He saw little point in setting people objectives or targets and then not granting them the ability to direct their actions to achieve those objectives.

Drucker recognised that his theory might conflict with the management style of the business. Authoritarian managers, for example, would probably resent the loss of power. Drucker suggested 'management by self-control rather than management by dominance'. This, he understood, might well involve changing the firm's whole management philosophy and corporate culture. With self-control comes self-discipline — the very essence of management by objectives assumes that workers want responsibility, want to contribute actively and want to help the firm.

Management by objectives is very much a part of McGregor's Theory Y management style and is closely linked to Herzberg's job enrichment motivator, both of which are dealt with in detail in Chapters 21 and 24.

Advantages of management by objectives

- **Motivation.** Managers know exactly what they must achieve and are able to prioritise activities and allocate time appropriately. In so doing, they are achieving their own and the company's objectives. In this sense, management by objectives acts as a motivator because individuals can track their own progress and measure this against agreed targets. Such delegation of responsibility is one of Herzberg's motivators.
- **Performance.** It provides performance indicators for the organisation. Targets act as a control mechanism because an individual's performance can be judged against targets. It is therefore easier to identify when perform-ance falls short of targets and in turn easier to decide what actions should be taken.
- **Common goal.** All staff should be working towards a common goal and therefore benefiting the organisation.

Disadvantages of management by objectives

- **Bureaucracy.** It is rather bureaucratic and time consuming in terms of the meetings needed to determine and agree targets.
- **Unsuitable targets.** Targets can quickly become out of date and unrealistic as circumstances change. If targets do not change in line with the changing conditions, this is likely to reduce the flexibility of a firm's response. Moreover, the process of setting targets does not guarantee that they will be

DID YOU KNOW?

Management and leadership styles have a huge influence on the philosophy and culture of an organisation. This is considered in detail in Chapter 24.

achieved, so more time might be spent setting them than trying to achieve them, especially if circumstances are constantly changing.

- **Short-termism.** Depending on the corporate culture, management by objectives can encourage short-termism to the eventual long-term detriment of the firm. In highly competitive working environments, where salaries and perks depend on sales and on beating one's colleagues' sales figures, targets can become narrowly focused on quantity, ignoring issues of appropriateness and ethics. For example, the overzealous or blatant misselling of various types of pensions, mortgages, insurance policies and warranties on electrical goods has led to long-term bad publicity for many firms. Similarly, schools are sometimes accused of concentrating too much on pupils' exam performance in order to achieve or exceed government targets or in order to compete successfully in local league tables, rather than on pupils' general education.

- **Low morale and stress.** Objectives that are imposed rather than agreed may reduce morale and, where overambitious targets are imposed, this can result in huge amounts of stress among employees.

DID YOU KNOW?	EXAMINER'S VOICE
Target setting is a skill in itself and requires extensive training.	Always consider the business context, how the environment in which the business operates is changing and the extent to which objectives are still appropriate.

Conclusion

Despite the evident advantages, the use of management by objectives has declined and is now actively rejected in many organisations, principally because it can be a constraint on management thinking. It can cause managers to miss business opportunities because they are focused too much on their targets. This is especially the case in a business environment that is changing rapidly. In such a situation, targets may restrict effort — the focus on targets may mean that workers are not using their initiative or responding creatively to situations.

However, management by objectives is still considered suitable for large firms operating in stable markets and where a regular and formal staff appraisal procedure is in place. In addition, the general issues emerging from the process of management by objectives are still vitally important in all business contexts: the principle that all employees are focused on achieving the common goals of the organisation, the importance of clear objective setting, the necessity of agreement rather than imposition, and the importance of delegating responsibility.

CHAPTER 18 Management by objectives

1 Briefly explain the term 'management by objectives' and its purpose. *(4 marks)*

2 Organise the following in the order in which they are likely to be set in an organisation: corporate aims, functional/departmental objectives, mission statement, corporate objectives, objectives for each section/team. *(5 marks)*

3 What is a mission statement? *(2 marks)*

4 Explain the significance of corporate aims. *(3 marks)*

5 Distinguish between corporate aims and objectives. *(3 marks)*

6 What does the mnemonic SMART stand for in relation to objectives? *(5 marks)*

7 Explain whether the following objective satisfies the SMART criteria: 'to increase sales by 3% over the next 18 months'. *(3 marks)*

8 Explain whether the following objective satisfies the SMART criteria: 'to improve market share in the near future'. *(3 marks)*

9 Explain two advantages to a firm of introducing management by objectives. *(6 marks)*

10 Explain two problems that might be encountered by a firm using management by objectives. *(6 marks)*

CASE STUDY Sainsbury's mission and objectives

The following extract, taken from Sainsbury's website, describes the company's mission and objectives.

Our mission

Our mission is to be the consumer's first choice for food, delivering products of outstanding quality and great service at a competitive cost through working 'faster, simpler and together'.

Our corporate objectives

To deliver a successful business longer term we are looking for profit growth through a balance of strong sales growth, reducing our cost base further and continuing margin improvement.

The development of our formats presents a bigger sales growth opportunity than we originally anticipated. We are committed to achieving industry leading margins, but it is too early to be precise about when. The market is dynamic and competition very active. We have choices about the rate of sales growth against margin targets. However, we are committed to delivering strong double-digit underlying profit growth in each year of our business transformation programme.

Source: adapted from the J. Sainsbury's plc website (www.j-sainsbury.co.uk).

Questions

Total: 50 marks (60 minutes)

1 Suggest how Sainsbury's corporate objectives could be rewritten to comply with the SMART criteria. *(6 marks)*

2 Examine the problems that might emerge for a business such as Sainsbury's if its objectives are not SMART. *(8 marks)*

3 The case study suggests uncertainty in relation to the precise detail of each of Sainsbury's objectives. To what extent does this contradict Drucker's management by objectives approach? *(15 marks)*

4 Briefly assess the implications for a business such as Sainsbury's of introducing a process of management by objectives. *(6 marks)*

5 To what extent would the process of management by objectives be helpful in motivating the workforce at Sainsbury's? *(15 marks)*

CHAPTER 19

Delegation and consultation

Building on the concepts first outlined in Chapter 17, the idea of delegation is examined and linked to the concepts of responsibility, authority, accountability and empowerment. An examination of the factors that influence the effectiveness of delegation is undertaken and its benefits and limitations are considered. The chapter then introduces the concepts of consultation and leadership styles, establishing the links between delegation and consultation and the different styles of leadership. Finally, it considers how delegation and consultation relate to structures such as quality circles and kaizen groups.

Delegation

 KEY TERM

delegation: the process of passing authority down the hierarchy from a manager to a subordinate.

In delegation, the subordinate is given the authority to make decisions connected with a particular task, but the manager remains accountable for decisions taken.

> **DID** YOU KNOW?
>
> It is often said that delegation can be both the most important but also the hardest thing for a manager to do well. However, James Crosby, ex-chief executive of the Halifax Bank, once said in answer to the question, 'What management wisdom is most overrated?', 'The importance of delegation — all too often a substitute for inability to do the job oneself.'

Responsibility, authority and accountability are important terms to understand in relation to delegation.

Responsibility

 KEY TERM

responsibility: being accountable for one's actions.

A person who is responsible for the performance of a department, section or team will be required to explain and justify performance that falls short of expectations and to ensure that things are put right. For example, a production manager may be responsible for ensuring that products are produced in the right quantity, to the right specification and on time. A personnel manager

may be responsible for ensuring that all employees receive appropriate training for their particular job. What the responsibilities are and to whom the subordinate is responsible are usually indicated in a job description.

Authority

 TERM

■ **authority:** the ability or power to carry out a task.

Subordinates must have the authority to undertake the various tasks delegated to them. It is therefore important that the manager has formally passed authority on to them and that the authority is clear and explicit. For example, if a manager, who was due to be away, did not give her assistant the authority to sign cheques or invoices or generally make decisions on her behalf, it is possible that the firm would grind to a halt. Thus if responsibility is delegated, it is important to ensure that appropriate authority is also delegated.

It is equally important to lay down clearly the limits to a subordinate's authority: for example, that a subordinate does not have the power to hire and fire in his manager's absence. Passing on authority is an issue that many managers find difficult, but if sufficient authority is not transferred, delegation will be unsuccessful.

Accountability

 TERM

accountability: the extent to which a named individual is held responsible for the success or failure of a particular policy, project or piece of work.

Despite delegating responsibility and authority, the manager is still accountable, both in law and in fact. He or she has chosen to delegate tasks to a subordinate, has recruited and trained subordinates and has made the decision that the subordinate is capable of exercising power efficiently. Thus accountability remains firmly at the top.

Delegation and empowerment

 TERM

empowerment: giving employees the means by which they can exercise power over their working lives.

The process of delegating tasks can be a way of motivating and empowering employees, by allowing them to exercise some power over their working lives and providing them with a degree of freedom to decide what to do and how to do it. However, empowerment can occur only if delegation is effective.

The following factors are likely to make delegation effective:
■ Delegation must be based on mutual trust between the manager and the subordinate.

 YOU KNOW?

If staff are empowered by more delegation, this links to Herzberg's motivation theory (see Chapter 21).

- It is important to select the most suitable person to delegate to — someone who will be able to complete the task efficiently and effectively. The person should be appropriately skilled, trained and informed about the particular task he or she will be responsible for.
- Interesting and challenging tasks should be delegated as well as the more routine. Managers should not delegate tasks simply because they dislike doing them, either because they are dull or difficult, or because the manager is overburdened with work.
- The tasks and responsibilities to be delegated need to be explained clearly and explicitly in order to avoid subordinates making mistakes or feeling unsure or insecure because of a lack of information. An effective support system should be provided — one that allows the subordinate to question and discuss issues connected with the delegated tasks. This should improve understanding and ensure that subordinates have the skills necessary to carry out their tasks.
- When delegating responsibility for carrying out a certain task, managers must also delegate the authority to carry it out and communicate this to others in the firm in order to avoid difficulties such as someone else questioning the authority of the subordinate. The limitations of the subordinate's authority should be made clear too.
- It follows that managers should avoid interfering with delegated tasks unless it is evident that things are going radically wrong. They must relinquish control in order to ensure subordinates feel that they are trusted and that the manager has confidence in them.

Advantages of delegation

- Delegation is necessary in all organisations because there is a limit to the amount of work managers can carry out themselves. Delegation reduces the stress and burdens of management and frees up time for managers to concentrate on more important strategic tasks.

DID YOU KNOW?

Research has shown that taking these six factors into account can improve the success of delegation fourfold.

e EXAMINER'S VOICE

Have you remembered that decentralised decision making is based on the delegation of authority? Therefore the advantages and disadvantages of delegation are similar to those for decentralised decision making.

- Delegation empowers and motivates workers. It provides subordinates with greater job satisfaction by giving them a say in the decision making that affects their work and by demonstrating trust in their abilities.
- Subordinates might have a better knowledge of local conditions affecting their area of work and therefore might be able to make better-informed decisions.
- Delegation may allow greater flexibility and a quicker response to changes, since if problems do not have to be referred to senior managers, decision making should be quicker.
- By giving subordinates the experience of decision making, delegation provides a means of grooming them for higher positions and is thus important for management development purposes.

Limits to delegation

- **Small firms.** In some small firms, managers delegate very little — often because they do not have the staff to delegate to or because they have set the business up on their own, are used to controlling all aspects of the operations and are therefore reluctant to relinquish control.
- **Customer expectations.** Often customers want to see the manager in charge, regardless of the fact that responsibilities may have been delegated further down the hierarchy.
- **Attitudes and approach of management.** The leadership style in an organisation will largely dictate the extent to which responsibilities are delegated down the hierarchy.
- **Quality of staff.** The extent to which responsibilities can be delegated will be influenced by the quality and skills of the staff who are employed.
- **Crisis situations.** In emergency or crisis situations where decisions need to be made quickly, delegation is less likely.
- **Confidentiality.** Where there is a need for confidentiality or extreme security, less delegation is likely to take place.

Consultation

 TERM

consultation: asking employees for their views on various issues that will affect them and the business.

 EXAMINER'S VOICE

Always remember to address questions in context, i.e. make sure that your answers relate clearly to the precise organisation that you are considering. This will assist you in gaining marks for application.

Employees' views may be taken into account before decisions are made. The important word here is 'may' and it is this that distinguishes consultation from delegation. Delegation means passing decision-making powers, responsibility and authority down the hierarchy. Consultation means taking into account the views of employees further down the hierarchy, but ultimately decision-making powers are kept at the top. One of the issues with a detailed consultation process is that decisions can take a long time to be reached.

Leadership styles

As mentioned above, the use of delegation and consultation in an organisation depends on the leadership style that management adopts. Leadership style in this context means the approach of management towards their staff. There are broadly four categories of leadership style that can be used to analyse behaviour. These are detailed in Figure 19.1.

Tannenbaum and Schmidt's continuum of leadership (see Figure 19.2) provides an alternative view of delegation and consultation in relation to different leadership styles. It attempts to categorise management approaches according to the extent to which management uses its authority and the amount of freedom subordinates are given.

Figure 19.1 Four styles of leadership

Democratic	Paternalistic
A democratic leadership style means running a business or a department on the basis of decisions agreed by the majority. In some situations this can mean actually voting on issues, but it is more likely to mean that the leader delegates a great deal, discusses issues, acts upon advice and explains the reasons for decisions. Democratic leaders not only delegate, but also consult others about their views and take these into account before making a decision.	A paternalistic leadership style is essentially an approach where management decides what is best for its employees. As its name implies, this style is similar to the approach that parents take with their children. A paternalistic approach is autocratic, although decisions are intended to be in the best interests of employees. The leader is likely to explain the reasons for his or her decisions and may consult staff before making them, but delegation is less likely to be encouraged.
Authoritarian	**Laissez-faire**
An authoritarian (also known as autocratic or dictatorial) leadership style is an approach which assumes that information and decision making should be kept at the top of the organisation. It is the use of power by giving out orders, rather than consulting or delegating. This may happen because managers have little confidence in the ability of their staff or because they are simply unable to, or prefer not to, relinquish power and control. It may, however, reflect significant pressures on the organisation that forces management to make rapid and difficult decisions. This is often the case in crisis or emergency situations, where an authoritarian approach is often the most effective.	A laissez-faire leadership style is an approach where the leader has minimal input in the decision-making process and essentially leaves the running of the business to the staff. The term comes from the French for 'leave alone' or 'let be'. Delegation occurs in the sense that decisions are left to people lower down the hierarchy, but such delegation lacks focus and coordination. This style often arises as a result of poor or weak leadership and a failure to provide the framework necessary for a successful democratic approach. However, there may be a conscious decision to give staff the maximum scope to use their initiative and demonstrate their capabilities. How effective it is depends on the staff themselves — some will love the freedom to use their initiative and to be creative whereas others will hate the unstructured nature of their jobs.

DID YOU KNOW?

According to Douglas McGregor, an authoritarian leadership style implies a Theory X approach on the part of the leader and an assumption that employees have little ability or desire to contribute fruitfully to the decision-making process. A democratic leadership style, on the other hand, is likely to imply a Theory Y approach (see Chapter 24, pp. 206–07).

EXAMINER'S VOICE

The section on 'laissez-faire' leadership is included for the purposes of comparison, but please note that it is not part of the AQA specification for A-level Business Studies. Examination questions will not make direct reference to 'laissez-faire' as a leadership or management style.

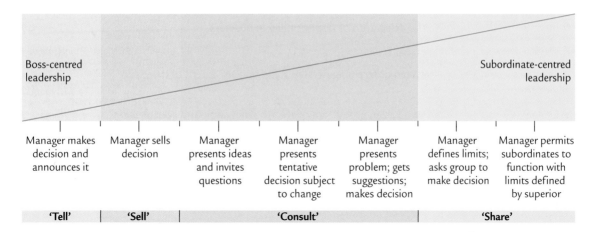

| 'Tell' | 'Sell' | 'Consult' | 'Share' |

Quality circles and kaizen groups

When organisations operate **quality circles**, this is an important part of the delegation and consultation process. The principal function of a quality circle is to identify quality problems, consider alternative solutions and recommend suitable outcomes to management (see Chapter 34). By delegating the responsibility for identifying problems to quality circles and then taking into account the solutions they put forward, organisations benefit operationally and financially. At the same time, they enrich the jobs of their workers, who appreciate the opportunity to show their knowledge and talents in a problem-solving environment.

Similar analysis can be made of **kaizen groups**, which meet regularly to discuss problems and solutions as part of the continuous improvement process (see Chapter 34).

Figure 19.2 Tannenbaum and Schmidt's continuum of leadership

DID YOU KNOW?

Job enrichment is part of Herzberg's motivational theory (see Chapter 21).

EXAMINER'S VOICE

Always try to relate your knowledge from one area of your study to your knowledge from another. For example, you will study quality circles and kaizen groups in the Operations Management part of your course, but they clearly relate here to the People in Organisations part of your course.

PRACTICE EXERCISE   Total: 50 marks (40 minutes)

1 Distinguish between delegation and consultation.   *(4 marks)*

2 Explain the purpose of both delegation and consultation.   *(5 marks)*

3 Distinguish between the terms 'responsibility', 'authority' and 'accountability'.   *(6 marks)*

4 Explain one advantage of empowering employees.   *(3 marks)*

5 Explain two factors that are likely to make delegation effective.   *(6 marks)*

6 Identify two limitations to the delegation of responsibility in business. *(2 marks)*

7 Identify the four main leadership styles. *(4 marks)*

8 Outline the relationship between different leadership styles and the extent of delegation and consultation. *(12 marks)*

9 Explain how quality circles and kaizen groups are related to delegation and consultation. *(8 marks)*

CASE STUDY   Peter's problems

Read the story below and answer the questions that follow.

Tuesday

Peter Smith is the sales manager of a textile firm in Lancashire. He is currently working on the draft of a document that will detail the current performance of the firm's various products in each of its sales regions, together with forecasts, based on market research findings, for the next 3 years. So far he has drafted some rough notes, identified the information he needs and asked his secretary to collect the information and have it ready for him first thing on Thursday morning, so that he can work on it on Thursday and Friday. The document will form the basis of a presentation he is due to make next Tuesday at the board meeting.

Peter's real passion is for selling, but since his promotion to sales manager, he finds that he does less and less of this and spends more and more time looking at figures, justifying performance and attending board meetings, none of which he particularly enjoys.

As well as a secretary, he has an assistant, Sam, who helps him in travelling around to meet the regional sales team and generally coordinating the regions. Sam is very keen to take on more responsibility; he is good with figures and would like to be more involved in the planning and reviewing process, which is mainly Peter's responsibility. At present Sam feels a little constrained by the fact that he spends most of his time on the road travelling.

Wednesday

At a local business forum meeting, Peter learns of a conference in Germany that will focus specifically on the long-term potential in eastern Europe for the types of product his firm produces and sells. The 3-day conference starts tomorrow. Peter feels that he needs to go, but he is aware of the important board meeting next Tuesday when he is due to present the document, which he has not yet really started producing. He decides that this is the right time for Sam to step in — after all, Sam has always said that he wants Peter to delegate more tasks to him. Here is his chance.

Peter gets back to the office at 3 p.m., with 20 minutes to spare before his next meeting, which will go on until late in the evening. He calls Sam in and tells him that he will be away for the next 3 days in Germany and that he wants Sam to cancel all his commitments for Thursday and Friday and to compile the document that Peter will need for the board meeting next Tuesday. Peter gives Sam his rough notes and explains the information that he has asked his secretary to get ready for early tomorrow morning. He tells Sam that he will go over the document on Monday to check it out and will talk to him then. He then dashes off to his meeting.

Sam is stunned. He has a number of appointments booked for the next 2 days, which are important and which he is reluctant to cancel. He is particularly concerned about missing tomorrow's kaizen group meeting, which will be discussing a number of proposals that he originally suggested. However, although producing the document is rather daunting, he is keen to have a go and therefore follows Peter's instructions, rescheduling his appointments for next week and deciding not to attend the kaizen group meeting.

Thursday

Sam arrives at the office early and goes to Peter's secretary for the information. She has half of the information, but says that the rest is with another manager who wants to speak to Peter before releasing it. Sam rings the manager to explain the task he has been set, but the manager refuses to provide him with the information, saying that the information is confidential and that Sam needs Peter's authorisation before he can have access to it.

Friday

Sam does his best to produce the document. However, he is not particularly happy with it and knows that there are significant gaps in it due to the lack of information. He has tried on a number of occasions to contact Peter in Germany, but has been unable to get hold of him. He is also aware that his lack of experience and lack of skill in terms of report writing mean that the document does not show the information in the best possible light.

Monday

Peter does not turn up until 2 p.m., having attended a meeting all morning. He finds Sam's report on his desk, together with a note. He ignores the note and scans the document. He then calls Sam into his office. 'This is awful — there are all sorts of gaps in the information and the format is wrong. I can't find the slides for the presentation either...'

Questions

Total: 50 marks (60 minutes)

1 Briefly explain **two** possible reasons why Sam would want Peter to delegate more tasks to him. *(6 marks)*

2 Explain **one** benefit that kaizen groups might bring to the textile firm in the case study. *(6 marks)*

3 Managers rely heavily on effective consultation and delegation. Evaluate this statement in the context of the above case study. *(15 marks)*

4 Analyse the style of leadership shown by Peter in the case study. *(8 marks)*

5 To what extent was Peter's failure to delegate authority the main cause of the difficulties that Sam faced in completing the report? *(15 marks)*

CHAPTER 20

Corporate culture and change management

Within this section on management structure and organisation, some important overall themes need to be considered. These themes include corporate culture, change management and the differing approaches adopted by small and large organisations. This chapter provides a brief outline of how these themes relate to the topics in Chapters 17–19.

Corporate culture

 KEY TERM

> **corporate culture:** the unwritten code that affects the attitudes and behaviour of staff, approaches to decision making and the leadership style of management.

There are many different business cultures. Examples include:

- **a goal-orientated culture** based on staff successfully meeting or beating performance targets (e.g. Honda and Toyota)
- **a bureaucratic culture** based on respect for seniority, official and often cumbersome procedures and communication channels — such organisations usually have tall hierarchical structures and tend to avoid risk (e.g. many government departments and local councils)
- **a growth-orientated culture** based on commitment to the product and the company (e.g. The Body Shop and Starbucks)

 DID YOU KNOW?

Culture is often described as 'the way that we do things around here', meaning the type of behaviour that is considered acceptable or unacceptable.

Culture thus influences the extent to which a business is centralised or decentralised and whether it has a narrow or tall hierarchical structure. However, as well as influencing organisational structure, culture will be influenced by it: for example, whether management is organised vertically by function or geographical or product categories and how many layers there are in the hierarchy. Culture will be influential when it comes to developing mission statements, and by affecting leadership styles in the business it will have a major effect on the degree of, and effectiveness of, delegation and consultation. The culture of an organisation will also affect the amount of resistance to change and therefore the ability of new management to impose its style or decisions on subordinates.

Change

Change is a constant feature of business activity. The key issues are whether potential change has been foreseen by the company — and therefore planned for — and whether it is within the company's control. For example, significant change will result if there is a huge growth in sales and hence growth in the size of the business. This is likely to require new management structures, more layers of hierarchy and new divisions or departments. In time this in turn may lead to the business becoming very bureaucratic, causing able and creative staff to leave. Alternatively, increased delegation to divisions or departments may have adverse effects on managers as they struggle to live up to their new responsibilities or fail to meet targets.

Unforeseen change is probably more of a problem. If a small business provides a service that suddenly becomes very popular, it may be in danger of overtrading, as it is unable to get the resources needed to support such growth adequately. Management may in turn begin to lose control unless it is well prepared. For example, managers may be unable to delegate because of a lack of appropriate staff or may be unwilling to delegate effectively because of an inability to 'let go' of power and to trust others. Yet appropriate planning could improve the situation by controlling the rate of growth and by creating an organisational structure that meets the needs of such growth, a leadership style that encourages delegation and staff who are trained to take on responsibility.

External change is usually the hardest to control or even influence, such as when there are changes in tastes or fashions, new laws or taxes, or increased competition. If the firm cannot influence such change, it must ensure that it is prepared to respond quickly and appropriately when it happens. Contingency plans can be drawn up to do just that, but where change develops into a crisis situation, an authoritarian leadership approach might be the most appropriate response, even if the usual style of management and the culture of the organisation suggest a more democratic and participatory approach.

Change management

 TERM

change management: the anticipation, organisation, introduction and evaluation of modifications to business strategy and operations.

The key underlying factor in change management is trust. Managers must give staff the skills and training to implement changes. In turn, staff must trust the motives and ability of the managers. In relation to the topics in Chapters 17–19, successful management of change therefore requires a number of elements.

Organisational structure

Successful change management needs an organisational structure that allows change to be implemented effectively. For example, United Biscuits moved from a geographical to a product category organisational structure and from a decentralised to a more centralised organisation in order to facilitate growth and expansion (see p. 155). An organisation may also change from a functional to a matrix structure (or to cross-functional teams) in order to innovate and relaunch products, as United Biscuits did in the case of Phileas Fogg (see p. 151).

Management

Sensitive handling will be essential if delayering is necessary. As this means removing a layer of management, it is likely to lead to redundancies and to resistance to change among all or some sections of the workforce. In order to reduce resistance to change, senior management should:

■ work hard to establish a sense of common purpose or mission and real trust between all levels of the hierarchy
■ explain and discuss the reasons for change with all levels of the hierarchy in order to achieve a consensus that such change is essential
■ consult widely on the options available for implementing the change, ensuring that employees' views are taken into account and, importantly, are *seen* to be taken into account in determining the eventual strategy

Leadership

Appropriate leadership should encourage job enrichment by effective delegation and consultation. This should improve staff motivation and trust, which in turn makes staff more willing to accept and possibly even welcome change.

> **DID YOU KNOW?**
>
> Research has shown that, in most organisations, middle managers are the staff who are most resistant to change. This is because middle managers have more to lose in any reorganisation than those below them in the hierarchy.

> **e EXAMINER'S VOICE**
>
> Corporate culture, change management and the approach of small and large organisations are important concepts to consider when answering questions on management structure and organisation. Remember to consider them in the context of any case you study, and to use them appropriately to develop your answers to questions asking you to analyse or evaluate.

PRACTICE EXERCISE 1 — Total: 50 marks (50 minutes)

1 Explain the term 'culture' in an organisational context. *(3 marks)*

2 Identify three different types of business culture. *(3 marks)*

3 Explain two possible effects of different cultures in an organisation. *(6 marks)*

4 How might the culture of an organisation influence the degree of resistance to change in that organisation? *(3 marks)*

5 Give two examples of foreseen change and two examples of unforeseen change. *(4 marks)*

6 Explain one possible impact of unforeseen change on a business. *(3 marks)*

7 State two examples of external change. *(2 marks)*

8 Why is external change so hard to control? *(3 marks)*

9 Explain the term 'change management'. *(3 marks)*

10 Briefly explain two aspects of business that might contribute to successful change management. *(4 marks)*

11 Outline the differing approaches of small and large organisations in relation to corporate culture and the management of change. *(6 marks)*

12 A small firm, with a simple functional structure, operates in a fast-growing, innovative product market. Discuss the factors that it should consider in relation to its future management structure and organisation. *(10 marks)*

PRACTICE EXERCISE 2
Total: 15 marks (20 minutes)

Corporate culture at Starbucks

Read the following extracts from Starbucks' website and answer the question that follows.

Starbucks' mission statement

Establish Starbucks as the premier purveyor of the finest coffee in the world while maintaining our uncompromising principles while we grow.

The following six guiding principles will help us measure the appropriateness of our decisions:

■ Provide a great work environment and treat each other with respect and dignity.

■ Embrace diversity as an essential component in the way we do business.

■ Apply the highest standards of excellence to the purchasing, roasting and fresh delivery of our coffee.

■ Develop enthusiastically satisfied customers all of the time.

■ Contribute positively to our communities and our environment.

■ Recognise that profitability is essential to our future success.

Starbucks' 'Job Centre'

Our success depends on your success. Our ability to accomplish what we set out to do is based primarily on the people we hire — we call each other 'partners'. We are always focused on our people. We provide opportunities to develop your skills, further your career, and achieve your goals.

At Starbucks, you'll find a commitment to excellence among our partners; an emphasis on respect in how we treat our customers and each other; and a dedication to social responsibility.

We look for people who are adaptable, self-motivated, passionate, creative team players. If that sounds like you, why not bring your talents and skill to Starbucks? We are growing in dynamic new ways and we recognise that the right people, offering their ideas and expertise, will enable us to continue our success.

'The Starbucks experience'

We are devoted to investing in supporting and engaging our partners in the constant reinvention of Starbucks. In fact the first guiding principle in our mission statement is to 'provide a great work environment and treat each other with respect and dignity'.

Imagine working for a company that constantly aspires to realise this principle. Chances are, it's like no place you've ever worked.

At Starbucks, diversity is an essential component of the way we do business. We believe so strongly in embracing diversity that it is the second guiding principle in our mission statement. We strive to create a diverse workplace in which every partner's voice is heard and in which all our partners will succeed while learning from one another. We believe that building understanding, respect and appreciation for different people contributes to our growth and to the growth of our partners.

Source: Starbucks' website (www.starbucks.com).

Question

On the basis of the information provided, analyse the possible nature of Starbucks' corporate culture and how this is likely to influence its management structure and organisation.

Motivation theory

In this chapter the term 'motivation' is defined. In accordance with the AQA specification, the works of four theorists on motivation are examined:

- *F. W. Taylor*
- *Elton Mayo*
- *Abraham Maslow*
- *Frederick Herzberg*

KEY TERMS

> **motivation:** the causes of people's actions — why people behave as they do.
>
> **motivation theory:** the study of factors that influence the behaviour of people in the workplace.

Scientific management and F. W. Taylor

F. W. Taylor (1856–1915) was an American engineer who invented **work-study** and founded the scientific approach to management. He considered money to be the main factor that motivated workers, so he emphasised the benefits of **piecework**, where workers are paid according to how much they produce. He argued that piecework provided high rewards for hard work, benefiting both the worker and the business.

KEY TERM

> **scientific management:** business decision making based on data that are researched and tested quantitatively in order to improve the efficiency of an organisation.

The principles of **scientific management** were laid down in Taylor's book, *The Principles of Scientific Management*, originally published in 1911. In it he stressed the duty of management to organise work, using the principles of **specialisation** and the **division of labour**, so as to maximise efficiency. According to Taylor, this was to be achieved by 'objective laws' based on 'science' that management and workers could agree upon. This in turn would reduce conflict between management and workers since, as he saw it, there could be no disagreement about laws based on 'science'.

Taylor recommended:

- extreme division of labour (with workers specialising in one very narrow task)
- payment by piecework
- tight management control

Division of labour means breaking a job down into small, repetitive tasks, each of which can be done at speed and with little training. By specialising in a particular task, individuals can quickly become expert at their job, leading to increased productivity.

Piecework means payment by results, i.e. payment per item produced. It provides an incentive to work hard but can encourage staff to concentrate on quantity at the expense of quality.

Tight management control ensures that workers concentrate on their jobs and follow the correct processes.

Taylor believed that these three features would be the main methods of improving productivity and efficiency.

Taylor's methods had considerable influence on business, most famously on the **mass production** processes introduced at the Ford Motor Company. However, his influence on the workforce was less successful. Extreme division of labour meant that jobs became more boring and repetitive. The lack of skills needed by workers also led to a loss of power for individual workers. This led to low morale and poor industrial relations, and had some influence on the growth of trade unions.

> **DID YOU KNOW?**
>
> Work-study is the measurement and timing of work processes in order to identify the best method and the most realistic output targets. First, a work-study consultant (or 'time and motion' person) would observe people at work and note down how the job was broken down into different actions and the sequence of these actions. Then the consultant would assess this to determine whether it was the most efficient method. Each action would then be timed and the motion and the effort used noted down. The presence of 'time and motion men' quickly became a cause of industrial relations disputes.

To an extent, Taylor saw human beings as machines with financial needs. No account was taken of individual differences and the fact that the approach determined by the time and motion study might not suit everyone. Ideas have moved on considerably since then. Money is obviously vitally important, but research has suggested consistently that money alone is not sufficient to create job satisfaction or to improve motivation and productivity.

The human relations school and Elton Mayo

Elton Mayo (1880–1949) was a follower of F. W. Taylor, but his experiments led him to conclude that scientific management could not explain important aspects of people's behaviour in the workplace. Many of his findings, including 'the Hawthorne effect', came from research he did at the Western Electric factory in Hawthorne, USA, and provided the foundations for the human relations school of management.

DID YOU KNOW?

The Hawthorne effect is the fact that workers' motivation and productivity are influenced by the degree of interest and recognition shown in them, and the groups to which they belong, by their managers.

Mayo's early research involved trying to measure the impact on productivity of improving the lighting conditions in the Western Electric factory. He followed Taylor's scientific principles by testing the changes in lighting conditions for one group of workers against a control group of workers who worked in a section of the factory with unchanged lighting. Productivity rose in the area where the lighting was improved, but surprisingly productivity also rose, and by a similar amount, in the area with unchanged lighting.

The results of further experiments conducted by Mayo brought into question Taylor's assumptions about the importance of money in motivating the workforce, and instead emphasised the importance of human relations in the workplace. Mayo's findings suggested the following:

- Recognition, belonging and security are more important in motivating employees than simply money and working conditions.
- Work is a group-based activity and employees should be seen as members of a group.
- Managers need to pay attention to individuals' social needs and the influence of the informal groups to which they belong, since these groups exert significant influence over an individual's attitudes.
- Managers must communicate with informal groups, ensuring that their goals are in tune with those of the organisation. This could occur by, for example, allowing them to become part of the decision-making process, which would in turn improve worker commitment and loyalty.
- Increases in output are due to greater communication and improved relations within informal groups.

Important developments resulted from Mayo and the human relations school. These included the introduction of social facilities at work, such as canteens and sports clubs, the appointment of personnel officers whose responsibility was the welfare of employees, and an increase in the quantity and quality of communication and consultation taking place between management and employees.

Maslow's hierarchy of human needs

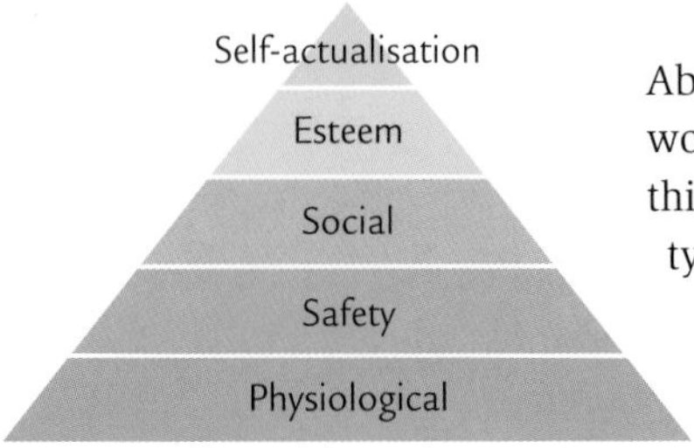

Figure 21.1 Maslow's hierarchy of needs

Abraham Maslow (1908–70) was an American psychologist whose work on human needs has had a major influence on management thinking. His **hierarchy of needs** suggests that people have similar types of need, which can be classified into a hierarchy. Needs range from lower-level ones, such as the need for food, clothing and shelter, to higher-level ones, such as the need for achievement and self-esteem.

Maslow's five categories of need are indicated in Figure 21.1. They are:

■ **Physiological needs**: the requirements for food, clothes and shelter; in relation to work, the need to earn an income in order to acquire these things and have reasonable working conditions.

■ **Safety needs**: the need for security and freedom from danger and anxiety; in relation to work, the need to have a secure job, a safe working environment, adequate pension arrangements and clear lines of accountability in relation to responsibilities.

■ **Social needs**: the desire for friendship, love and a sense of belonging; in relation to work, being part of a team, getting along with work mates and being provided with social facilities such as staff rooms and canteens.

■ **Esteem needs**: the need to have self-respect and respect from others; in relation to work, to have positive feedback, to gain recognition and status for achievement and to have opportunities for promotion.

■ **Self-actualisation**: the need to fulfil one's potential through actions and achievements. Maslow did not believe that this need could be satisfied fully and thought that people would always strive to develop further and achieve more.

Maslow believed that an unsatisfied need was a motivator of behaviour and that, while it remained unsatisfied, higher-level needs were unimportant. He therefore believed that, starting from the bottom of the hierarchy, each level of need had to be fulfilled before the next level became important. However, once satisfied, a particular level of need ceased to be important and the next level of unsatisfied need became a motivator.

This theory is intuitively appealing but it can be criticised. In relation to work, if people have insufficient income to enjoy adequate food, clothing and shelter, they are unlikely to be overly influenced by whether a job is permanent, whether it has good pension arrangements or whether their work mates make them feel welcome. However, once people satisfy their physiological and safety needs, it is questionable whether, for all individuals, social needs come before esteem needs. Many individuals are high achievers and are motivated by this sometimes to the exclusion of any desire to be part of a team or to get along with their colleagues.

Herzberg's motivation and maintenance

Frederick Herzberg (1923–2000) was an American psychologist whose research led him to develop the **two-factor theory** of job satisfaction and dissatisfaction. This theory suggests that some factors have the potential to provide positive job satisfaction while others can only really reduce dissatisfaction.

Herzberg called the factors that motivate and give job satisfaction **motivators**. They include:

- a sense of achievement
- recognition for effort and achievement
- the nature of the work itself — that it is meaningful and interesting
- responsibility
- promotion and improvement opportunities

All of these concern the job itself rather than issues such as pay, and all are likely to motivate workers and thus may improve productivity.

Factors that can reduce job dissatisfaction are called **hygiene** or **maintenance factors**. They include:

- company policy and administration, which includes paperwork, rules, red tape etc.
- supervision, especially if workers feel that they are over-supervised
- pay
- interpersonal relations, especially with supervisors and peers
- working conditions

All of these factors 'surround' the job; they do not concern the job itself. Ensuring that they are acceptable to the workforce prevents dissatisfaction rather than causing positive motivation. For example, improved canteen or staff room facilities and better pay are unlikely to motivate the workforce in the long term, but they will reduce the level of dissatisfaction. This is not to

say that hygiene or maintenance factors are unimportant or less important than motivators. They are clearly vitally important and if inappropriate will cause dissatisfaction, with severe consequences for the organisation.

Herzberg also distinguished between **movement** (when someone does something) and **motivation** (when someone wants to do something). If an individual works harder or puts in more hours because he or she is saving up for a holiday or a car, this is movement rather than motivation. Herzberg suggested that reward-based systems, such as bonuses, would provide only short-term motivation or 'movement'.

One of the main policy recommendations that stemmed from Herzberg's work is **job enrichment** — the attempt to motivate employees by giving them the opportunity to use their abilities and allowing them to exercise greater independence and authority over the planning, execution and control of their work. Chapter 22 returns to this concept.

Criticism of Herzberg's theory is mainly based on the fact that he drew conclusions about workers as a whole from a limited sample of 200 accountants and engineers. It is also criticised for making too little of the role of groups and teams in the workplace and the motivational influences they have on individuals. Despite this, many of Herzberg's ideas have been borne out in practice. For example, wage increases and changes to conditions of work are rarely sufficient to produce a highly motivated workforce. Equally, what are perceived to be inadequate wage increases and changes to working conditions can create immense dissatisfaction, often with dire consequences.

> **ℯ EXAMINER'S VOICE**
>
> Try to question the theories you have studied so that you can assess their value rather than only being able to describe them. For example, the research that led to Herzberg's two-factor theory is based on only a small sample of professionals. Maslow's theory makes broad assumptions about the fact that everyone has the same needs. Mayo's research is really about the result of group norms rather than individual motivation. Taylor's view that money, and in particular piecework, is the most important motivator, although discredited, is still practised in a number of organisations in the UK and extensively in less economically developed countries.

Links between Maslow and Herzberg

There are close links between some of the motivation theories studied in this chapter, especially those of Maslow and Herzberg.

Intrinsic and extrinsic rewards

Intrinsic rewards come from the job itself: for example, because of the degree of authority given to an individual at work or the sense of achievement gained from completing a task well. Intrinsic rewards are linked to Herzberg's motivators and the higher-level needs in Maslow's hierarchy.

Maslow's hierarchy of needs   Herzberg's two-factor theory

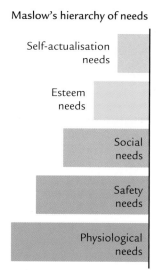

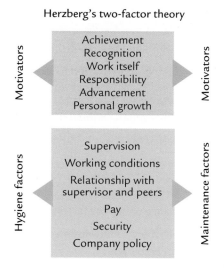

Figure 21.2
Links between Herzberg's and Maslow's theories of motivation

Extrinsic rewards are not directly related to the work itself but are associated with doing the job: for example, financial incentives, fringe benefits, good working conditions and interaction with people at work. Extrinsic rewards are related to Maslow's lower-level needs and Herzberg's maintenance or hygiene factors.

Needs as motivators

Herzberg's and Maslow's views about needs being the main driving force are similar, although Herzberg's emphasis on motivation corresponds with Maslow's higher-level needs. Figure 21.2 demonstrates the link between the two theories.

How useful are theories of motivation?

The answer to this question depends on the particular work situation. A traditional manufacturing organisation with a fairly authoritarian approach, a tall hierarchy and routine and monotonous work may find that money is a great motivator, allowing people to enjoy their social life and home comforts. This supports Taylor's view of what motivates people. It is also likely that in this situation Mayo's informal group influences and Maslow's social needs are important to the worker. Ensuring that Herzberg's hygiene or maintenance factors are appropriate will also be vital to avoid dissatisfaction.

However, in an organisation that employs large numbers of people with high-level skills and education, expectations are higher and jobs are more complex. Although rates of pay and working conditions are vitally important, workers expect more recognition, self-control, involvement in decision making and empowerment. In other words, they are influenced by Maslow's higher-level needs and Herzberg's motivators are important.

 EXAMINER'S VOICE

When you are evaluating, make sure that your conclusion is consistent with the evidence that you have presented and show why it is a natural conclusion from your arguments.

CHAPTER 21 Motivation theory

PRACTICE EXERCISE 1 — Total: 50 marks (40 minutes)

1 Briefly explain the views of F. W. Taylor and the scientific management school of thought. *(6 marks)*

2 Outline the main problems with these views in relation to motivating employees. *(6 marks)*

3 What is the 'Hawthorne effect'? *(4 marks)*

4 Briefly explain the views of Elton Mayo and the human relations school of management. *(6 marks)*

5 Identify and explain the various levels of Maslow's hierarchy of human needs. *(10 marks)*

6 Explain the relevance of Maslow's hierarchy of human needs in a work context. *(6 marks)*

7 Identify four of Herzberg's motivators. *(4 marks)*

8 Identify four of Herzberg's maintenance or hygiene factors. *(4 marks)*

9 Distinguish between the effect of Herzberg's motivators and that of his maintenance or hygiene factors on the motivation of employees. *(4 marks)*

PRACTICE EXERCISE 2 — Total: 20 marks (25 minutes)

Herzberg, Maslow and teachers

Despite the huge success of Herzberg's theory, there have been major criticisms of his research. These centre on the fact that the research took place in 1959 and covered a relatively small group of 200 accountants and engineers. A number of studies have tried to replicate the results, usually unsuccessfully.

One example concerned research with American teachers in primary and secondary schools. The findings from this research suggested that in relation to Herzberg's five main motivators, achievement ranked as the most important. However, the overall conclusion drawn from the research was that salary was the single most important influence on motivation and satisfaction at work, and that the teachers in the study perceived the amount of salary increase they received to be tied to achievement and the other motivators.

In relation to Maslow's hierarchy of needs, it appeared that the teachers in the study were less satisfied with their personal achievement of esteem (i.e. their self-respect and the respect they earned

INGRAM

from others) than with their achievement of self-actualisation (i.e. fulfilling their potential). The research concluded that fulfilling one's potential (self-actualisation) might provide the basis for self-respect and gaining the respect of others.

The research went on to suggest that this might explain why good teachers were leaving education and moving to other, higher-paying occupations, but also suggested that managers in schools should focus more closely on the esteem needs of teachers.

Questions

1 This passage shows how theories can always be challenged. Identify and explain other problems with the theories of Herzberg and Maslow, using examples from real organisations wherever possible. *(10 marks)*

2 Discuss how the 'esteem needs of teachers' in schools could be met more effectively by senior managers. *(10 marks)*

CASE STUDY Motivation at Taylor Woodrow

Taylor Woodrow plc employs around 6,000 people worldwide. Its primary business is house building through its Bryant brand in the UK and Monarch brand overseas. It is also involved in property development and construction.

Taylor Woodrow's culture is 'to ensure that its companies and employees continue to improve and develop in a culture of excellence'. It considers its unique selling point (USP) to be the skills of its workforce, relative to its rivals.

Some skilled trades people, such as bricklayers and plumbers, are employed by Taylor Woodrow. However, many are brought in on short-term contracts from other firms while the building is being erected. Taylor Woodrow encourages internal promotion for staff such as engineers, surveyors and architects, who can become managers.

Performance of the workforce is judged at three levels:

- individual workers
- teams
- the organisation as a whole

Individuals are set targets that they agree with their manager. This process also includes discussion of the employee's needs and hopes. Twice a year performance is measured against an agreed standard. Salaries and bonus payments are then decided in accordance with the individual's performance. This system of performance-related pay is popular with the workers, who prefer the fairness of a system that is not decided arbitrarily by a manager. Part of the annual pay award is linked to the overall success of the business.

The system is designed to encourage all staff to seek responsibility, and employees are encouraged to contribute ideas that will improve the company's efficiency.

The management theorist has shown that real motivation has to come from within an individual. Committed employees are people who believe that they have a shared purpose with their employer. As a result of its system, Taylor Woodrow's employees and the company are able to work towards a shared set of objectives, and are able to monitor their contribution to creating a successful organisation.

Source: adapted from *The Times 100 Case Studies* 2003.

Questions

Total: 50 marks (60 minutes)

1 Taylor Woodrow uses a system of management by objectives (MbO). Explain **one** difficulty that it may meet in using MbO as a way of motivating staff. *(6 marks)*

2 Identify and explain **one** aspect of Taylor Woodrow's approach that corresponds to the ideas of F. W. Taylor. *(6 marks)*

3 Select any **one** theory of motivation (except that of F. W. Taylor) and discuss the degree to which Taylor Woodrow appears to be using the ideas of that theorist. *(15 marks)*

4 Analyse **two** benefits that Taylor Woodrow might receive from improving the motivation of its workforce. *(8 marks)*

5 In house building and construction, many of the workers involved in a building project are *not* employees of the company, but are subcontracted. This means that they are used by the company for a set period of time in order to complete a particular project. To what extent does this make these workers more difficult for Taylor Woodrow to motivate than its own full-time staff? *(15 marks)*

Motivation in practice

Issues covered in this chapter include the link between culture and motivation and an examination of the relative merits of non-financial approaches to motivation. The motivation theories outlined in Chapter 21 are drawn on to scrutinise job enrichment, job enlargement, job rotation, empowerment and teamworking as practical ways of improving workforce motivation.

Culture and motivation

 TERM

corporate culture: the unwritten code that affects the attitudes and behaviour of staff, approaches to decision making and the leadership style of management.

One of the most important factors affecting motivation in an organisation is its prevailing culture. Culture can affect motivation both directly and indirectly. Elton Mayo's work identified the huge influence that group norms have on motivation and in particular the influence of group leaders on their teams. The culture of an organisation may encourage people to be chatty, sociable and laid back, or it may mean that they are conscientious, very serious and do everything by the book. Culture is also related to organisational structure, the number of layers in the hierarchy and the extent of delegation, all of which influence motivation (see particularly Chapters 17, 19 and 20).

Changing a culture in order to improve a firm's performance and the motivation of its workforce is difficult and very time consuming. Usually the types of people who are recruited to an organisation are those who suit its culture. For example, a business in a fast-changing market might recruit young, talented, creative risk-takers as opposed to more mature, experienced and safe individuals. The staff already working in the organisation will have a vested interest in maintaining its existing culture. Other factors that affect how a change in culture influences motivation are how effectively any change is communicated to staff, the provision of training in order to introduce change effectively, the extent to which senior management makes genuine changes to its approach, and whether senior managers who are recruited or promoted act to support the change.

Job enrichment and motivation

 TERM

job enrichment: a means of giving employees greater responsibility and offering them challenges that allow them to utilise their skills fully.

e **EXAMINER'S VOICE**

When answering questions on motivation it is important to show whose theory you are using, because different theories conflict. For example, money is seen as a motivator by Taylor but not by Herzberg.

Herzberg suggested that only job enrichment is likely to provide long-term job satisfaction. An enriched job should ideally:

■ introduce new and more difficult tasks and challenges at different ability levels, some of which might be beyond the employee's experience to date
■ give individuals a complete unit of work — in other words, a meaningful task rather than a repetitive part of a larger process, as advocated by Taylor
■ provide regular feedback on performance so that the employee knows immediately how well he or she is performing
■ remove some of the controls over the employee while retaining accountability
■ increase the accountability of the individual for his or her own work

Such systems have been introduced into many manufacturing organisations, most famously Volvo, Honda and Toyota, all of which completely reorganised their factories so that groups of workers could take charge of producing complete units of work and then check the quality of their own work. Not only did this give workers opportunities to satisfy their social needs, but also, as they were able to manage their own time and work, they had autonomy and responsibility for decision making.

Advantages of job enrichment

■ It develops workers' unused skills and presents them with challenges.
■ It allows workers to make greater contributions to the decision-making process.
■ It enhances workers' promotional prospects.
■ It motivates workers by ensuring that their abilities and potential are exploited and that individuals gain a high degree of self-control over the setting of goals and the identification of how to achieve those goals.

Problems with job enrichment

■ Although many workers will relish the challenges, others might find the whole process intimidating and may simply feel that it places additional pressure on them that they do not want.
■ It could be seen simply as a way to delegate responsibility down through

the hierarchy and to reduce the number of employees by delayering. In this sense, it could be viewed as an attempt to get more out of workers while paying them the same rate.

■ It may be costly and benefits may only result in the long term, as when reorganising the shop-floor and retraining the workforce in a manufacturing business.

■ Not all jobs lend themselves to enrichment. For example, refuse collection offers little scope for greater responsibility and challenges.

Job enlargement and motivation

AQA
AS Business Studies

DID YOU KNOW?

Job enrichment is closely based on Herzberg's ideas and McGregor's Theory Y approach to the management of the workforce (see Chapter 24).

KEY TERM

job enlargement: increasing the scope of a job, either by job enrichment or by job rotation.

In theory, job enlargement motivates workers through giving them greater recognition, improving their promotion prospects and increasing the feelings of achievement arising from the job itself. However, if enlargement is not used carefully, a firm can demoralise its workforce by giving them excessive workloads.

Jobs may be enlarged either through job enrichment or through job rotation:

■ **Job enrichment** is where the job is expanded vertically (known as **vertical extension**) by giving the worker more responsibility (see pp. 187–89).

■ **Job rotation** is where the job is expanded horizontally (known as **horizontal extension**) by giving the worker more tasks, but at the same level of responsibility.

Job rotation is a systematic programme of switching jobs to provide greater variety. Essentially it gives workers more varied work to do, but at a similar level of challenge. For example, a shop worker might spend 2 hours on the checkout, 2 hours filling shelves and another 2 hours in the warehouse.

Using job rotation gives a firm several advantages:

■ It is intended to relieve the boredom of the work and has the useful side effect of ensuring that if one person is absent, others can cover the job without difficulty.

■ Workers may be more motivated due to their wider range of skills and they will become more flexible.

■ There may be a greater sense of participation in the production process.

However, it has the following disadvantages:

■ Retraining costs will increase and there may be a fall in output because there is less specialisation.

■ It could be seen as simply involving a greater number of boring tasks but with a reduction in the social benefits of working, since groups will be constantly changing.

Empowerment and motivation

 KEY TERM

empowerment: giving employees the means by which they can exercise power over their working lives.

Whereas delegation might provide the authority for a subordinate to carry out a specific task, empowerment implies a degree of self-regulation and the freedom to decide what to do and how to do it. For example, Safeway and Zara not only delegate responsibility to local store managers, but also empower them with the scope to make judgements about what products to promote and what stock to carry.

Empowerment can be achieved through informal systems or through the more formal system of **autonomous work groups**. These provide workers with autonomy and decision-making powers, and aim to increase motivation while also improving flexibility and quality, thus adding value to the organisation.

Empowerment involves:

- recognising that workers are capable of doing more
- making workers feel trusted and confident to carry out jobs and make decisions without supervision
- recognising workers' achievements
- creating an environment where workers wish to contribute and to be involved

With such systems in place, empowerment is likely to lead to improved motivation, reduced labour turnover, reduced absenteeism and, in turn, an increase in productivity. However, the cost of training workers to take on responsibility and make decisions could be great, and managers need to be very good delegators if the process is to work effectively. In addition, there is a risk for the employer in providing a level of autonomy that may mean employees' actions are difficult to check effectively. There have been many examples of fraudulent activities in financial organisations where employees have been empowered. Nick Leeson and Barings Bank is a classic example of this.

 FACT FILE

Barings Bank, Britain's oldest and one of its most prestigious banks, was told on 24 February 1995 that huge trading losses in the Far East had wiped out its capital base. It was insolvent. Either a buyer had to be found or it would have to cease trading. Barings stood to lose over £600 million on dealings carried out by one man — Nick Leeson, a 28-year-old trader based in Singapore. The losses exceeded the £540 million of capital built up by the bank since 1762.

This happened because Barings switched from a traditional, centrally managed, low-risk operation to one in which bright young traders were empowered to push

for higher profits. Organisations need a culture that is understood by all staff, but as one Barings' employee was reported as saying, 'There were gung-ho aggressive stockbrokers on the one hand against myopic blue-chip bankers on the other.'

Although there are many good reasons for empowering staff by delegating authority to them, the Barings collapse shows the risks of delegating in a laissez-faire manner, with neither the controls nor the checks to ensure that staff are using power responsibly.

Source: adapted from Ian Marcousé, 'Lessons from Leeson', *Business Review*, September 1995.

From a more cynical viewpoint, empowerment could be viewed simply as a way of delayering and therefore cutting costs, i.e. removing a layer of management and delegating responsibility and authority further down the hierarchy. In a similar manner, it could be argued that workers are being given more responsibility but the same amount of pay.

Teamworking and motivation

 KEY TERM

> **teamworking:** a system where production is organised into large units of work and a group of employees work together in order to meet shared objectives.

Teamworking contrasts with systems where individual workers take on smaller, more fragmented processes, characterised by a high division of labour. A team of people working on a larger task, such as making a complete car rather than just a door, will need to be multi-skilled, well trained and motivated by more than the piece-rate rewards received by workers carrying out a single, repetitive task.

By using teamworking, an organisation gets a more motivated, flexible work-force that can cover absences more easily. When accompanied by other techniques such as job rotation and/or job enrichment and some degree of decision making, teamwork can enhance motivation and/or relieve boredom.

Teamworking can be linked to the theories of Mayo (group norms) and Maslow (social needs). It is also linked to autonomous work groups, quality circles and kaizen groups (see Chapter 34).

Conclusion

All individuals are different and the motivational factors that influence individuals will change over time depending on their particular circumstances. Some of the important questions raised by this chapter include:

- Will increased job satisfaction always lead to increased productivity? Individuals may be happier in their jobs and more ready to accept change, but no more productive than before.

CHAPTER 22 Motivation in practice

- Does less division of labour mean less control and, if so, is this a problem?
- Is it only factors at work that motivate individuals in a work context? Individuals' higher-level needs may be satisfied outside the workplace and the only thing they may want from work is their weekly wage or monthly salary.

FACT FILE

At First Direct, the telephone and internet bank, 'There is no difference between the organisation and its people,' according to Alan Hughes, chief executive. 'As far as the customer is concerned, the representative they speak to on the phone is First Direct.' So it is important that staff take a pride in their work. 'People don't want to be given hoops to jump through for rewards or beaten with a stick if they don't. People want to do a good job, and if we are all doing this, there is less staff turnover and greater customer satisfaction,' says Hughes.

A recent survey in the *Sunday Times* proves him right: almost 80% of staff say that they are proud to work for First Direct and that they feel they can make a valuable contribution to its success.

Source: *The Sunday Times 100 Best Companies to Work For*, 2 March 2003.

PRACTICE EXERCISE 1
Total: 55 marks (50 minutes)

1 Identify two problems for a business that might result from a low level of motivation among its employees. *(2 marks)*

2 Explain how the culture of an organisation can affect the motivation of its employees. *(4 marks)*

3 Explain the terms 'job enlargement', 'job enrichment' and 'job rotation'. *(6 marks)*

4 Explain two advantages to a business of introducing job enrichment. *(6 marks)*

5 Explain two problems that a business might encounter as a result of introducing job enrichment. *(6 marks)*

6 Explain how job enrichment is linked to the motivation theories with which you are familiar. *(6 marks)*

7 Explain one advantage and one disadvantage to a business of introducing a system of job rotation. *(6 marks)*

8 Explain the term 'empowerment'. *(3 marks)*

9 How might the empowering of its employees benefit a business? *(4 marks)*

10 Explain two benefits of teamworking to a business. *(6 marks)*

11 Explain how teamworking is linked to the motivation theories with which you are familiar. *(6 marks)*

Honda puts staff first

Honda, established in Japan in 1948 by Soichiro Honda, is the world's largest manufacturer of motor-cycles and engines and seventh-largest producer of cars. A British subsidiary was launched in 1965. The head office is in Slough, and there is a £1.2 billion manufacturing operation in Swindon. Strong team spirit and a can-do attitude are key features of life at Honda UK.

The company's principles are simple. Staff are told, 'Your growth is the key to Honda's growth.' Martin Sanders, general manager of power equip-ment, says that constant opportunities and high levels of responsibility keep people with the firm. 'Mr Honda's philosophy was that you work first for yourself and then for Honda,' he says. 'We employ people more than specialists, and the global company provides advice and assistance — but delegates decisions to local management.' He says that it is a strong culture; there is little rigid procedure or hierarchy, but there is a powerful team spirit and sense of empowerment.

Staff are offered tailored training and can move between three different business areas. A recent *Sunday Times* survey showed that 77% of Honda's staff believe that the company gives them opportunities to learn and grow, and 86% of employees feel they can make a difference.

Source: *The Sunday Times 100 Best Companies to Work For*, 2 March 2003.

Questions

1 Consider how 'a powerful team spirit and sense of empowerment' might benefit Honda UK.   *(10 marks)*

2 Discuss Honda's approach to its staff in terms of the motivation theories with which you are familiar.   *(15 marks)*

CHAPTER 23

Financial incentives

This chapter concentrates on the financial incentives that can be employed by an organisation in order to motivate its workforce. The relative merits of the following methods of providing financial incentives are compared: time rates/salary, piecework, performance-related pay (PRP), profit sharing, share ownership and share options, and fringe benefits.

Time rates

Salary and wage payment systems are time-based payment systems. Wages are normally paid weekly and are based on an hourly rate. Salary is normally paid monthly and is based on an annual rate. Salary in particular is used where it is difficult or impossible to measure work output and where tasks are complex and involved. Thus payment by time is in a sense a payment for input rather than output. For example, the sales assistants in a supermarket are paid a weekly wage for the hours that they work, not for the number of goods they sell. Bank tellers are paid a monthly salary; they are not paid on the basis of the number of accounts they open.

Of course, this means that effort is not guaranteed because staff could spend their time chatting or simply waste time. However, appraisal and supervision procedures, the need to achieve targets or simply completing the responsibilities of the job can be a sufficient check. The security provided by time rates may motivate, according to Maslow's hierarchy of needs.

Piecework

 KEY TERM

piecework (or piece rates): payment based on the number of items each worker produces.

Paying workers a rate for each item produced is an attractive way of providing them with an incentive to work hard. However, it can cause the following problems:

- It may encourage staff to concentrate on quantity at the expense of quality in order to boost their pay. To some extent a piece-rate system can reduce the supervision needed to keep workers on task, but greater levels of scrap and reduced focus on quality can cancel this out and simply add to costs.
- It may mean that the firm's output is heavily influenced by workers' needs rather than customer demand. For example, evidence suggests that

piece-rate workers speed up in July and again in December in order to boost their earnings for their summer holidays and for Christmas, even though this may not coincide with customer demand patterns.

- Herzberg considered that this type of reward system would reinforce behaviour, with repetitive tasks being emphasised and linked to pay. In this way, piece-rate systems are likely to increase resistance to change because change will tend to slow production in the short term.
- Herzberg also suggested that incentive systems such as piece rates and bonuses are in fact the most ineffective way to reward staff, since such systems do not change an employee's commitment or attitude to work, but simply and temporarily change what the worker does, i.e. they cause *movement*, not *motivation*.

DID YOU KNOW?

Sometimes workers are paid a small fixed amount of basic pay, which gives some security, and then a piece rate, which gives them the incentive to increase productivity.

Performance-related pay

KEY TERM

performance-related pay (PRP): a bonus or salary increase usually awarded for above average employee performance.

Under a system of performance-related pay, an employee performing well above average might get a 5% pay rise, while average achievers get only 2%. PRP is usually employed in situations where piece-rate systems are not appropriate because the work cannot be measured in a precise way. Decisions on PRP usually take place following an appraisal that assesses performance and the extent to which individual targets have been met.

There are a number of advantages of using a system of PRP:

- There are direct links between pay and effort.
- It may lead to a reduction in costs as a result of lower levels of supervision, an increase in productivity and an improvement in quality.
- There may be improvements in motivation and a possible reduction in labour turnover and absenteeism.
- PRP is a useful system for getting staff to work towards company objectives by establishing individual targets at appraisal that are linked to corporate objectives.

However, there are some serious disadvantages:

- It may become a serious source of conflict among staff who are receiving different bonuses for what they perceive to be the same effort.
- The effect on motivation is debatable because PRP is usually a very small proportion of salary.
- A major question is how performance can be measured, since PRP is often introduced into occupations where it is difficult to measure performance objectively.
- It can reduce the influence of trade unions and of collective bargaining, as decisions on pay are related to individuals.

Managers often favour PRP because they see it as a means of providing an incentive for staff to improve their performance and commitment, and a useful control mechanism. PRP is also used extensively to reward very senior management and chief executive officers. However, there is little research evidence to support the benefits claimed for it, and more emphasis is now put on group PRP.

> **FACT FILE**
>
> Taylor Woodrow plc is a construction company that builds property in the UK under the Bryant brand. It uses a form of PRP, which it calls 'performance and development review'. With this process it aims to create commitment and motivation among managers and employees. Each employee meets with his or her manager at a performance review. Prior to this meeting, the individual notes down his or her personal career objectives, training and development needs and the progress he or she has made in meeting previously set targets. This summary is passed to the individual's managers, who read it prior to the performance review meeting. At the meeting, the manager and employee agree targets for the individual and for the team in which they operate. At the same time, individual development needs are identified. This discussion takes account of Taylor Woodrow's corporate objectives and the objectives of the local branch or division, ensuring that the individual's targets are relevant to these. The meeting also assesses the individual's success against previous targets and identifies new targets. The outcome of all of this is to establish what are known as 'key result areas', which allow an individual's performance to be measured against agreed standards. Bonus payments then reflect the individual's success in achieving these targets.
>
> In 2000, 94% of Taylor Woodrow's surveyed employees favoured the performance and development review process, which identifies objective standards for measuring performance rather than relying on the subjective views of line managers.
>
> Source: adapted from *The Times 100 Case Studies*, 2003.

Profit sharing

> **KEY TERM**
>
> **profit sharing (or profit-related bonuses):** a financial incentive in which a proportion of a firm's profit is divided among its employees in the form of a bonus paid in addition to an employee's salary.

By relating employees' rewards directly to the performance of the company, profit sharing puts workers in a similar position to shareholders, linking them more firmly to company objectives and avoiding the individualistic approach of PRP systems.

The system has a number of advantages:

- It may help to reduce problems related to a feeling of 'them and us' between employees and management or shareholders.
- It may lessen resistance to change because the focus is on the profits of the whole organisation rather than an individual's job performance. Financial rewards only result if the organisation as a whole does well.

- If the profit share is large enough, it can provide staff with a personal incentive to keep costs down and productivity up in order to improve profits. For example, at John Lewis, the profit share has at times been over 20% of annual salary.

Problems with the system include the following:
- Unless the profit share amounts to a reasonable proportion of salary, employees are unlikely to consider it a significant incentive and hence it will have little or no effect on motivation and behaviour.
- As it is not linked to individual performance, it might encourage the **free-rider problem**, where certain workers put in less effort, knowing that all employees receive the same rewards.
- Rewards fluctuate with the performance of the company and this can cause uncertainty in financial planning if employees come to depend on them.
- Large payouts from profits may affect both shareholder dividends and profit retained for investment, with adverse consequences for the firm.

 FILE

In 2003 profit-related bonuses at the alcoholic drinks maker Bacardi-Martini were up to 15% of salary. In addition, there was free private health insurance (including family members), life insurance of four times salary and a final-salary pension for 50% of staff. Maternity pay is 100% for 18 weeks, with a phased return to work. 'We are a family business,' a company spokesman said. 'Our culture embraces not just our employees but also their families. We aim to manage our people as successfully as we manage our brand. Our employees are ambassadors for our company and everyone can make a difference.'

Source: *The Sunday Times 100 Best Companies to Work For*, 2 March 2003.

> **DID YOU KNOW?**
>
> Research evidence has shown that profit sharing, on its own, has little effect on performance, partly because individuals cannot believe that their own efforts will make a significant difference to the firm's profit level.

Senior management and chief executive officers are usually given bonuses that depend on profits or other measures of company performance. However, these are normally given as a form of performance-related pay. The assumption is that the performance of these individuals is considered a major influence on company profits and performance.

Share ownership and share options

 TERMS

share ownership: in this context, a financial incentive whereby companies give shares to their employees or sell them at favourable rates below the market price.

share options: a financial incentive in which chief executives and senior management are given the choice of buying a fixed number of shares at a fixed price, by a given date.

Share ownership is a means of encouraging workers and managers to identify more directly with company objectives, recognising that their rewards — share value and dividends — are dependent on company performance.

Share options, which are offered extensively to senior management, are becoming increasingly common. As an incentive, chief executives and senior management are often given the option to purchase a fixed number of shares, at a fixed price, by a given date. If the price of the shares on the stock exchange rises above this price, it would be in the individual's interest to buy the shares at the fixed price and sell them at the market price.

Example

As an incentive bonus, in January 2003, Susan Levitt was given a share option by her employer ABC plc, to buy 1,000 shares at £1.20 per share, the share option to be available until July 2005. In January 2003, the shares were trading at £1.00. Susan decided not to take up the share option at that time, as she would be paying more for the shares then they were worth on the market.

Since then the company has performed well and shares are now (September 2003) trading at £3.00 per share. Susan decides to take up the share option, buying the 1,000 shares at £1.20 each and then immediately selling them on the stock market for £3.00 each. Susan has therefore paid £1,200 for the shares and sold them for £3,000, making a profit of £1,800 on the deal. If she held the share option until July 2005, she would have to buy the shares for £1,200, regardless of their market value, or forgo the option.

Source: Gwen Coates, 'Money, motivation and management', *Business Review*, September 2003.

The benefit of share options is that they are believed to provide senior management with the incentive to perform at their very best. However, there are some problems:

- Some people suggest that it is likely to lead to short-termism, i.e. a focus on improving performance when the share option is due, in order to make a profit from the sale of shares, rather than a long-term commitment to improved performance.
- A criticism that has been prominent in the press in the last few years is that share options can lead to excessive financial rewards in the board-room, when the workforce may deserve just as much credit as the directors.

Fringe benefits

 TERM

fringe benefits: benefits received by employees in addition to their wages or salary.

Fringe benefits are a way of rewarding employees without actually increasing their wage or salary. Common fringe benefits include discounts when buying the firm's products, subsidised meals, the provision of sports facilities, a company pension scheme, a company car and private medical insurance.

FACT FILE

The new boss of Lloyds TSB has been awarded one of the country's most generous pay packages. Details of the package given to Eric Daniels, an American who becomes chief executive of the high-street bank in June 2003, are expected to spark renewed accusations of corporate excess in the country's boardrooms.

Daniels, who was previously Lloyds TSB retail director, will receive a 'housing allowance' of £100,000 a year paid in 12 instalments; up to £33,000 annually to cover the private school fees of his son; £25,000 to pay for his personal tax and financial planning advice; £1,000 a month for a car; and £175,000 for a deposit, should he buy a home worth more than £1 million.

These perks are in addition to Daniels' salary of £700,000, an annual bonus worth up to the same amount, and a golden hello worth more than

£1.5 million. Sir Peter Ellwood, his predecessor, is looking forward to a £400,000 a year pension despite the bank's recent lacklustre performance.

Shareholders are questioning whether such rewards are justified, especially at a time when share prices and profits are falling. But Lloyds TSB defended the package: 'This is what you have to offer to attract someone of Eric Daniels' calibre. The bonus scheme has tough performance-related conditions.'

Source: adapted from an article in the *Sunday Times*, 4 May 2003, reproduced in Gwen Coates, 'Money, motivation and management', *Business Review*, September 2003.

WHAT DO YOU THINK?

Interesting questions to consider include:
- Can any one individual make such a difference to the performance of a company as to justify such huge bonuses?
- What is the likely impact of such huge bonuses on the workforce, who in comparison receive very modest bonuses, if any?

EXAMINER'S VOICE

Remember when assessing or evaluating contentious points of view like this, always support your arguments with evidence and analysis.

All add to the cost of employing labour, but are expected to pay for themselves by encouraging staff loyalty and commitment, and also by reducing labour turnover. Substantial fringe benefits are more common at senior management level (see the fact file above), which in turn leads to conflict between workers and management, especially in so-called single-status firms (see Chapter 24).

Money as a motivator

Is money a major motivator? It is obviously important, but most evidence suggests that it is not a major motivator in the long term. Ask yourself why so many very wealthy people continue to work when financially they have no need to. Perhaps their reasons are related to Maslow's self-esteem and self-actualisation needs.

Money as a motivator can also lead to serious problems for both individuals and organisations:
- Rewards fluctuate with the performance of the company and this can cause uncertainty in financial planning if employees come to depend upon rewards.

EXAMINER'S VOICE

An important point to consider when deciding on appropriate motivational tools to employ is the timescale. It is relatively easy to motivate people with financial incentives in the short term (or create 'movement' according to Herzberg), but much harder in the longer term.

- If financial incentives are high and very firmly based on quantity, quality may be sacrificed in the drive to produce or sell more, with serious long term consequences for organisations. This is easy to understand in a manufacturing situation where actual products are being produced. But it is also apparent in the service sector. For example, the substantial monetary incentives provided to salespeople in the financial services sector (pensions, mortgages and insurance) to encourage them to increase the sales of these products has resulted in customers finding, years later, that they had been sold inappropriate products for their particular needs and have as a consequence lost vast amounts of money. Complaints have been made to the ombudsman over the misselling of pensions, mortgages and insurance by financial services companies, resulting in huge customer relations problems that have seriously affected their reputations.

- If rewards are based on individual performance, it can cause conflict between employees, especially where employees' contribution cannot be measured objectively and employees are doing the same job.

There are several reasons why financial incentives are used:

- Firms want to overcome or at least reduce resistance to change. By paying bonuses to those who retrain or learn new systems, a firm is likely to be able to implement change more easily.

- Many managers still see money as a major means of control.

- Firms are looking to meet short-term goals, and financial rewards are successful at encouraging what Herzberg termed 'movement'.

EXAMINER'S VOICE

Try to consider the reasons for wanting to motivate staff. Is it to increase production or is it to improve job satisfaction? Remember Herzberg said that 'A reward once given becomes a right', meaning that employees can get used to the financial rewards and take them for granted.

FACT FILE

Financial rewards at Lush, the handmade cosmetics retailer, stress individual responsibility and teamwork. Whenever staff outsell the same day last year by more than 10%, they are given £1 extra an hour, taking the basic pay to at least £5.50 an hour. Shona Macdonald, 37-year-old manager of the Brighton store, says: 'There is no limit to the bonus that you can make and Lush has the most generous scheme I have ever come across.'

Source: *The Sunday Times 100 Best Companies to Work For*, 2 March 2003.

PRACTICE EXERCISE 1

Total: 50 marks (45 minutes)

1 Explain what 'time rates' are and why they are usually used to pay clerical and administrative workers.
(6 marks)

2 Explain the meaning of 'piece rates' (piecework).
(3 marks)

3 Identify and explain two problems a business might encounter as a result of using piece rates to pay its employees.
(6 marks)

4 Explain the term 'performance-related pay' (PRP). *(3 marks)*

5 Briefly explain two advantages and two disadvantages to a business of using performance-related pay. *(8 marks)*

6 Identify and explain one advantage and one disadvantage to a business of using a system of profit sharing to reward employees. *(6 marks)*

7 Identify and explain one advantage and one disadvantage to a business of using share ownership as a means of providing financial incentives for employees. *(6 marks)*

8 What is a share option? *(3 marks)*

9 State three examples of fringe benefits that a business might offer its employees. *(3 marks)*

10 Explain two problems that might result from using financial incentives to motivate employees. *(6 marks)*

PRACTICE EXERCISE 2

Total: 15 marks (15 minutes)

TGI Friday's

TGI Friday's began as a 1960s New York singles bar. It was expanded by Dallas-based Carlson Restaurants and opened in the UK in 1985 after the franchise was bought by Whitbread.

The corporate identity is strictly enforced: kitchen staff replicate pictured dishes, every outlet has an American-diner look, and Jan Dalton, a typical manager, who works at the Kingston upon Thames branch, aims 'to create a consistent, good-value meal and great experience every time'. Four out of five staff feel that they contribute to the firm's success. They wear efforts on their sleeves, with metal pins given for meeting the company values of balance, enjoyment, excellence and integrity. 'People respond to a bit of personal recognition. They might joke about it, but they all wear them,' says Dalton.

Managers have the independence to set up their own reward schemes, offering free beer or a weekend's use of their company car, and 68% of staff think they have good benefits compared with other companies within the industry.

Salary is tied in with tests. Pay for many hovers around the minimum wage, but bar staff can almost double their £12,480 pay by passing tests to join the elite '100 club' for top-grade bartenders. Waiters keep tips, which can be £100 a night, sharing a proportion with cleaners and kitchen staff. There is an emphasis on internal promotion.

The firm offers a sharesave scheme and a buy-four-shares-get-one-free scheme (25% of staff own shares). Other benefits includes 9 weeks of full pay for staff on maternity leave plus a bonus of 9 weeks' pay 3 months after being recruited.

Source: adapted from *The Sunday Times 100 Best Companies to Work For*, 2 March 2003.

Question

To what extent do TGI Friday's motivational techniques depend upon financial incentives?

CASE STUDY Richer Sounds: 'all singing from the same hymn book'

Making work fun is a concept that the UK's largest hi-fi retailer, Richer Sounds, takes very seriously, according to Julie Abraham, its stock control director. 'I spent 4 years with IBM, where everybody did everything "properly". I came here, and people wear jeans and shorts in the summer. I wasn't sure if it was going to work for me but you just get hooked.' Julian Richer, the founder and chairman, was 19 when he opened his first store in 1978. He now has more than 50, as well as mail order and internet services. The Richer approach aims to achieve unparalleled customer service through highly motivated staff (or colleagues, as they are known).

Although the company has changed dramatically over the years, Richer still maintains a presence and ensures that his employees are kept motivated. 'We all know what we're working for and how our work fits in,' says Lol Lecanu, the marketing manager. 'Everybody is singing from the same hymn book, and the company made me understand my role and how I have an impact on the company.'

Communication is excellent, with all staff having ample opportunity to give feedback at seminars, suggestion meetings and branch dinners. Teresa Chapman, Richer's personal assistant, says: 'You can speak to people at all levels. If anyone wants to see Julian, he'll see them as soon as he can. That's policy.' The business has a very open communications policy to ensure there is always awareness and discussion among colleagues. Results and performance ratings of stores and of individuals, for example, are regularly measured and examined. This means that colleagues are very much aware of how they are performing and that their efforts are being noticed.

Salaries are high for the retail industry: a senior sales assistant can expect £18,000. The perks are also impressive: the loan of holiday homes in locations such as St Tropez and Venice; trips in the company jet; free massages, facials and pedicures at Christmas. There is even a take-your-pet-to-work scheme.

Colleagues are encouraged to take on new responsibilities, and promotion from within is the norm; the majority of head office staff have worked on the shop-floor. 'The beauty of Richer Sounds is that it is willing to recognise people's potential, and allow them to develop into a role that they may not have previously considered,' says Lecanu, who started her career 11 years ago with a summer job on the shop-floor. 'I think if I had been a store manager for another company and wanted to be a marketing manager, I don't think many companies would have taken me seriously.'

When it comes to motivating staff, Richer is a great believer in measuring performance and then recognising and rewarding achievement. All customers, for example, are asked to rate the quality of the service they have received; salespeople who are rated excellent receive a bonus, while those rated poor are penalised. Each colleague's rating is measured regularly and performance is discussed.

Colleagues are also encouraged to contribute to the suggestions scheme, which has a cash bonus of at least £5 for each idea. It has been remarkably successful, producing on average 20 suggestions a year from each employee.

Does the approach work?

There is no point in providing a range of incentives or adopting a particular management approach unless it actually improves business performance. In the case of Richer Sounds the results are impressive: as well as its incredibly high sales per square foot, Richer Sounds has extremely low rates of labour turnover, absenteeism (1–2%) and theft. In a recent *Sunday Times* survey, an impressive 90% of colleagues found their teams 'fun to work with', 91% of staff had faith in Julian Richer's leadership, 87% thought he was inspirational and 98% said that the company had strong principles for treating customers well.

Source: adapted from *The Sunday Times 100 Best Companies to Work For*, 2 March 2003, and Andrew Gillespie, 'On the Richer scale', *Business Review*, November 1998.

Questions

Total: 50 marks (60 minutes)

1 Identify and explain **one** form of financial incentive used by Richer Sounds to motivate its workforce.

(6 marks)

2 Analyse **two** non-financial incentives that are used in Richer Sounds and explain how they motivate staff.

(8 marks)

3 Salaries at Richer Sounds are relatively high for the retail industry. Evaluate the extent to which this is what motivates its staff.

(15 marks)

4 Explain **one** possible disadvantage of giving managers the independence to set up their own reward scheme.

(6 marks)

5 Discuss whether it is easier to motivate workers with financial incentives in the short term rather than in the longer term.

(15 marks)

Leadership and management style

In this chapter the difference between leadership and management is explained and different styles of management and leadership are contrasted: authoritarian, paternalistic and democratic. McGregor's Theory X and Y management styles are compared. The chapter also compares team-based management styles to the more traditional 'them and us' approach and relates this to the concept of single status. It concludes by examining the factors that influence the optimum style of management and leadership.

KEY TERMS

leadership: deciding on a direction for a company in relation to its objectives and inspiring staff to achieve those objectives.
management: getting things done by organising other people to do it.

Management is a science which can be taught and leadership is an art which cannot. Leaders can be found and encouraged but they exist only because they have certain inherent factors...Today because employees have as much information as their managers, leadership is even more vital. Ten years ago a successful company could have got away with only a quarter of its managers having leadership; now it has to be more then 50%.

Ian Smith, managing director of *Oracle*

There is no inherent quality which turns those who get to the top into leaders. Most will remain managers concerned with the day-to-day activity of the organisation, unable or unwilling to elevate and give vision to their followers.

John Hunt, *Managing People at Work*

Source: both quotations from Hugh Thompson, 'Leadership must be on the ball', *Daily Telegraph*, 14 December 2003.

Management styles

Management styles are the manner and approach of the head of an organisation or department towards his or her staff. They are sometimes called leadership styles because a leader's manner will affect the leader's personal relationships with employees. For example, some leaders will inspire loyalty, some respect and some fear. Management style will dictate the extent to which delegation takes place and whether employees are consulted on important decisions.

EXAMINER'S VOICE

Laissez-faire management is not explained in this chapter because it is not included in the AQA specification for A-level Business Studies. However, it is included in Figure 19.1 (see p. 168).

Four main categories of management style are used widely for purposes of analysis: democratic, paternalistic, authoritarian (or dictatorial) and laissez-faire. These were introduced in Chapter 19 (see p. 168).

Authoritarian management

 TERM

authoritarian management: a Taylorite style of management in which communication tends to be one-way and top-down.

Authoritarian management takes McGregor's Theory X approach (see pp. 206–07), using rewards for good behaviour and performance, and penalties for bad performance. Authoritarian managers employ formal systems with strict controls. The advantages of this approach are that there are clear lines of authority and it can result in quick decisions. However, it can cause frustration and resentment because the system is so dependent on the manager and because of the non-participation of workers in the decision-making process.

Paternalistic management

 TERM

paternalistic management: a management style in which employees are consulted but decision making remains firmly at the top.

The paternalistic management style reflects Mayo's work on human relations and the lower- and middle-level needs of Maslow's model. The workforce is treated as a family — there is close supervision, but real attempts are made to gain the respect and acceptance of employees. This is really a type of author-itarian management style, but with the manager trying to look after what he or she perceives to be the needs of his or her subordinates. The main advantage is that workers recognise that the manager is trying to support their needs.

Democratic management

 TERM

democratic management: a management style involving two-way commu-nication and considerable delegation.

Democratic management is related to Maslow's higher-level needs and Herzberg's motivators and follows McGregor's Theory Y approach (see pp. 206–07). Usually managers and employees take decisions jointly, or workers are consulted and their views are taken into account.

The major advantage of democratic management is that the participation of workers in decision making allows input from people with relevant skills and knowledge, which may lead to improved morale and better-quality decisions. However, the decision-making process might be slower because of the need to consult and discuss, and there might be concern as to where power lies and whether loss of management control is a danger.

 YOU KNOW?

Participative leadership styles involve consulting with subordinates and evaluating their opinions and sugges-tions before making a decision. Devolved leadership styles are similar to participative leadership styles.

McGregor's Theory X and Theory Y

Douglas McGregor (1906–64) was an American psychologist whose book, *The Human Side of Enterprise* (first published in 1960), popularised his view that managers can be grouped into two types: Theory X and Theory Y.

McGregor conducted research into the attitudes of managers towards their employees. He found that the majority of managers assumed that their workers did not enjoy work, did not want to work and were motivated primarily by money; he termed this type of management approach **Theory X** and noted that it was likely to be self-fulfilling. It is an authoritarian approach in which the manager tells workers what to do and supervises them doing it. Such an approach can be useful in a crisis situation or in organisations with many constantly changing or part-time workers, who need clear instructions and clear supervision.

The alternative, minority view that emerged from McGregor's research was that managers assumed that workers enjoyed work, wanted to contribute their ideas and wished to gain satisfaction from employment. He termed this a **Theory Y** approach. It is likely to be a democratic style in which the manager delegates responsibility and authority, and therefore involves staff much more in decision making.

A Theory X manager assumes that workers:

- are lazy, dislike work and are motivated by money
- need to be supervised and controlled or they will underperform
- have no wish or ability to help make decisions or take on responsibility
- are not interested in the needs of the organisation and lack ambition

In describing Theory X, McGregor commented:

> Behind every managerial decision or action are assumptions about human nature and human behaviour. A few of these are remarkably pervasive:
>
> 1. The average human being has an inherent dislike of work and will avoid it if he can.
> 2. Because of this human characteristic, most people must be coerced to get them to put forth adequate effort towards the achievement of organisational objectives.
> 3. The average human being prefers to be directed, wishes to avoid responsibility, has relatively little ambition, wants security above all.
>
> Source: Douglas McGregor, *The Human Side of Enterprise*, 1987.

A Theory Y manager assumes that:

- workers have many different needs, enjoy work and seek satisfaction from it
- workers will organise themselves and take responsibility if they are trusted to do so
- poor performance is likely to be due to boring or monotonous work or poor management
- workers wish to, and should, contribute to decisions

According to McGregor, in Theory Y:

> The expenditure of physical and mental effort in work is as natural as play or rest...

> The average human being learns, under proper conditions, not only to accept but to seek responsibility...

> The capacity to exercise a relatively high degree of imagination, ingenuity and creativity in the solution of organisational problems is widely, not narrowly, distributed in the population...

Source: Douglas McGregor, *The Human Side of Enterprise*, 1987.

e EXAMINER'S VOICE

Try to integrate topics. In considering styles of management, relate the use of a particular management style to the level of motivation among the workforce, or to the suitability of a particular motivational tool, or to a particular motivational theorist.

McGregor's Theory X approach is clearly linked to the views of Taylor and to Adam Smith's idea of 'economic man'. In practice, many firms use this approach, especially at shop-floor level where money and control may be the main tools of influence. The Theory Y approach is clearly linked to Maslow's higher-level needs and Herzberg's motivators. It was also a forerunner of much of the later Japanese approach to management (see Chapter 34).

DID YOU KNOW?

'Economic man' (a term coined by Adam Smith) is an assumption that human behaviour is based on rational economic motives, principally the desire for financial reward.

'Team-based' versus 'them and us' styles and single status

Increasingly, firms are employing workers in teams. This is resulting in significant changes to the role of managers. They are seen more as facilitators and supporters than as supervisors, and are there to help teams of employees fulfil their potential and meet company objectives. For this changing role to be effective, managers and employees must have trust and confidence in each other's abilities and be focused on meeting company objectives. To gain this trust, managers need to delegate responsibility to workers to enable them to take full control of their own work. This is a major move away from the more traditional 'them and us' approach. In the latter approach, managers did not communicate regularly with workers — their job was to instruct and closely supervise workers, who obediently carried out tasks without question.

Some organisations try to overcome 'them and us' differences by treating all staff equally. For example, all employees, at whatever level of the organisation, may be known as associates (Rover) or colleagues (Richer Sounds and Asda). This emphasises the idea of the whole organisation being a team. This is usually linked to a move away from traditional hierarchies and their focus on status.

KEY TERM

single status: an approach in which all staff are given the same terms and conditions of employment.

In some organisations, such as those described above, firms have abandoned separate canteens and car parks for management and they pay salaries to all staff (but at different levels depending on their skills and responsibilities). All staff are, in effect, treated in the same way. Organisations adopting this type of approach, which includes many of the major Japanese manufacturing companies, are known as **single-status firms**.

> **WHAT DO YOU THINK?**
>
> The increase in single status has not changed the fact that chief executives and other senior management are still receiving huge bonuses and pensions compared to their employees. Why?

In recent years, the distinctive features of the Japanese approach to management have had an enormous influence on management thinking and management style. The approach is a democratic style of management, with an emphasis on trust between managers and workers, and extensive delegation of responsibility and authority to teams of workers. This is complemented by the development of highly skilled and well-trained workers who are able to take responsibility and control their own work and quality. The methods used include kaizen/continuous improvement groups and quality circles (see Chapter 34).

What is the most appropriate management style?

One approach to deciding what is the most appropriate management style is to consider the extent to which the needs of the task or the needs of the people involved are dominant. Much of the research in this area suggests that managers are likely to be focused either on tasks or on relationships with people. Intuition suggests that authoritarian managers are more likely to be focused on tasks, while democratic managers are more likely to be focused on relationships. However, it is more likely that the particular circumstances of the company will dictate the most appropriate approach. For example, if a company is facing massive competition and declining sales, its management will probably be very task focused because the company's survival is at stake. This is likely to be the case even if management is usually very democratic in its approach.

> **e EXAMINER'S VOICE**
>
> There is not complete agreement on the best style of management/ leadership. Base your arguments on the circumstances.

> **DID YOU KNOW?**
>
> Culture, by affecting leadership and management styles in an organisation, will be a major influence on the degree and effectiveness of delegation and consultation. The culture of an organisation will also affect the amount of resistance to change and therefore the ability of new management to impose its style or decisions on subordinates.

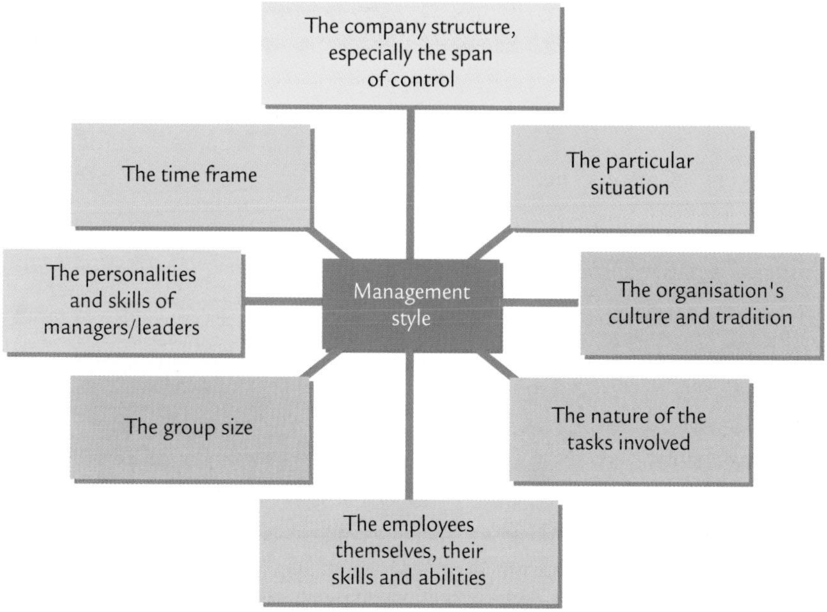

The company structure, especially the span of control

The time frame

The particular situation

The personalities and skills of managers/leaders

Management style

The organisation's culture and tradition

The group size

The nature of the tasks involved

The employees themselves, their skills and abilities

Figure 24.1
Influences on the choice of management style

A broader approach is to suggest that the question of which is the most appropriate management style depends on a number of different factors, as shown in Figure 24.1.

Using this framework, it is easy to see that the most appropriate style of management should change according to circumstances and it may well be a mixture of all the factors shown. For example, in a crisis situation an autocratic style can be the most appropriate. In a stable situation, with well-trained, skilled and experienced staff, a democratic style of management is likely to be best. Probably the worst situation is where an authoritarian approach is used with highly skilled and experienced staff in normal circumstances, as this is likely to alienate staff. Equally, a very democratic or even laissez-faire style of management in an emergency situation, or where workers are inexperienced and unskilled, is likely to lead to real problems.

It might be difficult for managers to change their style to suit different situations, either because of their personalities or because of internal or external constraints on the organisation. Furthermore, employees might feel insecure if managers constantly change their style as the situation changes.

DID YOU KNOW?

Management style can greatly influence the attitudes and motivation of employees. McGregor's Theory X and Y clearly indicates this, while Herzberg's motivators suggest that a democratic management style is the most appropriate to motivate workers.

EXAMINER'S VOICE

Remember to apply the styles of management to the case you are given.

CHAPTER 24 Leadership and management style

1 Distinguish between leadership and management.   *(6 marks)*

2 Describe the main characteristics of McGregor's Theory X manager.   *(6 marks)*

3 Describe the main characteristics of McGregor's Theory Y manager.   *(6 marks)*

4 Outline the main characteristics of an authoritarian management style.   *(4 marks)*

5 Outline the main characteristics of a paternalistic management style.   *(4 marks)*

6 Outline the main characteristics of a democratic management style.   *(4 marks)*

7 Distinguish between team-based styles of leadership and a 'them and us' approach.   *(6 marks)*

8 What are single-status firms?   *(5 marks)*

9 Discuss the extent to which there is a link between the Theory X manager and the authoritarian and paternalistic management styles.   *(9 marks)*

HSA Healthcare

HSA Healthcare is a financial services company which provides health plans and hospital benefits for individuals and families. Although it has been in business for 80 years and has an excellent reputation with the public, when Des Benjamin, its chief executive, arrived in 2000 he found it 'Dickensian'. The offices had not been redecorated for decades — they were all 'brown, brown, brown' — and equipment was scarce: three members of staff would share a phone. Even worse, the company had an autocratic management style. Staff looked downtrodden and, with little or no training, had low confidence, low expectations and low ambitions.

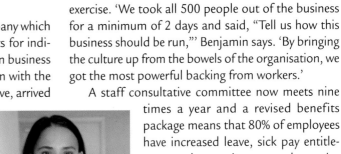

A new board of directors initiated a cultural change exercise. 'We took all 500 people out of the business for a minimum of 2 days and said, "Tell us how this business should be run,"' Benjamin says. 'By bringing the culture up from the bowels of the organisation, we got the most powerful backing from workers.'

A staff consultative committee now meets nine times a year and a revised benefits package means that 80% of employees have increased leave, sick pay entitlement and paternity pay, and superior parental leave. All staff are eligible for individual performance-related bonuses, and 80% of them for profit-related pay.

Source: *The Sunday Times 100 Best Companies to Work For*, 2 March 2003.

Question

Using the above information about HSA Healthcare, explain how a change in management style can influence the motivation of the workforce.   *(8 marks)*

PRACTICE EXERCISE 3   Total: 25 marks (30 minutes)

The Japanese of Europe

Thanks to Sven Goran Eriksson and his success as coach of the England football team, Swedish management style is in the news. Similarities with Japanese styles of management, such as reaching decisions through a consensual process (agreement among everybody involved), have led to the Swedes being referred to as the Japanese of Europe. Research work by Julian Birkinshaw of the London Business School suggests that Swedish management style has a number of distinctive characteristics:

■ It is very consensus oriented and fairly pragmatic. Egos do not get in the way of making good decisions.

■ It is a funny combination of very plain-speaking discussions as well as very polite ones, whereas in England we tend to talk around issues and can often be quite confrontational.

■ It is ultimately an empowerment model: that is to say, dissent is encouraged and senior managers listen to junior people and seek their opinions. These things together mean that good decisions are made.

Birkinshaw says that empowerment is a more natural process in Sweden than in the UK or the USA because research suggests that the Swedes prefer group ideas rather than individual decisions. They are also relatively non-hierarchical: 'the power distance between the top of society and the bottom is relatively small'.

TOPFOTO

However, there can be problems with the Swedish management style, according to Birkinshaw:

> The risk is perhaps an obvious one, that, if you let go and empower people to do as they see fit, you are putting an awful lot of trust in the individual. If it backfires, well think of Nick Leeson and Barings Bank. You are basically acting on trust.

Source: BBC News, 6 September 2001 (www.bbc.co.uk).

Questions

1 Assess the nature of Swedish management style in relation to your knowledge of different management styles and of McGregor's Theory X and Y.   *(10 marks)*

2 To what extent is the Swedish management style appropriate for (a) a football manager such as Sven Goran Eriksson and (b) the manager of a busy call centre?   *(15 marks)*

CHAPTER 25

Introduction to human resource management

This chapter provides a brief introduction to, and overview of, human resource management (HRM). 'Hard' and 'soft' HRM are defined and the concept of HRM is compared to that of 'personnel management' using the principles of horizontal and vertical matching. The personnel functions are identified and the key factors influencing HRM are studied.

Hard or soft human resource management?

Some commentators suggest that there are two types of human resource management: 'hard' and 'soft'.

- **'Hard' human resource management.** Hard HRM treats employees as a resource, just like any other resource, to be monitored and used in an efficient manner in order to achieve the strategic objectives of the organisation. This type of HRM includes workforce planning, analysing the current need for employees, predicting the future demand for employees, predicting the future supply of employees and predicting labour turnover.
- **'Soft' human resource management.** Soft HRM views employees as valuable assets to be developed. Because of their skills and expertise, they are a major source of competitive advantage for the firm and hence of vital importance in achieving the strategic objectives of the organisation. This type of HRM focuses on motivational issues and organisational culture, leadership approaches and industrial relations.

Human resource management or personnel management?

Since the 1980s, **human resource management** has tended to replace **personnel management** in describing the function within business that focuses on the selection, appraisal, development and reward of people. Referring to people as human resources might sound mechanical, but in fact the objective of the approach is really the opposite. The intention is to emphasise a total strategy related to a firm's most valued resource, rather than the set of functions that a personnel management department was commonly

e EXAMINER'S VOICE

HRM is possibly the most widely misunderstood part of the AS course. Check that you understand this concept and can apply your understanding to case studies.

expected to undertake. Table 25.1 indicates some of the main differences between human resource management and personnel management.

The personnel management approach	The human resource management approach
• is tactical	• is strategic
• is short term and responds to policies introduced in other areas of the organisation	• is long term and leads policies in other areas of the organisation
• tackles issues separately with no overall framework	• places issues within a clearly defined and integrated framework that benefits the organisation
• tends to operate in organisations with traditional ways of working, where there is little employee involvement in decision making	• emphasises the importance of involving employees in decision making
• may operate in traditionally unionised organisations	• encourages single-status agreements and places less emphasis on the role of trade unions
• focuses on getting identical rewards and conditions for groups of individuals	• focuses on individual contracts and payment and reward systems
• tends to specialise in all of the personnel function activities — recruitment, selection and training etc.	• tends to devolve personnel function activities, such as recruitment, selection and training, to departmental managers, concentrating instead on developing policies, planning, monitoring and evaluating

Table 25.1 Human resource management versus personnel management

Horizontal and vertical matching

Two principles, known as **horizontal matching** and **vertical matching**, serve to highlight further the difference between HRM and personnel management.

Human resource management takes the view that each individual policy adopted in the management of people, such as recruitment, training and payment systems, should fit with every other policy used in the area. This is the principle of horizontal matching within the work of the personnel function itself. For example, an attempt to introduce flexible working needs to be considered in relation to the introduction of appropriate payment systems, training methods and appraisal systems.

Figure 25.1 illustrates how all of the policies adopted by HRM fit together. This demonstrates horizontal matching. For example, individuals are selected, they perform their tasks and they are appraised. Appraisal leads to reward and payment, which in turn has an effect on performance. Appraisal also leads to training and development, which in turn affects performance and can lead to selection for a more senior position.

Figure 25.1 HRM policies and horizontal matching

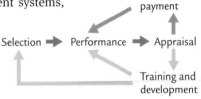

Source: adapted from C. J. Fombrun, N. M. Tichy and M. A. Devanna, *Strategic Human Resource Management*, John Wiley, 1984.

Human resource management policies should fit with the overall strategic position of an organisation. This means that how people are managed is determined largely by the goals the company has set itself and that employees are organised to ensure that these goals are met. This is achieved by vertical matching between HRM policies and outcomes, and the corporate objectives and long-term direction of the company as a whole. Thus a company that is attempting to expand significantly may consider moving towards a more decentralised structure and will need an HRM strategy that takes account of this in relation to the staff it recruits and promotes and in relation to training and payment systems.

Figure 25.2 illustrates the idea of vertical matching. It demonstrates how the approach of HRM is integrated into the long-term competitive position of the firm by linking the individual HRM policies and outcomes developed in Figure 25.1 with the goals of the organisation as a whole.

Figure 25.2 HRM *and vertical matching*

HRM policies ➡ HRM outcomes ➡ Organisational outcomes

Personnel functions

The real difference between human resource management and personnel management relates to the overall approach or philosophy adopted rather than to the activities that are undertaken. These activities remain the same whether undertaken by the personnel department or the human resource department or by delegation to other departments, and can be considered as part of the personnel function of the organisation.

The key activities covered by the personnel function are:
- human resource or workforce planning
- recruitment and selection
- training and development
- appraisal
- consultation
- collective bargaining
- wage and salary systems
- fringe benefits
- disciplinary and grievance procedures
- health and safety issues
- employment legislation

Factors affecting human resource management

As with any other aspect of business, human resource management will be affected by a whole range of issues both inside and outside the organisation:
- The financial constraints in an organisation may affect human resource

management in terms of what plans it will be able to implement in relation to staff training and development.

- In the case of financial constraints, the HRM section may not be as adversely affected if the corporate culture is such that human resource management has a high profile and human resources are recognised as a valuable asset that needs to be trained and developed.
- If the organisational structure changes — for example, if it becomes flatter or if delayering takes place — this will have a major impact on human resource management.
- Trade unions and the relationship between employers and workers will influence human resource management in its drive to introduce change, such as flexible working practices.
- The introduction of new technology will lead to changes in the amount and type of labour required and training requirements. It will also have an impact on workers' motivation.
- How a business develops or expands will influence human resource requirements if, for example, unprofitable areas are closed down or the focus of the business changes.
- The actions of competitors can lead to changes. For example, if there is a shortage of skills in a particular area, poaching of workers may occur and salaries may be forced up.
- Changes in the market and the economy will cause changes in demand for products and services, which in turn will lead to changes in the demand for labour in an organisation — a need to expand in certain areas and cut back in others.
- Government legislation in relation to equal opportunities and conditions of employment will affect human resource management.
- The structure of the population will affect human resource policies: for example, the UK's ageing population and the desire, or need, on the part of the elderly to work longer.

---

1 Briefly explain the importance of human resource management in an organisation. *(5 marks)*

2 Distinguish between 'hard' and 'soft' human resource management. *(6 marks)*

3 State two activities or issues that are included under 'hard' human resource management. *(2 marks)*

4 State two activities or issues that are included under 'soft' human resource management. *(2 marks)*

5 Explain three differences between human resource management and personnel management. *(9 marks)*

6 What is horizontal matching in relation to human resource management? *(4 marks)*

7 What is vertical matching in relation to human resource management? *(4 marks)*

8 Briefly show how a firm's human resource management policy is linked to its company goals. *(4 marks)*

9 List five activities covered by the personnel function in an organisation. *(5 marks)*

10 Identify and explain three factors that might influence human resource management in an organisation. *(9 marks)*

Personnel management versus human resource management

Each of the following two situations corresponds to either the personnel management approach or the human resource management approach.

Situation A

Mike works in an engineering firm where most of his time is taken up with recruitment, training and development, and disciplinary issues. He has an assistant who does most of the interviewing with managers from the relevant departments that require staff. Mike handles most of the disciplinary and grievance work. The disciplinary procedures mean that the appropriate departmental managers issue a first warning, but Mike is responsible for any subsequent warnings and further action. This action is taken in the presence of the departmental manager and also the trade union representative. Mike spends a great deal of his time negotiating and consulting with the trade union repre-

sentatives on a range of issues related to pay and conditions. In addition, he and his assistant meet with individual workers to discuss their particular problems. Mike or his assistant visits each departmental manager daily to discuss any problems and to obtain information about absenteeism. They also use these visits as an opportunity to talk to the workers and to deal with their problems.

Situation B

Amanda works in an insurance company and has a number of assistants. The aim of the insurance company is to provide its customers with quality advice and service at competitive prices. Amanda's boss is a director of the company and is mainly concerned with strategic issues and how their work fits in with the broad corporate objectives. Amanda's department has its own set of objectives. These

include reducing the levels of labour turnover and absenteeism for the company as a whole by 10% within the next year. Because of the competitive nature of the industry, they are also looking at ways of restructuring the way people work in order to improve efficiency. Amanda and her staff spend much of their time considering these issues, assessing current policies and practices, coming up with proposals, and involving employees in designing and evaluating them. Most of Amanda's time is spent with either her own staff or other departmental managers. She monitors absentee rates, labour turnover rates and a range of other personnel indicators on spreadsheets that are updated daily on her computer. Amanda's department provides advice to departmental managers, coordinates recruitment advertising and provides the associated paper work and correspondence, but it leaves responsibility for interviewing, appraising, disciplining and dismissing employees etc. to departmental managers and their staff.

Questions

1 Examine which of the two situations above matches the personnel management approach and which one matches the human resource management (HRM) approach. Justify your choices. *(10 marks)*

2 Use your answer to question 1 and the information in the two situations to discuss how HRM emphasises the use of employees as a major strategic resource. *(12 marks)*

3 How might the aims of an organisation be converted into human resource targets or requirements? *(8 marks)*

CHAPTER 26

Workforce planning

This chapter looks at how businesses analyse their existing workforce and forecast their future workforce needs. The internal and external factors influencing human resource requirements are discussed, leading on to a consideration of how workforce plans operate at company, local and national levels.

e **EXAMINER'S VOICE**

Workforce planning is a widely misunderstood term. It is specifically about matching the numbers of employees and the skills of the employees to a company's needs. In case studies look for evidence of planning, or lack of it.

KEY TERM

> **workforce planning (or human resource planning):** the method by which a business forecasts how many and what type of employees it needs now and in the future, and matches up the right type of employees to the needs of the business.

Workforce planning helps organisations to foresee change, to identify trends and to implement human resource policies. It is an important part of the overall strategic plan and should be centralised to ensure a whole company view.

Efficient workforce planning requires managers to question the existing employment structure at every opportunity: for example, when an employee leaves the firm, when an employee is promoted internally, when there is an increase in workload or when a new product or new technology is developed that requires employees with different skills.

The stages of workforce planning

Workforce planning involves three important stages: analysing current employees, forecasting future workforce requirements, and planning the internal and external supply of labour to meet these requirements.

Analysing current employees
It is vitally important to keep personnel records up to date in order to analyse current employees. This involves identifying how many workers there are, what type (e.g. full time or part time), and their characteristics in relation to age, length of service, qualifications, staff turnover rates and reasons, promotion patterns and retirement rates.

Forecasting future workforce requirements
Forecasting workforce requirements is important and should be done for the short term (e.g. to cover sick leave or maternity leave), medium term and long term (e.g. to meet future growth or expansion overseas). Forecasting, which should be constantly reviewed and updated, should provide estimates of how many workers are needed, what type of workers are needed, in which location they are needed and when they are needed.

Ineffective human resource forecasts can lead to any or all of the following problems, which are likely to increase costs and reduce productivity:

- recruitment and selection difficulties
- inadequately trained employees
- morale and motivation problems
- high levels of labour turnover and absenteeism
- redundancies

Organisations forecast their human resource needs by analysing both internal and external factors.

Internal factors

The following internal factors provide information about the human resources that a company needs:

- managers' local knowledge and their analysis of skill requirements
- the budget available
- past records on recruitment and promotion
- the organisation of work (e.g. cell production and teamwork or traditional production-line work)
- the impact of reorganisation, merger or takeover
- labour turnover rates
- exit interviews (discussions with staff to discover why they left)
- workers' productivity and the use of technology

External factors

External factors that are relevant to a company's human resource requirements can be either local or national.

The local factors are:
- working population
- skill and education levels
- unemployment levels
- competition
- travel to work patterns
- availability of housing and amenities
- cost of living

The national factors are:
- demographic changes related to age, gender, sector and socioeconomic groups
- the level of demand for the organisation's products
- changes in government policy

Planning the internal and external supply of labour

By analysing the current workforce and the future demand for labour, a firm can draw up plans relating to both the internal and external supply of labour.

Internal supply

The internal supply of labour is influenced by:

- **Internal promotional opportunities.** An individual promoted from within already knows about the business, its practices and culture, and will be able to adapt more quickly and easily than a newcomer. However, internal promotion usually creates another vacancy that has to be filled.
- **Training and development.** This might be particularly useful if changes are needed in skills and expertise due to, for example, a change in demand for the product.
- **Changing employment conditions.** This could occur because of increasing flexibility, the introduction of annualised hours rather than weekly hours, the use of job rotation, or the use of more part-time workers and job sharing.
- **Retirement and staff turnover.** Too high a rate of retirement among the older members of the workforce can be problematic, since a lot of experience and firm-specific knowledge will disappear from the firm. On the other hand, if a reduction of staffing is needed, a firm can offer incentives for early retirement or voluntary redundancy, which might help to maintain positive employee–employer relations during a difficult period. High staff turnover might be an indication of poor motivation and needs further investigation.
- **Legal requirements.** If, for example, redundancy is being planned as a result of a reduction in the scale of the business or a decision to delayer the organisation, acceptable procedures need to be introduced and adhered to.

External supply

The external supply of labour is influenced by both local and national factors.

Local factors include the following:

- The availability and cost of housing. For example, housing in London and some rural areas is so expensive that it is very difficult for some firms to attract labour.
- The ease and availability of transport. For example, it is difficulty to attract labour in some rural areas if workers do not own a car. Equally, parking and congestion charges for those travelling into large urban areas such as London are often very expensive.
- Local unemployment rates.

The following national factors are important:

- Government legislation in relation to employment.
- Government policy in relation to training and subsidies that might be available.
- The skills available and how these are distributed regionally: for example, the pottery skills of the workforce in Staffordshire.
- The degree to which flexible working (e.g. working at home) is the norm.

TOPFOTO

- Trends in population: for example, the ageing population in the UK and the impact of this on the workforce.
- National unemployment rates.

Overcoming labour shortages

Shortages in the supply of labour can be overcome in a number of ways:

- Outsourcing. This is the transfer of internal activity to a third party. It gives a firm the opportunity to use expertise not otherwise available in the organisation, to offload low-level administrative work and to free employees to undertake more interesting work. Areas of work that are commonly outsourced include: recruitment, especially the initial stages of dealing with enquiries and applications and carrying out standard assessment; training; and payroll activities.
- Introducing training programmes or retraining existing employees to ensure that there are appropriately qualified staff.
- Increasing mechanisation/automation to reduce the need for staff.
- Offering better terms and conditions of employment to attract more or better applicants.
- Rescheduling work or increasing overtime in order to meet changes in demand in the short term.

> **DID YOU KNOW?**
>
> The government's definition of the workforce planning process is 'activity that improves the level and application of skills, so as to achieve greater success for individuals and employers, and, ultimately, enhanced sectoral and national competitiveness'.

PRACTICE EXERCISE 1
Total: 50 marks (40 minutes)

1 Explain the term 'workforce planning' or 'human resource planning'. *(4 marks)*

2 Why is workforce planning becoming more important in business? *(4 marks)*

3 Identify three important stages in workforce planning. *(3 marks)*

4 Explain two problems that might result from an inability to assess accurately the future labour needs of a firm in relation to type and number of workers. *(6 marks)*

5 Identify two internal and two external factors that might influence human resource requirements. *(4 marks)*

6 State and explain two factors that might influence the internal supply of labour in a firm. *(6 marks)*

7 Identify and explain one local factor that might influence the external supply of labour to a firm. *(4 marks)*

8 Identify and explain two national factors that might influence the external supply of labour to a firm. *(6 marks)*

9 Outsourcing is one method of overcoming a shortage in the supply of labour. Explain the term 'outsourcing' in this context. *(5 marks)*

10 Identify and explain two other methods of overcoming a shortage in the supply of labour to a firm and therefore achieving labour targets. *(8 marks)*

PRACTICE EXERCISE 2 — Total: 40 marks (50 minutes)

Workforce planning

The UK Clothing Industry

This is an extract from the Workforce Development Plan 2001–05 for the UK clothing industry, showing how workforce planning takes place at the industry level.

Introduction

A highly skilled workforce at both managerial and technical level is absolutely vital if the industry is to grow over the coming years. Equally important is finding flexible and accessible skills development solutions to support the many small and medium-sized enterprises within the sector.

This plan sets out the main priorities for the clothing industry in the next 5 years.

The industry

The UK clothing industry produces a wide range of apparel from high fashion to ties and hats and from relatively low-cost, mass-market clothing to high-cost, branded or fashion-house garments. It employs around 140,000 people in some 4,500 companies. The sector has restructured considerably over the past 20 years and this process is continuing.

Change

In the last 20 years, import penetration has doubled and the industry has experienced a number of forces for change, which include: powerful customers such as Marks and Spencer, Next, Tesco and Asda; international price competition; the need to get products from overseas for certain types of production; the consequent proportionate reduction in the need for lesser-skilled grades and corresponding increase in the need for those with higher-level skills; current lack of skilled staff; rapid change in consumer taste and fashion; opportunities and challenges from technology and IT developments.

Employment

In the 20 years between 1973 and 1993, employment in the UK clothing industry fell by 53%. Further employment shrinkage in the next 5 years is likely to be concentrated mainly at the lower and lesser-skilled end of the employment spectrum. The opposite end of this process will be the proportionate growth of the demand for higher technical skills centred on IT, advanced manufacturing technologies and traditional handcraft skills. The industry is 70% female — mostly concentrated in the operative sections of the workforce — and has a relatively high proportion of owners who are from ethnic minorities (around 35%).

Skills gaps

(Skills gaps occur when employers believe that members of their existing workforce need additional skills in order to meet changing demands.)

The clothing industry is experiencing a wide range of skills gaps in the existing workforce. These can be summarised as being primarily within those occupations in the technical clothing skills area and in the management skills area. There are gaps in technical skills ranging from handcrafted tailoring to high-tech garment technology, and at the management level from team-management skills to marketing. Another area in which highly detailed skills gaps have been identified is in both corporate and individual-level IT skills.

Skills shortages

(Skills shortages occur when employers cannot find enough appropriate people to fill vacant positions in their workforce.)

Key current and anticipated skills shortages are: highly skilled sewing machinists; handcraft tailors and cutters; pattern cutters; high-quality finishers (including pressing).

Strategic issues

The major strategic issues for the industry over the next 5 years can be summarised as: increasing the amount of management training; creating provision for widespread higher technical-level training; designing cost-effective mechanisms for training; remedying barriers to effective recruitment such as industry image.

Source: adapted from CAPITB Trust, Sector Workforce Development Plan, 2001–05.

The National Health Service

This is an extract from a government consultation document on the workforce in the National Health Service (NHS).

Introduction

The NHS has dedicated, hard-working staff. We need more of them. The government is committed to expanding the NHS by expanding the number of doctors, nurses and other health professionals. But alongside expansion must come reform, to change the way staff work, the way they are trained and how they are educated.

Where are we now?

Current arrangements are *not*:

- built around service needs and the skills required to deliver them
- well integrated with service and financial planning
- holistic in their approach, looking across primary, secondary and tertiary care or across staff groups
- responsive to service changes and developments
- supportive of multi-disciplinary training, education and working

What changes need to be made?

- Greater integration of workforce planning and development with service and financial planning.

- More flexible deployment of staff to maximise the use of their skills and abilities.

The emphasis needs to be on:

- teamworking across professional and organisational boundaries
- flexible working to make the best use of the range of skills and knowledge that staff have
- streamlined workforce planning and development which stems from the needs of patients, not the needs of employees
- maximising the contribution of all staff to patient care and doing away with barriers that say only doctors or nurses can provide particular types of care
- modernising education and training to ensure that staff are equipped with the skills they need to work in a complex, changing NHS
- developing new, more flexible careers for staff of all professions
- expanding the workforce to meet future demands

And we need to do this not just because it is the right thing to do but because it will provide patients with the care they have the right to expect. Care must be delivered quickly, by skilled professionals, who listen to patients and provide the best possible treatment and care.

Source: adapted from 'A health service of all the talents: developing the NHS workforce', a consultation document published by the Department of Health, 2000.

Questions

1 How can organisations anticipate their changing labour needs in advance? *(10 marks)*

2 How might organisations benefit from advance planning of their workforce? *(10 marks)*

3 Read the extract on the UK clothing industry. Analyse how an individual firm in the clothing industry might benefit from the findings and recommendations of the workforce development plan. *(10 marks)*

4 Read the extract on the National Health Service. Why might it be important that the workforce planning document for the NHS was sent out to staff and other stakeholders for consultation before it was decided to go ahead with introducing the system? *(10 marks)*

CHAPTER 27

Recruitment and training

Having identified their workforce needs, firms must then ensure that an appropriate labour force is acquired. This chapter describes and examines the various processes involved:
- *how workers are recruited, comparing the benefits of internal and external recruitment*
- *the alternative methods of selection that can be used*
- *types of training: induction, on- and off-the-job training and their purposes and relative merits*
- *the potential for market failure*

Recruitment

Recruitment is about identifying the need for new employees, attracting the 'best' candidates for the job and then selecting the most suitable candidate in order to meet the staffing requirements of the organisation.

The recruitment and selection process can be summarised as shown in Figure 27.1. It requires the following stages.

Workforce planning

The human resource requirements of the organisation need to be determined by the use of workforce planning techniques (see Chapter 26). Many organisations decide to fill vacancies that occur without really considering whether there are alternatives to recruitment and selection. Good human resource management will consider alternatives, including redeployment of existing staff, increased use of overtime, employment of temporary workers, introduction of new technology and outsourcing of certain functions.

Job descriptions

Once it is established that recruitment and selection needs to take place, job analysis should be undertaken. This is where the tasks, skills, responsibilities, duties and performance level required are analysed and a job description is produced. The job description tells candidates what is expected in the job and helps the firm to identify the qualities needed in the individual to be selected for the job. It consists of the job title, the main purpose of the job, who the job holder is answerable to, the main duties and tasks contained in the job, and any authority the job holder has.

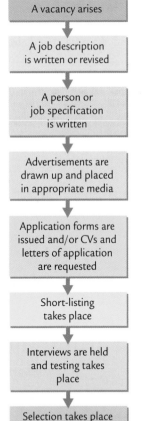

Figure 27.1 *A summary of the recruitment and selection process*

A vacancy arises

A job description is written or revised

A person or job specification is written

Advertisements are drawn up and placed in appropriate media

Application forms are issued and/or CVs and letters of application are requested

Short-listing takes place

Interviews are held and testing takes place

Selection takes place and an appointment is made

Person (job) specifications

A person (or job) specification is then drawn up. This provides details of the ideal candidate by listing the essential and desirable characteristics of that person. It is used to identify the criteria that should be used in short-listing and then in selecting the best candidate from those who apply for the position.

There are a number of different formats for a person specification. One that is widely used is Alec Rodger's seven-point plan. This uses the following criteria to describe the person most suited to the job: physical make-up, attainments or achievements, general intelligence, special aptitudes, interests, disposition or personal manner, and personal circumstances. These factors are then ranked as either essential or desirable and applicants are judged against them at interview.

Deciding on internal or external recruitment

Decisions must then be made about whether to consider **internal** or **external** sources of candidates.

Arguments in favour of recruiting internal candidates include the following:
- The employee's abilities are known already.
- Internal promotional opportunities are motivating for the workforce.
- The recruitment and selection process is quicker.
- A shorter induction period is required.
- It is less expensive.
- It reduces the risk of employing the wrong person.

Despite these advantages, internal promotion usually creates another vacancy further down the hierarchy.

In contrast, external recruitment brings the following advantages:
- It tends to provide a larger choice of well-qualified applicants.
- It brings in 'new blood' with new ways of thinking.
- It overcomes jealousies that may occur if one member of a group is promoted above his or her colleagues.
- It can help a firm to improve its understanding of how other firms operate.

Advertising media

Decisions must then be made about the most appropriate advertising media to use in order to attract the most suitable candidates.

There are many different kinds of advertising media:
- National and local newspapers.

EXAMINER'S VOICE

Opportunity cost is a concept that is relevant in every area of business, including this one. It is in a firm's interest to recruit the best person for the job at a minimum cost in terms of time and resources.

MACINTOSH DESIGNER

We are looking for a creative Macintosh designer to join our current team working on various educational titles across a range of subjects — from resource packs for teachers to magazines and revision guides for students.

The successful candidate must have a degree or equivalent in graphic design and at least two years' work experience of Quark and Illustrator, with Photoshop a useful bonus. A thorough understanding of production for print is essential and a background in magazine design would be an advantage.

We offer an attractive salary, five weeks' holiday and the opportunity to join a dynamic company located in

Freelancers Required

G&S Design is looking for freelance designers and freelance artworkers to work within a team of designers on a number of blue chip accounts.

The successful candidates will be approachable, self motivated, have a degree or equivalent in graphic design and excellent knowledge of all the usual packages.

They will also have experience working in a team and at least three year's experience in graphic design.

Interested?

Send your CV to Griffin&Seller@design.com

www.creativecountry.

CREATIVE ARTWORKER Oxo

Expanding educational publisher of books an magazines seeks a literate artworker with g design sense.

You will have previous experience of dealing complex projects involving textflow and styl and will be able to work closely with the ed creative teams to meet tight deadlines with sacrificing accuracy.

You will have acquired an expert knowledge and Illustrator (with Photoshop a useful bor sound understanding of repro after a minim years' experience. This post will suit a stror artworker with excellent Mac skills.

SENIOR INTERACTIVE DESIGNER

Greens Conferencedesign is looking for a conceptually driven Senior Designer

You will have at least 3 years' previous ex

- Trade or professional magazines.
- Job centres, which help people to find jobs locally and can also direct individuals to government-funded training schemes for young people and the unemployed, such as the New Deal and Modern Apprenticeships.
- Commercial employment agencies, which will provide shortlists of candidates for interview. Because the agencies do the advertising and initial short-listing, this removes the administrative burden from the firm. However, agencies charge quite large fees and often deal only with temporary staff.
- Specialist careers centres such as the army.
- University 'milk rounds', where companies visit universities to recruit students who are about to graduate.
- Local schools/colleges.
- Local radio, national television and the internet.
- Internal newsletters, notice boards and billboards.
- Word of mouth.
- **Headhunting**, where recruitment consultants seek the right person for a job. This tends to be used to recruit very senior managers and top-ranking professionals. The main advantage of headhunting is that headhunters may find someone who is ideal for the job, but who is not actually looking for work and would therefore not notice an advertisement. However, headhunting is expensive because it is very labour intensive.

The following article, which appeared in the *Sunday Times*, argues that advertisements are much more effective than agencies in the recruitment process:

> The advertising of jobs works best for employer and prospective employee alike. For the employer it means access to a wide range of motivated, qualified applicants, and for the prospective employee it means access to a huge job market that could never be offered by headhunters and recruitment agencies.

Unfortunately, many companies in the recruitment industry don't believe in advertising and do all they can to discourage employers from publicising their jobs. These range from the headhunters — who would rather have a researcher call up 10 or 20 people — to the agencies, which would rather pick a few names from their files and charge the employer 25% of the candidate's salary.

You might think that employers would care about this, but many think that calling up an agency or headhunter is easier. They don't want to handle all the responses to the advertisement, or there is nobody to do the interviewing, or they just can't be bothered. But some employers are beginning to realise they are spending a fortune on these methods of recruitment and getting little in return.

Source: adapted from 'Never mind the agencies, ads are just the job', *Sunday Times*, 21 September 2003.

Application forms and CVs

Candidates attracted by the vacancy will be asked to send in a completed application form and/or curriculum vitae (CV) and letter of application. An application form provides information in a standard format, making it easier to pre-select candidates. Although CVs include similar information (details of the individual, their qualifications, their experience and why they are suitable for the job), they can vary considerably and hence may be more difficult to compare.

Short-listing

The best candidate for the job must then be selected. This is usually done by assessing candidates' application forms or CVs against the criteria set out in the person specification. The result will be a short-list of a small number of applicants. References from previous employers or tutors are then requested in order to confirm information about candidates' abilities, skills and experience.

Interviews and other methods of assessment

Suitable candidates will then be called for interview and/or asked to take part in other methods of assessment. Research suggests that, although interviews are the traditional and still the most popular method of selection, they are not necessarily the most effective in indicating how well an individual will perform in a job. This is because interviewers tend to be swayed by appearance and personality, and are often overly influenced by first impressions.

For this reason, other selection techniques are often used in addition to interviews. These include:

- **Aptitude and attainment tests.** These measure how the applicant copes when presented with a particular business situation or how good the applicant is at a particular skill such as word processing, a foreign language or basic arithmetic.
- **Psychometric or personality tests.** These measure the personality, attitude and character of applicants: for example, whether they are team players or

loners, whether they are passive or assertive, how good their problem-solving skills are, how good they are at dealing with the unknown, how creative they are, and so on. These tests are more common for graduate and management-level jobs. There are criticisms about the effectiveness of psychometric tests, such as whether it is wise to want all managers to have particular, and therefore similar, characteristics and the extent to which people answer questions truthfully or simply give answers that they think will get them the job.

- **Assessment centres.** Here a group of candidates are invited to a particular location for a day or a few days for an in-depth assessment. They are likely to be observed performing a range of tasks, including oral and written activities, role-play, teamwork, presentations, simulations and case studies that reveal their leadership skills, their team-working skills, their problem-solving skills etc.

Research suggests that this latter method is the most effective one for predicting successful job performance. However, it is a very expensive and time-consuming method and tends to be restricted to large firms and government departments, and to the selection of those people who are likely to fill senior positions in the future — for example, high-flying graduate trainee programmes.

In general, the assessment method used should be the one that is the most appropriate for ensuring that the most suitable candidate is selected. Whichever method is used, it is increasingly the case that the human resource department provides support to the functional departments, allowing departmental or line managers to be much more involved in the recruitment and selection decisions.

Appointment

Once the best candidate has been selected and informed of the decision, he or she must confirm that they accept the position. At this point it is good practice to debrief those short-listed candidates who were not successful. Explaining why they were not successful can be of immense practical value to them if done sensitively and constructively. In relation to the whole process of recruitment and selection, it is vitally important that firms take into account the legal implications of equal opportunities legislation, including sex discrimination, equal pay, race relations, disability discrimination and age discrimination. This not only avoids legal challenges to decisions, but also ensures that the best candidate is appointed to the job.

INGRAM

Factors affecting methods of recruitment and selection

Methods of recruitment and selection depend on a number of factors, including:

- the level of the job within the organisation, whether shop-floor or senior management level

- the size of the organisation, whether a large multinational or a small shop
- the resources available to fund the recruitment and selection process
- the cost of any particular method — recruitment and selection can be a very expensive process and includes the cost of advertising, the cost of administering, perhaps, thousands of applications, and the time spent short-listing, interviewing and assessing
- the supply of labour — whether there are plenty of potential applicants with relevant skills and experience or whether there are very few
- cultural factors and the extent to which these dictate that internal recruitment and promotion is the norm

The importance of effective recruitment and selection

Ineffective selection can cause increased labour turnover, which in turn leads to additional costs in terms of further advertising, interviewing and training. Effective recruitment and selection could lead to lower labour turnover, lower costs, improved productivity and more highly motivated employees.

 YOU KNOW?

The Chartered Institute of Personnel and Development (CIPD) asked over 10,000 organisations to work out what it costs them every time an employee leaves. The average cost of payroll and personnel time, recruitment, interview time, placement fees, training, 'unproductive' time, induction and loss in customer service and satisfaction came out at £3,456 for each person.

Training

 TERM

training: the provision of work-related education, either on-the-job or off-the-job, involving employees being taught new skills or improving skills they already have.

Training is the process of instructing individuals about how to carry out tasks directly related to their current job. **Development**, on the other hand, involves helping individuals to realise their full potential. Development covers general growth and is not necessarily related specifically to employees' existing posts.

Training needs

The need for training essentially arises when the knowledge and skills required by the firm exceed or differ from those that workers currently possess. Training is often a response to some sort of change, whether internal or external. Possible changes are:

- the development and introduction of new products
- restructuring of the firm
- the development and introduction of new technology
- changes to procedure, including improvements to customer service

DID YOU KNOW?

DID YOU KNOW?

Many business initiatives are constrained by limited finance and this area is no different. Thus the broad objective of training and development is generally to ensure the best possible return on the firm's investment in people.

- high labour turnover
- low morale
- changes in legislation

Benefits of training

Training offers the following benefits to employees and the firm:

- It helps new employees reach the level of performance expected of experienced workers.
- It ensures that employees have the necessary skills, knowledge, attributes and qualifications for the job, both at present and in the future.
- It develops a knowledgeable and committed workforce, with increased motivation and job satisfaction.
- It increases efficiency and productivity, enabling the firm to produce high-quality products and services, which may in turn lead to improved profits.
- It can identify employees' potential and thus increase employees' job prospects and chances of promotion.
- It reduces costs in the long term by, for example, reducing the number of accidents and injuries, reducing wastage and poor-quality work, and increasing workers' productivity.
- It encourages employees to deal with change more effectively and to be more flexible: for example, about the introduction of new technology.
- It encourages employees to work towards the organisation's aims and objectives.
- It improves the image of the company. Customers will have more confidence in well-trained staff, and a better image will attract more able recruits.

Induction training

 KEY TERM

induction training: education for new employees which usually involves learning about the way the business works rather than about the particular job that the individual will do.

The aim of induction training is to help new employees settle in quickly, in order to ensure that they reach the level of performance expected of experienced workers. It includes familiarising new recruits with the layout of the business, health and safety issues, security systems, key personnel, the hierarchical and departmental systems, the main policies of the organisation, job descriptions, the culture of the organisation, the organisation's history and development, terms of employment including disciplinary rules, employees' benefits and services, and physical facilities. In general, an effective induction programme is likely to:

- reduce labour turnover
- improve employees' understanding of both the corporate culture and the situation in which the organisation is placed

- mean that employees contribute to the organisation more quickly
- increase motivation

External or internal training?

External training, such as joining a college course on business management or supervisory training, is appropriate if there are only a few employees with a specific training need and if the training requirements are not specifically linked to the organisation. External training gives employees the opportunity to meet people from other organisations, allowing for an interchange of ideas and a broadening of understanding. It can also make employees feel valued and increase motivation.

Internal training is appropriate if training needs are specific to the individual organisation — for example, if employees need to learn how to use a new computer system.

On-the-job or off-the-job training?

KEY TERMS

on-the-job training: where an employee learns a job by seeing how it is carried out by an experienced employee (also known as 'sitting by Nellie').
off-the-job training: all forms of employee education apart from that at the immediate workplace.

On-the-job training is likely to be cheaper than off-the-job training, as existing employees and equipment can be used. Such training takes place in a realistic environment, therefore avoiding any problems about adjusting between, say, a college environment and a work situation, and there is also no loss of output. However, the quality of training depends on the ability and willingness of the instructor, and the time available. The employee who is chosen to be an instructor might be unable to teach the proper skills, or might have developed bad habits or short-cuts that are passed on to the trainee. In addition, the work situation might be noisy and stressful, and not helpful for effective learning.

Off-the-job training may be conducted internally — for example, in a conference room — or externally, at a college. Either way there is less immediate pressure from work. Employees might attend college during working hours either through day release or block release, or in the evening or at weekends. The training will be focused on skills, attitudes and theories that relate to work, and is likely to include generic skills and knowledge that are useful at work, rather than job-specific content.

Off-the-job training often uses specially trained experts to do the teaching. This may result in training being more highly valued by employees, leading

> **DID YOU KNOW?**
> Cost will be a major constraint in determining the most appropriate method of training.

DID YOU KNOW?

The culture of the organisation will influence the recruitment, selection and training and development process, as will the leadership styles and approaches of senior management.

EXAMINER'S VOICE

As with any area of business, when evaluating, weigh up the evidence and consider the context.

to increased motivation. If it is also external, off-the-job training will give employees an opportunity to meet staff from other organisations and to learn about their systems. In general, it is more straightforward to estimate the costs of such training and it is easier to monitor progress. However, it can be expensive and there is a question as to whether the skills learned can be transferred effectively to the actual work environment.

How can training be evaluated?

Evaluation of training is reasonably easy if the outcome can be observed by, for example, the effective use of a computer system or the production of a product, but it is more difficult in relation to management training courses. In such situations, questionnaires are needed to assess people's views and perceptions before and after the course and perhaps at a later point. In relation to customer care courses, mystery visitors can be used, who act as members of the public to check on how staff are responding to customers after their training. Training can also be evaluated by monitoring improvements in the quality of output, reductions in labour turnover, increases in candidates coming forward for internal promotion and reductions in accidents, mistakes and wastage.

Training and market failure

Much has been written about the efficiency of the 'market'. This is where the forces of supply and demand operate unhindered by government interference. In the labour market, the supply of labour comes from people wanting jobs and the demand for labour comes from organisations wishing to employ people.

Market failure occurs when the interaction of supply and demand fails to allocate resources in the most efficient way or to produce goods that are wanted. Markets also fail when **externalities** such as pollution are not fully accounted for. For example, firms that pollute the atmosphere by their industrial activity, fail to pay for their actions and therefore make private profit at the cost of social welfare. In these cases, it is argued that governments should intervene.

A similar analysis can be applied to training and the issue of poaching trained workers. Poaching employees means attracting workers who have already been trained by another firm. If firm A wants workers with particular skills that can only be acquired with training, it might attempt to poach them from firm B, which has already trained its workers in that particular skill. Poaching would mean attracting workers by offering higher salaries. This saves firm A the cost of the training process, but means that firm B has wasted its resources in training the workers who have now left.

If done widely within an economy, poaching might lead employers to stop or reduce their training of employees. They will realise that it is pointless

training employees who subsequently leave the firm, and will consider it more cost effective to hire ready-trained staff. Then if those staff leave, the firm does not lose out as a result of having paid for their training.

In this way, the market leads to inefficiencies rather than efficiency, and it may be desirable for the government to intervene by, for example, providing tax incentives for firms that train their own staff. Without some sort of government intervention, such market failure will damage the skill level and therefore the competitiveness of the workforce.

In general, research suggests that firms in the UK fail to invest sufficiently in training and development, viewing training as a cost and failing to consider the long-term benefits to the organisation and to the individual. In addition, training programmes tend to be developed in response to current problems rather than in anticipation of future knowledge and skills requirements.

e EXAMINER'S VOICE

'Market failure' is a term that will be met again in the external influences section of the course. It describes any situation in which the market does not operate well. Other examples occur when there is a lack of competition in a market, although such examples may cause problems for consumers rather than the businesses.

PRACTICE EXERCISE 1
Total: 60 marks (50 minutes)

1 Identify six stages in the recruitment and selection process. *(6 marks)*

2 Explain two advantages of recruiting an internal candidate for a job and two advantages of recruiting an external candidate for a job. *(12 marks)*

3 What is a headhunting organisation? *(3 marks)*

4 Identify and explain two different methods of selecting individuals for a job. *(6 marks)*

5 Identify and explain two factors that will influence the method of recruitment and selection used. *(6 marks)*

6 Explain the importance of effective recruitment and selection to an organisation. *(5 marks)*

7 Distinguish between training and development. *(4 marks)*

8 Outline the benefits to a firm of providing an effective induction training programme. *(6 marks)*

9 Compare the benefits to a firm of on-the-job training and off-the-job training. *(6 marks)*

10 Briefly explain the term 'market failure' and outline why the poaching of trained workers by firms is likely to lead to market failure. *(6 marks)*

Searching for stars on the shop-floor

When you have 300,000 employees, there is a fair chance that some of the talented people in the workforce will be overlooked. The possibility of anyone making it from shop-floor to boardroom is negligible.

At Tesco, all but one member of the board has risen from within the company. The message at Tesco is that nobody gets overlooked when it comes to finding out who has the capacity for self-improvement and the ability to contribute more to company performance.

David Fairhurst, a human resources director at Tesco, says that last year 800 shop-floor staff were promoted or fast-tracked. 'How you bring people up is a key factor for us,' he says. 'We look for talent from top to bottom.'

In 'Capitalising on Talent', a survey in which more than 400 human resources managers took part, 94% said they believed that employing talented people improved the bottom line, 84% confessed that talent lay undiscovered in their organisations and 77% admitted that their company did not have a strategy for managing talent.

At Tesco, managers are trained in talent spotting and are expected to have regular meetings with their staff, whose aspirations are carefully considered. They are encouraged to remember what happened when they were spotted and how they were given a chance.

'We make talent spotting an everyday activity for managers,' says Fairhurst. 'We show people how to create the right environment for talent to flourish. We want to find the people who are going that extra mile and improving the business. It's essential in a rapidly expanding company.'

All the information that is gathered moves up layer by layer to the board, which gets a complete picture of the staffing resources available. This is matched to a forecast of staffing needs. 'If we know what we have got and what we need, we can take a broad view of where investment in people and training is needed,' says Fairhurst.

Earlier this year, when the board reviewed the projections for investment in new stores, it saw that there would be a shortfall in managers. The answer was to accelerate the development of senior team managers. Tesco selected 50 people, 38 of whom were internal candidates, and sent them on an 8-week intensive training programme designed to fast-track employees to store-manager level. The programme covers weekend and evening work, sessions at Sandhurst military academy, leadership training and all the procedures and policies that candidates are likely to have to deal with.

Source: adapted from an article in the *Sunday Times*, 21 September 2003.

Question

Discuss the benefits and the problems that Tesco is likely to face if it continues to recruit the majority of its senior management from within the company.

PRACTICE EXERCISE 3   Total: 30 marks (30 minutes)

Recruitment and training at Starbucks

Read the following extracts from Starbucks' website and the information on Starbucks' corporate culture on pp. 175–76 before answering the questions that follow.

Job centre

Starbucks Coffee Company is an Equal Employment Opportunity employer. All qualified applicants will receive consideration for employment without regard to race, national origin, gender, age, religion, disability, sexual orientation, veteran status, or marital status.

Career moves

Learn about retail management at Starbucks via our multimedia presentation.

Job opportunities

Learn more about retail careers available at Starbucks.

The Starbucks experience

Training and education

We guide all new partners through an extensive orientation and fundamental training programme to provide a solid foundation for career advancement at Starbucks. Some of our educational programmes are:

- **Coffee education.** A course focusing on the Starbucks passion for coffee and understanding our core product.
- **Learning to lead.** A three-level programme for baristas (bar staff) to develop leadership skills. The programme also includes store operational and effective management practice training.

- **Business and communication.** The Starbucks Support Centre (SSC) offers a variety of classes ranging from basic computer skills to conflict resolution, to management training.

Total pay (compensation, stock, benefits and savings)

Starbucks Total Pay package is referred to as 'Your Special Blend' because it is unique to each partner. Partners who work full time or part time (20 hours or more per week) may participate in a variety of programmes, and make choices based on individual needs and interests.

Depending on the job and personal situation, a partner's total pay package may include:

- healthcare benefits (medical, prescription drugs, dental and vision)
- retirement savings plan
- referral programmes and support resources for child and eldercare
- discounted Starbucks merchandise

And, of course, all partners get a pound of coffee each week.

Staff comments

'It's a really good benefits package. But the best thing about the benefits is that they're personalised. You can pick and choose what you want in your benefits package.' (Dija, district manager)

'The training is great. I'm always learning something new through Starbucks.' (Jeff, district manager)

Source: Starbucks website (www.starbucks.com).

Questions

1 To what extent does the recruitment and training information presented here suggest that Starbucks views human resource management as an integral part of its corporate strategy? *(15 marks)*

2 The information provided here is available on the Starbucks website. Discuss how effective the internet is likely to be as a medium for advertising jobs and recruiting staff, compared to more traditional sources. *(15 marks)*

Human resource management

The following 1-hour case study is based on Chapters 24–27. It integrates leadership and management styles with human resource management.

CASE STUDY Prentiss plc

Li Lam sat back contentedly. She had been with Prentiss plc for exactly 2 years and she could tell from their reactions that the board were convinced that her changes had improved the efficiency of the company. This meant that they were more likely to support her proposals that:

- all future recruitment and redundancy should fit in with the human resource strategy that she had devised
- training budgets and programmes should have her approval and match the strategic needs of the company, before being implemented by the department managers

When Li had first got the job of 'Personnel Manager' (a title that would be replaced by 'Director of Human Resources' if her plan was agreed) she had been astounded at the lack of value placed on the role by her fellow managers. The previous personnel manager had only ever been involved in placing job advertisements and organising the interviews and paperwork involved in recruitment. He had been responsible for the training budget but had never exerted control over the managers who used the budget to support the limited training that took place.

As soon as she was appointed, Li got busy. She gathered together evidence that supported her view that some of Prentiss plc's financial difficulties were due to the lack of planning in human resources. For example, 18 months prior to her appointment the

company had lost an important contract because it had been short of staff (and yet just before her appointment it had been forced to make redundancies). Training seemed to be a disaster area and most of the training that had taken place in the previous year had been in response to customers' complaints about faulty products. Extensive training had been provided to make sure that the products left the factory in perfect condition, only for the same problem to occur again. The quality problems turned out to be due to a storage problem in the warehouse.

At first Li found it difficult to obtain the information that she needed. Her early attempts to talk to the production line workers and warehouse staff met with some resistance. Her fellow managers warned her away from the staff canteen, encouraging her to stay in the management dining room (the prices were higher but their generous salaries could cope). Even the working hours made it difficult for communication. Production staff were reluctant to talk during working hours because it affected their piece-rate payment and casual conversation was hard: anyone in overalls was banned from the office block and the management car park was a long way from the bus stop and the workers' car park.

Initially Li had encouraged her fellow managers to consult more and delegate responsibility more fully, rather than use the authoritarian leadership style that they preferred. They all worked exceedingly long hours because subordinates had little understanding of the business other than their own, narrowly defined jobs. This situation led to the firm lurching from crisis to crisis with managers taking decisions without consulting others simply because immediate action was needed. However, Li did reluctantly accept that at times their approach was sensible as most of the junior managers appeared to be clueless. The marketing department was particularly prone to individuals making their own decisions 'in order to get a bargain on a prime slot in a newspaper or on television'.

At first Li decided that training was her top priority, but the managers were reluctant to plan training. The operations manager, Ed Wilkie, summed up their attitude: 'This industry suffers from market failure in relation to training. Why bother training?' As a result, Li organised various off-the-job training programmes, particularly targeted at his department. His opposition soon disappeared because his workers developed higher levels of skill and started to suggest better ways

of running the factory. Despite his reservations, Ed experimented with some of these ideas and found that they helped efficiency and improved the morale of the workers. His new found enthusiasm for training rubbed off on the other managers, allowing Li to switch her focus to the firm's recruitment methods.

Li introduced a system that required managers to justify their need for any new recruit, both in the short run and long run. She also liaised with the managers to try to identify possible shortages or surpluses of workers so that they could anticipate any problems. A new system of recruitment was introduced whereby all staff had to be recruited through one of two approaches (see Table 1). Approach 2 is only used if Approach 1 fails to provide a choice of two or more candidates.

Li would have preferred to have introduced this system after her new training programme had been operating for longer but she was impatient. At her own job interview she had promised to 'make human

Table 1 Approaches to recruitment at Prentiss plc

Approach 1	Approach 2
■ Line managers identify workers with potential for career advancement through annual reviews of each employee.	■ Advertisements are posted in the local newspaper, the company website and on the designated company noticeboard. (For more senior positions, an appropriate specialist magazine is also used.)
■ Selected workers receive additional training to allow them to take on a more senior position.	■ Applicants are long-listed using a system that rates their background and experience to the needs of the job.
■ If a position in the company becomes vacant, the human resources division identifies any staff who have received appropriate training for that particular position and invites them to apply.	■ The long-list of ten candidates is cut to a short-list of five candidates, based on the rating system and the references received.
■ If there is more than one individual with suitable training, 1-hour interviews with two senior managers are held to select the most appropriate candidate. If there are no suitable internal candidates or if there is only one suitable individual, then the post is advertised externally (with the individual candidate being asked to apply).	■ The short-listed candidates spend a day at the company headquarters and are assessed in the following ways: — a practical test to examine their skills — a psychometric test to assess their personality — a group exercise to ascertain their leadership skills and ability to work within a team — informal meetings with staff to get feedback from the colleagues that the successful candidate will be working with — a 1-hour interview with an interview panel of two senior managers and the prospective employee's line manager
	■ The final decision is taken by the interview panel after they have received the results of the other four elements of the selection process.

resource management a strategic part of the business rather than something concerned with day-to-day operations'. It had taken her a year to get to this stage and she needed a further year of operation to prove that her system would improve Prentiss plc's efficiency.

The year passed and the results exceeded her expectation. She was looking forward to the next board meeting. It was scheduled exactly 2 years to the day that she had been appointed and she believed that she could persuade the board to recognise the growing value of human resource management.

Questions

Total: 50 marks (60 minutes)

1 What evidence is there in the case study to suggest that Prentiss plc does *not* follow a policy of 'single status'? *(6 marks)*

2 Analyse **two** instances within the case when Prentiss plc might have benefited from the authoritarian leadership style of its managers. *(8 marks)*

3 Li Lam encouraged the board of Prentiss plc to introduce a more carefully planned approach to human resource management. Evaluate the advantages and disadvantages of this approach for Prentiss plc. *(15 marks)*

4 The operations manager believed that 'this industry suffers from market failure in relation to training'. Explain the possible significance of this market failure for Prentiss plc. *(6 marks)*

5 Discuss the relative merits for Prentiss plc of the two approaches that it used for recruitment (as outlined in Table 1). *(15 marks)*

Operations management

❝I like work: it fascinates me. I can sit and watch it for hours.❞

Jerome K. Jerome

CHAPTER 28

Operations management and productive efficiency

This chapter introduces the concept of 'operations management' and looks at the meaning of productive efficiency, linking it to the topics covered within the 'people in organisations' section of the book. The difficulties in using one specific measure of efficiency are shown, leading to an investigation of alternative ways of measuring efficiency. The chapter concludes with a study of the main ways to improve efficiency and thus the UK's international competitiveness.

Operations management

KEY TERM

operations management: the process that uses the resources of an organisation to provide the right goods or services for the customer.

In the context of the above definition, 'right' means 'what the customer wants'. It may therefore vary between customers — for example, it may mean quality and price to one customer, but convenience and flexibility to another.

Customers have many requirements, so operations management looks at a variety of issues. The following issues are studied in the AS course:

- production methods — to examine whether the most efficient has been selected
- scale of operation — to study its impact on the cost effectiveness and quality of production of a good or service
- stock control — to provide for the needs of customers quickly and cheaply
- quality and its achievement within an organisation
- waste reduction and flexibility — to minimise costs and serve the needs of the buyer

Some additional issues are covered in the A2 specification:

- research and development of new products — to serve the changing needs of the market
- network analysis — scheduling production to minimise the time taken to produce a good or service
- information technology and its impact on business operations
- location of business — to meet the needs of the business and its customers

DID YOU KNOW?

Although operations management originated in the production of goods, over two-thirds of UK spending is on services, so operations management has been widened to apply to both goods and services.

This chapter examines the issue of productive efficiency.

Productive efficiency and productivity

KEY TERMS

productive efficiency: a measurement of the cost of producing 1 unit of a good or service. The lower the unit cost, the greater is the level of efficiency.
productivity: a measurement of the efficiency of an organisation in terms of its ability to convert its inputs (factors of production) into outputs.

There is no single agreed measure of productivity because firms use different inputs, but all firms use labour, so labour productivity is the most common measure. It is given by the following formula:

$$\text{labour productivity} = \frac{\text{output of units (per annum)}}{\text{number of employees}}$$

Thus a company producing 300 units with 15 staff has a labour productivity of 20 units per employee.

> **EXAMINER'S VOICE**
>
> Productivity should not be confused with production, which is the total output of a firm. If the company discussed here cuts production to 250 units, but only employs 10 workers, then labour productivity has increased (to 25 units per employee) because the number of employees has fallen by a much larger percentage than the output (production).

There is a close link between productive efficiency and labour productivity. If each worker produces more output, it could lead to lower labour costs per unit produced. However, this is not necessarily true.

Productivity and people

It is impossible to look at operations management in isolation from other functions of a business. Balancing the need for quality against the need for cost-effectiveness is a part of operations management, but marketing is also responsible for assessing the best balance between quality and price. Similarly, the finances of a firm will influence the methods of production chosen.

However, the closest links are between people and operations management. In the first section of Module 2, among other topics, you have already studied:

- motivation in theory and in practice (Chapters 21 and 22)
- leadership styles (Chapter 24)
- workforce planning (Chapter 26)
- recruitment and training (Chapter 27)

WHAT DO YOU THINK?

Can you think of reasons why productive efficiency may fall even though labour productivity has risen? Here are some clues:

- wage levels
- machinery versus labour
- other costs

Difficulties in measuring productivity or productive efficiency

The formula for measuring productivity given earlier appears to offer a straightforward way of comparing organisations, but there are a number of problems in using it for purposes of comparison:

- **Is the measure of 'output' standardised?** Nissan's Sunderland factory was the most productive car plant in Europe in 2002, with labour productivity of 99 cars per annum per employee. Not surprisingly, on this measure, no luxury car-maker featured in the top 20. This problem could be overcome by comparing revenue productivity (i.e. not 99 cars but £990,000 of cars).
- **How can multi-product firms be compared?** A company such as Nestlé produces a wide range of products, with varying degrees of difficulty in their production. Therefore it is not reasonable to compare jars of baby foods with jars of coffee.
- **Which employees do you include in the calculations?** It is accepted that managerial and sales staff should be included. However, many firms now use subcontracted and agency staff who are not included in the calculations, so those firms appear to have higher productivity per full-time employee. In this case, productive efficiency (unit cost) is more useful than labour productivity.
- **How do you measure individual staff?** Part-time staff can be converted to full-time equivalents (FTEs). Changes to 'productivity' caused by changes to working hours can be dealt with by measuring the input of labour in 'man hours'.

To overcome some of these problems, firms can use measures that take into account the value of outputs and costs of inputs:

$$\text{value added} = \text{sales revenue} - \begin{array}{l}\text{purchases of materials} \\ \text{and bought-in services}\end{array}$$

Comparisons of value added to the number of employees are an alternative way of measuring productivity, recognising in particular the key role of some staff in adding value to a product rather than in increasing the physical level of units produced.

Other ways of measuring efficiency

Customers do not always perceive price to be the critical factor in deciding on the purchase of goods and services. The effective satisfaction of other criteria can therefore be considered as a sign of efficiency. Five areas of efficiency (described as 'advantages') that firms could possess, relative to their rivals, have been identified. These are:

- the cost advantage — to enable competitive prices to be charged
- the quality advantage — to meet customer needs for product reliability and performance
- the dependability advantage — to service customer wants accurately

- the speed advantage — to react quickly to customer needs
- the flexibility advantage — to vary the offer to customers as appropriate

Improving productive efficiency and international competitiveness

In order to improve productivity and productive efficiency within the UK, the government has set up a special Competitiveness Unit to examine ways in which British firms can improve their performance.

The government believes that minimising unemployment is an important strategy in achieving greater efficiency, as anyone who is unemployed is not contributing towards UK production (measured by gross domestic product, GDP). In addition, the Competitiveness Unit has identified five key factors that improve labour productivity and thus the UK's productive efficiency. These factors are outlined below.

- **Investment in new equipment and technology.** Machinery and computers can improve the speed, reliability and quality of products, and still provide flexibility. Labour and other costs can be reduced.

FACT FILE

In the UK a lot of investment has been described as 'inward investment': that is, investment by foreign multinational companies in the UK. In 2002 the UK dropped from fourth to seventh place in the international inward investment league, falling behind China, Germany and France. This is partly because of the UK's failure to adopt the European single currency, but also because eastern European countries are becoming more attractive bases for global businesses and had attracted investment away from the UK.

Source: DTI

- **Improving staff skills through education and training.** A skilled and educated staff will be more adaptable and flexible, able to cope with change more readily, and possess more creativity and innovative talents.
- **Making markets more competitive.** Forcing or encouraging UK companies to compete in markets in which there are no barriers to competition will lead to companies discovering the most effective ways to fight off competition. In this way, their efficiency is improved.
- **Innovation through investment in research and development.** The pace of change requires companies constantly to update and broaden their product range. Product life cycles are becoming shorter, and new ideas must be incorporated into products.
- **Enterprise.** Encouraging people to establish small firms and become their own bosses creates a culture of independence, hard work and flexibility, which helps to supply the needs of larger organisations while providing alternative products and services.

Within a particular organisation there are numerous actions that could be taken to improve productivity. The suitability of the techniques for each firm will depend on its strengths and weaknesses, and the opportunities and threats that it faces (see SWOT analysis in Chapter 51).

PRACTICE EXERCISE 1

Total: 30 marks (25 minutes)

1 What is meant by the term 'operations management'? *(4 marks)*

2 Explain the difference between 'productive efficiency' and 'productivity'. *(4 marks)*

3 Explain three reasons why it is difficult to compare the productivity of different organisations. *(9 marks)*

4 Analyse two possible reasons why labour productivity might vary between different countries. *(8 marks)*

5 Describe the link between motivation and productivity. *(5 marks)*

PRACTICE EXERCISE 2

Total: 60 marks (55 minutes)

Based on the information in this chapter and your understanding of business, answer the following questions.

1 Select three areas of operations management and explain how they each can be used to improve the performance of a business. *(18 marks)*

2 Look at the information in the following table.

	Firm A	Firm B
Units of production	10,000	20,000
Sales revenue	£300,000	£500,000
Number of employees	5	8
Total costs of production	£240,000	£440,000

Calculate the following measures for both firm A and firm B:
a Labour productivity measured in units of production. *(4 marks)*
b Labour productivity measured in sales revenue. *(4 marks)*
c Productive efficiency. *(4 marks)*

3 Discuss the main reasons why it would be difficult to compare the efficiency of two rival hairdressers. *(15 marks)*

4 Study factors that improve productive efficiencies (see p. 243) and evaluate the most appropriate methods that would assist **one** of the following:
- a car manufacturer
- a mobile phone network provider
- a magazine producer *(15 marks)*

CHAPTER 29

Economies and diseconomies of scale

What are the benefits and problems of large-scale enterprises? This chapter explains how economies and diseconomies of scale can be measured. It distinguishes between economies/diseconomies that can be quantified and those that can only be assessed by more qualitative attributes.

 TERMS

> **economies of scale:** the advantages that an organisation gains due to an increase in size. These cause an increase in **productive efficiency** (a decrease in the average cost per unit of production).
>
> **diseconomies of scale:** the disadvantages that an organisation experiences due to an increase in size. These cause an increase in the average cost of production.

Economies of scale

Fixed costs, such as the depreciation of machinery and administrative expenses, must be paid, regardless of the number of units that an organisation produces and sells. This enables large firms that utilise their equipment effectively to produce at much lower costs per unit.

Variable costs, such as labour and raw materials, can be combined more effectively in a large firm, also leading to a saving in unit costs.

Internal economies of scale (often abbreviated to 'economies of scale') can be classified under a number of headings. Three examples of economies are:

Technical

- Modern equipment that will improve efficiency can be installed. This should lower unit costs and improve the quality and reliability of the product or service.
- Mass production (flow) techniques can be employed to improve productivity.
- Highly trained technicians can be employed to improve the reliability of the production process.
- Large-scale transportation can reduce distribution costs per unit.
- The purchase of computer systems can improve efficiency in both production and administration.

> ### EXAMINER'S VOICE
>
> Remember that, as output increases, the total costs will also increase. It is the average cost (unit cost) that falls as output rises when economies of scale are being achieved.

e **EXAMINER'S VOICE**

There are many economies of scale. Because the AQA AS Business Studies specification is concerned with the principle rather than with details, it is only necessary to
recognise the three economies of scale described (technical, specialisation and
purchasing). However, unit costs can also fall because of:
■ marketing economies — more effective marketing
■ financial economies — cheaper loans and easier access to funds
■ research and development economies — spending to discover new products or to find
easier ways to produce goods
■ social and welfare economies — improved facilities to motivate workers
■ administrative economies — more cost-effective administration

■ Improvements in communication systems through new technology can
enhance customer service and the working environment, improving the
company's operations and its reputation.

Specialisation

■ Large firms can afford to employ specialists with particular skills. In smaller
organisations, staff tend to take on a wider variety of tasks, and specialist
skills, when needed, are bought from outside at a relatively high price.
■ Production techniques can be adapted to encourage division of labour
(specialisation) in large firms.
■ A small firm is unlikely to be able to pay a high enough salary to attract the
best staff, so larger firms should be more efficient. Training to improve
specialist skills is also easier in large firms.
■ If staff are able to specialise, they are likely to become even more skilled in
their role, again increasing the efficiency of the firm.

DID YOU KNOW?

In recent years, Tesco has removed control of distribution (transportation) from many
of its suppliers and taken control itself. Tesco used to pay suppliers a price that
included delivery to its stores or warehouses, but it found that smaller suppliers were
too small to benefit from cheap transport. Tesco now uses its specialisation in transportation to save money. It buys the supplies at the factory gate price (FGP), picks up
the goods from the factory and delivers the goods itself. Over two-thirds of Tesco's
supplies are now purchased in this way, with only the very large suppliers delivering
directly to Tesco. Tesco's huge buying power also means that it can buy additional
transport cheaply at short notice, giving it a competitive and flexible system.

Purchasing

■ Large firms can buy in bulk. This reduces costs because suppliers can
produce in large quantities and thus lower their own costs, and suppliers
can offer greater discounts in order to guarantee a contract with a large
customer. In September 2003, B&Q was able to cut costs by 4% by
bargaining with suppliers, having announced that it would be reducing the
number of suppliers from 8,000 to 5,000.

■ Specialist purchasing departments or specialist buyers can be employed, allowing the company to research and negotiate the best purchases.

Purchasing economies of scale can have a huge impact on costs. Asda used to pay $14 per metre for 50,000 metres of material to make men's jeans. After the company was taken over by Wal-Mart, purchasing rose to 6 million metres per annum and the price fell to $4.77 per metre.

DID YOU KNOW?

In some cases, economies of scale can depend on the size of orders as much as the overall level of sales. In 1995 Daily Bread, a sandwich supplier, had been trading for 10 years with a relatively low level of growth. It was saved from possible liquidation by a large contract with a firm for 300 sandwiches daily. Previously, to sell 300 sandwiches would have meant supplying many different customers and incurring heavy transport costs. From that point onwards, the business decided to concentrate on wholesale deliveries to large customers only, and it now has annual sales of £7 million.

FACT FILE

Ian Higgins, chief executive of Empire Interactive, a games publisher and developer, says that when the company was founded in 1987 its first game cost £4,000 to produce. The group's most recent title cost almost £2 million.

In response to this trend, Empire Interactive became a public limited company in 2000, following other games producers such as Eidos, the business behind Lara Croft.

'The rise in costs has been driven by technology,' according to Higgins. 'You used to be able to produce a game with a couple of people – a programmer and an artist. These days you need a team of 20, 30 or even 40. That includes programmers, artists, sound engineers, producers and so on.'

This is leading to changes in the industry. Firms need to be big to survive and it is vital that the work of the different individuals is coordinated carefully to avoid delays in releasing new products. Despite these potential diseconomies of scale, large firms can gain from technological economies of scale. They also have stronger bargaining power when dealing with retailers.

As recently as 2000 there were over 300 computer games publishers in the UK, but the need for high technology and cost effectiveness means that individuals with bright ideas are excluded from the market, unless they can get employment with a publisher. The need for expensive research and development means that only large firms can remain competitive.

Source: Empire Interactive

Diseconomies of scale

As organisations grow, they may suffer disadvantages that lead to a lowering of efficiency and higher unit costs of production. These are known as **diseconomies of scale** or **internal diseconomies of scale**. Some examples are given below.

Coordination
■ There may be a loss of control by management as an organisation becomes more complex, particularly if the organisation becomes more geographically spread or management experiences an increasing workload.
■ Individuals are less likely to follow organisational policies if the level of control is reduced. This happens in larger organisations because managers have larger spans of control and there are more levels of hierarchy.
■ Large firms often have more rigid and inflexible policies, imposed to limit

the loss of control described above. Greater control can improve efficiency, but by limiting the delegation of power to subordinates a firm will reduce its ability to respond quickly to changing customer needs.

Communication

- Too many levels of hierarchy in a business can reduce the effectiveness of communication. Messages can be distorted (as in Chinese whispers) and it is possible that communications do not reach everyone. Sometimes the time taken for a message to reach an individual can cause problems for the firm.
- Difficulties also occur as spans of control widen. It becomes much more difficult for managers to meet with subordinates and, again, urgent communications may be delayed or missed.
- In large firms, inappropriate methods of communication are likely to be used, as standardised, large-scale approaches are more common.
- Employees who do not receive or feel involved in communications may feel unvalued and demotivated.

Motivation

- It is more difficult to assess the needs of many individuals. Even if motivational methods are used, it is less likely that the managers will know the best approach for each subordinate.
- In large firms there may be less time for recognition and reward.
- Large hierarchies create feelings of distance between decision makers and employees. If staff do not feel involved, they may feel demotivated.
- Large firms often have the financial wealth to introduce schemes to motivate employees, but can lack the management time to provide the recognition required to make sure that staff feel rewarded.

Other diseconomies of scale

- Technical diseconomies, where production on a very large scale becomes very difficult to organise as efficiently as smaller-scale production.
- Excessive bureaucracy. As organisations grow, the number of levels of management increases and this may slow down decision making and add to the costs of production.
- Industrial relations problems and higher staff turnover and absences as a result of the factors described above.
- Less flexibility and innovation, which means firms may not continue to meet the changing needs of their customers.

 FILE

The huge size of some car plants led to diseconomies of scale in the 1970s. Poor coordination meant huge wastage of materials and poor quality control. The difficulties in communication and the boring nature of jobs led to many days lost through absenteeism or disputes between workers and managers. These problems have been reduced by modifying jobs and giving workers more responsibility, but also car manufacturers have reduced the size of individual factories.

> **ⓔ EXAMINER'S VOICE**
>
> These problems occur in firms of all sizes. They are only diseconomies of scale if they have been caused by the large size of the organisation rather than by other factors, such as poor management.

Car manufacturers need to find a balance between economies and diseconomies of scale. Professor Garel Rees at the Centre for Automotive Industry Research believes that car firms need to make 3 million cars a year to be cost-competitive. He forecasts that firms such as MG Rover, Fiat and even Peugeot Citroën are unlikely to survive, unless they merge with other manufacturers.

Quantifying economies and diseconomies of scale

Table 29.1 quantifies the effect of both economies of scale and diseconomies of scale. It shows how, initially, the unit (average) costs of production fall as the company increases its output. This occurs for three main reasons:

- The fixed costs stay the same (and so fixed costs per unit fall) as output rises.
- Variable costs increase at a slower rate because division of labour enables the organisation to combine its factors of production more efficiently.
- The firm can benefit from the economies of scale described earlier.

However, once the output rises beyond 9 units, diseconomies of scale outweigh economies of scale. Although economies such as bulk buying may be helping to lower unit costs, problems such as co-ordination are having a larger impact and so overall the unit costs are beginning to rise.

Units of output	Fixed costs (£)	Variable costs (£)	Total costs (£)	Average (unit) costs (£)
0	240	0	240	–
1	240	200	440	440
2	240	340	580	290
3	240	420	660	220
4	240	476	716	179
5	240	520	760	152
6	240	570	810	135
7	240	642	882	126
8	240	736	976	122
9	240	849	1,089	121
10	240	1,000	1,240	124
11	240	1,201	1,441	131
12	240	1,476	1,716	143

Table 29.1
Economies and diseconomies of scale

Distinguishing the quantifiable from the qualitative

A business will not find it easy to calculate its most efficient production level in the manner suggested in Table 29.1. This is because it is difficult to **quantify** (put into numbers) the exact implications of a change in scale. **Qualitative judgements** (based on opinions rather than exact numerical data) will also be needed.

As a general rule it is easier to quantify economies of scale. Gains from specialisation can be calculated by working out the productivity of the specialist, perhaps in comparison to non-specialist workers or smaller firms. The introduction of technical improvements, such as a new production line or computer system, can also be investigated to see if efficiency has improved. However, it is very difficult to assess the exact causes of any changes, so qualitative judgements (based on opinions) will need to be made. Arguably, purchasing economies are the easiest to quantify. As indicated earlier in the

chapter, Asda knows that, by buying in larger quantities, it is able to save $9.23 a metre — a 66% reduction in cost.

Diseconomies of scale are much harder to quantify. If staff are less motivated or communications become less efficient, then costs will increase and customers will be lost, but it is impossible to pinpoint how much these diseconomies actually cost the firm. It is also possible that the problems were caused by other factors.

Firms use information on economies and diseconomies of scale in order to plan their most efficient size, but exact guidelines cannot be established and opinions change over time. Thirty years ago the emphasis was on large-scale operations to get the benefits of economies of scale; in the last 20 years, greater flexibility has been demanded, so many firms have demerged or split themselves into smaller operations to avoid diseconomies of scale. For example, Racal, the company that created Vodafone, viewed any operation with more than 800 staff as too large and had a policy of splitting any division that exceeded this size. This led to Vodafone being split away from Racal Tacticom, the division that dealt with mobile communications for military purposes.

FACT FILE

General Electric (GE) is a firm that finds its economies of scale easier to quantify than its diseconomies of scale. GE is a $130 billion-a-year business that covers aircraft engines, financial services, lighting, locomotives, medical instruments, plastics, television — and much more.

In one week in October 2003, GE bought three companies: Universal Studios (to combine with its NBC subsidiary) and two healthcare companies (Amersham in the UK and Instrumentarium in Finland).

GE has calculated that its healthcare division will be able to save up to $400 million a year, as a result of its increased scale. The company's healthcare division has grown by 30% in one week, allowing GE to provide medical equipment on a much larger scale. In addition to technical economies of scale, the medical division has purchased expertise that will allow greater specialisation in personalised medicine. GE's massive purchasing power enabled it to outbid its main rivals — Siemens and Philips — in the bid for Amersham. GE chief executive, Jeff Immelt, argues that the price paid for Amersham shares (800 pence, compared to a rival bid of 720 pence) will be repaid in the first year from the purchasing economies available to the newly enlarged health division. A further $400 million of additional profit is expected after 3 years.

Diseconomies of scale have proved harder to quantify. The wide spread of GE business activities has been difficult to coordinate and overall sales in 2002/03 grew by only 2%. Sales of GE's industrial products actually declined by 5% in the year. Immelt's strategy is to change the core of the business from its industrial products to activities with higher profit margins, such as financial services, film and television, and healthcare. Unfortunately, the breadth of the business makes it difficult to control the organisation as a whole.

Immelt has given greater independence to subsidiaries, so that specialists are employed to run each area of activity. This comes at a cost — the top five key employees each earned in excess of $7 million last year. According to Immelt, 'We believe very much in people and are investing in their skills.'

To improve decision making, better communication and coordination are specific aims for GE, but it has not been able to measure the financial costs of problems arising from its huge size. To date GE has coped with its size much better than many rival companies that have been too slow to adapt to changes in the market.

Source: General Electric website (www.ge.com).

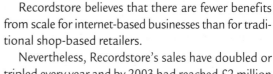

1 At what level of output is the company in Table 29.1 (see p. 249) at maximum productive efficiency? *(2 marks)*

2 Using Table 29.1, calculate the fixed costs per unit at the following levels of output:
  a 4 units *(2 marks)*
  b 12 units *(2 marks)*

3 Analyse two possible *economies* of scale that might occur in a national newspaper publisher, or another firm of which you have knowledge. *(8 marks)*

4 Analyse two possible *diseconomies* of scale that might occur in a national newspaper publisher, or the other firm that you chose in question 3. *(8 marks)*

5 To what extent is it more difficult to quantify diseconomies of scale than economies of scale in an organisation such as a supermarket? *(12 marks)*

6 Discuss the possible benefits and problems for Asda as a result of its decision to buy its materials from the USA rather than the UK. *(16 marks)*

CASE STUDY **Recordstore**

The past

In 1997 Russel Coultart, Simon Moxon and Tony Matthews set up Recordstore. Its market was online sales of CDs and records, with an emphasis on dance music. The business builds 'mini stores' online for small record companies and their artists. Its artists and bands include U2, Moby, Travis, Robbie Williams and Paul Weller.

Its lack of size means that Recordstore, according to Coultart, 'cannot compete with Amazon or HMV, with their greater opportunities for economies of scale. We sell items that the stores will not stock because our customers want more niche products and not the latest releases.' Its focus on devoted fans rather than casual customers means that many of its sales are merchandise such as tour T-shirts and calendars, rather than just music. Online sales of music have doubled in the last 2 years and now represent 5.5% of record sales within the business.

TOPFOTO

Recordstore believes that there are fewer benefits from scale for internet-based businesses than for traditional shop-based retailers.

Nevertheless, Recordstore's sales have doubled or tripled every year and by 2003 had reached £2 million per annum. The 13 staff have clearly defined jobs as label managers (linking with the record companies), computer programmers, customer-service advisers and warehouse workers. In 2001 there were eight staff helping to create sales of £500,000.

The future

Recordstore made losses every year until 2002, but achieved breakeven in 2003. Chief executive Russel Coultart has set challenging targets for the future. The plan is to achieve sales of £20 million by 2008. The firm believes that it is too small to make consistent profits at present.

In order to prepare for such growth, Recordstore is moving to a new office in trendy Notting Hill. This will give the

company three times as much floor space. It is also investing £80,000 in a new computer system to handle the 500,000 product lines it will offer by 2008.

Recordstore prefers to place orders with record companies once a customer agrees a purchase, but the record companies are reluctant to agree. As a result, Recordstore has stock levels of £15,000 at any one time – roughly 1 month's supply. How much stock to keep and where to keep it are decisions that have not yet been taken.

In addition, Recordstore has plans to cut down on the number of record labels whose products it stocks, but the owners have been too busy on day-to-day matters to investigate this idea.

The business is planning to recruit a fourteenth employee, as existing staff have heavy workloads. The owners have helped to relieve the pressure by taking on some of the work, but this has meant less time for planning the future of the business. Coultart is also intending to recruit a fifteenth person, a personal assistant for himself, to improve communication and the management of the organisation. However, he is reluctant to give up his day-to-day involvement in a business that he set up because of his love of music.

The potential of the business has been recognised by venture capitalists, who have injected £230,000 of capital into the business in return for 30% of the shares. Another investor is Bob Geldof. He approached the business to set up an online store for his own website, and was so impressed that he decided to invest and agreed to act as a business adviser.

Source: adapted from a report by Derren Hayes in the *Sunday Times*, 27 April 2003.

Questions   Total: 50 marks (60 minutes)

1 Calculate the change in labour productivity between 2001 and 2003 (output is measured as sales revenue).   *(4 marks)*

2 Analyse **two** economies of scale that might have benefited Recordstore as it grew between 1997 and 2003.   *(8 marks)*

3 Evaluate the reasons why there is considered to be less scope for economies of scale for an internet-based music retailer, such as Amazon, than there is for a traditional record shop, such as HMV.   *(15 marks)*

4 Examine **two** benefits for the business of recruiting the fourteenth and fifteenth workers referred to in the article.   *(8 marks)*

5 Discuss the main diseconomies of scale that may affect Recordstore during the next 5 years.   *(15 marks)*

CHAPTER 30

Capacity utilisation

In this chapter 'capacity' is defined and the concept of 'capacity utilisation' and its measurement are introduced. The possible causes of under-utilisation of capacity and its impact on an organisation are discussed, and different approaches to increasing capacity utilisation are suggested, focusing in particular on rationalisation and subcontracting.

KEY TERMS

capacity: the maximum total level of output or production that a business can produce in a given time period. A company producing at this level is said to be producing at **full capacity**.

capacity utilisation: the percentage of a firm's total possible production level that is being reached. If a company is large enough to produce 100 units a week, but is actually producing 92 units, its capacity utilisation is 92%.

under-utilisation of capacity: when a firm's output is below the maximum possible. This is also known as **excess capacity** or **spare capacity**. It represents a waste of resources and means that the organisation is spending unnecessarily on its fixed assets.

Measuring capacity utilisation

Capacity utilisation measures the extent to which the company's maximum possible output is being reached. It can be calculated using the following formula:

$$\text{capacity utilisation (\%)} = \frac{\text{actual output per annum (month)}}{\text{maximum possible output per annum (month)}} \times 100$$

A company capable of producing 3,500 units but actually producing 2,800 units is working at 80% capacity:

$$\frac{2,800}{3,500} \times 100 = 80\%$$

It could increase production by 700 units or 20%. This is known as its **spare capacity**.

Capacity utilisation can be measured over any chosen time period. For some organisations it may be most appropriate to calculate it on a daily basis, but weekly or monthly calculations may be more relevant to other firms.

There is no one ideal target percentage, but many people believe that 90% capacity utilisation is a sensible level. At 100% there is no scope for

maintenance and repair, or to deal with emergency situations that may occur. However, every percentage point below 100 represents 'unused' resources and higher fixed costs per unit produced.

Causes of under-utilisation of capacity

There are several reasons why a firm may be operating at below its maximum possible output.

- **New competitors or new products entering the market.** It has become increasingly popular to open coffee houses in recent years, in response to higher demand. However, the growth of competition has been so high that there is now excess capacity in the market, so the average turnover for each outlet has begun to fall. A similar situation has occurred with pizza restaurants.
- **Fall in demand for the product as a whole due to changes in taste or fashion.** McDonald's has been forced to close some of its restaurants because of a fall in demand caused by consumers wanting more variety and healthier food.
- **Unsuccessful marketing.** Benetton grew rapidly in the UK, partly as a result of brand awareness created by its advertising. Its decline coincided with negative publicity related to some of the controversial images that it used in its posters.
- **Seasonal demand.** The tourist industry must build facilities to accommodate visitors at peak times of the season. Attractions such as Alton Towers therefore have excess capacity during the winter months. Within the working day, organisations such as cafés and fitness clubs will also have varying levels of spare capacity.
- **Over-investment in fixed assets.** Globally, there was a considerable expansion of car production plants in the 1980s, as manufacturers expected sales to rise quickly. A rate of growth slower than expected has meant that there is spare capacity worldwide, with many factories operating well below full capacity.
- **A merger or takeover leading to duplication of many resources and sites.** The integration of Time and Tiny Computers to form Computer World meant that in many towns there were two shops both selling the same stock and unlikely to be reaching full capacity. Over time such a business will sell off smaller sites to overcome this problem.

The impact of under-utilisation of capacity

Under-utilisation of capacity helps a firm to cope with unexpected problems or increases in demand, but it can increase costs.

Disadvantages of under-utilisation

- Firms have a higher proportion of fixed costs per unit. If utilisation falls, the fixed costs must be spread over fewer units of output. This leads to higher unit costs.

UNITED COLORS OF BENETTON.

FACT FILE

Woolworths is a business that usually operates with high levels of spare capacity. The 10-week period leading up to Christmas Day accounts for 40% of the group's sales and all of its profits. Typically, it recruits more than 6,500 extra staff and installs over 1,000 additional tills, in order to make sure that it can cope with the increased demand at Christmas time.

- These higher costs will lead to *either* lower profit levels *or* the need to increase price to maintain the same profit levels, and therefore to lower sales volume.
- Spare capacity can portray a negative image of a firm, suggesting that it is unsuccessful. For an organisation such as a club or retailer, where the low utilisation can be physically seen, this may put customers off and lead to lower sales.
- With less work to do, employees may become bored and demoralised, lowering their motivation and efficiency. If the problem appears to be permanent, it may even lead to workers worrying about losing their jobs.

FACT FILE

Under-utilisation of capital is a greater problem for organisations with high fixed costs. The Channel Tunnel was opened in 1994 with a capacity to take 14 million passengers annually. Eurotunnel's original 5-year plan predicted that it would have 13 million customers by 1999. In 2003 the figure stood at 7 million. These disappointing figures mean that Eurotunnel will be unable to pay the interest charges on the huge loans that it needed to finance the tunnel. Fierce competition from ferries, and more recently from low-cost airlines, has had a major effect on passenger numbers. In 2003 price offers and promotions cut the average price by 20%, but led to only a 4% increase in passengers.

Advantages of under-utilisation

- Spare capacity means that there is more time for maintenance and repair of machinery, for training and for improving existing systems. During a period of spare capacity, a business may spend the available time improving its set-up and skills, making it better prepared for an increase in trade.
- There may be less pressure and stress for employees, who may become overworked at full capacity.
- Under-utilisation allows a company to cope with a sudden increase in demand. Businesses in expanding markets will increase their capacity beforehand, so that their sales are not limited by the size of the factory or shop.

Summary

Overall, it is often felt that 90% capacity is ideal, as this gives the firm an opportunity to repair and maintain equipment. It also gives some flexibility in response to changes in demand. However, for seasonal businesses or those expecting rapid growth, a lower percentage would be sensible.

Ways of achieving high capacity utilisation

Achieving full capacity utilisation is a matter of balancing demand and supply of products.

Demand

If a business has spare capacity, it can attempt to improve its marketing mix in order to increase demand. McDonald's has widened its product range in

order to overcome its problem of spare capacity. Hotels regularly offer off-peak special deals to increase capacity utilisation at these times.

On rare occasions, a firm may suffer from the opposite problem — a capacity shortage. For the Last Night of the Proms at the Royal Albert Hall, there is always a high demand for tickets. The organisers therefore charge a higher than usual price in order to reduce the demand to a reasonable level and to maximise sales revenue. Theatres and concert halls regularly try to anticipate the level of demand for tickets at different prices. With this knowledge they can set prices so that the demand for tickets matches the number of seats available, hence achieving full capacity and high sales revenue.

Supply

If a business has spare capacity, it might decide to follow a policy of **rationalisation**.

KEY TERM

rationalisation: a process by which a firm improves its efficiency by cutting the scale of its operations.

Rationalisation leads to a cut in the capacity of a firm and thus to a reduction in its maximum output. If a firm is capable of producing 200 units but actually produces only 96 units, its capacity utilisation is only 48%. If it rationalises and halves its capacity to 100 units, it will have a much more efficient level of capacity utilisation (96%). Over the years, Woolworths has reduced the size of many of its stores for this reason.

FACT FILE

It is possible for a firm to have both spare capacity and a capacity shortage at the same time. McDonald's is planning to close 160 restaurants in the UK between 2003 and 2005 because of an overall fall in demand. However, although it has spare capacity in large city centres, its research reveals that there is a demand for more McDonald's restaurants in suburban and outlying areas — for example, on major roads. Similarly, closures in the USA, the UK and France are taking place at the same time as plans for expansion in Italy and Spain.

Ways of reducing capacity

- **Selling off all or a part of its production area.** This will cut fixed costs and is likely to be used if a company believes that its spare capacity problem is long term. For example, both Ford and Vauxhall have shut car production plants in the UK because they have too many factories worldwide. However, selling off production facilities will not be the best strategy if the under-utilisation is a short-term problem. It will be very difficult to increase production again if the factory has been sold.
- **Changing to a shorter working week or shorter day.** This will save costs and cut production, but it may lead to lower motivation and a higher turnover of staff.

- **Laying off workers.** This will save more money and reduce costs, but fixed costs will remain high if this is the only action taken. If demand then rises, there will be problems of recruiting new staff — these are likely to have less understanding of the job and lower skill levels.
- **Transferring resources from another area.** If spare capacity exists elsewhere in an organisation, resources can be shifted from one area to another. Retailers will often shift staff temporarily from less busy stores to new ones to help cope with the high demand in the opening weeks.

Ways of increasing capacity

For some firms, it is their shortage of capacity that causes them difficulties. This problem can be overcome by taking the opposite actions to those listed above:

- **Building or extending factories/plants.** For example, for the Last Night of the Proms a video link to Regent's Park is used to take extra customers. Successful retailers such as Tesco and New Look have extended the number and sizes of their branches.
- **Asking staff to work longer hours.** Many firms offer overtime pay at higher rates or give contracts to staff that allow them to request longer hours during times of peak demand.
- **Recruiting new staff.** This is appropriate if there is a long-term need for higher output.

Some firms overcome capacity problems by creating a flexible workforce. **Core workers** are employed to meet regular demand; fluctuations can be met by introducing staff on flexible, short-term contracts.

Subcontracting

 TERM

subcontracting: when an organisation asks another business to make all or a part of its product.

Many businesses use subcontracting as a way of reducing capacity utilisation problems. By asking other firms to supply goods, the original firm can increase supply to match demand without the need to increase its own factory size. Similarly, it can reduce supply to match a fall in demand by reducing the amount of work that it subcontracts, without making any changes to its own factory size. Many council services, such as waste management, are subcontracted to private firms like Cleanaway and Biffa. Private firms subcontract specialist services, such as catering, to other organisations.

Advantages of subcontracting

- Businesses will be able to react to changes in demand more quickly if they have access to a number of different firms' production plants.
- Subcontractors may be more specialised and therefore more efficient in a particular line of activity. A car manufacturer buys tyres from a specialist firm such as Michelin, rather than making its own, inferior tyre.

- Subcontracting lets a firm focus on its core business and helps it to avoid becoming involved in activities in which it is less competent.

Disadvantages of subcontracting

- Firms must recognise that the quality of their service is no longer directly under their own control. An unreliable subcontractor may influence the reputation of a business. Customers will blame a supermarket if its own-label cornflakes are of poor quality, even though the supermarket did not produce them.
- Excessive subcontracting erodes a company's operations base and its ability to initiate research and make changes.
- The opportunity cost of subcontracting should be evaluated. The producer wants to make a profit, so it is possible that it will be more expensive to subcontract than produce in-house.
- Subcontracting may require a firm to give confidential information to a supplier, such as details of its methods and patents.

 FILE

Electricity generation is an industry in which capacity utilisation is a major issue. At peak times in the year (such as the Queen's Speech on Christmas Day or at the end of a particularly exciting episode of *EastEnders*), huge demands are placed on the national grid as everybody rushes to the kitchen to make a cup of tea. However, at off-peak times, such as the middle of the night, there is very low demand for electricity and most power stations are not needed. It is also very difficult to store electricity — less than 5% of all electricity is supplied from 'stock'.

To reduce this problem, the national grid came up with a very imaginative solution. At Llanberis in Gwynedd, Wales, the largest man-made underground chamber in the world was created in order to generate electricity. Built into the side of a mountain is a pumping station and electricity generation plant. Water flows from a mountain-top lake down through the plant and this is used to generate electricity. The water then flows into a lake at the bottom of the mountain, from where it is pumped back to the lake at the top. The plant, which opened in 1984, is able to generate more than 10% of the UK's total electricity.

In terms of physics, the plant is very inefficient — pumping the water back to the mountain-top lake uses up more electricity than the plant is able to generate from the water flowing down through the mountain. However, from a business viewpoint it is very efficient.

At night, when capacity utilisation of the national grid is very low, electricity from other power stations is used to pump the water back to the top. Then, at peak times, when there is a shortage of capacity, the water flows down the mountain, adding 10% to the national supply of electricity.

A similar business principle is used in Niagara, on the border between Canada and the USA. During the day, hydroelectric power is generated by diverting over 50% of the natural flow of water from the Niagara river into power stations. At night (when the tourists have gone home) this is increased to more than 75% (leaving less than 25% to cascade over the falls), so that even more electricity can be generated. In 2003, this scheme was not enough to prevent major power cuts in New York, a consequence of the shortage of capacity in the USA's electricity industry. It has even been suggested that Niagara Falls could be turned off at night to help the situation!

High levels of capacity utilisation mean that electricity supplies are vulnerable if problems occur. Until the 1980s, the respective governments owned electricity generation in the UK and USA. Since privatisation, electricity has been run by limited companies seeking to make profits for their owners. A consequence of this has been a reduction in levels of spare capacity. In the UK, spare capacity has fallen from 28% to 16% since privatisation. In the USA, it has fallen from 15% to 3%.

Source: based on an article by Steve Connor in the *Independent*, 16 August 2003, and various other sources.

PRACTICE EXERCISE

Total: 30 marks (30 minutes)

1 In 2002/03 Tesco introduced a number of cost-saving measures. One measure was to try to increase the amount of stock carried by each lorry. The average lorry can carry a maximum of 26 pallets of stock. During 2002/03 the average load increased from 22.5 pallets to 24 pallets per trip.
  a Calculate the capacity utilisation at the beginning of 2002/03. *(2 marks)*
  b Calculate the percentage of spare capacity at the end of 2002/03. *(2 marks)*

2 Explain two implications of under-utilisation of capacity for a business. *(6 marks)*

3 Explain three factors that might create high levels of capacity utilisation. *(9 marks)*

4 What is meant by capacity shortage? *(3 marks)*

5 What is considered to be an ideal capacity utilisation? *(1 mark)*

6 Explain the meaning of 'rationalisation'. *(3 marks)*

7 How can subcontracting help a firm's capacity utilisation problems? *(4 marks)*

CASE STUDY Capacity utilisation in selected industries

Hotels and restaurants

In the UK **hotels** market in the 1990s, there was a lack of capacity in the budget hotels market but excess capacity in other hotels. As a consequence, there was a rapid expansion of rooms in the early years of the twenty-first century. The budget sector in 2002 consisted of 850 hotels containing 52,000 rooms. Figures for 2002 show occupancy rates at a high level for this sector of the industry, with an average of 40,000 rooms occupied at any one time. In London, occupancy rates were even higher, although this is considered to be the result of a lack of supply as much as a high level of demand. Hotel owners were able to increase prices by 11% in 2002 without affecting capacity utilisation. Hotels calculate that reasonable profit levels can be achieved with capacity utilisation at 60%, so expansion plans are in place in many budget hotel chains. It is estimated that there will be approximately 1,350 budget hotels with 75,000 rooms in total by the end of 2005.

The non-budget sector of the hotel industry traditionally operates with spare capacity for most of the year, but a capacity shortage at other times. Hotel owners attempt to achieve more even levels of capacity utilisation through flexibility in their prices and through the introduction of additional attractions and packages at times when spare capacity is expected to be high.

With the exception of 'fast food', most types of **restaurants** are dominated by small firms. For this reason, changes in demand are quickly matched by changes in supply, as new restaurants open.

This has been most noticeable in coffee bar outlets, which have increased by more than 65% in the last 5 years (although this type of outlet is dominated by larger chains such as Starbucks and Costa). The lack of capacity in this sector now appears to have been eliminated.

Overall the rapid growth in 'eating out' that first took place in the 1980s has now ended, with a slight decline in recent years. The demand for eating out is only marginally higher now than it was in 1990, but with more restaurants in existence, capacity utilisation is lower.

Retailing

Retailers of **electrical goods** have experienced the following features in their market:

- Increased demand brought about by new products and technology, especially digital technology. This has led to a high growth in demand for certain products.

- However, some consumers appear to be delaying purchases until they are sure of the benefits of this new technology.

- Relatively few new shops being opened, as the trade is dominated by two or three large retailers. The number of shops is therefore growing more slowly than consumer demand.

- Some reluctance to replace existing electrical products, as consumers have been concerned about their future incomes in the light of predictions of job losses in the UK.

In the **food and drink** sector, specialist shops and convenience stores have been losing sales to supermarkets and, to a lesser extent, garage forecourts. However, the number of closures of small grocery retailers has fallen, as these shops are being bought by larger businesses and added to their chains of stores.

Source: Industrial Economics Team, Barclays plc.

Questions

Total: 50 marks (60 minutes)

1 Calculate the capacity utilisation of budget hotel rooms in 2002. *(3 marks)*

2 The total number of budget hotel rooms is expected to reach 75,000 by the end of 2005. These hotel chains require 60% capacity utilisation to meet their profit targets. By what percentage will the demand for budget hotel rooms need to increase between 2002 and 2005, if 60% capacity utilisation is to be achieved? *(5 marks)*

3 There is a shortage of capacity in the budget hotels market in London. Analyse **one** implication of this situation for customers. *(6 marks)*

4 Study the features of the electrical goods market. Discuss the possible effects of these features on the level of capacity utilisation of an existing electrical goods retailer. *(15 marks)*

5 Examine **one** reason why an industry dominated by small firms, such as the restaurant trade, may adapt to changes in demand more quickly than an industry dominated by large firms. *(6 marks)*

6 With reference to hotels and restaurants, evaluate the extent to which prices might vary as capacity utilisation changes. *(15 marks)*

CHAPTER 31

Methods of production

The main methods of production — job, batch and flow — are studied in this chapter. The trade-off between productivity and flexibility is demonstrated and the factors that influence the method chosen are analysed. Capital-intensive and labour-intensive approaches to production are also compared. Finally, the implications for the UK's international competitiveness of the methods and approaches taken are examined.

Classification of production methods

Methods of production are classified in three ways:

KEY TERMS

job production: the manufacture of a one-off, specialised product, made individually to a certain specification (e.g. an athletics stadium or designer dress).

batch production: a method of production in which groups of products go through the various stages of production together, until the products are completed (e.g. bread and cakes).

flow production: a method of production based on manufacturing a product by using a continued flow of assembly. Once an individual product completes a stage of its production, it moves on to the next stage (often on a conveyor belt system) and is replaced on the conveyor by the next product, which is assembled in the same way (e.g. cars and radios).

Job production

In job production, items are often (but not necessarily) made to the consumer's own specifications. For example, people may request that some furniture is designed in a way that matches their specific needs. Unit costs of production are relatively high, as it is not possible to repeat processes continually. As people become richer, they are more likely to want these individual, personalised products.

As job production involves a one-off process, there is a high degree of flexibility. For example, the travel industry has recognised that fewer people want package holidays and it is now helping travellers to plan individualised (but more expensive) trips to different destinations.

Employees are usually more highly skilled than in other methods of

 FILE

General Welfare for the Blind (GWB) is an example of an organisation using job production. Set up in 1854 to produce quality beds and mattresses, it currently employs 28 people, 13 of whom are partially sighted or blind. Its unique selling points are individuality and quality.

It produces about 1,000 beds a year. Each one is an individual job and will have up to three workers dedicated to its production; two work on the bed base

and one on the mattress. The mattress will take up to a day to make, depending on its individuality, and only one of the stages involves the use of machinery. The bed bases take longer, but GWB offers a lead time of about 2 weeks.

The firm is regularly used by antique dealers, who need mattresses for non-standard bed sizes. The client list also includes celebrities such as Richard Branson and Misteeq, and designers who are looking for an unusual shape and design for their beds.

Source: Working Lunch, BBC, 21 February 2003.

production, to enable them to adapt to different customer requirements. The interest level is higher, so employees tend to be more motivated. However, production times are longer and output levels are lower than in firms using other methods.

Batch production

Passing a number of products together through each stage of the production process enables a firm to produce variations of similar products at the same time, such as jam doughnuts and apple doughnuts being produced in the same batch.

Unit costs are lower than for job production, as greater usage of machinery is possible. Production times are usually decided by the nature of the product: for example, a loaf of bread will bake for 2.5 hours but a batch of beer will take 2 weeks to ferment.

Flow production

In flow production, at any point in time a number of products will be at different stages of production. After all stages have been completed, the final product emerges from the end of the line. The large scale of flow production has led to the term **mass production** being used for this approach to manufacturing.

Products are more standardised than in job and batch production, although computerised production lines often give flexibility to the components added at different stages. Overall, there is generally less flexibility in the types of product that can be made in comparison to other methods.

Unit costs are lower, however, as items can be produced quickly using the same pieces of equipment for each product, giving scope for economies of

	Pros	Cons
Job production	• High added value, special-order products. • Interesting work; motivated staff. • Zero or low stock levels. • Easy to organise and control. • Good quality, usually. • More personalised production.	• Labour-intensive process and the skills involved mean high labour costs. • Long lead times. • High levels of work-in-progress. • Inefficient use of capital. • Little scope for economies of scale.
Batch production	• Some flexibility in product specification. • More effective utilisation of capital than in job production. • Some motivation for workforce, as jobs are less routine than flow production. • Ideal for perishable products.	• High levels of stocks of raw material and work in-progress. • More boring than job production for the workforce. • Long lead times possible. • Difficult to plan efficiently.
Flow production	• More efficient use of capital equipment. • Large-scale production leading to economies of scale. • Standardised quality. • Low-cost, unskilled labour. • Produces low-cost products.	• Routine jobs lead to demotivated staff. • Standard product, lacking in variety. • Inflexible to changes in taste. • Quality errors and disruptions to production can be very costly. • High capital costs, initially.

scale. It is also possible to save costs by employing unskilled labour. Many businesses have moved flow production to countries where labour forces are less skilled but are happy to accept lower wages. For example, Dyson ended the UK production of its vacuum cleaners in September 2002. In August 2003 Dyson announced that assembly of its washing machines would also be transferred to Malaysia.

Table 31.1 The relative merits of the methods of production

Table 31.1 sets out the advantages and disadvantages of each method of production.

Choosing the method of production

There are a number of factors that influence firms in their choice of production method, but the key issue is the need for productivity and/or flexibility. In general, flow production increases labour productivity and efficiency, by helping firms to produce standardised items at the lowest possible unit cost. In contrast, job production is much more flexible and can be adapted to the needs of the customer, but this takes away the benefits of mass production and leads to higher costs.

The actual method chosen will be influenced by several factors:

■ **The product.** Individual products such as a house extension require the flexibility offered by job production, so that the extension is compatible with the needs of the customer. Many food products must go through set processes (such as cooking) that take a fixed time, so they are most efficiently produced in batches. Standardised items that do not need individuality, such

as nails and screws, are ideally suited to flow production, as the main requirement is low price. A customer would not want to pay more for his or her furniture because the nails have been individually crafted.

■ **The size of the firm.** Small firms may be unable to finance the machinery needed for flow production. Their best chance of survival is to be flexible, making goods with high 'added value', such as unique pieces made by job production. Large firms, however, can afford to buy the expensive equipment needed for flow production. This will enable them to lower unit costs and so undercut the prices of smaller competitors, which may be forced out of the market.

■ **The type of 'product'.** Tertiary production (production in service industries) is often tailored to the individual needs of the customer, and thus tends to be job production. Even fairly standardised services such as window cleaning and hairdressing must be geared to the requirements of the customer.

■ **The market.** If customers require cheap, standardised products, flow production will dominate the industry. However, demand for varied, personalised products will suit job production. The market for men's suits is dominated by mass-produced items, as there is enough variety of design to suit the majority of the market, but some customers will pay extra for the flexibility in size, quality and design offered by tailor-made suits.

> **FACT FILE**
>
> Portakabin Ltd uses a mixture of batch and job production when it provides temporary accommodation. Batch production is used to provide the basic structure and standard fittings for a building. At the same time, the foundations for the new building are prepared at the customer's site. The items are then delivered to the site, where job production is used to add the special features required by the customer.

Capital-intensive and labour-intensive production

> **KEY TERMS**
>
> **capital-intensive production:** methods that use a high level of capital equipment in comparison to other inputs, such as labour. A fully automated factory, such as Fiat cars, and a nuclear power station are examples of capital-intensive production.
>
> **labour-intensive production:** methods that use high levels of labour in comparison to capital equipment. Many service industries such as retailing and call centres use a large number of people in comparison to equipment.

A business will weigh up a number of factors before deciding whether to use capital- or labour-intensive production. The most significant factors are as follows.

The method of production

In general, flow production and batch production need capital equipment if the firm is to maximise the benefits from using them. Consequently,

these methods will usually encourage a firm to choose capital-intensive production methods.

In contrast, job production depends much more on the skills of the workers and uses labour-intensive methods. So a firm using job production is likely to spend much more on its labour force.

The relative costs of labour and capital

Labour is relatively expensive in western Europe as compared to other parts of the world. As a result, firms that operate in this area will benefit from replacing labour with capital equipment. Fewer and fewer people in western Europe are now employed on production lines, as firms have automated production (replaced workers with machinery). In other parts of the world, labour is much cheaper to use and so production lines are more labour intensive. This situation has led to multinational corporations moving production from western Europe to other parts of the world where labour is cheaper.

Another consideration is the reliability of labour and capital. Industrial relations problems in industries such as car manufacturing led firms to decide that capital-intensive production methods were more cost effective because disruptions to production were very expensive. Conversely, unreliable equipment may encourage firms to choose labour-intensive production.

> **DID YOU KNOW?**
>
> At one time the ten multinational corporations that exported the most products to the USA all had one thing in common — they were American companies! In most cases, these firms had moved the location of their production plants to nearby countries such as Mexico, where labour costs were much lower. They then transported the goods into the USA, where they could be sold at lower prices than products actually made in the USA.

The financial position of a business

Capital equipment is very expensive to buy. It may not be possible for small businesses or firms with cash-flow difficulties to purchase the equipment needed for capital-intensive methods. As a consequence, these firms will choose labour-intensive production, which may cost more in the long run, but which is more affordable in the short term.

The product

The more standardised a product, the greater are the advantages of capital-intensive production. The more individualised a product, the greater is the need for labour.

The customer

If customers want personal contact, this may limit the scope for capital intensity. The banking industry has lowered its costs by automating many of

its processes, but many of its customers prefer the more sociable nature of a branch to the automated cash point. NatWest has used its 'labour intensity' as a selling point in its marketing campaigns.

Methods of production: implications for international competitiveness

For the UK to compete with other countries, its firms must choose efficient methods of production. Figure 31.1 compares the productivity of UK firms with those in other countries.

Figure 31.1 GDP per worker and per hour worked in 1999

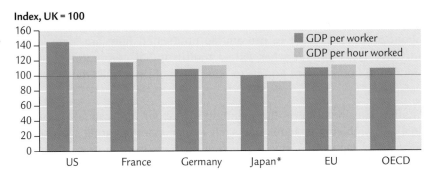

Index, UK = 100

(* GDP per hour for 1998)   Source: DTI calculations based on Harley and Owen (1998).

Key production or operational factors that influence international competitiveness are as follows:

■ **Investment in new equipment and technology.** Capital-intensive methods improve the speed, reliability and quality of products, and can still provide flexibility.

■ **Improvements in the quality of labour skills.** A skilled and educated staff is more adaptable and flexible, is able to cope with change more readily, and possesses more creativity and innovative talents. This helps the UK to compete in fields where individuality and creativity are important to the customer.

■ **Management services/work study approaches.** Scientific approaches to factory layout, which identify activities, analyse potential improvements and scrutinise the time taken to complete tasks, provide the foundation for improvements in productivity.

■ **Modifying factory layout and design.** Modifying the production line to incorporate improvements in technique, such as cell production, total quality management and just-in-time methods, also improves productivity (see Chapters 32–34).

■ **Strategic planning.** The pace of change requires companies to update and broaden their approaches constantly. Product life cycles are becoming shorter, and new ideas must be used to keep customers loyal. Efficient production methods are giving managers more time to concentrate on strategies rather than supervision of operations.

■ **Flexibility of production.** Keeping pace with changing consumer tastes helps a business to fight off competition. By adopting flexible methods, firms are able to modify their products or services, so that they meet the changing needs of consumers, who will thus remain loyal to the business.

PRACTICE EXERCISE

Total: 50 marks (40 minutes)

1 Explain the following terms:
  a batch production
  b flow production
  c job production *(9 marks)*

2 Explain two benefits of batch production. *(6 marks)*

3 Explain two problems of flow production. *(6 marks)*

4 Explain two disadvantages of job production. *(6 marks)*

5 Explain why the size of a firm might influence the type of production method chosen. *(5 marks)*

6 Briefly explain two factors that might influence a decision to use job production. *(6 marks)*

7 Distinguish between capital-intensive and labour-intensive production. *(4 marks)*

8 Explain one factor that would encourage a firm to use labour-intensive production. *(4 marks)*

9 Explain one factor that would encourage a firm to use capital-intensive production. *(4 marks)*

CASE STUDY Production methods at Nestlé

Chocolate production combines elements of batch and flow production. Take, for example, the stages involved in the production of Nestlé's Rolos.

TOPFOTO

Although cocoa originated in Central and South America, 66% of the world's supply now comes from Africa. During the early stages, cocoa farmers use **batch production** methods and production is very **labour intensive**.

1 Ripe pods are cut from the trees and the beans removed.

2 Batches of beans are then allowed to ferment in piles for about 6 days.

3 The beans will by now have turned brown. The batches are dried in the sun and then sold to manufacturers.

Chocolate manufacturers then take over the production process. Over three-quarters of the chocolate consumed in the UK is supplied by Cadbury, Nestlé and Mars; their main manufacturing plants are in Birmingham, York and Slough respectively.

The remaining processes are much more **capital intensive** than the stages outlined above. The next steps are as follows:

1 Cleaning the beans.
2 Winnowing — extracting the beans from their shells and heating them.
3 Roasting — to release the flavour.
4 Grinding — to produce cocoa paste.
5 Blending — mixing varieties of cocoa paste to achieve the right flavour, quality and hardness.

Nestlé and other chocolate manufacturers then use **flow production** to produce the chocolates. For Rolos, this means a continuous flow production line. The chocolate is poured into a mould. The chocolate then hardens and the filling is poured in, to be followed by the chocolate base. The remaining stages involve the addition of packaging so that the finished products leave Nestlé's production line ready for transportation.

When chocolate was first introduced into the UK, manufacturers used batch production. But as demand increased, the larger manufacturers moved into mass production using flow production techniques.

In the UK, very little chocolate is made through job production. Nestlé has occasionally used job production to support public relations activities. In general, however, Nestlé does not use job production, as it is much more expensive. Even Thorntons, whose reputation is based on the individuality of its chocolates, uses mass production and batch production methods, although on a much smaller scale. The main examples of job production at Thorntons are when specially requested lettering is added to a basic product. This type of job production is possible only because Thorntons owns the retail outlets.

Source: adapted from *The Times 100 Case Studies.*

Questions

Total: 50 marks (60 minutes)

1 Briefly explain **two** disadvantages that might occur because of the use of batch production by cocoa farmers. *(6 marks)*

2 Analyse **two** factors that Nestlé should consider before deciding to use flow production for a new product. *(8 marks)*

3 The early stages of chocolate production are labour intensive and take place overseas. The later stages are capital intensive and are based in the UK. Discuss the possible reasons for these differences. *(15 marks)*

4 Explain why Thorntons' ownership of retail outlets makes it easier for it to use job production than it is for Nestlé, which is only a manufacturer of chocolate. *(6 marks)*

5 Discuss the main reasons why job production is so rare in the production of chocolate products. *(15 marks)*

CHAPTER 32

Stock control

The key aspects of stock control are studied in this chapter. The idea of opportunity cost is outlined and used to show the relative merits of keeping high and low stock levels. The notion of stock control charts is introduced in order to explain important concepts such as buffer stocks, re-order levels and maximum stock levels. Stock wastage is explained and approaches to reducing wastage such as stock rotation and 'just-in-time' are examined.

Stocks are items that firms need to produce for, or supply to, customers. They can take three different forms:

- **Raw materials** — components or ingredients that will be used in the making of the good.
- **Work-in-progress** — part-finished products. For a business using flow production (see Chapter 31), it is common for some goods to be undergoing the production process at any given point of time.
- **Finished goods** — completed products that are owned by the firm until a sale has been agreed.

KEY TERMS

stock control: the management of levels of raw materials, work-in progress and finished goods in order to reduce storage costs while still meeting the demands of the customer.

opportunity cost: the next best alternative forgone. If a firm decides to hold higher stock levels, the opportunity cost is the use to which the firm would have put the money. Using money to hold high stock levels could lead to a reduction in the marketing budget or a decision not to replace a member of staff who has left. If more warehousing is needed, it may mean less space to display the products to customers.

What is the ideal level of stock?

It is very difficult to know the optimum level of stock. There are advantages to holding high stock levels and low stock levels, as shown in Table 32.1. Businesses must weigh these up before deciding on stock levels.

The ideal level of stock will therefore depend on circumstances:

- **Low** stock levels are sensible if a company is located in an area in which rents are high, has a perishable product and suffers from cash-flow problems.
- **High** stock levels would suit a business that gains large cost savings by bulk buying of a product that has unpredictable peaks in demand.

EXAMINER'S VOICE

Opportunity cost is a very important concept in business studies and is not just limited to decisions on stock levels. *Every* action in a business has a next best choice that was not selected. Opportunity cost is also relevant to everyday life, as any decision means that an alternative decision was not made.

Advantages of high stock levels	Advantages of low stock levels
• Customers' demands are met promptly. • There is no loss of goodwill caused by **stock-outs** (running out of stock). • Sudden increases in demand can be dealt with efficiently. • Production lines are not halted because of shortages of raw materials. • Companies can benefit from purchasing economies and from technical economies resulting from large, continuous production runs.	• Reduced warehousing costs are possible. • Opportunity cost is low. • Security and pilferage costs are lower. • Perishable products are less likely to deteriorate and problems of **obsolescence** (a product becoming outdated) are minimised. • Cash-flow problems due to cash being tied up in stocks are less probable.

Table 32.1
Advantages of high and low stock levels

Controlling stock levels

In order to monitor stock levels, a business will use a **stock control chart**. An example is shown in Figure 32.1 on p. 271. The following ideas are essential to understanding how a stock control chart works.

Buffer stocks

KEY TERM

buffer stocks: the minimum level of stocks targeted by an organisation. The buffer stock level should be enough to cover for sudden increases in demand or unexpected problems in getting stocks, such as a transport problem with a supplier.

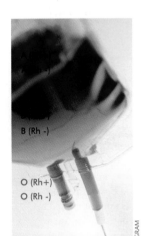

B (Rh -)

O (Rh+)
O (Rh -)

INGRAM

As firms try to save costs by minimising storage costs, it is becoming common for suppliers to make smaller but more regular deliveries of stock, so buffer stock levels are falling. However, high stock levels are still maintained in some organisations. For example, publicity about the dangers of smallpox led to an announcement that hospitals were holding high levels of smallpox vaccine, in case of an emergency. There has also been concern about low stocks of blood in hospitals.

Re-order level

KEY TERM

re-order level: the stock level at which an order is placed for new stock.

The re-order level will depend on three factors:
- the **lead time** of the supplier — how long the supplier takes to deliver once an order has been placed
- the demand for the product — the higher the demand, the higher the re-order level must be
- the buffer stock level — a high buffer stock usually needs a high re-order level

A lot of stock control is automated. In many shops, each time an article is sold the computer will register the fact that the stock level has fallen by 1 unit. When the number of items sold reduces the stock level to the re-order level,

the computer (which will be linked to the supplier's computer) will automatically place an order for new stock.

Maximum stock level

 TERM

maximum stock level: the highest amount of stock that the company is able to store.

Table 32.1 shows the advantages of holding high and low stock levels: these will be the factors that influence a firm's decision on how large a storage space it requires.

Figure 32.1 shows a stock control chart where everything operates in a predictable manner. The company starts with a stock level of 100 (its maximum stock level). Stock is used up at a rate of 30 units per week. After 1 week the re-order level (70 units) is reached and 60 units are ordered. The lead time is 1 week, so the 60 units are delivered at the end of the second week. At this point the stock has reached the buffer stock level of 40 units, so the stock level jumps to 100 units (40 in stock + 60 just delivered). This process then repeats itself every 2 weeks.

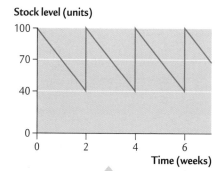

Figure 32.1
Stock control chart

WHAT DO YOU THINK?

What happens when stock control does not operate so smoothly? Look at Figure 32.1 and think how it would be changed in each of the following situations:
- There is an increase in demand by consumers, so stock levels reduce more quickly.
- There is a decrease in demand by consumers, so stock levels reduce more slowly.
- The business forgets to re-order when the re-order level is reached.
- A problem at the supplier or a transport difficulty means a delay in the delivery of stock (an increase in the lead time).
- The amount ordered is too high.
- The amount ordered is too low.

Some or all of these issues are dealt with in case study 2 on p. 275.

Stock wastage

 TERM

stock wastage: a measure of the loss of stock within a business.

There are a number of causes of stock wastage:
- raw materials being wasted during storage and production
- defects in production
- pilferage or theft
- damage to stocks during storage and production
- obsolescence (products becoming outmoded or being kept beyond their sell-by date)

Stock rotation

KEY TERM

stock rotation: using old stock before new stock to make sure that stock wastage is kept to a minimum.

Under stock rotation, warehouses are designed to make sure that new stock is not placed in a position where it blocks access to older stock. In shops, shelves are stacked so that the new stock is placed behind the old stock, to avoid the chances of products perishing.

DID YOU KNOW?

Many manufacturers and retailers are attaching tiny radio transmitters to items of stock (especially clothing) so that their exact location can be found at any point in time. This helps them to detect old stock that may have been left at the back of the shelf or in a warehouse. Although the radio transmitters only have a range of 5 metres, they have worried civil liberties groups as, in theory, they could be used to trace people's movements. They could also be used to detect thefts and pilferage. The European Central Bank is planning to put them into euro banknotes.

Improving the efficiency of stock control

Many firms now realise how vital stock management is in their operations. Traditionally, businesses kept high stock levels 'just in case' they were needed. However, this led to the need to sell off unwanted stock in 'sales' at the end of the year. Japanese firms led the way in challenging this idea, arguing that it was a waste of space and stock, costing the company money. This led to the introduction of **just-in-time** measures.

Just-in-time stock control

KEY TERM

just-in-time: a Japanese philosophy that organises operations so that items of stock arrive just at the time they are needed for production or sale. The ultimate aim is to eliminate the need for stock, although in practice this is not always ideal.

This form of stock control has a number of implications:
- Costs of raw materials are likely to be higher, as smaller but more frequent orders are placed. This means that there are fewer economies of scale for the purchaser.
- Problems may be experienced in getting raw materials on time. Any delays can halt the production line or mean disappointed customers. For this reason, firms prefer to deal with suppliers located nearby. For example, when Honda decided to locate in Swindon there were no significant suppliers of car components, but many suppliers have moved there to be close to Honda, which uses just-in-time.

- Costs of storage and insurance fall as stocks are delivered directly to the production line or placed immediately on to the shelves. Similarly, stocks of finished goods are sent out of the factory immediately, reducing the need for large areas of storage. This frees up space for more productive use. Typically, supermarkets used to devote two-thirds of their space to storage. Just-in-time deliveries have led to much of this space being changed to selling space, allowing a supermarket to serve far more customers from the same-sized building.
- There is less likelihood of stock perishing or becoming obsolete because goods spend little or no time in the warehouse.
- Production areas are less cluttered with work in progress and working environments may become safer.

FACT FILE

Although there are long-term benefits from introducing just-in-time stock control, in the short term it can cause difficulties for companies and their suppliers. Traditionally, Ford held stocks of completed cars equal to 80 days of sales. In 2003 it cut this to 70 days, a decision that led to real difficulties for many of its smaller suppliers whose products, in effect, were not ordered for 10 days, and for Ford's workers, whose working hours were temporarily cut.

PRACTICE EXERCISE

Total: 50 marks (40 minutes)

1 Identify the three different forms of stock. *(3 marks)*

2 Explain two advantages of holding high levels of stock. *(6 marks)*

3 Explain two problems of holding high levels of stock. *(6 marks)*

4 a Explain the meaning of the term 'opportunity cost'. *(3 marks)*

   b Briefly illustrate a business example of the concept of 'opportunity cost'. *(4 marks)*

5 Briefly explain three factors that will influence the re-order level of a product. *(6 marks)*

6 State four possible reasons for stock wastage. *(4 marks)*

7 What is meant by just-in-time stock control. *(2 marks)*

8 Explain two benefits of just-in-time stock control for a manufacturer. *(6 marks)*

9 Explain two problems of just-in-time stock control for a retailer. *(6 marks)*

10 Why might suppliers dislike supplying to a company that operates on a just-in-time basis? *(4 marks)*

CASE STUDY 1 Peacocks: the firm where cutting costs is a hanging matter

Stock control is not just about the levels of stock. Businesses must also meet the needs of their customers and make sure that stock control is cost effective.

The problem

Cost cutting is a challenge at Peacocks, the value clothing chain store with about 350 stores across the UK. Value clothing shops depend a great deal on low prices to sell their goods. At the low-price end of the clothing market, high sales volume is needed to make up for lower profit margins. Any idea that can save money will have a big impact on Peacocks' profits.

Corporate objectives

Two years ago, the board of Peacocks realised that they needed to reduce costs, so David Apjohn-Williams, a senior manager, was given the task of visiting a number of major discount retailers in the USA. There he discovered Plasti-form, an Australian manufacturer of clothes hangers. With worldwide manufacturing and distribution, Plasti-form is able to deliver hangers directly to clothes manufacturers around the world. The garments are placed on the hangers and delivered directly to the shop.

In effect, the hangers allowed Peacocks to introduce a new system of stock control.

The main benefits of this system are:

- Time is saved unpacking the clothes in Peacocks' shops, as they can be placed straight on to the display racks.
- Perhaps more importantly, Plasti-form hangers come with colour-coded price tags, which slip easily on to the top of each hanger. This eliminates time spent by the shop assistants trying to locate the price tag.
- Peacocks believes that the brightly coloured price tags improve the look of the store and make it easier for customers to find the right product.
- The hangers can be re-used — each hanger is returned to the manufacturer and, on average, is used six times before it becomes a part of the recycling heap.

- Shop assistants can identify levels of stock for each garment more easily, so it is possible to reduce stock levels.

Plasti-form agreed to set up distribution centres near Peacocks' overseas factories, which are mainly based in China, Hong Kong, Sri Lanka, Pakistan, Bangladesh, India and Morocco. After a successful trial in its Cardiff store, Peacocks spent £1.5 million (just over £4,000 per store) on modifying its stockrooms and stores so that the new system could be introduced.

The result

Chief executive Richard Kirk detailed the cost savings expected by Peacocks as a result of the new system: 'We will save £2 million per annum from reduced labour costs as about 400,000 hours of staff time will be saved. Furthermore, Plasti-form hangers cost 5p each, as opposed to the 13p Peacocks forked out for its old hangers.' It is estimated that over £300,000 per annum will be saved on hangers.

Peacocks also hopes that the system will result in big sales increases. The colour-based price tag system means that customers can locate their size more easily. Shop staff are able to identify missing sizes more quickly and replenish the stocks so that customers' needs can always be met. In the Cardiff trial, sales revenue grew by 10%. If this were to be repeated nationally, then Peacocks' sales would grow from £160 million in 2002 to £176 million in 2003. (In fact, in 2003, sales at Peacocks stores rose to £181 million — and to £230 million, if Bonmarché stores are included.)

The future

As Peacocks works on low profit margins, these cost savings have had a noticeable impact on profit. Peacocks has recently purchased Bonmarche, another cut-price retailer, and is expanding its number of shops. The new hangers will help to cut Peacocks' stockholding costs further, which are much higher than clothing stores that concentrate more on fashion and thus rely more on just-in-time stock systems. In Peacocks both the maximum and buffer stock levels have been reduced as a result of the new system. In 2002 Peacocks' average stock level was equal to 40% of annual sales; by 2003 this had been reduced to 28%. This has greatly assisted both cash flow and profit.

In the year following the introduction of the new hangers, the profit margin on Peacocks' products more than doubled from 2.8% to 5.7%, with overall profit rising from £5.3 million to £13.7 million, although it is impossible to discover how much of this improvement resulted from the new system.

Source: based on an article by Sally Patten in *The Times*, 6 August 2002, and information from the website of the Peacock Group plc.

Questions

Total: 50 marks (60 minutes)

1 Analyse **one** reason why a 'value' clothing store might pay more attention to the importance of stock control costs than a fashion retailer. *(6 marks)*

2 Explain **one** possible disadvantage to *Peacocks* of its new system of stock control. *(6 marks)*

3 Analyse **two** factors that might explain why *Peacocks* does not use just-in-time in its stock control. *(8 marks)*

4 Discuss the main reasons why the new hangers helped *Peacocks* to reduce its maximum and buffer stock levels. *(15 marks)*

5 To what extent is it possible to calculate how much of *Peacocks'* increased profits came from the new stock control system? *(15 marks)*

CASE STUDY 2   Stock out of control

Mich Magni looked at the stock control chart and wept. He couldn't understand where it had all gone so horribly wrong. For 20 years his company had successfully survived in the competitive world of pizzas. At first it had been easy. The local demand in his home town of Bedford had given him a firm base on which to expand, and the excellent transport links had encouraged him to extend his target market into London and the Midlands.

Magni Pizzas produced a range of frozen pizzas, but its main business was in supplying freshly made pizzas to supermarkets. Magni purchased ready-made pizza bases from a local supplier, Bedford International Pizza Bases (BIPB) plc, and transformed them into completed pizzas by adding a variety of different toppings. There had been difficulties in facing up to competition from larger food manufacturers, but in recent years the market for more expensive, individually made pizzas had grown, and Mich's business had secured valuable contracts with two of the UK's largest supermarkets. This had persuaded him to set up the new factory, which was fully automated. The ingredients were delivered regularly, in small batches, and fed straight into the production line. Each day's production schedule was based on weekly orders from the supermarkets, so that Mich's firm had sufficient time to buy in the stock needed.

The new factory opened in October and operated smoothly for the first 2 months. After 20 years in the business and the successful expansion of his firm, Mich decided to take a long holiday in Naples, visiting relatives and friends whom he had not seen for many years. Mich's brother Hugo was placed in temporary charge.

Mich returned to Bedford in late January. Hugo had been very evasive on the telephone and Mich sensed that something might be wrong. The plane touched down at 6 p.m. on Sunday evening; by 8 p.m. Mich was in the factory trying to find some clues to Hugo's behaviour. Mich was disturbed when the first two letters that he opened were from his new supermarket customers, threatening to end the contracts 'unless immediate action is taken to improve the reliability of deliveries'. Unfortunately, the only other item that he could find was a stock control chart, showing the stock levels of pizza bases delivered by BIPB (Figure 32.2).

Stock levels of pizza bases

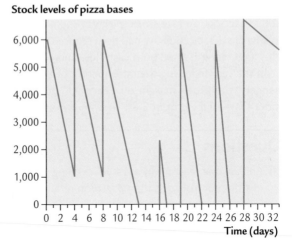

Figure 32.2 *Stock levels of pizza bases*

Mich studied the chart, trying to piece together the events of the past month or so.

Questions

Total: 55 marks (65 minutes)*

*Question 1 has been included to test understanding of some key stock control terms. The remaining questions are set out in the style of a Unit 2 examination. Allow 60 minutes for completion if question 1 is not included — the maximum marks will be 50 in this case.

1 In the first 8 days, stock control operated smoothly. Use this information and Figure 32.2 to work out the value of:
   a the maximum stock level *(1 mark)*
   b the buffer stock level *(1 mark)*
   c the re-order level, assuming a lead time of 2 days *(3 marks)*

2 Briefly explain **two** factors that might have caused the company to run out of stock on day 13. *(6 marks)*

3 Explain why the stock-outs (absence of stocks) during the period between days 17 and 28 were caused by different factors from those that led to the stock-out on day 13. *(8 marks)*

4 Explain **two** possible reasons for the change in the chart after day 28. *(6 marks)*

5 Discuss the implications of the situation shown in the chart for Mich's business. *(15 marks)*

6 To what extent could the problems shown have been prevented? *(15 marks)*

CHAPTER 33

Quality control, improvement and assurance

As economies grow richer, customers place a much greater emphasis on quality when purchasing products or services. This chapter scrutinises the concept of quality and compares the different approaches that organisations can take to improve quality: quality control based on inspection or quality assurance based on self-checking. Total quality management (TQM) is considered as an approach to quality assurance. The role of quality standards (such as BS 5750 and ISO 9000) and benchmarking as means of guaranteeing and improving quality are considered.

Quality

 TERM

> **quality:** those features of a product or service that allow it to satisfy (or delight) customers.

Quality is subjective — a matter of personal opinion — and views of it will vary from individual to individual. In most cases, quality can be seen as a tangible factor, such as speed or durability, but some customers place emphasis on intangible factors, such as the assurance provided by a firm's name.

Tangible measures of quality

- **Appearance.** For fashion clothing, this would be considered the all-important measure.
- **Reliability.** Machinery will be in constant use, so reliability is needed.
- **Durability.** A firm hiring lorries would expect strength and a long-lasting vehicle.
- **Functions (added extras).** Mobile phones are made more attractive by the range of additional functions offered.
- **After-sales service: cost, promptness and effectiveness.** High-quality after-sales service is needed for a firm's IT network, as breakdowns will be very costly.
- **Repair and maintenance needs.** A car that requires less servicing and few repairs would be considered to be of high quality.

Intangible measures of quality

- **Image and brand.** Cadbury is seen as a good brand, even though it has diversified well beyond its original products.
- **Reputation.** An organisation such as *The Times* newspaper has developed a reputation for quality.
  - **Exclusiveness.** Brands such as Chanel are able to use their name to introduce new products and charge high prices because the customer assumes that they are of high quality.

These factors may relate to other values, such as the firm's treatment of its staff or the environment or ethical issues. For example, Nestlé's image has suffered in recent years because of its marketing of products such as baby milk in less economically developed countries.

The value of quality systems

In deciding whether to introduce quality systems into its operations, a firm must weigh up the costs of having a system against the costs (both direct and 'hidden') of not controlling quality. These costs are set out in Table 33.1.

Table 33.1 Assessing the value of quality systems

The costs of a quality system	The costs of not controlling quality	
	Direct	'Hidden'
• designing and setting up	• reworking	• lost customers
• monitoring	• rechecking	• staff overtime
• scrapping of waste	• query handling	• lost reputation/loyalty
• new machinery	• lost revenue	• machine downtime
• training		• fall in employee morale

The remainder of this chapter examines the various methods by which organisations can seek to provide quality.

Quality control

KEY TERM

quality control: a system that uses **inspection** as a way of finding any faults in the good or service being provided.

Traditionally, quality inspectors were employed by organisations to check the accuracy of completed work, and also the quality of goods received from suppliers. This approach was taken because it was believed that:

- Many workers would not take responsibility for quality and needed close supervision (a Theory X view).
- Specialist staff were needed to recognise the suitability of a product for consumers or the production line.

Benefits of inspection

- Inspection at the end of the process can prevent a defective product reaching the customer, thus eliminating a problem with a whole batch of products.

- It is a more secure system than one that trusts every individual to do his or her job properly.
- Inspectors may detect common problems throughout an organisation, so mistakes can be put right more efficiently. It is possible that an incorrectly trained group of workers will not realise that their work does not reach the right level of quality.

Problems of inspection

The idea that an inspector (rather than a worker directly involved in production) should be 'responsible' for quality has lost favour, for three main reasons:

- By placing responsibility for quality failures on the inspector, it does little to encourage individuals to improve the quality of their output.
- Employing an inspection team is an expense that could be viewed as unnecessary if the products are produced 'right first time'.
- Giving workers responsibility for their own work helps to increase the interest, variety and responsibility within a job, and thus helps to motivate workers.

Quality assurance

For the reasons given above, many companies have moved from quality control to **quality assurance**, and from checking by inspectors to **self-checking**.

 TERM

> **quality assurance:** a system that aims to achieve quality by organising every process to get the product 'right first time' and prevent mistakes ever happening.

While quality control is based on the end product or service, quality assurance concentrates on the *process* of production. The idea of self-checking is crucial to quality assurance.

Benefits of quality assurance

- Ownership of the product or service rests with the workers rather than with an independent inspector, giving them greater responsibility.
- Theorists such as Herzberg argue that there are positive effects on motivation due to this sense of ownership and recognition of the worker's job.
- Costs are reduced because there is less waste and less need for reworking of faulty products. Under inspection it is possible for a fault to occur at the first stage of production and yet for many more components to be added before the product is deemed unsuitable.
- With all staff responsible for quality, there should be a higher and more consistent level of quality, which can lead to marketing advantages for the firm.

Because quality assurance processes make individual workers responsible for their job, they should also allow workers to reject any partially completed item that they receive from the person before them in the supply chain, if it lacks quality. An individual will not want to be blamed for a faulty product if the fault lies with the previous person on the production line or in the office. This system effectively means that inspection now takes place at the beginning and end of every part of the production process, greatly reducing the possibility of a faulty end product.

The most widely recognised quality assurance system is **total quality management**.

Total quality management

 TERM

> **total quality management (TQM):** a culture of quality that involves all employees of a firm.

Under total quality management, organisations consist of **quality chains** in which each person treats the receiver of their work as if they were an external customer, and adopts a target of 'right first time'. In this way, every department of a firm contributes to the quality of its products and services.

This philosophy has developed from Japanese companies, but ironically the person generally considered to be the main instigator of this philosophy was an American engineer, Dr W. E. Deming. His 14-point plan applies to management in general, but is particularly applicable to quality management:

1 'Right first time' — aim for defect prevention rather than detection.
2 Provide a consistent, clear message on quality.
3 All staff must share a commitment to continuous improvement and change.
4 Build partnerships with suppliers (many companies have extended this to apply to the supply chain within an organisation).
5 Constantly improve.
6 Educate and train staff to take responsibility for their own quality.
7 Supervisors should encourage and help.
8 Encourage change by eliminating the 'fear of failure' factor when introducing improvements.
9 Integrate departments and share problem solving.
10 Set clear, achievable goals.
11 Avoid setting global standards of work.
12 Help employees to take pride in their work.
13 Train and educate.
14 Establish a structure and culture to support these aims.

Arising from this philosophy, company TQM systems usually possess common features:
- commitment to the needs of the customer

- close links with all members of the 'supply chain'
- personal responsibility for actions among all employees
- company-wide policies applicable to all staff
- an emphasis on teamwork
- clear measures of quality
- information gathering to support these measures
- well-used, two-way communication systems

By combining these characteristics, a business should be able to recognise the quality needs of its customers and satisfy them in a consistent and flexible manner. TQM also provides the background for a good working environment for the firm's staff.

Quality improvement

In the words of Sir John Harvey Jones, the former head of ICI, 'If you are not making progress all the time, you are slipping backwards.' In a dynamic business environment, quality improvement must be a constant challenge, as any business that believes it has produced the highest-quality product will soon be overtaken by its rivals.

In order to improve quality continuously, a firm relies on the following:

- **Market research.** The standard for 'quality' is set by the customer, who is therefore the best place to start. Comments from consumers and feedback from the market guide a firm towards making improvements to products that are needed to keep its customers satisfied. Organisations such as the Department of Trade and Industry (DTI) also provide data on the factors and features that are most valued in the marketplace.
- **Research and development.** Within an organisation, teams of staff investigate new products, innovations and processes with the aim of providing a higher-quality product in the most cost-effective way.
- **Kaizen groups.** Kaizen is a Japanese term meaning 'continuous improvement'. It is a philosophy whereby improvements are made through a series of small, incremental changes, based mainly on the ideas of people within the organisation. Kaizen groups of employees suggest possible improvements to production or quality, according to their observations on how things can be improved within a firm. Kaizen groups are an example of lean production and their focus is not just on quality improvement. Consequently, they are examined in more detail in Chapter 34.

INGRAM

EXAMINER'S VOICE

The decision to select a specific approach to improving quality may depend on the work-force. Do they have the skills to operate quality assurance? Would they be motivated by more responsibility? Has the existing approach worked?

Quality standards

 TERMS

BS 5750: a British Standards award granted to organisations that possess quality assurance systems that meet the standards set.

ISO 9000: the international standard of quality assurance that is equivalent to BS 5750.

BS 5750 and ISO 9000 both aim to increase quality throughout an organisation. To achieve them, firms must show that they have quality systems that cover the quality of their working methods, services and processes as well as the quality of their products. The focus is on prevention (or rapid detection) of defects, ensuring that adequate support systems are in place and good teamworking exists.

The benefits of these awards are:
- marketing advantages from the acknowledgement of higher quality standards
- assurance to customers that products meet certain standards — some organisations insist on these awards before agreeing to trade with a firm, as this helps to guarantee the quality of their supplies
- greater employee motivation from the sense of responsibility and recognition
- financial benefits in the long term, from the elimination of waste and the improved reputation of the firm

Many firms also acknowledge that the procedure needed to gain and keep these awards makes them focus more fully on the needs of their customers.

A criticism made of these standards is that they emphasise procedures rather than the end product. As long as a firm has a clear process for setting standards and proves that it is keeping to these procedures, it will achieve BS 5750 or ISO 9000. However, its definition of acceptable quality may be different from that of another company. Consequently, BS 5750 guarantees that a firm has standards and keeps to them; it does not guarantee that the standards are higher than those of a company without the award.

Benchmarking

 KEY TERM

> **benchmarking:** the process of setting competitive standards, based on the achievements of other firms, against which an organisation will monitor its progress. The benchmarking organisation tends to focus on the companies that are best in its industry ('best in class'), but for specific functions a company may compare itself with organisations in other industries.

The benchmarking process
The benchmarking process involves the following stages:
1 Select the processes and/or activities to be benchmarked.
2 Identify the best in class, against which to benchmark.
3 Gather data from both organisations and analyse any performance gaps.
4 Establish reasons for these gaps and set targets for improvement.
5 Agree and implement new strategies and review the results.
6 Continue the process. Benchmarking should be seen as a never-ending process.

 **EXAMINER'S VOICE**

The usefulness of benchmarking will be limited by the opportunities for access to other firms' data.

Benefits of benchmarking

- A firm can gauge what it is possible to achieve and compare this to its own level of performance. This process will help the firm to recognise how much potential for improvement exists.
- Data from other firms can provide ideas and inspiration to help the organisation to improve its quality and efficiency. Often, these ideas can be applied to many areas of an organisation besides the one involved in the original comparisons.
- Cost advantages achieved through more efficient methods and reduced wastage can improve an organisation's competitiveness.

Although these benefits can be achieved through other methods, the main benefit of benchmarking is that it tends to offer a much quicker solution than other approaches, especially those that depend on an organisation's own resources.

Possible reasons for the failure of benchmarking

- It may not be possible to introduce an approach that has been successful in one firm into another organisation. For example, a successful method in a decentralised organisation may not be effective in a centralised company.
- There may be a lack of belief by staff, who may be demoralised by the challenge of achieving what they consider to be unrealistic targets. Targets for improvement should be agreed and not just based on those achieved by the best competitor.
- The benchmarking study itself may become the focus of activity, rather than the implementation of strategy. Energy must be put into following up the consequences of benchmarking.
- There can be difficulties in gathering reliable information — in particular, other organisations may be reluctant to share their data. Benchmarking is more likely to succeed if organisations share each other's data.
- If it is seen as a copying exercise, benchmarking may be counterproductive because the business will not look into the reasons for its own underperformance.

Internal benchmarking

It is not necessary for benchmarking to involve comparisons with outside organisations. Because of the limited competition in its market, Mothercare believes that the best way to improve is to use different approaches in its own stores and compare the results. The most successful stores become the benchmark for other stores, which then copy the approach that brought success. As a result, Mothercare has made changes such as store refurbishment, changes in product ranges and reductions in variety where a broad range was not cost effective. For instance, Mothercare now stocks five baby car seats rather than 23.

EXAMINER'S VOICE

The AQA specification states that for the section on controlling operations there will be a focus 'on qualitative understanding of the issues, *although there may be a requirement to analyse data*'.

You are therefore advised to answer question 5 of the case study on p. 285 in order to practise this skill.

> **FACT FILE**
>
> Benchmarking does not necessarily involve comparisons with a business in the same industry. For example, Coca-Cola and Nike are acknowledged for their marketing skills, and are often used by organisations seeking to improve their benchmarking. When Amancio Ortega, Spain's richest man and the founder of Zara, wanted to introduce a system of rapid distribution, he ignored the fashion industry and examined DHL, the courier company.

PRACTICE EXERCISE

Total: 60 marks (50 minutes)

1 Define 'quality'. *(3 marks)*

2 Give four examples of tangible measures of quality. *(4 marks)*

3 Give two examples of intangible measures of quality. *(2 marks)*

4 Briefly explain two advantages of a successful quality system. *(6 marks)*

5 Describe the differences between quality control and quality assurance. *(6 marks)*

6 Explain why more firms are moving from quality control to quality assurance. *(6 marks)*

7 What does the acronym TQM stand for? *(3 marks)*

8 State five features of a TQM system. *(5 marks)*

9 What is a kaizen group and what is its significance for quality improvement? *(7 marks)*

10 What is wrong with the following statement: 'BS 9000 is the British Standard awarded to organisations that possess quality assurance systems that meet the standards set. The international equivalent is ISO 5750.' *(3 marks)*

11 Explain one benefit and one weakness of the quality standards system. *(6 marks)*

12 Explain the meaning of the word 'benchmarking'. *(3 marks)*

13 Explain one benefit and one problem of benchmarking for a business. *(6 marks)*

CASE STUDY Constance Products plc

Jake Turner was determined to succeed. Since his appointment as operations director at Constance Products, he had vowed that he would restore the company's tarnished image.

Jake's first action had been to dismantle the firm's quality control inspection at the end of production. With the backing of managing director, Sarah Hall, Jake had presented his ideas to the workforce.

Each worker would become responsible for his or her own quality and any worker could stop the production line if he or she felt that there was a problem. The workers were particularly pleased to hear that the production line would be closed down for 2 weeks to enable it to be redesigned and that they would be given training in the new quality assurance procedures.

The first few weeks were a disaster. Everyone produced slowly to avoid mistakes, but gradually productivity improved. For Jake, the subsequent improvement in quality was the most pleasing result, but the workers saw it differently. After 9 months they were finding that greater responsibility meant a more interesting job. Sam Bulmer, the human resources manager, was overjoyed at the increased morale within the workforce and the fall in staff turnover, and people were looking forward to the productivity bonuses that were being anticipated in 3 months' time.

Sarah was not satisfied, however. She believed that there was still room for improvement.

Constance Products was based in County Durham and its customer base was Scotland and the north. Sarah had been approached by the managing director of Bremmen plc, a London-based rival, with a view to establishing a benchmarking exercise. Sarah had agreed, as the two firms were not direct competitors. However, she was worried by the results. 'Their production is geared towards individual jobs rather than the mass market that we target. Whereas 40% of their staff are graduates, we have only 5% of our employees with degrees. I am not convinced that our workers can adapt to their approaches.'

Bremmen appeared to be more efficient in most categories and Sarah was concerned that the company might target expansion into the north as a direct result of the benchmarking exercise.

Sarah presented the benchmarking results to the board of directors (Table 33.2).

Measures of quality	Constance Products plc	Bremmen plc
Distribution		
Delivery time (days)	1.8	1.0
% of deliveries on time	93	99
Production		
Lead time (days)	6.6	2.3
Quality		
Scrap rate (%)	1	5
Rating of customer satisfaction (%)	88	93
Customer complaints (%)	3	5

Table 33.2 *Benchmarking exercise: Constance Products plc and Bremmen plc*

'These are the six measures of quality that are most important to our customers. In my opinion we need to strengthen two of these measures of quality in the next 6 months, or else Bremmen may start targeting our area for expansion.'

Questions
Total: 50 marks (60 minutes)

1 Explain how the system of quality control formerly used at Constance Products helped to ensure high quality. *(6 marks)*

2 Analyse the reasons why a shift to quality assurance led to 'increased morale within the workforce'. *(8 marks)*

3 Evaluate the problems that Constance Products might face as a result of changing its approach from quality control to quality assurance. *(15 marks)*

4 Using the information in the case study, explain **one** problem of benchmarking that affected Constance Products. *(6 marks)*

5 Sarah believes that two of the six measures of quality identified in the benchmarking exercise need to be improved within the next 6 months. Identify the **two** measures that should be improved and discuss the reasons for your choices. *(15 marks)*

CHAPTER 34

Methods of lean production

This chapter looks at some of the main elements of lean production:
- *cell production — its purpose and methods*
- *just-in-time (briefly linking lean production to the detail on just-in-time methods provided in Chapter 32)*
- *time-based management, notably shorter product development times and simultaneous engineering*
- *continuous improvement (kaizen) and the principles of gradual change and staff involvement in change*

It concludes with a comparison of mass production and lean production approaches.

> **KEY TERM**
>
> **lean production:** production based on the range of waste-saving measures inspired by Japanese manufacturing companies.

Cell production

> **KEY TERM**
>
> **cell production:** the splitting of a continuous flow production line into self-contained units or clusters. Each unit produces a completely finished article, or a significant element of it, leading to improvements in the commitment of the workforce.

Typically, a flow production line is modified so that teams of workers can share a series of tasks or a section or stage of production. These teams are empowered (given independence) to decide on their targets and approaches to work, although these must be consistent with the overall aims of the organisation.

The purpose of cell production
The exact purpose of cell production varies according to the business. It has been introduced to overcome difficulties experienced by companies using mass production methods, although modern factories are often designed to allow for cell production from the outset. Possible purposes are:
- To improve workers' motivation by providing them with job rotation and job enrichment (see Chapter 22).

- To give employees the opportunity to complete a more satisfying range of output, in order to avoid the boredom and related problems caused by narrow specialisation and simple routine jobs. Volvo introduced cell production in order to reduce the levels of absenteeism and trade union action, which were blamed on boredom at work.
- To improve the quality of the product or service. By giving more independence and responsibility to employees, firms have been able to improve the quality of their work.

Cell production may not suit all situations. In order for it to work, it may be necessary to:

- Improve the layout and design of the production line (and possibly the product) so that separate cells can operate on their particular stages or tasks.
- Ensure that there is a balancing of time between the different activities within the cell, to avoid excessive waiting times (and hence waste).
- Check that the level of production is enough to justify the allocation of resources to a cell. On a small-scale production line, there may not be enough savings to make cell production economically feasible.
- Change materials-handling systems so that components or ingredients can be delivered directly to the cells in a cost-efficient way.

Benefits of cell production

Cell production has a number of potential benefits:

- The closeness of the cell members should improve communication and help to avoid problems caused by misunderstanding or non-receipt of messages.
- Workers should become more flexible (multi-skilled), thus increasing their adaptability to future changes in production.
- There should be greater motivation, arising from the variety of work, teamwork and greater responsibility.
- Product quality should improve as 'ownership' of the product is felt by the cell.

Collectively, these benefits may also increase the efficiency and productivity of production, but this is not guaranteed. Moving away from flow production can lead to lower levels of production, despite the benefits shown, as cell production does not always enable a business to use its machinery as intensively as a more traditional style of production.

Teamworking

Teamworking involves the use of teams such as production cells or autonomous (independent) work groups. These teams are given greater responsibility so that the workers can take critical decisions and solve problems, often setting their own objectives.

Teamworking provides opportunities for job enlargement as workers are often allowed to take on a variety of different tasks within the team. Teams may also benefit from the specialist skills of individual team members which can increase productivity.

Teamworking has been closely linked to motivation:

- Mayo's Hawthorne experiments revealed the importance of team and group norms.
- Maslow recognised social needs as a potential motivator which teams often provide in the workplace.
- Herzberg noted the importance of working with others, although in his two-factor theory it was seen as a maintenance factor — i.e. a demotivator if not provided for adequately — rather than as a motivator.

Teams can also create 'synergy' — a situation in which the combined results of a team of individuals is greater than the individual parts. This can be seen in teamwork in professions such as architecture, where ideas from different architects can create buildings far superior to those that would be designed if each architect worked independently.

Just-in-time

 KEY TERM

just-in-time: a Japanese philosophy that organises operations so that items of stock arrive just at the time they are needed for production or sale. The ultimate aim is to eliminate the need for stock, although in practice this is not always ideal.

The concept of just-in-time was introduced in Chapter 32 as a method of stock control. This section builds on Chapter 32 in order to show the significance of just-in-time to lean production.

Purposes of just-in-time

The main aim of just-in-time is to reduce waste by eliminating the need for high levels of stock. This can enable a business to reduce costs by cutting warehouse space and staffing costs linked to the warehouse. Lower stock levels also reduce the losses to a firm caused by pilferage (theft), damage during storage, or products perishing or becoming obsolete (out-of-date).

Just-in-time techniques save time, too, as stock can be delivered straight to the production line or shelves, ready for use, saving on the time spent moving them between the 'goods in' area to the warehouse and then on to the production line/shelf. Time may also be saved because the space saved may mean that the production line is more compact, reducing distances between different stages of production, and avoiding some of the problems of stock cluttering up the factory that can be commonplace in factories not using just-in-time methods.

Just-in-time also aims to provide flexibility for customers. Companies with zero stock levels are more willing to respond to changes in customer tastes as they will not suffer from unsold stock if there is a sudden shift to the production of new goods.

A central business aim is to 'add value'. Stock in a warehouse is not adding value to the business; it only adds value when it forms part of the finished product. Just-in-time places stock straight onto the production line where it immediately adds value.

Just-in-time methods are often described as a system based on 'pull' rather than 'push'. Traditionally, businesses made products which were 'pushed' through the production process in the hope that they would then sell in the market place. The driving force behind the decision to manufacture was the firm's desire to sell a product. Just-in-time is linked to customers' needs instead. Customers place an order which leads to the product being made (the product is 'pulled' through the production process by the desire of the customer to have a particular design on a particular date). The push system led to stocks of finished products waiting to be sold. The pull system means that there is a customer waiting for the finished product, eliminating the need for high stock levels.

> **DID YOU KNOW?**
>
> The move to flexible production is being driven by consumers. Companies such as Dell have led the way in providing fast, customised products for consumers. In the travel industry, the fastest-growing sector is the provision of tailor-made holidays built around the requirements of the individual customer.

Requirements of a just-in-time system

To operate efficiently, just-in-time requires careful planning and organisation. For it to work a firm needs:

- Excellent communications and high levels of cooperation and flexibility from suppliers. (Ironically, to guarantee just-in-time deliveries to their customers, some suppliers need to keep high levels of stock in case of problems.)
- Reliable and flexible employees who are prepared to modify their workloads to cope with sudden increases in activity. Many organisations have needed to agree new contracts and working conditions with their employees, as rigid job descriptions prevented the success of just-in-time methods. Workforces have also changed to include more short-term or part-time workers who can help a business to cope with sudden changes in workload.
- A flexible approach to managing workers, so that employees see tangible benefits (such as financial rewards or time off) from their greater flexibility. A benefit that has suited both employees and employers has been increased training to allow workers to become **multi-skilled** (able to do a wide range

of jobs). This has increased job opportunities for workers and flexibility for the organisation.

- Suitable equipment so that machinery can be adapted quickly to changing needs. Many production lines can be changed in this way. For example, to change their production, cinemas only need to insert a different film, so they can plan their schedules on a short-term basis according to customer demand. Car manufacturers can modify the fittings, colours and components of a particular model of car so that six different versions of a model are completed in sequence. These are then driven straight on to the transporter, for delivery to the garage whose customers ordered those styles of car.

Just-in-time and people

Just-in-time links closely to people management. Greater responsibility is placed on individual employees. Many factories give authority to production line workers to stop the production line if they detect that a delivery of new stock is likely to endanger the quality of the finished product.

Flexibility is also key. Workers in the factories of suppliers must be prepared to complete a job at short notice, if an organisation wants an immediate delivery. Similarly, workers at the organisation must react quickly to sudden changes in the requirements of their customers. Multi-skilling and job enrichment have become essential features of organisations, so that the workforce has the ability and authority to meet urgent requests from customers without the need to consult with and involve other staff or managers. It is also possible that well-trained, highly-skilled staff will be able to anticipate changes in the market and prepare the business in a pro-active manner, rather than constantly reacting to changes after they have happened.

The minimising of waste in production

A central element of lean production is the identification of waste and its elimination. There are many sources of waste that can be reduced by lean production methods.

Product waste

- **Over-production.** 'Just-in-case' production and stock control systems mean that products are pushed through the production line in the hope that they will be sold. By introducing just-in-time methods, a firm can pull stock through the system in response to a known demand, so it is unlikely that finished stocks will be wasted because of a lack of customers.
- **Reject products.** Quality assurance means that faults are prevented (or detected earlier), reducing the wastage of raw materials and work-in-progress during manufacturing.
- **Over-ordering of materials.** This should not present a problem in lean production, as orders are placed (just-in-time) when the firm knows exactly how many items need to be made.

Time waste

- **Movement of materials.** Lengthy movement of materials between warehouses is reduced as they are delivered directly to the production line, with the finished product going straight to the customer.
- **Planning and decision making.** Involving teams in planning and decision making should mean that efficiency is improved by the ideas generated.
- **Bottlenecks.** These should be eliminated, as the flexibility of the workers means that additional staff can be used to deal with problem areas. In Japanese companies it is common for managers to wear overalls, so that they can assist in production if problems occur.

Time-based management

> **time-based management:** an approach that recognises the importance of time and seeks to reduce the level of 'unproductive' time within an organisation. This leads to quicker response times, faster new product development and reductions in waste, culminating in greater efficiency.

In some organisations, time is used as a selling point — the ability of the firm to respond to a customer request can give firms a competitive advantage. The AA, RAC and other motoring organisations see quick response times as a means of improving customer loyalty. They pay particular attention to the needs of female motorists and families, who might be considered to be in need of a more rapid response. Organisations use the flexibility of their staff and other resources and approaches, such as just-in-time, in order to respond quickly to customer needs.

More specific applications of time-based management can be seen in the form of shorter product development times and simultaneous engineering.

Shorter product development times

Constant changes in customer demands and the high failure rate among new products mean that companies that can produce new products quickly are able to stay competitive. Sainsbury's has been slow to react to changes in the marketplace and has lost market share as competitors have recognised the benefits of diversifying into non-grocery products such as clothing. Continual market research enables firms to identify potential trends and so change their product range.

Flexible production methods can also allow firms to modify their products quickly in response to the market. Information technology has helped businesses to modify and adapt their processes very quickly.

Simultaneous engineering

To help them to develop new products more quickly, firms have introduced simultaneous engineering. This takes place when all of the areas involved in a project to introduce a new product are planned together. Everything is considered simultaneously (at the same time) rather than in a series of stages. Simultaneous engineering has the following characteristics:

- Product teams are set up to include people in all areas that are relevant to the new product — design, development, production, marketing etc.
- Suppliers are involved in the new product development process so that potential delays can be anticipated and avoided.
- A teamwork approach is used with all areas working on the project at the same time. In this way, the needs of the marketing department can be included in the design; or difficulties in getting suitable materials can be identified and changes made to avoid this problem.

The end result is that the new product is brought to the market much more quickly and the need for re-engineering (modifying the product) because of a problem being discovered is reduced. The firm can therefore beat its competitors in the race to produce the newest version of a product.

Continuous improvement (kaizen)

 TERM

> **kaizen:** or '**continuous improvement**' is a policy of implementing small, incremental changes in order to achieve better quality and/or greater efficiency. These changes are invariably suggested by employees and emanate from a corporate culture that encourages employees to identify potential improvements.

Kaizen can operate through individuals or by using **kaizen groups** or **quality circles** — groups designated to identify potential productivity and quality improvements. It is considered to be a cost-effective means of steady improvement because all employees of an organisation support its aims.

The key features of kaizen are as follows:

- It relies on many small steps, rather than on fewer, more significant changes from approaches such as research and development, in which sudden changes are introduced.
- It uses everyday ideas from ordinary workers rather than major technological or dramatic innovative changes.
- It usually focuses on methods rather than outcomes, assuming that improved methods and approaches will guarantee a more effective outcome.
- It employs the talents of the workforce rather than requiring expensive equipment, and encourages staff to use their talents to seek improvements.

Kaizen is based on two main principles:

- **Gradual change.** Kaizen relies on many small changes rather than sudden leaps. Britain's industrial revolution in the nineteenth century was characterised by a number of dramatic leaps forward, caused by major inventions or innovations such as the spinning jenny in the textile industry and the steam engine for transportation and energy creation. In contrast, the kaizen approach concentrates on finding lots of small improvements. Over time the sheer volume of improvements leads to major advances.

- **Staff suggestions.** Because continuous improvement relies on staff identifying ways in which efficiency can be improved, it is more likely to be successful if staff are given opportunities and encouraged to express their opinions. It also works better if the workforce is more educated and skilled, and thus able to recognise potential weaknesses in the firm's existing approach.

 FILE

The Big Food Group received 3,200 suggestions in the first year of its 'Big Ideas' scheme. A hundred of these new ideas were implemented, saving the company a total of £354,000. In return, the staff with the best ideas were allowed to drive the company Jaguar for a month.   Source: www.thebigfoodgroup.com

A comparison of lean production and mass production

Interpretations of lean production vary and, in the UK in particular, many organisations have chosen to use some (but not all) of the methods described above.

Lean production	Mass production
● short lead times	● longer lead times
● minimal stock levels	● high stock levels
● 'right first time' quality	● quality inspection of finished product
● elimination of unnecessary processes	● no close scrutiny of unnecessary processes
● high levels of worker responsibility	● low levels of worker responsibility
● multi-skilled workers	● specialist or unskilled workers
● excellent two-way communications	● one-way communications
● frequent, small deliveries from suppliers	● fewer, large-scale deliveries from suppliers

Table 34.1 Features of lean production and mass production

Benefits of lean production

Lean production has been widely adopted because it creates a variety of advantages for firms. These include:

- increased productivity as better methods are identified by staff and greater flexibility prevents bottlenecks and idle time on the production line
- a more motivated workforce as a result of their greater skills and more interesting jobs, with greater chances of recognition and responsibility

 EXAMINER'S VOICE

You may be asked to contrast lean production with more traditional methods such as mass production. The brief summary in Table 34.1 shows how different they are.

- increased worker participation in decision making leading to better, more informed ideas and methods
- reduced waste and stockholding costs, improving firms' cash-flow positions
- higher quality and a greater variety of goods and services that are continuously improved for the customers' benefit

e EXAMINER'S VOICE

People in organisations and operations management are very closely linked, and lean production techniques are linked to theories of motivation. The whole process of lean production is focused on giving employees more autonomy and responsibility, particularly for product quality and control over their own work situation. Rotation of job roles provides variety and less likelihood of boredom or monotony. Project teams lead to improved communications, which can lead to improvements in motivation. These factors are linked in with Herzberg's motivators, the higher-level needs in Maslow's hierarchy and Mayo's human relations school of motivation.

Why do some firms use traditional methods?

Lean production does not always guarantee benefits. Many firms choose more traditional production methods so that they can benefit from bulk buying. If demand is predictable, they will know how much to produce and may not need any flexibility. Moreover, unexpected demand is not always dealt with more efficiently by using flexible methods.

The surprisingly hot weather in the summer of 2003 is a case in point. John Lewis sold out of fans at the peak of the heat wave because it was operating on lower stock levels than in the past. Manufacturers were then unable to make enough fans to meet demand. Similarly, Carlsberg had to import lager from abroad because the low stock levels in the UK were insufficient to cope with the sudden increase in demand.

FACT FILE

An example of a business that employs lean production techniques is easyCar. Its goal is to simplify the product that it offers and pass the benefits on to customers in the form of lower prices.

- Customers are expected to return the car in a clean condition (or pay £10 for cleaning).
- An empty-to-empty fuel policy is used, to save on staff costs for refuelling.
- 90% utilisation of cars is achieved.
- Only one type of car is stocked at each branch.
- Customers must make their own way to and from the easyCar base — no delivery or collection is arranged.
- A free mileage level is set — additional charges are made if these limits are exceeded.
- Bookings are made through the company website or a call centre.
- Cancellations are not refunded.
- Marketing costs are reduced by displaying the company name on each car.

Source: easyCar website (www.easycar.com).

PRACTICE EXERCISE
Total: 50 marks (45 minutes)

1 Study the fact file on easyCar (p. 294) and identify the characteristic of lean production that the company uses most often. Justify your choice. *(5 marks)*

2 Explain how cell production can help to motivate the workforce. *(6 marks)*

3 a In the teaching profession, analyse the reasons why teamworking may be more effective than empowering individual workers. *(8 marks)*

   b Explain one advantage and one disadvantage of empowering teachers. *(6 marks)*

4 Select any organisation and identify one example of time wastage and one example of wastage of another resource. Explain how the organisation could reduce the waste that you have identified. *(8 marks)*

5 Explain the meaning of the phrase 'time-based management'. *(3 marks)*

6 How can simultaneous engineering improve the efficiency of a business? *(4 marks)*

7 What is a kaizen group? *(4 marks)*

8 Select any organisation of your choice and explain how continuous improvement could be used to improve its profitability. *(6 marks)*

CASE STUDY 1 A comparison between Marks and Spencer and Zara

Marks and Spencer represents the traditional, mass production approach to fashion retailing. Zara, a Spanish company, is an example of lean production in this trade.

Marks and Spencer buys in large quantities and enjoys the benefits of mass production. However, because it is 'pushing' garments into the stores, it is taking a risk that its idea of this year's fashion may differ from its customers' views. For this reason, Marks and Spencer has been most successful in

providing high-quality items where fashion has been less important (such as socks). If fashion changes quickly, Marks and Spencer struggles because its high-quality, high-price strategy becomes irrelevant. Marks and Spencer has tried to change into a more fashionable store, but has met resistance from both existing and potential customers. There are concerns that the average age of its customer base has been rising.

In contrast, Zara's approach is based on speed and economy. Zara's 'designers' are crucial to the company's success. They must decide on the stock to be produced, although this is mainly choosing which items to copy from the popular designer items in shows and celebrity events, and then simplifying them so that they can be made quickly and cheaply. This is a demanding role, as designers need to combine a sense of fashion with considerable understanding of the manufacturing process. Design time is minimised and production and distribution take about 5 days. A few copies of each item are delivered to each store, in a limited range of sizes and colours. The decisions on

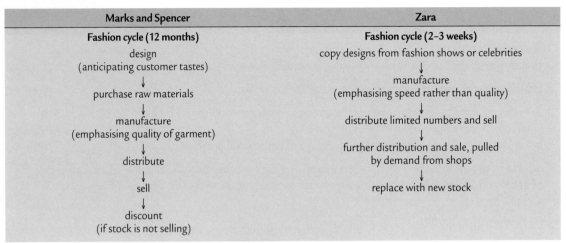

Marks and Spencer	Zara
Fashion cycle (12 months)	**Fashion cycle (2–3 weeks)**
design (anticipating customer tastes)	copy designs from fashion shows or celebrities
↓	↓
purchase raw materials	manufacture (emphasising speed rather than quality)
↓	↓
manufacture (emphasising quality of garment)	distribute limited numbers and sell
↓	↓
distribute	further distribution and sale, pulled by demand from shops
↓	↓
sell	replace with new stock
↓	
discount (if stock is not selling)	

Table 34.2 The fashion cycle at Marks and Spencer and Zara

whether to order further stock are made by shop managers, who can identify which items are selling well. Thus there is less risk of unsold stock — a major problem for Marks and Spencer.

For Zara quality is low, but with new stocks in the shops every 2–3 weeks it is unlikely that the garments will be worn long enough for quality to become a problem. Zara has also found that customers visit its stores more frequently, because they know that a completely new batch of stock will have arrived. In addition to empowering the designers and shop managers, Zara has given more independence to its workshops, which deliver directly to the shops in most cases. The differences in approach between Zara and Marks and Spencer are summarised in Table 34.2.

Zara has been flattered by the number of businesses benchmarking against the company. Visits from senior managers of businesses such as Marks and Spencer are a testament to the success of Zara's approach to fashion retailing. From its humble origins in La Coruña in 1975, Zara has grown to an international business with over 650 stores in 44 different countries, including 20 in the UK.

Sources: Various, including www.inditex.com; www.marksandspencer.com

Questions

Total: 50 marks (60 minutes)

1 Analyse **two** benefits to Marks and Spencer arising from its use of traditional mass production methods. *(8 marks)*

2 Explain why Marks and Spencer's approach is more suited to socks than to fashion items. *(6 marks)*

3 Evaluate the advantages and disadvantages to Zara of its shorter product development times. *(15 marks)*

4 Zara's supply of clothing operates on a 'just-in-time' basis. Explain **one** factor that might lead to problems in using this approach. *(6 marks)*

5 To what extent is the use of people-centred management crucial to the success of Zara? *(15 marks)*

CASE STUDY 2 Herman Miller

Herman Miller is a supplier of office furniture that has successfully introduced lean production. Traditionally, Herman Miller supplied large businesses, but in the 1990s it recognised that small businesses were likely to become a growth area for office furniture. Smaller businesses were more concerned about price and speed of delivery, and less worried about choice of colours and fabrics.

There was a culture of delay in the whole office furniture industry. A typical order would be planned to take 8 weeks, but even then Herman Miller delivered one-third of all orders after the deadline. This led to compensation claims and meant that loyalty among customers was very low. A great deal of time had to be spent finding new customers to replace those who had been disappointed with the firm.

Another expense was stock. Herman Miller carried high levels of stock, just in case they were needed by customers, but poor stock management meant that entire orders were delayed if one critical piece of the order was missing, so these stock levels did not really help to reduce delivery times.

An order for furniture would typically go through these stages:

1 From customer contact to order. This process took up to 3 months as Herman Miller attempted to identify potential manufacturers whose products would meet the needs of the customer.
2 From order to delivery. The manufacturer would receive the order from Herman Miller and, within 4–8 weeks, the manufacturer would deliver the goods to a warehouse.
3 From warehouse to installation. Herman Miller would collect the items, take them to the customer's site and install them.

In 1995 Herman Miller introduced a new system called SQA, based on lean production.

Salespersons are now able to use a laptop to show a three-dimensional view of the office layout from any angle and modified to include or exclude different items of furniture. This helps customers to plan layouts and furnishing that meet their specific needs much more effectively. The costs of any changes to the order can also be calculated on the laptop. This reduces stage 1 from up to 3 months to 1 or 2 days.

At the press of a button, the order can be sent directly to the furniture manufacturer. Previously these manufacturers had been reluctant to begin production because amendments were often made, but now the orders are final, so manufacturers no longer delay production. Average manufacturing time (stage 2) is now only 2 weeks.

The expense of warehousing has been eliminated. With definite completion dates now agreed, the manufacturers deliver directly to the customers, eliminating the cost of warehousing (and thus stage 3) completely.

Since the introduction of SQA, late deliveries have fallen from 33% of all orders to 0.3%, even though promised delivery times have fallen from 8 weeks to 2 weeks.

Staff morale, especially among salespersons and the office fitters, has increased dramatically. The irregular and unpredictable arrival of furniture under the old system meant that, in the past, Herman Miller used a very structured authoritarian approach to the installation and fitting of the furniture. The certainty that all of the furniture will now be delivered has enabled Herman Miller to adopt cell production techniques. Each team of fitters is given responsibility for deciding on the best approach to take, and teamwork methods are employed. With more and more jobs being one-off orders, customised to the

specific layout and requirements of the customer, greater variety and responsibility have been added to the office fitters' jobs. Individuals or teams are now responsible for the quality of the installation.

The higher level of enthusiasm among the workforce has led Herman Miller to consider the introduction of kaizen groups.

Since SQA was introduced, customer satisfaction levels have increased, annual sales growth has been a remarkable 25% per annum, stock levels have been halved and profit margins have increased.

Source: adapted from the MMC Views website (www.mmc.com).

Questions

Total: 50 marks (60 minutes)

1 Analyse **two** features of SQA that allowed Herman Miller to reduce waste. *(8 marks)*

2 Evaluate the importance of time-based management to Herman Miller. *(15 marks)*

3 Explain why the introduction of SQA made it easier to introduce cell production. *(6 marks)*

4 Explain whether a higher level of enthusiasm is helpful if kaizen groups are to be introduced. *(6 marks)*

5 The introduction of lean production led to higher staff morale at Herman Miller. Discuss the main reasons for the improvement in morale resulting from the adoption of certain lean production methods. *(15 marks)*

People in organisations and operations management

This case study integrates the basic 'operations management' concepts covered in Chapter 28 with the 'people' concepts dealt with in Chapters 21–27.

CASE STUDY   NaB

Nat and Bisham had been warned about rapid expansion but wanted to take the risk. Their first two factory shops selling a variety of clothing had been so successful that they had decided to open ten others within 3 weeks of each other. Their investors had insisted on this dramatic action as they were convinced that other businesses would copy the idea before the NaB name became widely recognised as the original provider. The idea of taking the order from the customer and then making the individualised product straight away, while the customer waited, was unique within their area of business. It was vital that they spread beyond their roots in Yorkshire before rivals entered the market.

According to the NaB organisation chart, Nat was responsible for the Sheffield branch and Bisham ran the shop in Leeds, but in practice they were so busy with strategic planning that they had delegated responsibility to other staff. However, they had set up very different systems in the two branches.

In Sheffield, Nat took a much closer interest, partly because she lived above the shop. Most of the staff had worked in the shop since its opening 24 months ago and they had reacted well to Nat's democratic leadership style. From the beginning, decisions had been made by the team rather than by Nat, who argued that she knew no more about running a shop than her employees. Nat was a firm believer in job enrichment and also rotated jobs around so that all of the staff could do each job within the shop.

Although the relaxed atmosphere in the Sheffield shop sometimes frustrated Bisham, it did not seem to discourage the shoppers. The six workers ('colleagues', as Nat described them) achieved a total sales turnover of £760,000 per annum, and the average unit cost per item sold was only £13.20. This had surpassed the targets set by Nat and Bisham and each worker had received a bonus in the form of a share of the profit made by the branch.

Bisham was much more experienced in the retail trade than Nat. In the first year, he had advised Nat, but had not really been involved directly in the business. When they decided to open in Leeds, Bisham gave up his old job and became manager of the Leeds store. Bisham described himself as a paternalistic leader. 'By setting clear guidelines and watching each worker carefully, I am able to get the best out of them.' Each employee had one specialised job, according to his or her abilities. In the 2 weeks before opening the store, each employee spent a week of training in the Sheffield store and a week at a specialist retail training centre.

At the end of the first year of trading, Bisham was disappointed. He had expected Leeds to be a more profitable store than Sheffield. Sales revenue of £670,000 from a full-time staff of five employees suggested greater productivity, but the average unit cost was high at £13.90. The performance-related pay, linked to sales achieved by each employee, seemed to motivate staff, but customers commented

unfavourably on the atmosphere in the shop. The only major factor that he could discover was that the store in Leeds suffered from much higher staff absences. Perhaps he had just been unlucky with illnesses.

Nat and Bisham realised that, with ten new stores, they would need to look much more closely at their human resource management. Workforce planning enabled them to assess the number and types of staff needed, and their first task was to appoint the shop managers.

Only half of the stores were within easy travelling distance, so they decided to use external recruitment methods. In the end, advertisements in local newspapers were used rather than adverts in specialist retail magazines. Naturally, Bisham and Nat encouraged existing staff to apply for these posts too and were pleased to note that most of their workers chose to apply. Bisham received a shock during the interviews to appoint the new store managers. Five of the appointments made were internal candidates, but only one came from the Leeds store. The Sheffield staff had been much more impressive at interview.

Questions

Total: 50 marks (60 minutes)

1 Calculate labour productivity in (a) Sheffield and (b) Leeds. *(4 marks)*

2 Analyse possible reasons why productive efficiency is lower in Leeds even though labour productivity is higher. *(8 marks)*

3 Discuss the ways in which the leadership styles in NaB influence the efficiency of the organisation. *(15 marks)*

4 Analyse the possible reasons why NaB believed that workforce planning was more important once the company expanded beyond two stores. *(8 marks)*

5 To what extent were Nat and Bisham successful in applying ideas from motivation theories in order to improve the efficiency of the business? *(15 marks)*

Units 2 and 3

Introduction

Unit 1 (Marketing and Accounting and Finance) is tested by a 1-hour stimulus-response examination. Two articles are included in the examination and the questions asked are based on the data in the article. The 30-minute 'case studies' at the end of the Marketing and Accounting and Finance sections of Module 1 (on pp. 88–90 and pp. 141–44) are based on this style of paper.

Unit 2 (People in Organisations and Operations Management) and Unit 3 (External Influences and Objectives and Strategy) are tested differently. A pre-released case study of 2,500–3,000 words is issued approximately 8 weeks before the examination. The questions for both Units 2 and 3 are based on this case study. You can investigate the case and use it as you wish to plan your examination, including adding comments and notes. However, you cannot take it into the examination room. On the day of the examination, a fresh, identical copy of the case study is handed out with the questions. Therefore it is vital that you are familiar with the story behind the case study. It will save time if you do not need to refer to the case study constantly during the examination, although for detailed information such as statistics it is advisable to refer to the information in the case study before answering a question.

To give you the opportunity for examination practice, two sample pre-released (pre-issued) case studies are included in this book. Although you may wish to try to spot potential questions, it is not advisable to rely on this strategy. Partially to demonstrate the dangers of this approach, *two* separate Unit 2 examination papers, based on the first case study, are included on p. 307. Because the case study also tests Unit 3, *two* separate Unit 3 examination papers are also included on p. 308.

Do not attempt the Unit 3 examination papers until you have reached Chapter 51. (You may wish to attempt both Unit 2 and Unit 3 examinations at the end of the course.)

The second sample pre-released case study is printed on pp. 430–34 (after Chapter 51). Again, it is followed by two sets of Unit 2 questions and two sets of Unit 3 questions. You may want to attempt the Unit 2 (but not the Unit 3) questions at this point of the course.

CASE STUDY   Ethel the Pork Pie

A. Background

Godfrey Glenn and his wife Gemma agreed. Changes had to be made to the farm. The farm's location, close to Stonehenge on Salisbury Plain, offered opportunities to attract tourists, but the Glenns were determined to keep farming.

Over 85% of the farm's sales were from pig farming. Godfrey was relieved that many of the recent crises in farming, such as mad cow disease and foot-and-mouth, had not affected his farm. However, he was aware that specialising in one product brought benefits and problems. His workforce was able to develop very high levels of skill in pig farming, in comparison to the employees of some of his neighbours, whose staff found it difficult trying to adapt from animal farming to other tasks on a daily basis. In addition, in comparison to neighbours with less specialised farms, he was able to buy materials in bulk and to purchase more expensive but more productive equipment that met the specific needs of pig farming. In fact, most of the remaining 15% of his income came from hiring out specialist equipment to neighbouring farms that were too small, or too diversified, to be able to purchase the equipment themselves.

Pig farming was not very much affected by changes in the business cycle, but it was very vulnerable to changes in inflation rates and exchange rates. Competition was very fierce right across Europe. There were many suppliers all producing the same product, and so price was a major selling point. Although Godfrey never exported his pigs, if other farmers found it difficult to sell abroad it led to more competition (and lower pork prices) in the UK. Economic forecasts for the next 4 years were as shown in Table 1.

It was after a meeting of the local farmers' union that Godfrey decided to make a change. A representative of the nearest food-processing plant, in Yeovil, gave a talk in which he argued that the supermarkets were making most of the money from each animal that was processed, but the figures that he quoted made Godfrey think. The food-processing company was making a lot more money than his farm for every pig that it processed.

B. GG Ltd is formed

Godfrey did some preliminary market research. All of the local farms sent their animals a long distance to Yeovil and a local processor would reduce the costs of transport and the distress caused to the animals from long journeys. Best of all, the profit would be kept in the local community. Godfrey identified some buildings on his own farm that could be adapted and he got quotes from some local builders to show how much it would cost to set up an abattoir and food-

Table 1 Economic forecasts for the UK and EU

	Economic growth, UK (%)	Economic growth, EU (%)	Inflation, UK (%)	Inflation, EU (%)	Exchange rate (value of £ in €s)
Next year	1.5	2.3	1.7	1.5	€1.42
2 years' time	1.3	2.0	1.4	1.2	€1.32
3 years' time	2.5	1.7	1.6	1.1	€1.24
4 years' time	4.3	2.4	2.3	1.5	€1.36

processing plant. Gemma, who did the farm's accounts, calculated that the initial cash payments needed to set it up would be recovered in just under 3 years if all of the farmers within an 8-kilometre radius of the Glenns' farm used the facility. Armed with these calculations he visited his bank. The manager was very sympathetic and agreed to a generous overdraft facility. He also put Godfrey in contact with some venture capital providers. As a result, GG Ltd was formed. GG Ltd would be a separate company from the farm (Glenn's Farm Ltd) which was owned equally by Godfrey and Gemma.

Table 2 shows the ownership of GG Ltd at the time of the setting up of the company (year 1) and 1 year later (year 2). All of the finance to convert the buildings into a food-processing plant was provided by the two venture capital providers. Reg Tidworth, an experienced abattoir manager, was appointed to organise the day-to-day operations and a part of his reward system was the gift of 4% of the shares in the business.

It was decided from day 1 that the two businesses would run separately. The farm workers would have no involvement in the food-processing plant — Reg would be responsible for recruiting the labour force.

The first year was a disaster. Building work was delayed and cost much more than expected. The overdraft reached its maximum allowed level. Fortunately the two venture capital providers agreed to put more money into the business in return for an extra 4% of the shares each.

Eventually, in the second year of GG Ltd's existence, the new plant was completed.

C. Reg's whirlwind start

Initially things went well. Reg was a superb organiser. He had planned the recruitment according to God-frey's original calculations, making sure that there were enough staff to meet demand if the customer levels equalled all of the farms within an 8-kilometre radius. For senior positions he advertised in towns with food-processing plants; the remaining positions were filled from advertisements in local newspapers and a contact in Latvia, who eventually provided most of the employees. The selection process included

	% of shares		
Owner	Year 1	Year 2	Comments
Godfrey Glenn	24	20	Provider of land and buildings
Gemma Glenn	24	20	Joint provider of land and buildings
Vinnie Tcher-Capital	24	28	Venture capital provider
3 j ltd	24	28	Venture capital provider
Reg Tidworth	4	4	Operations manager

Table 2 Ownership of GG Ltd

practical tests as well as an interview, as Reg knew from experience that some staff would dislike the working conditions. To compensate, Reg offered a payment system based on piece rate. If the processing plant was busy, the employees would earn much higher hourly wages than Godfrey's farm workers earned. This fact was noticed by the workers, and two of the farm's most valued employees, Jim and Pete, took jobs in the processing plant, much to Godfrey's annoyance. He wondered whether he had given Reg too much freedom in his decision making.

Reg made sure that everybody in the food-processing plant had clearly defined jobs and he provided excellent induction and on-the-job training courses for the new employees. Each employee had a large manual that described their jobs, the company rules, and how to handle issues that might arise. He also continually posted around the buildings instructions that appeared to cover every possible event. Godfrey even spotted a notice instructing employees what to do in the event of a direct hit by a nuclear bomb — but this turned out to be a practical joke by one of the employees.

Godfrey was very impressed by Reg's quality control procedures. Reg seemed to be everywhere, checking and inspecting every stage of the process to make sure that no mistakes were made.

The food-processing plant was a distinct contrast to the farm. On the farm, the employees had all worked there for many years, and Godfrey left them alone to decide on their tasks. At busy times he was just one of the workers and all of the farm workers instinctively knew what was needed. Godfrey would discuss the priorities with his farm workers in a morning briefing, and they would decide among themselves how and by whom the job would be completed.

In the food-processing plant it was very different. Each stage of the process was the responsibility of one worker, and regular practice meant that the workers became very quick and efficient. The foreman was able to complete each task and covered for any tea breaks or absences.

D. Problems and dilemmas

The plant ran smoothly for the first 2 months. The first sign of a problem was when Jim and Pete pleaded to be allowed to have their old jobs back. Godfrey was puzzled. GG Ltd was running very efficiently on paper. Far more farmers were using it than he had originally estimated, and the piece-rate system was providing a very good weekly wage for the employees. Admittedly, the employees were working long hours, but Jim and Pete had always worked hard, so he did not believe that this could be the problem.

Godfrey fixed a meeting with Reg, Jim and Pete. Jim and Pete had no specific complaints — they just found the jobs boring in comparison to the farm, where they had been trusted to make their own decisions. In addition, whereas Godfrey showed his appreciation of the work that they did, Reg did not. But most significantly, they had enjoyed coming to work because they had been a team. Pete even confessed to missing his daily contact with the pigs. 'I knew the pigs better than my current workmates. Now I spend the whole day in one place, doing my job. The only chance I get to talk to anyone is when the plant closes down at lunch time.' Reg argued that Pete should have realised this. 'You can't make food processing interesting. That's why the pay is better than it is on the farm.' Pete and Jim started to argue that it was possible. On the farm, Godfrey had set up a kaizen group and Godfrey followed a policy of continuous improvement. The farm workers had regularly offered suggestions, many of which had been adopted. Godfrey had been surprised by how many of these ideas seemed to have benefited the farm rather than the workers; the farm had become more efficient as new ways of doing jobs had been introduced by the kaizen group. However, Reg was

adamant that the processing plant was different. 'It's a boring job which people do for the money. Kaizen groups will only raise people's hopes — they won't improve anything.' After a long discussion, Reg and Godfrey agreed that Jim and Pete could return to their old jobs on the farm.

The processing plant continued to work efficiently, but Godfrey did worry about it. Reg was like a whirl-wind, everywhere at once, dealing with problems, making decisions and checking the finished products before they were transported. Godfrey noticed that the only substandard products returned by customers had been produced on the day that Reg was visiting a supplier.

Gemma noticed the next problem — a lot of staff were not being paid for working on Fridays. She checked with Reg, worried that there was insufficient business to keep the plant operating at full capacity. He did not seem to be at all worried. 'They say they are ill on Fridays, but I think it's just laziness. The piece rate pays them a good weekly wage, so they don't bother turning up on Fridays. It happened at the last two food-processing plants that I managed. Don't worry — I knew this was going to happen and so I never book in so much work for the plant on Fridays.'

Godfrey was concerned. He had expected 90% capacity utilisation and was worried that low usage of the plant on Fridays would add to the unit costs. He also noticed an increase in the number of workers leaving — 40% of the original workers had left and it had been hard to replace them locally. Fortunately, the Latvian contact had supplied more workers. The Latvian workers seemed to be keen to work long hours, although Godfrey suspected that this was partly because the cottages that they lived in (rent free) were very damp. Once they had become the majority of the workforce, the Friday problem disappeared.

The accounts of GG Ltd were excellent. Sales of the processed food were much higher than expected and the profit made by GG Ltd was more than the farm had made in all of the last 10 years put together. This was a very pleasant surprise, as Godfrey had forecast a big loss at this stage.

Reg came to see him at the end of the financial year and asked, 'When do I get my 4% of the profit?'

Godfrey was bemused. He had never agreed to give Reg 4% of the profit. Reg explained, 'I've got 4% of the shares, so I get 4% of the profit.' Now it made sense to Godfrey, and he explained that shareholders only got a share of the profit if the company decided to declare a dividend. Reg had not attended the annual general meeting at which a 0% dividend had been agreed, ironically so that retained profit could be used to buy some new machinery that Reg had requested. Godfrey felt guilty. Reg had worked hard and Godfrey had been surprised that he had never demanded any bonuses or additional payments.

The following day Reg handed in his resignation. Godfrey and Gemma eventually persuaded him to withdraw his resignation, but only after promising him a substantial bonus payment. 'We'll take it from the farm's accounts,' promised Godfrey. 'Gemma can add you to the list of casual workers.' They both knew that this was illegal, as Reg was not an employee of the farm, but they were desperate to reward Reg for his excellent work.

Gemma argued, 'The plant has helped to bring a lot of jobs and wealth into the community. We have had complaints about the huge lorries driving through the local villages, and the waste from the food-processing plant has ended up in the local river a few times, but I believe that we have helped the area overall, and much of this is down to Reg.' (Gemma would have been less sympathetic if she had known that Reg was taking a percentage of the earnings of all of the Latvian workers in return for giving them jobs.)

E. From batch to flow, and into retailing

At first the processing plant used batch production processes, operating on a just-in-time basis. A batch of animals would be delivered and processed as soon as they arrived. This meant that there was no need to keep stock. The absence of storage areas also meant that the finished food was sold immediately. Once the supermarkets realised that GG Ltd had no storage, they started to offer lower prices. An emergency meeting of the five shareholders was held and they decided to build a storage area immediately.

Reg then proposed that they also bought new equipment: 'I've been turning away a lot of business because our present equipment means that we can only process one batch at a time. Farmers are having to book their delivery times 3 weeks in advance at the moment. If we had large storage areas and a continuous flow production line, we could keep food processing going for 24 hours a day on Mondays to Fridays. Farmers could deliver when they like and we could store the finished products until we can negotiate a good price from the supermarkets.'

'We could even set up a farm shop,' said Godfrey. 'The village store has just closed down, so we could sell other items as well. If we make the shop visible from the A303, we can attract a lot of passing trade from motorists and people visiting Stonehenge.'

The shop (Stonehenge Stores) was a big success, especially in the summer. Gina, the Glenns' daughter, ran the store and noticed that passing holidaymakers were happy to pay much higher prices for the products, as long as they were clearly identified as genuine, local produce. The food-processing plant started to use its own brand name and packaging for the farm shop.

F. Ethel, at last

The next big break for the Glenns occurred at the National Pig Competition. 'Ethel' swept the board to earn the accolade of 'Pig of the Year'. In an unprecedented round of voting, Ethel became the first pig to ever achieve perfect 6s from every judge. For Ethel an even bigger break came 2 weeks later.

Pop Group Idols had finished its television run and the public had voted the Trolls, a local Wiltshire group, as their favourites. The group's first single 'Placid Thing' had gone straight to number one and *Top of the Pops* beckoned. For some bizarre reason, the group was looking for a pig to feature in its performance. Pete's son was the bass guitarist and he persuaded Godfrey to let Ethel join in. Suitably attired in earplugs (to cut out the sound) and sunglasses (because of the bright lights), Ethel played the part of 'placid thing' brilliantly. Overnight she became a cult figure. Ethel went on tour with the band, but following protests from animal rights pressure groups

Godfrey decided to bring her back to the farm. Privately, he did not share their concerns. He had worked with pigs all of his life and he knew that Ethel enjoyed the limelight. In fact, on her return to the farm she was very grumpy.

Three weeks later Ethel was dead. It was front-page news in the tabloids and Gina came up with a cunning plan. 'Why not turn Ethel into pork pies? We could call them Ethel Pork Pies and guarantee that they are 100% Ethel. Ethel would have wanted it.'

Godfrey was not sure on this last point but eventually agreed, despite Gemma's opposition. That weekend, a special consignment of Ethel Pork Pies was produced and on Monday they were offered for sale in the farm shop. The first customer to notice them was a big fan of the Trolls, and within hours the message had got round. The next day there was a huge traffic jam on the A303 with people queuing to buy the remaining Ethel Pork Pies.

There was a huge public outcry about the idea of personalising a pork pie. Godfrey did not help his cause by attending a television debate and arguing that 'Ethel was always going to end up as a pork pie.' It annoyed him that people living in towns seemed to be happy to eat meat, but were unable to cope with the processes that this involved. As if in answer to his critics, the next week saw the introduction of Big Ted, Napoleon and then Snowball pies. For every animal rights protester at the farm shop, there were four or five customers eagerly queuing for a personalised pork pie, and willing to pay a very high price for the privilege.

It was Godfrey's granddaughter who eventually changed his mind. 'Why did you let people eat Ethel?' was a simple question, but he could not answer it. He realised that he was beginning to see high profits as more important than his animals — something he had vowed would never happen. Despite huge protests from customers, Snowball was the last ever personalised pork pie.

Unit 2: People in Organisations and Operations Management

PAPER A

Questions

Total: 50 marks (60 minutes)

1 Explain **one** disadvantage that might arise from Reg's decision to use inspection as the main method of quality control. (*Section C*) *(6 marks)*

2 Analyse **two** possible reasons for using on-the-job training rather than off-the-job training in the processing plant. (*Section C*) *(8 marks)*

3 Briefly explain why GG Ltd stopped using just-in-time methods in the processing plant. (*Section E*) *(6 marks)*

4 Using information from the case study, discuss the relative merits of flow production and job production. *(15 marks)*

5 To what extent did Godfrey and Reg use different leadership styles? *(15 marks)*

PAPER B

Questions

Total: 50 marks (60 minutes)

1 Outline **one** possible problem for the farm arising from Godfrey's willingness to delegate. *(6 marks)*

2 Analyse **one** economy of scale that benefited the Glenns' farm and **a different** economy of scale that helped GG Ltd. *(8 marks)*

3 To what extent might the processing plant (GG Ltd) have benefited from the introduction of a policy of continuous improvement? *(15 marks)*

4 Briefly explain how Godfrey's approach to motivation was based on Herzberg's theory of motivation. *(6 marks)*

5 Discuss the effectiveness of Reg's human resource management. *(15 marks)*

Unit 3: External Influences and Objectives and Strategy

PAPER A

Questions

Total: 50 marks (60 minutes)

1 Analyse the reasons why the Glenns set up a separate private limited company (GG Ltd) to run the food-processing plant. (*Section B*)   *(8 marks)*

2 Explain **one** example of Godfrey acting in a socially responsible manner in his relationship with the local community.   *(6 marks)*

3 Discuss the possible impact on GG Ltd of the forecast changes in the exchange rate for the next 2 years. (*Section A*)   *(15 marks)*

4 Briefly explain **one** instance in the case where the aims of a business had not been agreed among its owners.   *(6 marks)*

5 To what extent would a SWOT analysis have helped the Glenns when deciding whether to diversify into food processing?   *(15 marks)*

PAPER B

Questions

Total: 50 marks (60 minutes)

1 Explain why changes in the business cycle had a relatively small impact on the farm.   *(6 marks)*

2 Organisations are often influenced by UK and EU law on health and safety. Explain **one** possible implication for GG Ltd of health and safety legislation.   *(6 marks)*

3 Evaluate the major problems of 'start-up' faced by GG Ltd.   *(15 marks)*

4 Examine **two** areas of conflicting aims between different stakeholders of **Glenn's Farm Ltd** or **GG Ltd.**   *(8 marks)*

5 To what extent did Godfrey behave ethically in his involvement in the two businesses?   *(15 marks)*

External influences

❝ I want to work for a company that contributes to and is part of the community. I want something to believe in. **❞**

Anita Roddick

CHAPTER 35

The market and competition

This chapter examines the external environment and its influence on businesses by introducing PEST analysis. It then moves on to an explanation of the market and how different market conditions influence business behaviour. Market conditions are also examined through Porter's five forces model. The concepts of fair and unfair competition are explained and the impact of excess capacity and capacity shortage within a market are studied.

Although business studies is concerned with the internal operations of a business, such as marketing, finance and accounting, human resource management and operations management, it is also vital to understand and appreciate that all business takes place within a much wider context than the business itself. This is illustrated in Figure 35.1.

Figure 35.1
The business and its environment

First, a business operates within a competitive environment. The nature of this competition varies from industry to industry, but almost all firms face some level of competition. The number of competitors, for example, dictates the extent to which a business can raise or lower its prices, and the amount of advertising it is likely to undertake.

Second, a business operates within a general business environment. This involves the broader influences that affect all businesses, including issues such as the impact of changes in government policy on business, how legislation influences business behaviour, and the extent to which changes in consumers' lifestyles affect the types of product that are demanded.

PEST analysis

 TERM

PEST analysis: a framework for assessing the likely impact of the **political**, **economic**, **social** and **technological** factors in the external environment of a business.

The use of PEST analysis enables all the different influences in the general business environment to be classified into four categories. Table 35.1 summarises some of the issues that could be considered in each category.

There are alternatives to the PEST framework, such as PESTLE and STEEP analysis, but these simply extend the division of categories to be considered. (The L stands for **legal** factors and the second E stands for **environmental** factors.)

This chapter focuses on the competitive environment of the firm, while later chapters in this section consider the various issues covered in a PEST analysis.

Markets and market structure

KEY TERM

market: a situation where buyers and sellers come together.

PEST category	Examples of issues in each category that might affect business
Political factors	• government economic policies • government social policies • the extent of government intervention • legislation
Economic factors	• the business cycle • interest rates • exchange rates • the level of inflation • the level of unemployment • membership of the EU
Social factors	• environmental issues • ethical issues • the impact of pressure groups • the influence of different stakeholders • changing lifestyles
Technological factors	• new products • new processes • the impact of change • the costs of change

Table 35.1
PEST analysis

Some markets are very competitive with lots of small firms operating in them, each selling only a very small proportion of total market sales. Other markets tend to be dominated by a few large firms, each selling a significant proportion of the total market sales. The size of a market is measured either by volume (the number of units sold) or by value (the money spent on all the goods sold).

In practice, defining the nature of a market is quite complex. For example, is British Gas in the gas provision market or in the fuel provision market? This will determine whether it sees itself as competing only against other gas suppliers or against all fuel suppliers, including those supplying coal, electricity and oil. Similarly, do newspapers compete only with other newspapers or with all other news sources, including the internet, radio, and cable and satellite television? The managing director of Waterman Pens is famously quoted as saying, 'We are not in the market for pens, but executive gifts.' Thus he redefined the company's competitors as Dunhill and Rolex, rather than, or in addition to, Parker and Bic.

Market structure

In general, four different market structures explain the broad range of competitive environments in which most firms operate. These range from monopoly situations where, in theory, there are no competitors, to perfect competition where there are many competitors.

KEY TERM

monopoly: in theory, a single producer within a market, but in practice a firm with a market share of 25% or more.

The potential danger of monopolies is that they will exploit the consumer. If there is little or no competition in providing a particular product or service, and therefore few or no alternative supplies of it, monopolists could charge high prices and offer poor service, and they might simply waste scarce resources by being inefficient.

Where monopolies exhibit or are likely to exhibit any of these characteristics, the government investigates them and can require them to change their behaviour and subject them to massive fines. When the former nationalised utilities, including gas, electricity and water, were privatised, regulators such as Ofwat and Ofgas were appointed to control them, in order to ensure that they did not abuse their monopoly position.

Before the 1980s, the UK had a number of true monopolies in the form of the nationalised industries, including British Coal, British Gas, British Steel, British Rail and other utilities such as electricity and water. Subsequently, all of these industries were privatised and opened up to competition so that today in the UK, true monopoly situations are rare. However, firms with more than 25% of the market continue to exist because it is extremely difficult for a new firm to enter the market of a monopolist owing to high barriers to entry. Barriers to entry include:

- the high capital costs required to set up a new business in markets in which existing firms are monopolies
- possible patents that allow existing firms to 'monopolise' the market legally
- the loyalty of customers to existing firms
- the need to achieve large economies of scale quickly in order to be able to charge a competitive price

DID YOU KNOW?

Monopsony means a single buyer, as opposed to a monopoly, which is a single seller. A single buyer of a product has a lot of power over the supplier of the product. For example, they can force the supplier to lower price, they can delay payment or they can impose stringent quality standards, and the supplier can do little in response since there are no alternative buyers with which to trade. This situation often emerges in practice when a small firm, such as a pig farm making its own sausages, sells all of its products to a large firm, such as one of the major supermarket chains.

KEY TERM

oligopoly: a market dominated by a small number of large firms known as oligopolists.

Oligipoly markets may seem to be extremely competitive because each producer competes fiercely in order to maintain or increase its share of the

particular market. However, if one oligopolist reduces price, the others follow suit and so no firm gains. Similarly, a business that increases price may lose market share, as the other oligopolists may not copy this strategy. Therefore, competition is usually in the form of 'non-price' competition, such as special offers and advertising.

KEY TERM

cartel: a group of firms that come together to agree price levels and output levels within an industry.

Cartels are illegal in the UK, but they are often difficult to detect. If they are found out, legal action can be taken to force them to change their behaviour and a fine of 10% of revenue can be required. In September 2003, the government conducted an investigation into price fixing by a number of prominent independent schools that were alleged to be colluding in the setting of their school fees. At the time of writing (March 2004), the investigation has not been concluded.

Predicting the behaviour of oligopolies is complex because each firm is aware that whatever action it takes will result in a reaction from its competitors. It must therefore guess this possible reaction and take it into account before undertaking any action itself.

As markets mature and successful firms take over or merge with less successful firms, more markets inevitably become oligopolies. Then, as with monopolies, oligopolies continue to exist because of high barriers to entry.

KEY TERM

monopolistic competition: this occurs when there is a large number of firms competing within a market, each having enough **product differentiation** to achieve a degree of monopoly power and therefore some control over the price they charge.

This can result from the development of brand names or local reputation. For example, a hair salon might have an excellent reputation and a loyal clientele, which enable it to charge higher prices than other hair salons in the vicinity. A local café or bar might have developed a reputation as the place to be for 18–25-year-olds, even though its prices are much higher than the pub next door.

It is easy for a new firm to enter this type of market because the set-up costs tend to be relatively low and the nature of the market is such that there is a constant flow of businesses.

KEY TERM

perfect competition: this exists where there is a large number of sellers and buyers, all of whom are too small to influence the price of the product.

All the sellers produce homogeneous (identical) products and are 'price takers', meaning they accept the ruling market price. The buyers all have perfect

DID YOU KNOW?

Many oligopolies are in fact monopolies under the government's 25% market share definition.

knowledge: for example, they know the price being charged in the market. There is perfect freedom of entry into and exit from the market for firms.

Like the theoretical monopoly of a single firm, perfect competition is rarely evident in practice and tends to be simply a model against which the behaviour of firms in the real world can be compared.

Table 35.2 summarises the different types of market conditions in which businesses operate.

> ### *e* EXAMINER'S VOICE
>
> When you answer case study questions about particular market situations, try to decide what type of market structure is evident (e.g. whether oligopolistic or monopolistic competition). Then apply your knowledge of the characteristics of the relevant market structure in answering the question: for example, how a particular market structure will affect the profitability and likely success of the firm, and how it might affect the firm's objectives and strategy.

Table 35.2
Market conditions

Characteristic	Perfect competition	Monopolistic competition	Oligopoly	Monopoly
Number and size of firms	Many and small	Many and small	Few and large	One, in theory*
Nature of product	Identical	Differentiated	Differentiated	Unique
Examples	Foreign exchange market, stock market, fruit and vegetable market	Hairdressers, plumbers, cafés and insurance companies	Supermarkets, banks and motor vehicle manufacturers	Nationalised industries (pre-1980s), Royal Mail (for letters)
Barriers to entry	None; it is easy to enter or leave the market	None; it is easy to enter or leave the market	High barriers to entry	High barriers to entry
Effect on business	Price takers Cost efficiency needed for survival No real scope for marketing Very low profit margins	Some control over price Cost efficiency is important unless the firm has a strong USP Benefits from marketing Low profit margins	Non-price competition High overheads High profit margins but aim to achieve USP through branding High spending on promotion Collusion can occur between firms	Price setter Can become complacent Power depends on importance of the product and its alternatives High profit margins

*In theory, a monopoly is a single producer; in practice, a monopoly is a firm with a market share of 25% or more.

Porter's five competitive forces

An alternative or additional way of analysing market conditions is to draw on Michael Porter's idea of **competitive forces**. Some firms struggle to survive or are forced out of business, while others prosper, grow and become very profitable. Why? Michael Porter identified five features of markets that determine how a successful firm might cope with its competitors. These are shown in Figure 35.2.

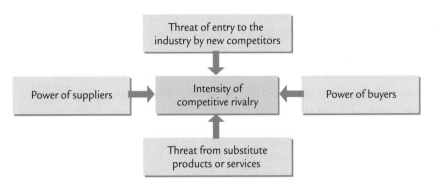

Figure 35.2
*Porter's five
competitive forces*

When using this model to analyse a firm's position, the following questions should be posed.

Intensity of competitive rivalry
■ Are there a large number of small firms competing fiercely in the market, or are there a few large firms controlling the market?

Threat of entry to the industry by new competitors
■ Can new firms enter the market in response to high profits or are there significant barriers to entry? These might include patents, contracts tying wholesalers or retailers to existing manufacturers, and the need for a large capital base.

Threat from substitute products or services
■ Is the product unique and in high demand, or are there substitute products produced by other firms that can be used as alternatives?

Power of suppliers
■ Are the firm's inputs supplied by a single firm or cartel such as OPEC (Oil Producing and Exporting Countries) or by a large number of competing suppliers?

Power of buyers
■ Does the firm sell to a single powerful buyer, such as a major supermarket chain, or to a large number of individual customers?

Porter's model can be used to assess a firm's strategy in an attempt to create the right conditions for it to have a clear competitive advantage over its rivals. If, for example, a supplier has too much power over a firm, one possibility is for the firm to find alternative sources of supply. Equally, if the firm currently sells to a single buyer, its strategy might be to find more buyers in order to reduce the power of any one buyer.

Competition

All firms in the UK operate in a competitive environment of some sort, but this has not always been the case. Prior to the 1980s, a number of large state

monopolies or nationalised industries existed that had no competition. It is therefore useful to consider the advantages and disadvantages of competition with other organisations.

The advantages of competition are based on the fact that, in order to gain market share, firms need to offer the cheapest or the best-quality products to customers. This usually means that they try to:
- improve efficiency
- improve cost-effectiveness
- improve the quality of products and services
- reduce waste by attempting to become more efficient

However, the disadvantages of competition include the following:
- If competition is based on price, product quality might be sacrificed.
- Huge resources are devoted to competing with other firms, such as the cost of advertising, which uses resources that could have been spent on producing cheaper or better products.
- Some businesses will inevitably be forced out of the market, with the economic and human consequences of redundancy and unemployment.
- The competitive process tends to mean that successful businesses take over, or merge with, unsuccessful ones. This in turn leads to the existence of a smaller number of larger and larger businesses: in other words, to the growth of more oligopolies and to increasing concentration rather than competition.

Fair versus unfair competition

The more competitive the market, the less opportunity there is for profit as firms try to cut costs and prices in order to attract customers. Where there is little competition but a strong demand, supernormal profits may be made, i.e. profits well above what could be 'reasonably expected'. Such profits are often a sign of unfair competition.

> **KEY TERMS**
>
> **fair competition:** where firms compete on equal terms in a way that offers consumers the best choice of products and prices.
> **unfair competition:** where firms do not compete fairly by acting in a way that restricts consumer choice in the short or long run.

Examples of unfair competition include:
- monopolies charging high prices because of a lack of competition
- oligopolies agreeing to restrict supply and/or fix high prices (e.g. supermarkets and independent schools have been accused of colluding in a bid to set high prices or fees)
- producers only supplying retailers that promise not to stock rival products or that agree to stock the whole range of a supplier's products
- predatory pricing by large firms (i.e. a policy of undercutting the prices charged by a small firm in order to force it out of the market)

> **DID YOU KNOW?**
>
> The degree of concentration refers to the number of firms that produce and sell a given proportion of the market share in an industry. For example, if the largest three firms in an industry have 60% of the total market share compared to another industry in which the largest five firms have 10% of the total market share, the former industry would be considered as heavily concentrated compared to the latter.

In practice, it is often difficult to establish immediately whether competition is fair or unfair. A company may offer lower prices because its costs are lower (fair competition), but if it eliminates competition and then increases its prices, this is unfair competition. If unfair competition is likely to be 'against the interests of consumers', it is possible that the Competition Commission will intervene to stop a firm's actions.

e **EXAMINER'S VOICE**

Students sometimes get side-tracked into discussing ethical and moral issues in relation to fair and unfair competition, rather than considering the issue more formally as indicated in the examples above.

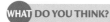 **WHAT DO YOU THINK?**

The granting of a patent generally guarantees a monopoly for 20 years. This could be seen as a reward for the research and development undertaken by the company and as allowing the company time to enjoy a return (which could mean huge profits) on its investment. Is this unfair? Without such patent-related monopoly power, much research and development might never take place. If people demand a particular product and are prepared to pay high prices for it, is it unfair for a company to charge them a high price? Does it depend on the nature of the product and whether it is a basic necessity or a luxury?

Excess capacity and capacity shortage

KEY TERMS

excess (or spare) capacity: a situation where, in the market as a whole, maximum output of all firms is greater than the demand for the product.
capacity shortage: a situation where, in the market as a whole, the demand for the product exceeds the maximum possible supply or output of all firms.

Capacity utilisation for individual firms is covered in Chapter 30. The market for a particular product or service can also suffer from spare/excess capacity or capacity shortage. This can in turn affect the degree of competition and therefore market structure by influencing whether firms decide to enter the market. Table 35.3 summarises the possible impact of excess capacity and of capacity shortage in the market.

Table 35.3
The impact on a firm of excess capacity and capacity shortage in a market

Possible impact of excess capacity in a market	Possible impact of capacity shortage in a market
Excess supply means that prices are likely to be low as companies try to sell their products.	Excess demand means that prices are likely to be high
As firms are working at low capacity utilisation, fixed costs per unit are high, leading to higher unit costs.	As firms are working at full capacity, fixed costs per unit are low, leading to lower unit costs.
Higher unit costs mean lower profit margins.	Lower unit costs mean higher profit margins.
Restructuring of the company might occur in order to dispose of surplus land or plant and to get rid of excess labour.	Investment programmes might be undertaken in order to acquire new fixed assets in order to increase capacity.
A greater focus on marketing is needed, as higher sales will reduce unit costs.	Given the excess demand and high capacity utilisation, there is less need for marketing.
Some existing firms will leave the market as profit margins fall, and others may try to diversify into new markets.	New firms will try to enter the market in order to reap the benefits being gained by existing firms.

> **DID YOU KNOW?**
>
> Market conditions can be linked with most marketing strategies and tactics. For example, the marketing mix may need to be adapted to the market situation (e.g. non-price competition for oligopolies), and the length of the product life cycle may depend on the level of competition. Similarly, links can be made with operational issues. For example, economies of scale are more accessible for monopolists than for firms in very competitive situations, but are not so likely if there is spare capacity.

PRACTICE EXERCISE   Total: 50 marks (40 minutes)

1 Distinguish between the theoretical definition of a monopoly and the legal definition. *(4 marks)*

2 Describe the main characteristics of a market that is an oligopoly. *(4 marks)*

3 Why is it often difficult for new firms to set up in monopoly or oligopoly markets? *(5 marks)*

4 Distinguish between a monopoly market and a market that is characterised by monopolistic competition. *(6 marks)*

5 What are the main characteristics of perfect competition? *(4 marks)*

6 Distinguish between fair and unfair competition. *(5 marks)*

7 Explain three examples of unfair competition. *(9 marks)*

8 Why is it difficult to assess whether competition is unfair? *(5 marks)*

9 Explain the difference between excess capacity and capacity shortage in a market. *(4 marks)*

10 Why might a capacity shortage in a market be beneficial to a firm? *(4 marks)*

CASE STUDY **Market mapping**

Introduction

It is impossible for one industry to provide all of the market features required for the study of AS Business Studies. As a consequence, three 'mini case studies' are presented below, each supporting one or two questions. Overall, these five questions equate to a 1-hour case study on 'The market and competition'.

The first two mini case studies describe market conditions in two sectors — the jewellery and watches sector, and the organic foods sector. The information is adapted from various Keynote reports (source: www.keynote.co.uk). The third mini case study looks at concentration ratios in selected industries.

PHOTODISC

The jewellery and watches market

The UK jewellery and watches market was worth £2.97 billion in 2002. The growth in sales enjoyed during the 1990s has declined in the new millennium, as global economic uncertainty has led to a decrease in consumer spending.

The jewellery and watches market is highly competitive in terms of both supply and retail. Recent years have seen the emergence of several luxury-goods and high-fashion conglomerates* into the market, which possess strong brands that are supported by substantial financial resources. However, this has had the consequence of overcrowding — particularly in the watches sector — and is putting pressure on the small and medium-sized operations that make up the majority of the UK industry.

This overcrowding has led to excess capacity in the industry as the number of manufacturers and retailers has increased at a faster rate than the demand for watches and jewellery. Analysts predict that some smaller firms will be forced out of the industry eventually, unless they can find a niche market for their products. The high-fashion conglomerates are able to purchase the more expensive locations in the high street and can afford to spend much more money on advertising in order to promote their brands and achieve brand loyalty.

Shifts in consumer demography and buying motives have led to renewed design and marketing initiatives. Companies are targeting young, high-earning, brand-conscious customers, who are increasingly regarding jewellery and watches as fashion and lifestyle purchases, rather than symbolic and sentimental ones. Fashion watches are the sector's fastest-growing segment, while jewellery companies — traditionally less brand focused than the watches sector — are increasingly investing in aggressive brand-building strategies in an attempt to remain competitive.

The organic foods market

In the year ending April 2002, the retail market for organic foods grew by an estimated 19.7% in value terms. This is a substantial increase, but represents, nevertheless, a slowing growth rate from previous years. In 1999/2000, for example, the market rose by 55.1% as a number of important launches and

---

* A conglomerate is a firm that has joined with another firm in a different line of business to create a larger company.

relaunches took place. However, according to various organisations, such as Organic Monitor and the Soil Association, organic foods sales still only account for between 1.5% and 2% of total foods sales. This is a much lower penetration level than in some other European countries, such as Austria, Denmark and Switzerland.

A dominant and increasing share of organic food sales is accounted for by the major grocery multiples — principally Tesco and the original champions of organics, Sainsbury's and Waitrose — which are now stocking between 1,000 and 1,200 organic lines. Growth is at the expense of small grocery multiples, independents, health food shops and direct sales outlets, such as box schemes, farm shops, farmers' markets and the internet.

The organic foods market has always been characterised by a large number of small but now well-known producers. However, strong market growth has now attracted some major international food companies, such as Heinz, Masterfoods, Muller Dairy, Gerber, RHM, Arla and Unilever Bestfoods. These have often entered the market by acquiring and autonomously running small manufacturers, although some have simply produced organic variants of their brands. Between 2002/03 and 2005/06, market growth for organic foods is forecast at between 13.9% and 17.7% per year.

Concentration ratios

The level of competition in a market is indicated by how many firms are operating in it — the more firms, the more competitive the market. However, it could be that although many firms are operating in a

Industrial sector	Market share of the largest five firms in the industry (%)
Computers/office equipment	71.2
Motor vehicles	62.9
Domestic electrical appliances	46.4
Meat products	5.7
Clothing	4.3

Source: S. Davies and D. Lyons (1996) *Industrial Organisation in the EU*, Clarendon Press, Oxford.

Table 35.4 *Five-firm concentration ratios in the EU*

market, the market is dominated by just five firms, each having a significant market share. For example, an industry with 500 firms in it might at first glance appear very competitive, but if the largest five firms have 90% of the market, then the market is likely to be oligopolistic. A method of identifying this is to use 'concentration ratios'. Thus, the five-firm concentration ratio identifies the total market share of the five largest firms in an industry. This provides a good indication of the type of market structure present in the major part of the market.

Questions

Total: 50 marks (60 minutes)

1 Explain the implications of the excess capacity in the jewellery market for the customers in that market. *(6 marks)*

2 To what extent might the traditional small jewellery and watch operators be considered to be suffering from unfair competition from 'luxury-goods and high-fashion conglomerates'? *(15 marks)*

3 Briefly analyse the market conditions for organic foods using Porter's five forces model. *(8 marks)*

4 Using the data in Table 35.4, identify and briefly explain the market structure that is likely to be present in:
 a the computer/office equipment industry *(3 marks)*
 b the meat products industry *(3 marks)*

5 Using your understanding of the motor vehicle and clothing industries, discuss the reasons why the motor vehicle industry is so highly concentrated compared to the clothing industry. *(15 marks)*

CHAPTER 36

The business cycle

This chapter introduces the idea of macroeconomics before briefly explaining the use of index numbers. It then considers the circular flow of income and the business cycle and its causes, such as spending on durables, changes in stock level and investment decisions. The chapter also considers the different phases of the business cycle and their implications for business.

Chapters 36–40 consider macroeconomic issues relating to business. The study of macroeconomics is concerned with the total (or aggregate) level of spending (or demand) in the economy, the total or aggregate level of production (or supply) in the economy, national employment and unemployment levels, the general level of prices, and the rate of interest and the exchange rate. It is, in effect, concerned with making the most efficient use of an economy's resources.

KEY TERMS

macroeconomics: the study of the whole economy.
microeconomics: the study of the individual parts of the economy.

Index numbers

Many pieces of information, particularly sales records and economic data, are presented as index numbers. The use of index numbers simplifies comparisons between the different items over time. To demonstrate this, consider which of the products in Table 36.1 has experienced the fastest rate of growth in sales between 2001 and 2003.

Sales of product C have declined, so it is clear that this has been the most disappointing product.

Sales of product B have increased by the greatest number, but does this mean that it has performed better than product A?

Product A has more than doubled its sales in the 2 years, but product B has less than doubled its sales. In this respect, product A has performed better than product B if the firm's main objective is growth.

Index numbers are used to make it easier to compare numbers that would otherwise be difficult to compare. They are constructed as follows:

- A base year is selected. The sales volume (or value) in this year is given an index number of 100 (a figure from which it is easy to calculate percentage changes).

Table 36.1
Volume of product sales

| | Year | | | Change from |
	2001	2002	2003	2001 to 2003
Product A	150	285	345	+195
Product B	600	780	990	+390
Product C	250	225	215	−35
Product D	40	70	120	+80
Product E	80	100	128	+48

■ Figures in later years are calculated as a percentage of the base-year figure.
■ The index number is calculated as follows:

$$\frac{\text{actual sales volume in selected year}}{\text{actual sales volume in base year}} \times 100$$

Thus sales of product A were 150 units in 2001 and 285 units in 2002. The index number for 2002 is thus:

$$\frac{285}{150} \times 100 = 190$$

Similarly, the index number for product A in 2003 is:

$$\frac{345}{150} \times 100 = 230$$

This shows the percentage growth in sales between the base year and the year being studied. For product A, growth between 2001 and 2003 has been from 100 to 230, an increase of 130. As a percentage, this is:

$$\frac{130}{100} \times 100 = 130\%$$

	Year		
	2001	**2002**	**2003**
Product A	100	190	230
Product B	100	130	165
Product C	100	90	86
Product D	100	175	300
Product E	100	125	160

Base year (2001) = 100.

Table 36.2 *Index number of product sales*

Completing the calculations for all of the products in years 2002 and 2003 gives the results detailed in Table 36.2.

At a glance it can be seen that product A has grown much faster than product B. It also shows that product D has had the fastest growth rate, and that the growth rate of product E is only slightly less than that of product B (although it was much less in terms of volume).

Index numbers are used where it is more important to compare percentage growth rates than the actual volume of change. They can be used to calculate and compare information on the business cycle, exchange rates, inflation and unemployment.

The circular flow of income

The circular flow of income (Figure 36.1) illustrates the interrelationship between the main parts of the macro economy — that is, between producers and firms, consumers and households, and the government and other countries.

Firms receive revenue or consumer spending (C) in exchange for the goods and services that they provide. This revenue is used to pay incomes (Y) to workers and to other factors of production, in return for their contribution to the production of the goods and services available for sale.

The income of households (Y) is either spent on consumer goods and services that are produced by UK firms (C) or withdrawn from the circular flow. Income withdrawn from the circular flow is used to buy imported goods from abroad (M), is saved (S) or is paid to the government as taxation (T).

The revenue received by firms comes either from consumer spending (C), or from injections. Injections include investment spending by other firms (I) (e.g. when they purchase capital goods such as a JCB digger or a lorry), government spending (G) (e.g. paying for the building of a new school or hospital) or export sales abroad (X).

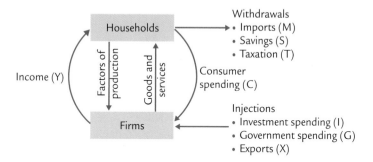

Figure 36.1
A simple circular
flow of income

Introducing the business cycle

KEY TERM

business (or trade) cycle: the regular pattern of ups and downs in demand and output within an economy.

Business cycles have been occurring for as long as records about demand and output have existed, and it is possible to identify periods of booms and slumps since the industrial revolution. Economists differ about what they estimate to be the length of the average cycle — some suggest 8–11 years, others as little as 3–4 years, and some even as long as 50 years. Regardless of these differences, there appear to be definite ups and downs in the business cycle, although in the long term the economy tends to grow, giving each successive cycle an upward trend.

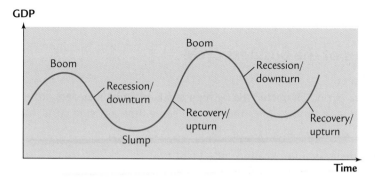

Figure 36.2
The business cycle

The length and magnitude of each stage of the business cycle varies. Some are short-lived, lasting only a few months, while others are as long as 3–4 years. This is illustrated in Figure 36.3, which shows the business cycles in the UK from 1950 to 2002.

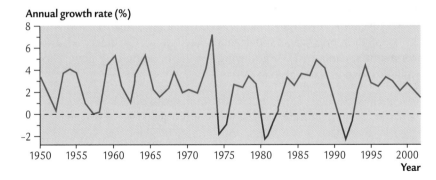

Figure 36.3
Business cycles in the UK,
1950–2002

Annual growth rate (%)

Possible causes of the business cycle

Possible causes of the business cycle include the following:

- Changes in business confidence, which lead to changes in the level of investment in fixed assets. Usually a business replaces fixed assets that have worn out, but mostly it uses existing fixed assets. If the business believes that its sales are going to increase, it will buy more fixed assets and, overall, this could mean a large increase in orders to the producer of the fixed assets. (The opposite applies if confidence is low, as the business will perhaps cancel all orders to replace assets that have worn out.)
- Periods of stock building and then de-stocking. Again, these depend on the confidence of the firm in its ability to sell the stock.
- Irregular patterns of expenditure on consumer durables, such as cars, washing machines and televisions. These are influenced by the level of interest rates and consumer confidence in the economy, and by the need to replace old items.
- Government 'stop–go' policies. These aim for growth just before an election in order to create a favourable economic environment, but often require anti-inflationary policies to control the economy soon afterwards because people are spending lots of money.

Phases of the business cycle

DID YOU KNOW?

De-stocking is where a firm attempts to reduce its stockholding by cutting orders of materials or by cutting production levels. This is usually undertaken by organisations at the beginning of a recession when orders begin to fall.

KEY TERM

boom: period characterised by high levels of consumer demand, business confidence, profits, investment at the same time as rising costs, increasing prices and full capacity.

There are several implications of a boom:

- Consumer demand is likely to be greater than supply, leading to increases in prices.
- A shortage of resources means that costs rise. For example, wages may need to increase in order to attract and/or keep skilled workers; this may in turn lead firms to increase their prices.

- High capacity utilisation may lead firms to look for ways to increase output and fund new investment.
- An overall increase in profits may mean high retained profits and dividends.

KEY TERM

recession (or downturn): period characterised by falling levels of consumer demand, output, profit and business confidence, little investment, spare capacity and rising levels of unemployment.

FACT FILE

Firms producing capital goods such as machinery and plant tend to suffer most in a recession because other firms cut back on their orders dramatically if they expect to sell fewer items. However, in a boom they benefit most because businesses must buy new equipment etc. in order to keep pace with new demand. In effect, these industries are more likely to experience dramatic changes than businesses producing consumer goods, especially essential products such as food.

e EXAMINER'S VOICE

Remember, when analysing the impact of a particular phase of the business cycle on a firm, to consider the organisation and its products. If a firm is producing and selling inferior goods, for example, it may find that it benefits during a recession as incomes fall. Don't ignore the context of the case study.

DID YOU KNOW?

The official definition of recession is a fall in GDP for two consecutive quarters.

Some of the implications of a recession are as follows:
- Falling demand and therefore excess stock may lead to reduced prices.
- Falling demand and reductions in output may lead to low profits or even losses being made and workers being laid off.
- Liquidations as a result of falling demand and losses may mean fewer suppliers and/or fewer consumers.
- Bad debts might mean tighter credit control and eventually less trade.
- High unemployment and therefore falling incomes may lead to a fall in demand for some goods and/or a switch in demand to inferior goods and possibly a search for new markets.
- Low investment as a result of falling demand may lead to a serious decline in firms producing capital goods.

KEY TERM

slump: characterised by very low levels of consumer demand, investment and business confidence, an increasing number of businesses failing and high unemployment.

'Slump' is a rather vague term, sometimes used interchangeably with depression; **essentially it means a very severe recession**. A full-scale depression is much rarer — an example is the Great Depression of the 1930s.

A slump has the following implications:

- The lack of demand means that firms are content to charge low prices, concentrating on sales volume rather than sales revenue. It is possible that deflation (falling prices) may occur across the whole economy.
- The low level of demand means that factories are likely to close, leading to large-scale redundancies and unemployment.

KEY TERM

recovery (or upturn): period characterised by slowly rising levels of consumer demand, rising investment, patchy but increasing business confidence and falling levels of unemployment.

Some of the implications of a recovery are as follows:

- Increasing demand for consumer goods may lead to some increase in profits and to new businesses starting to appear.
- The time lag before capital investment begins may mean that the pace of recovery for different firms is uneven.
- Business confidence is growing, which may mean more investment in fixed assets and more borrowing.
- Spare capacity will be used, but if there are subsequent shortages, costs may increase and potential bottlenecks may arise.

Business confidence

Business confidence can be a key influence on the business cycle. Firms' decisions regarding their labour force needs, investment plans and stock levels are likely to be significantly influenced by their assumptions about potential success and hence about their confidence. Many commentators believe that a high level of business confidence can become a self-fulfilling prophecy — an optimistic outlook leads to higher levels of investment spending and stock building, which in turn cause the economy to grow. For this reason, governments often try to describe the economy in positive terms so that confidence will increase.

DID YOU KNOW?

Business confidence is measured regularly by the CBI's Quarterly Survey. The Department of Trade and Industry (DTI) also publishes insolvency statistics — data on the number of businesses that stop trading because of financial difficulties. These are used as a means of analysing business confidence.

KEY TERMS

gross domestic product (GDP): the total value of a country's output over the course of a year.

gross national product (GNP): the total value of a country's output over the course of a year plus net income from abroad (i.e. income earned on

overseas investment less the income paid to foreigners investing in the UK economy). The growth in real GNP per head of population is the main measure of economic growth.

consumer durables: goods that are owned by households, but which are not instantly consumed by them (e.g. cars, hi-fi equipment, televisions, refrigerators and washing machines).

stock: raw materials or components, work-in-progress and finished goods.

capital (or investment) goods: items that are purchased by firms because they help them to produce goods.

PRACTICE EXERCISE 1 — Total: 50 marks (45 minutes)

1 What is macroeconomics? *(3 marks)*

2 Draw the circular flow of income and explain the interrelationship between households and firms. *(6 marks)*

3 Identify three withdrawals from the circular flow, and explain how one of these withdrawals takes money out of the circular flow. *(6 marks)*

4 Why might demand and output in the economy as a whole fluctuate in a cyclical manner? *(5 marks)*

5 Explain the causes of the recession phase of the business cycle. *(6 marks)*

6 Analyse the effects of the boom phase of the business cycle on business. *(8 marks)*

7 Compare the different implications of a recession for a firm selling:
  a an inferior good *(4 marks)*
  b a luxury product *(4 marks)*

8 Business confidence is a major factor in influencing the business cycle. Why is this the case and how might it be measured? *(8 marks)*

PRACTICE EXERCISE 2 — Total: 50 marks (50 minutes)

Refer to Figure 36.3 (see p. 324) and answer the following questions.

1 What evidence is there to suggest that UK governments used 'stop–go' policies in the 1950s and 1960s? *(6 marks)*

2 Evaluate the implications for a manufacturer of kitchen equipment of the unpredictability of the length of the business cycle in the 1970s and 1980s. *(15 marks)*

3 What evidence is there to suggest that the current government's strategy is aiming to reduce the fluctuations in the business cycle? *(6 marks)*

4 Analyse the possible business opportunities available to a clothing retailer during an upturn or recovery in the business cycle. *(8 marks)*

5 Figure 36.4 shows predictions made for economic growth, with expert opinions ranging from those predicting a strong recovery to those expecting low growth.

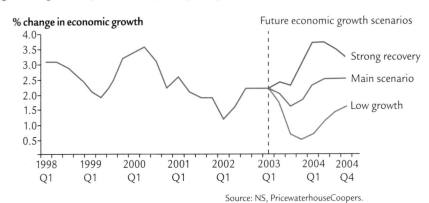

Figure 36.4
GDP growth scenarios

Source: NS, PricewaterhouseCoopers.

Discuss the difficulties facing a house builder when trying to use economic growth scenarios for 2003/04 to judge future sales of houses.

(15 marks)

CHAPTER 37

Interest rates

This chapter looks at interest rates and considers the following questions:
- *How are they set?*
- *What impact do they have on demand for goods?*
- *How do they influence costs?*
- *What is the link between interest rates and exchange rates?*

KEY TERM

interest rates: the cost of borrowing money and the return for lending money. They also measure the **opportunity cost**, to both individuals and firms, of spending money rather than saving it and receiving interest.

A firm that is considering an investment project will take into account whether the financial return from the project exceeds the interest that must be paid if the money to fund the investment is borrowed. It will also consider the interest that could be earned elsewhere if the firm's own funds are used to fund the investment project.

Interest rates are also an important tool of government economic policy. By influencing the cost of borrowing and the reward for lending, the government can influence spending in the economy and therefore the rate of inflation, the level of employment, the rate of exchange of pounds sterling and the level of exports and imports.

DID YOU KNOW?

Opportunity cost measures cost in terms of the next best alternative forgone. For example, the cost of an evening spent revising could be the missed opportunity of attending a concert or of earning money by working in a supermarket.

EXAMINER'S VOICE

Opportunity cost is an excellent concept to use when analysing a range of issues. Make sure that you understand its meaning and can apply it to different situations.

Who sets interest rates?

Before 1997, interest rates were set by the Chancellor of the Exchequer, a member of the government. Under this system, there was always some concern that interest rates might be used for political gain. For example, increases in interest rates might be delayed or interest rates might be reduced just before an election in order to gain political popularity for the government.

Since 1997, the control of interest rates has been the responsibility of the Monetary Policy Committee (MPC), headed by the governor of the Bank of England. The MPC is responsible for maintaining price stability in the UK. It meets monthly to consider interest rate changes and is free to decide the

level of interest rates necessary to meet the target for inflation set by the government, which is currently 2% or less (recently reduced from a target of 2.5%).

Implications of changes to the rate of interest

If interest rates rise, the effects on demand include the following:

- People with mortgages on their property will have less discretionary income available (i.e. actual income available to spend on goods and service). This is a more significant factor in the UK than in other European countries because the UK has one of the highest proportions of owner-occupiers (people owning their own homes) in Europe. In contrast, Germany has a high proportion of people privately renting their homes.
- The sales of consumer products that are bought on credit (e.g. expensive, durable items such as cars, furniture and electrical goods, and luxuries such as holidays) are likely to fall. This is because repayments will now be more expensive and because these goods tend to be income elastic.
- Saving will tend to become more attractive than spending because of the interest earned. This may cause a further drop in sales.
- If interest rates become too high, the increased cost of borrowing may delay investment or actually reduce the level of investment. This is because the return on projects is less likely to exceed interest payments that must be made on borrowed funds or that could be received by investing the firm's own funds elsewhere. This results in a fall in demand for capital goods, such as machinery, as firms become less confident.

This fall in demand for both consumer and capital goods will reduce the rate of economic growth.

In addition to these effects on demand, a rise in interest rates will have further effects on costs and pricing:

- An increase in the interest payments on loans will have a significant effect on firms that have borrowed a lot of money. As interest payments are part of fixed costs, then fixed costs for these firms will rise. This will in turn increase unit costs and the breakeven point (see Figure 37.1).

Figure 37.1 The effect on breakeven of a rise in fixed costs resulting from a rise in interest rates

Costs, revenue (£)

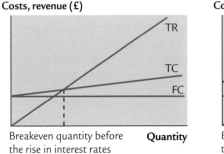

Breakeven quantity before the rise in interest rates

Costs, revenue (£)

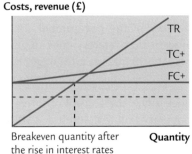

Breakeven quantity after the rise in interest rates

As fixed costs increase due to a rise in interest rates, the breakeven quantity rises.

£

Price level	
Profit margin	Profit margin falls
Unit costs	Unit costs rise
Original cost	After cost increase

Figure 37.2 *The effect on profit margins of a rise in unit costs resulting from a rise in interest rates*

- As unit costs rise, there will be a fall in profit margins, i.e. the difference between unit costs and the price of the product (see Figure 37.2), unless price is increased.

If interest rates fall, the reverse effects will apply:

- People with high levels of borrowing will have more discretionary income to spend and so there will be an overall increase in spending in the economy.
- Consumer goods that are bought on credit, such as cars and furniture, will experience an increase in demand because the interest payments will fall.
- Savings will become less attractive because interest rates earned on savings will fall. This may lead to consumers deciding to spend more of their incomes rather than saving money.
- Investment in capital projects and machinery may rise because the cost of borrowing will fall and so the spending will be easier to finance.
- Overall costs will fall, especially in businesses that have high levels of borrowing. This may lead to an increase in profits for these firms.

Interest rates and their influence on exchange rates

An increase in interest rates means that it becomes more attractive to invest in the UK. There is therefore more foreign investment in the UK. If firms wish to invest in the UK, they need pounds sterling. This means an increase in demand for pounds and therefore an increase in the price or the **exchange rate** of pounds. Figure 37.3 summarises this process.

The impact on firms of changes in exchange rates is discussed in Chapter 38.

DID YOU KNOW?

The exchange rate for the pound is the price of the pound in terms of other currencies. Just as demand and supply can influence the price of goods and services, so they can also influence the price of the pound.

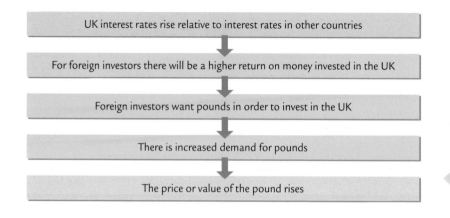

UK interest rates rise relative to interest rates in other countries
For foreign investors there will be a higher return on money invested in the UK
Foreign investors want pounds in order to invest in the UK
There is increased demand for pounds
The price or value of the pound rises

Figure 37.3 *The effect of an increase in interest rates on the exchange rate*

1 Explain the term 'interest rates'. *(2 marks)*

2 How are interest rates set in the UK? *(3 marks)*

3 Identify and explain three different ways in which a fall in interest rates is likely to affect demand for consumer goods. *(9 marks)*

4 Explain how a rise in interest rates is likely to affect demand for capital goods. *(3 marks)*

5 Explain how a change in interest rates might affect profit margins. *(4 marks)*

6 How could profit margins be maintained if interest rates cause unit costs to rise? Show this by redrafting Figure 37.2 (see p. 331). *(7 marks)*

7 In the breakeven chart in Figure 37.1 (see p. 330), how could the firm keep its breakeven quantity at the original level, given that the increase in interest payments has increased total costs? Redraft Figure 37.1 to show this. *(8 marks)*

8 If interest rates fall, what is likely to happen to the value of the pound? *(4 marks)*

Figure 37.4 shows the changing level of interest rates since 1998. How the economy performs in 2003/04 will dictate the extent to which, and in which direction, the Monetary Policy Committee (MPC) will change interest rates. The graph provides three possible scenarios for interest rates in the near future, depending on whether there is strong growth in the economy, low growth or growth similar to current levels.

Source: NS, PwC scenarios using modified Taylor rule.

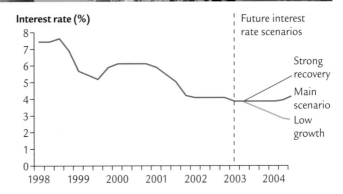

Figure 37.4 Interest rate scenarios

1 Explain why the MPC is expected to set lower interest rates if growth is low and high interest rates if growth is high. *(6 marks)*

2 Describe the trend in interest rates since 1998 and explain the possible effects of this trend on the value of the pound. *(6 marks)*

3 Discuss the possible impact of the 'strong recovery' interest rate scenario in Figure 37.4, on a luxury hotel chain in the UK. *(9 marks)*

4 To what extent might all firms benefit from the low interest rate shown in the 'low growth' scenario in Figure 37.4? *(9 marks)*

CHAPTER 38

Exchange rates

This chapter explains the notion of exchange rates and examines the different strategies used by governments to manage exchange rates. The effects of exchange rate changes in different situations and on different organisations are analysed.

KEY TERM

▪ **exchange rate:** the price of one country's currency in terms of another.

There is an exchange rate for pounds sterling against all other currencies, although the ones most commonly quoted are the rate against the euro, the US dollar, the Japanese yen and also against a 'basket of currencies' (an average of a number of major currencies).

Exchange rate policies

Exchange rate policies are strategies that the government can adopt in order to determine the exchange rate of the country's currency. There are three broad policies available.

KEY TERM

flexible or freely floating exchange rates: the demand for and the supply of the currency determine the exchange rate.

As with any 'product', if lots of people want (demand) it, the price will go up. On the other hand, if there is too much available (being supplied), then the price will fall as it is easy to obtain. The demand for pounds comes from those who wish to buy UK goods and services (i.e. UK exports) or invest in the UK. The supply of pounds comes from those who need foreign currency in order to purchase foreign goods and services (i.e. imports to the UK) or invest abroad. Thus the exchange rate is influenced by the level of demand for exports and imports and the level of foreign investment.

DID YOU KNOW?

The foreign exchange market is a good example of **perfect competition** (see Chapter 35). The products are identical: for example, one dollar is exactly the same as another dollar. There are many buyers and sellers, all of whom are too small to influence the price on their own. Everyone buying and selling a particular currency knows the price, so sellers are unlikely to try to charge higher or lower prices than their competitors.

KEY TERM

managed exchange rates: the Bank of England or central bank intervenes in the foreign exchange market in order to influence the exchange rate.

PHOTODISC

For example, the Bank of England would buy pounds if market pressures forced the exchange rate of sterling down below the level that is deemed to be acceptable for the economy. Buying pounds increases the demand for the currency and therefore increases its price. Similarly, the Bank of England would sell pounds if it were concerned that the exchange rate of sterling was getting too high for the economy, thus increasing its supply and reducing its price or the exchange rate.

> **KEY TERM**
>
> **fixed exchange rates:** the government decides to fix the value of its currency permanently in relation to other currencies.

This happened when 11 European Union countries fixed their exchange rates in relation to each other's currency on 1 January 1999 in preparation for the introduction of the euro. If the UK decides to join the European single currency (i.e. to adopt the euro), it too will fix sterling in relation to the euro prior to introducing the euro and subsequently withdrawing pounds.

> **DID YOU KNOW?**
>
> 'Euro' (€) is the name given to the single European currency introduced on 1 January 1999. The currencies of the 11 countries adopting the euro were fixed permanently to each other on that date. Euro notes and coins were introduced on 1 January 2002 and by 30 June 2002 individual currencies were no longer legal tender. Greece, the twelfth country, joined the Euro in 2001.

The UK has a free exchange rate system, although if the exchange rate of sterling rises too high or falls too low, the government may request the Bank of England to intervene and 'manage' the exchange rate until it reaches an acceptable level.

Changes in the exchange rate

An *increase* in the exchange rate can result from any of the following:

- An increase in exports increases the demand for the currency.
- A reduction in imports decreases the supply of the currency.
- High interest rates attract savings from abroad and therefore increase demand for the currency.
- If speculators expect a currency to increase in value in the future, this is likely to cause an increase in the demand for the currency now. Then, when its value does rise, speculators will sell the currency and make a profit.
- If foreign multinationals wish to invest in a country, they will need to buy its currency, which in turn will increase the demand for it.
- The government may buy the currency in order to support its value, as in managed exchange rate policies.

A *decrease* in the exchange rate is caused by the opposite factors: for example, a decrease in the demand for the currency caused by a decrease in exports, an increase in supply caused by an increase in imports, and so on.

Implications for business of changes in exchange rates

Assuming that profit margins remain the same, an *increase* in the exchange rate increases the price at which exports sell, but reduces the price at which imports are bought. This affects a firm's revenue, competitiveness and profitability. The extent to which this affects export sales and the purchase of imports depends on the price elasticity of demand:

- If the price elasticity of demand for exports is inelastic, an increase in their price, due to a rise in the exchange rate, will mean increased revenue from export sales.
- If, on the other hand, demand is price elastic, an increase in export prices is likely to lead to a fall in sales and in revenue.
- If imports are price elastic, consumers are likely to purchase more of them, possibly substituting them for UK-produced goods.
- Alternatively, where firms purchase imported raw materials, their costs may fall, which could lead them to reduce the price of their finished products or simply increase their profit margins.

It is, however, important to note that the level of exports and imports is influenced not only by exchange rates, but also by a range of other factors, including reputation and quality, after-sales service, the reliability, design and desirability of the product, the overall packaging provided and payment terms.

Exchange rates can be very volatile, as indicated in Figure 38.1. Changes in the exchange rate make it difficult for firms to predict the volume of overseas sales or the price they will receive from their overseas transactions. Because this increases the level of risk, it is likely to discourage overseas sales. In order to avoid the effects of changes in the exchange rate, it is possible to buy currency in advance at a guaranteed fixed rate, but this is expensive and may reduce profits.

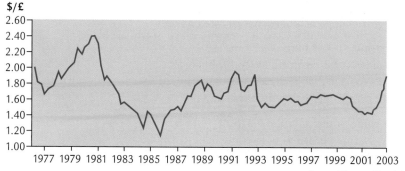

FACT FILE

In late 2003/early 2004 there was a dramatic rise in the $/£ exchange rate. On 18 November 2003 the pound reached $1.70, by 18 February 2004 it had increased to $1.90. Brent Hoberman, chief executive of lastminute.com, reported that 70% more flights to New York were booked in January than December as tourists flocked to the USA.

EXAMINER'S VOICE

Price elasticity of demand is an important concept in this area, so do ensure that you understand the concept and the implications of different elasticities on a firm's revenue.

Figure 38.1 *The dollar/sterling exchange rate, 1976–2003*

Source: *Thomson Financial.*

Unpredictable exchange rate changes also create administrative and marketing problems. For example, the information on published price lists may change, as may the prices quoted on advertising material.

Impact of exchange rates on exporters

Examples 1 and 2 show the impact of changes in exchange rates on a UK car exporter.

Example 1: the effect of a change in exchange rate on the price and competitiveness of an exporter

The figures used here are for illustration only and are not intended to reflect the actual value of the currencies involved. In this example, profit margins per unit remain fixed at £2,000 but the selling price abroad changes as the exchange rate changes.

Currently £1 = €1.60.
In the UK a car costs £8,000 to produce.
It sells for £10,000 in the UK.

At the current exchange rate, it sells for €16,000 (10,000 × 1.60) in Spain.
Similar models in Spain sell for €17,000.
The UK car is competitively priced.

The value of the pound rises to £1 = €1.75.
The UK car now sells for €17,500 (10,000 × €1.75) in Spain.
The UK car is no longer competitively priced.

The value of the pound falls to £1 = €1.50.
The UK car now sells for €15,000 (10,000 × 1.50) in Spain.
The UK car is very competitively priced.

Thus it can be seen that in this situation a *rise* in the value of the pound leads to a *less competitive* export price, while a *fall* in the value of the pound leads to a *more competitive* export price.

Example 2: the effect of a change in exchange rate on the profitability of an exporter

In this example, selling price abroad remains fixed at $20,000, but profit margins change as the exchange rate changes.

Currently £1 = $2.00.
In the UK a car costs £8,000 to produce.
It sells for $20,000 in the USA (£10,000).
Profit margin per car is therefore £2,000.

The value of the pound rises to £1 = $2.5.
The revenue per car is now equivalent to £8,000.
Profit margin per car is therefore zero.

The value of the pound falls to £1 = $1.6.

The revenue per car is now equivalent to £12,500.
Profit margin per car is therefore £4,500.

In this situation, the *rise* in the value of the pound leads to a *smaller profit margin*, while a *fall* in the value of the pound leads to a *larger profit margin*.

Impact of exchange rates on importers

In both examples 1 and 2, the best result for the exporter is brought about by a fall in the exchange rate. But what effect will exchange rate movements have on an importer of raw materials? This is shown in Example 3.

Example 3: the effect of a change in exchange rate on an importer of raw materials

Currently £1 = €1.60.
An importer who buys 1,000 units from France at a cost of €32 each will pay €32,000. At the current exchange rate this is £20,000.

The value of the pound rises to £1 = €2.
The UK importer will now need to exchange only £16,000 in order to get €32,000 to buy the raw materials. Therefore, the *rise* in the exchange rate has made it cheaper for the importer to buy raw materials.

The value of the pound falls to £1 = €1.28.
The UK importer will now need to exchange £25,000 in order to get €32,000 to buy the raw materials. Therefore, the *fall* in the exchange rate has made it dearer for the importer to buy raw materials.

Thus a change in the exchange rate, by affecting the price of imports and exports, will affect the extent to which a firm remains competitive and profitable in both its overseas and domestic markets. The exact impact will be different for exporters and importers and will also depend on whether price is the main factor when buying a good.

FACT FILE

Carrie Bradshaw, the shopaholic heroine of *Sex and the City*, buys her Jimmy Choos on Madison Avenue. Now it is no longer a ridiculous idea for Britons. A standard pair of Jimmy Choo stilettos costs £360 in London. In New York, the same shoes retail at $575. At the new exchange rate of $1.90 to the pound, that's £302, a saving of £58.

Buy a couple of pairs, throw in a handful of CDs, and maybe pick up an Apple iPod (£249 in the UK; £158 in the US) and you've saved enough to pay for your flight and a couple of nights in a Manhattan hotel.

These bargains on offer across the pond may be good news for shoppers, but firms in Britain and the euro-zone watching their exports become more expensive for American buyers are not so thrilled. The dollar's 20% decline over the past year is causing alarm in European capitals.

Of course, the process also works in reverse — it is now more expensive for Americans to visit Britain. This fact is alarming the British tourist industry, but Will Whitehorn, a director of Richard Branson's Virgin Group, thinks there is little reason to worry. 'Nobody in the US is in the least bit bothered about this,' he says. 'Only 11% of adult Americans have a passport after all. It's only rich Americans who go abroad and they are rich enough not to be too affected by this.'

Source: adapted from an article in the *Guardian*, 20 February 2004.

PRACTICE EXERCISE 1
Total: 50 marks (45 minutes)

1 What is an exchange rate? *(2 marks)*

2 Explain the meaning of 'freely floating exchange rate'. *(3 marks)*

3 State and explain three reasons why a currency might increase in value. *(9 marks)*

4 List two reasons that might cause a currency to fall in value. *(2 marks)*

5 When the exchange rate rises:
   a How might a firm ensure that its prices abroad do not rise? *(3 marks)*
   b Why would a firm not always choose to take the action that you have chosen in 5(a)? *(3 marks)*

6 What is the effect of a fall in the exchange rate on the price of exports and the price of imports? *(6 marks)*

7 If a firm is dependent on imported raw materials, what will be the possible impact of a fall in the exchange rate on its costs and pricing? *(4 marks)*

8 Why might a system of fluctuating exchange rates cause difficulties for a firm involved in exporting or importing? *(4 marks)*

9 The current exchange rate is £1 = $1.50. A firm sells 10,000 units abroad at a price equivalent to £6.00. If the exchange rate rises to £1 = $2, what effect will this have on its sales revenue? Explain your answer. *(5 marks)*

10 The exchange rate of a currency rises by 10%. To what extent would an exporter of goods with an elastic demand be affected differently from an exporter of goods with an inelastic demand? *(9 marks)*

PRACTICE EXERCISE 2
Total: 50 marks (50 minutes)

1 Study Table 38.1 and answer the questions that follow.
   a Describe the changing value of the pound sterling against the three currencies given in Table 38.1. *(6 marks)*
   b If a component purchased from Japan in 1996 cost 17,000 yen, how much would that have been in sterling? Assume that the Japanese supplier did not alter the yen price of the component between 1996 and 2000. What would its sterling price have been in 2000? *(6 marks)*

Year	US dollar	Japanese yen	Euro
1996	1.56	170	1.21
1997	1.64	198	1.45
1998	1.66	217	1.49
1999	1.62	240	1.52
2000	1.50	264	1.60

Source: *Economic Trends*, various dates.

Table 38.1 *Sterling exchange rates, 1996–2000*

   c In 1996, the price of a particular product in the UK was £500. What would its price have been in euros? Assume that the sterling price of the product did not change between 1996 and 2000. What would its euro price have been in 2000? *(6 marks)*
   d Discuss the possible impact of the changes in exchange rate shown in the table on a firm that imports essential components for production from Japan and sells its finished products mainly in Europe. *(15 marks)*

2 The data in Table 38.2 show changes in the exchange rates of four countries in recent years, using 1995 as the base year.

Compare and contrast the impact of the exchange rate changes shown on the following firms:

a a UK business that exports to Germany and also exports to the USA *(6 marks)*

b a UK business that imports from Japan and also imports from the USA *(6 marks)*

c a UK business that sells its products worldwide on the basis of quality and service rather than price *(5 marks)*

	1994–96	1997–99	2000–02
USA ($)	101	121	132
Japan (yen)	94	90	103
Germany (DM)	97	98	95
UK (£)	102	125	129

Source: *Thomson Financial.*

Table 38.2 *Exchange rate indices, averages for each period (1995 = 100)*

CHAPTER 39

Inflation

Inflation is the focus of this chapter which examines the following questions:
- *What is inflation?*
- *How is it measured?*
- *What are the main causes of inflation?*
- *How are businesses affected by inflation?*

KEY TERMS

inflation: an increase in the general level of prices of goods within an economy. Inflation also means that there is a fall in the purchasing power of money.

deflation: a decrease in the general level of prices of goods within an economy or a rise in the purchasing power of money.

It is important to be able to distinguish between **real** and **money or nominal values**. Real income broadly measures what you can buy with your income. If prices increase by 2% over a year (in other words, the cost of living rises by 2%) and your money or nominal income also increases by 2% over the same period, then your real income (i.e. what you can buy with your income) has remained the same. Thus real income increases only if the nominal or money value of income rises by more than the rate of inflation over the same period. If money income rises by 10% and prices rise by 3%, then real income has risen, since you can now buy more with your income. But if money income rises by 2% and prices rise by 5%, then real income has fallen, since you can now buy less with your income.

Measuring inflation

The retail price index

Until 2003 inflation in the UK was measured by the **retail price index (RPI)**. This shows changes in the price of the average person's shopping basket. It is calculated using a weighted average of each month's price changes. It starts with a study of people's spending patterns, to try to assess the average household's weekly expenditure. Weights are allocated to different categories of goods according to the degree of importance attached to them and the proportion of income spent on them by an average family.

For example, household spending on food makes up approximately 12% of the total, so food as a category would carry a weight of 0.12 within the RPI. Then if food prices rise by 10%, this adds 1.2% to the overall RPI (10% × 0.12). From this it can be seen that the bigger the proportion of household income

spent on a particular category, the greater the effects of any price change on the overall inflation figure. The RPI is an **index number**, which means that a base year is given the value of 100 and all future price increases are calculated in relation to this reference point (see pp. 321–22).

For example, if the RPI in year 1 is given the value of 100 and if, between years 1 and 2, inflation rises by 20%, the RPI in year 2 will be 120 (i.e. a 20% increase on 100). If, between years 2 and 3, inflation rises by 25%, the RPI in year 3 will be 150 (i.e. a 25% increase on 120). If, between years 3 and 4, inflation rises by 33.3%, the RPI in year 4 will be 200 (i.e. a 33.3% increase on 150). This figure of 200 shows that prices in year 4 are double those in year 1 (when the value was 100).

A major problem with the RPI as a measure of inflation is that it is based upon the average household's spending pattern. However, many people whose annual increases in government benefits or pensions depend on the level of the RPI have quite different spending patterns from the average household. For example, pensioners in general spend twice the proportion of their income on heating as the average household. So if electricity and gas prices rise by 10% in a year when most other prices have risen by only 3%, the figure reflecting general price rises in the RPI will fail to reflect the rate of inflation experienced by pensioners.

RPIX and CPI (HICP)

A variant on the retail price index (RPI) is the **RPIX**. This measures inflation in the same way as the RPI, but excludes mortgage interest payments. The previous inflation target of 2.5% set by the Chancellor of the Exchequer used the RPIX. This measure, also known as 'the underlying rate of inflation', is used to ensure that the rate of inflation reflects the cost of living not only of owner occupiers, but also of those living in rented accommodation.

In Europe a different measure of inflation is used, known as the **harmonised index of consumer prices (HICP)** or the **consumer price index (CPI)**. The Chancellor of the Exchequer introduced this measure in December 2003. In general, the CPI (HICP) tends to be approximately 0.5–0.75 percentage points below the RPIX, but this can vary. This means that the new CPI inflation target has been set lower (at 2%) than the previous target of 2.5% set for the RPIX. The CPI gives a more accurate view of inflationary pressures and will be necessary if the UK decides to join the euro. In the UK, the term CPI has been adopted rather than the term HICP which is favoured on the Continent, but they both measure inflation in the same way.

An important short-term drawback of the HICP (CPI) is that it does not yet include a measure of housing costs, such as council tax or house prices.

For example, the sharp rise in UK house prices over recent years means that the RPIX has been substantially higher than the HICP (CPI); in August 2003, the HICP was at an annual rate of 1.4% and the RPIX was at 2.9%.

Figure 39.1 illustrates the differences between the three measures of inflation.

Figure 39.1
Annual inflation rates in the UK, 2001–03

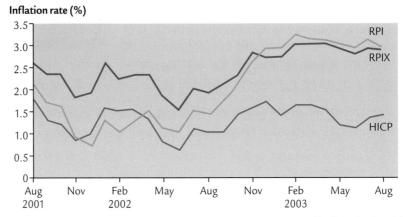

Source: Office for National Statistics.

Causes of inflation

In general, the causes of inflation can be divided into two types: cost-push and demand-pull, to distinguish between prices being pushed up by rising costs or being pulled up because demand has outstripped supply. In addition, emphasis is now placed on the role of expectations in generating inflation.

KEY TERM

cost-push inflation: occurs when there is an increase in the costs of production (including wages, raw materials, fuel, taxation and interest rates) that forces firms to increase their prices in order to protect their profit margins.

For example, this could be due to trade unions achieving wage increases that are greater than productivity increases, or it could be due to a massive increase in the price of an essential fuel, such as oil.

KEY TERM

demand-pull inflation: the process by which prices rise because there is excess demand in the economy.

Excess demand occurs if consumers' income increases but there is no corresponding rise in output on which to spend this increased income. If interest rates are low and more borrowing, by consumers or firms, is encouraged, this will have the same inflationary effect.

Just as an increase in demand for a particular product might lead to an increase in its price unless there is a corresponding increase in supply, so

✐ EXAMINER'S VOICE

Don't make the mistake of thinking that a fall in the inflation rate means a fall in prices. It simply means a slowing down of the rate at which prices are rising. Falling prices could only be occurring if the inflation rate was negative. This has not happened in the UK for over 70 years.

AS Business Studies

demand-pull inflation can be explained as a situation when aggregate (or total) demand in the economy increases without a corresponding increase in aggregate supply in the economy. This leads to an increase in the general level of prices because aggregate supply cannot increase beyond the point where firms are working at full capacity.

 **KEY** **TERM**

inflationary expectations: views about what will happen to the rate of inflation in the future.

As a rule, people expect a period of rising inflation to continue into the future. For example, if the rate of inflation has risen from 1% 2 years ago, to 2% last year and then to 3% this year, people are likely to expect inflation to be 4% next year. If this is the case, they are likely to try to negotiate a pay rise of 4% now in order to avoid a fall in their real income if inflation does rise to 4%. If they are successful, this will add to costs and will help to bring about a 4% rate of inflation.

In practice, the causes of inflation are difficult to disentangle. As prices rise, for whatever reason, people negotiate wage increases to maintain their standard of living, anticipating future levels of inflation and thereby helping those levels to come about. An **inflationary spiral** is the way in which price rises in one sector of the economy cause price increases in another, in a continuous upward spiral. Pay increases become price rises, which in turn lead to demand for further pay increases, which cause further price rises, and so on. Figure 39.2 shows the rates of inflation in the UK since 1979.

Inflation (RPIX) % change

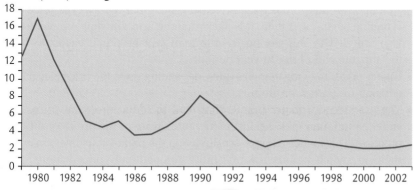

Figure 39.2
UK annual inflation rates (%), 1979–2003

KEY **TERM**

hyperinflation: a situation where the value of money decreases so fast that people lose confidence in it.

As a result, people start to barter or to make use of other commodities, such as gold, which have their own intrinsic value, or to use an internationally

Section 1 *Economic opportunities and constraints*

343

dependable foreign currency such as the US dollar. There is no precise level of inflation that means it is hyperinflation. It is more the case that price rises become so rapid and uncontrollable that confidence in the currency is lost and people are reluctant to enter into transactions with it.

> **DID YOU KNOW?**
>
> The best-known example of hyperinflation occurred in Germany in the 1920s, when prices were rising every day and paper money rapidly became worthless. By 1923 the annual rate of inflation had reached a mind-boggling 7,000,000,000,000%, and in 1924 the German currency was replaced by a new currency. More recently, a number of South American countries have suffered from hyperinflation. For example, inflation in Brazil peaked in 1993 at 1,200% and in Russia it reached 2,500% in 1992.

Hyperinflation has severe consequences for society because it not only affects people's willingness to enter into transactions, but also leads to a major redistribution of income in favour of those with debts and with non-financial assets, and against those dependent on fixed incomes, such as pensioners and those relying on their savings.

Effects of inflation on business

Some of the effects of inflation can be positive for individual firms or consumers, but in general the effects are negative.

- Inflation tends to encourage borrowing if interest rates are less than the rate of inflation. For firms with heavy borrowing, inflation reduces the real value of the sum they owe, making it easier to repay the loan towards the end of its life. For example, if a firm borrowed a large sum of money 10 years ago, and if inflation has been increasing such that the average price level is double what it was then, it is likely that the firm's income or revenue has also doubled in this period, so the loan will be much easier to repay towards the end of the 10-year period.
- Higher prices may mean lower sales, depending upon the price elasticity of demand for particular products.
- The producers of major brands that tend to sell at premium prices may suffer as inflation makes consumers more aware of the prices of different products. This increased price sensitivity on the part of consumers may lead them to switch brands towards more competitively priced items. As a result, brand owners will either cut their price premiums or greatly increase their advertising expenditure in order to try to regain customer interest and loyalty.
- Just as consumers become more aware of prices, so workers become far more concerned about the level of their real wages because, unless they obtain a pay rise at least as high as the rate of inflation, their real income will fall. Therefore industrial action often increases in inflationary periods as workers and trade unions negotiate hard for pay increases. As a consequence, industrial relations tend to deteriorate.

- Suppliers may demand higher prices for the goods and services they supply, adding further to a firm's costs and putting more pressure on the firm to increase its own prices.
- If inflation in the UK is relatively higher than inflation in other countries, the international competitiveness of UK firms may be reduced.
- As the future is uncertain, forecasts and planning will be less reliable.
- If the Monetary Policy Committee (MPC) of the Bank of England takes action to reduce inflation by increasing interest rates, this is likely further to reduce demand and sales.

> **e** **EXAMINER'S VOICE**
>
> Under time pressure it is easy to forget or confuse terms. Check carefully whether the question is about the exchange rate, the inflation rate or the interest rate.

PRACTICE EXERCISE 1 — Total: 40 marks (35 minutes)

1 Explain the terms 'inflation' and 'deflation'. *(4 marks)*

2 What is the consumer price index (CPI)? *(3 marks)*

3 If the CPI in year 1 stands at 175 and in year 2 stands at 183.75, what has been the inflation rate between the 2 years? *(3 marks)*

4 Explain one problem in using the CPI. *(3 marks)*

5 Distinguish between cost-push and demand-pull inflation. *(6 marks)*

6 If the rate of inflation in 2000 was 2.1% and my annual salary in 2000 increased by 2.5%, was I better off? Explain your answer. *(4 marks)*

7 Explain why inflationary expectations are likely to cause inflation. *(5 marks)*

8 Explain one benefit that inflation might have for firms and individuals. *(3 marks)*

9 Identify and explain three adverse effects of inflation on a firm. *(9 marks)*

PRACTICE EXERCISE 2 — Total: 50 marks (50 minutes)

1 Look at Table 39.1, which gives inflation rates for selected countries.

Country	Consumer price inflation (%)		
	2002	2003	2004
USA	1.6	2.3	1.9
UK	2.2	2.8	2.3
Spain	3.1	3.1	2.7
Ireland	4.7	4.2	3.3
Japan	−0.9	−0.5	−0.6
Russia	15.1	14.0	11.0

Table 39.1 Inflation rates for selected countries, 2002–04

a Explain what the rates of inflation quoted for Japan indicate about price levels in that country. *(4 marks)*

b Why might these levels of inflation have helped to cause a recession in Japan? *(6 marks)*

c As a UK company trading in all of these countries, discuss the possible implications of their differing inflation rates for the competitiveness of your product. *(12 marks)*

2 Refer to Figure 39.1 (see p. 342).

  a What has happened to actual prices (as measured by the RPI) during the period covered by the graph? *(6 marks)*

  b If the RPI in September 2003 was 182.5, up from 181.6 in August 2003, what was the rate of inflation between August and September? *(4 marks)*

3 Refer to Figure 39.2 (see p. 343).

  a Consider the likely impact of inflation on a firm producing consumer durables such as televisions and other electrical goods in 1980 and in 2002. *(8 marks)*

  b Inflation in the UK has been low and stable for the last 10 years. To what extent might a firm be adversely affected by such low inflation? *(10 marks)*

CHAPTER 40

Unemployment

Unemployment exists when someone seeking work is unable to find a job. In this chapter it is studied in the context of the business world. The main types/causes (structural and cyclical) are explained, the role of the government in the control of unemployment is introduced and the effects of unemployment on business are considered.

Types of unemployment

Structural unemployment

> **KEY TERM**
>
> **structural unemployment:** long-term unemployment resulting from a change in demand, supply or technology in the economy, which produces a fundamental decline in an industry.

Structural unemployment is often concentrated in regions that have been heavily dependent on certain industries. For example:

- The coal industry in Wales and other areas of the UK suffered from a fall in demand as coal was replaced by other fuels. Employment in the UK coal industry fell by 94% between 1978 and 1998.
- The shipbuilding industry in the northeast suffered from a fall in demand for shipping as foreign competition hit sales. Employment in the UK shipbuilding industry fell by 86% between 1978 and 1998.
- The steel industry also suffered from foreign competition, resulting in a fall in employment of 82% between 1978 and 1998.
- The textile industry in Lancashire and Yorkshire suffered from competition from low-wage economies.

TOPFOTO

Cyclical unemployment

> **KEY TERM**
>
> **cyclical unemployment:** unemployment resulting from an economic downturn or recession in the business cycle.

Cyclical unemployment can be expected to last for as long as the recession itself, which might be for 1–2 years. Figure 40.1 illustrates that, like economic growth, unemployment tends to follow a cyclical pattern.

The impact of cyclical unemployment will vary according to individual firms and their products, but might include the following:

*Figure 40.1
Unemployment in the UK,
1970–2002*

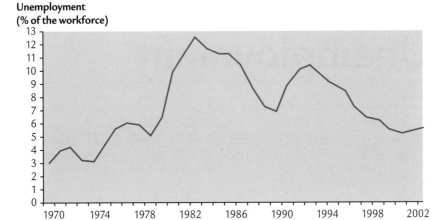

Unemployment
(% of the workforce)

- In theory, the sales of luxury products will decline significantly as income declines, whereas firms selling inferior goods may gain increased sales as people cut back on luxuries.
- Firms selling products in a growing market may be able to ride out the effects of recession, but on the other hand, firms selling products with low profit margins may suffer as price becomes a more important element of the marketing mix.
- Capital goods firms and construction firms are likely to experience the greatest problems as business confidence falls and there is less demand for their products.

Seasonal unemployment

Seasonal unemployment tends to be of a temporary nature and disappears in the next 'season'. For example, people working in the tourism industry and in the building and construction industry are often laid off during the winter when there is less demand for their service.

Frictional unemployment

Frictional unemployment is also known as 'search' unemployment and occurs in the time between losing one job and finding another when people are temporarily unemployed. Government can reduce frictional unemployment by improving the quality of service in job centres so that people who are newly unemployed are able to find work more quickly.

 **EXAMINER'S VOICE**

The AQA specification only requires recognition of cyclical and structural unemployment. However, two other forms of unemployment are widely recognised: seasonal unemployment and frictional unemployment.

Tackling unemployment

There is little any government can do to alleviate structural unemployment in the long term, other than offering retraining opportunities and incentives to relocate for those made redundant. However, some governments will 'protect' industries to reduce this type of unemployment. The European Union is accused of 'protecting' agriculture among member countries through the Common Agricultural Policy.

TOPFOTO

Module 3 *External influences*

However, a government that wishes to prevent or relieve cyclical unemployment could take counter-cyclical economic measures or encourage wage flexibility, so that company wage bills fall automatically during recessions, without requiring redundancies.

Counter-cyclical economic policies are an attempt by the government to smooth out fluctuations in economic activity. When the economy is in a boom period, the government may try to stop it booming further, or 'overheating', by reducing government spending on goods and services in order to reduce aggregate demand. In a period of recession, government may follow the opposite course and increase government spending in order to increase aggregate demand.

In a recession there is more unemployment, so government spending has to rise in order to pay for more unemployment and social security benefits. In a boom period, unemployment falls, so government spending on social security and unemployment benefits also falls. These changes are known as **automatic economic stabilisers** because their effect is to move the economy towards stability. Other aspects of government spending are not automatic, such as the decision to increase or decrease the amount of road building or the building of new hospitals and schools. The difficult issue here is getting the timing right. For example, if the government believed the economy was coming out of recession, it might decide to reduce government spending on roads. If the recovery did not happen as expected, however, the reduction of incomes in the road-building industry would make the recession worse.

Implications of unemployment for business

A high level of unemployment has the following implications for businesses:

- Consumer incomes fall, leading to lower sales and possibly redundancies. Alternatively, low incomes may lead to a higher demand for inferior goods.
- Workers have less bargaining power as alternative jobs are harder to find, which may lead to lower wage levels. In addition, people may be more willing to work for lower wages in order to get a job.
- Cost-saving exercises may be undertaken, which in the short term may lead to cost efficiencies, but in the longer term may lead to problems. For example, reducing training and delayering an organisation will eventually lead to a lack of skills and expertise, and wider spans of control.
- The reduction in demand is likely to lead to cutbacks in investment, which in turn may lead to a further decline in employment.
- The reduction in demand may require businesses to rationalise, which may in turn lead to takeovers and mergers.
- Because more skilled and experienced people are available for work, businesses may benefit from reduced training needs.
- Due to high levels of unemployment, lower wages are likely to be the norm. In turn, these will lead to lower costs and possibly lower prices.

> **DID YOU KNOW?**
>
> Minimum wage legislation limits the extent to which firms can push down wages during a period of high unemployment.

PRACTICE EXERCISE 1   Total: 40 marks (35 minutes)

1 Explain the term 'structural unemployment'. *(3 marks)*

2 Give two examples of structural unemployment. *(3 marks)*

3 Explain one way in which the government can reduce the impact of structural unemployment. *(3 marks)*

4 Explain the term 'cyclical unemployment'. *(2 marks)*

5 What can the government do to reduce cyclical unemployment? *(6 marks)*

6 Explain the term 'seasonal unemployment' and give two examples of it. *(5 marks)*

7 Explain the term 'frictional unemployment'. *(3 marks)*

8 Identify and explain three adverse effects of unemployment on firms. *(9 marks)*

9 Identify and explain two possible benefits to firms of the presence of unemployment. *(6 marks)*

PRACTICE EXERCISE 2   Total: 30 marks (30 minutes)

1 Refer to Figure 40.1 (see p. 348). Describe the extent to which the pattern of unemployment reflects the business cycles shown in Figure 36.3 (see p. 324). *(8 marks)*

2 Look at Figure 40.2, which shows the pattern of regional unemployment in the UK in 2002–03.

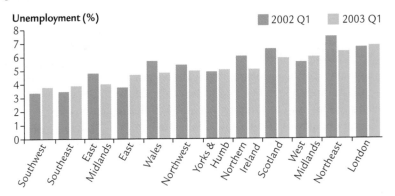

Figure 40.2 Regional unemployment in the UK

Source: NS.

  a Briefly explain why there are differences in levels of unemployment between different regions of the UK. *(6 marks)*

  b Analyse the possible impact of these unemployment data on two different firms, one of which produces and sells its products in the southeast of England while the other produces and sells its products in the northeast of England. *(8 marks)*

  c The UK has experienced relatively low rates of unemployment in recent years. Analyse the possible problems resulting from this for a firm operating in the financial services industry. Assume that the firm requires highly skilled and well-qualified staff. *(8 marks)*

CASE STUDY

Macroeconomic issues

CASE STUDY Harewood Ltd

Introduction

Tessa Harewood opened the newspapers excitedly. Following the takeover of T. J. Laing Ltd, she was now the chief executive of the UK's fifth-largest sports goods supplier.

It was a gamble. Harewood Ltd had built up a tremendous reputation for its sportswear, and sales were growing fast, helped by Tessa's decision to move all of the production of its sportswear to India. However, Tessa found it difficult to foresee a time when Harewood Ltd could displace some of the major international sportswear suppliers. On that basis the takeover made good sense.

T. J. Laing specialised in equipment manufacturing. However, the company had been plagued by problems. The fitness equipment was manufactured in a factory in Birmingham, but more and more competitors had moved production to Asia or eastern Europe, where wage costs were lower. T. J. Laing had responded by specialising in the higher-quality, technically sophisticated end of the market, but the current recession had hit sales of these products significantly.

The other division of T. J. Laing was racquet production. Production of racquets was based in China, but difficulties with quality and delivery had led to heavy financial losses.

Year 1

Tessa's first action was to start producing racquets in two more places. Harewood Ltd opened a new factory in Portugal. In Birmingham, Tessa used some of the spare capacity in the fitness equipment factory to produce racquets. Only 30% of racquet production was left in China, with 60% in Portugal. After delivery costs had been allowed for, the production in Portugal was only slightly dearer than China. The remaining 10% was manufactured in Birmingham — mainly the more expensive racquets — but there was also scope to produce other racquets just-in-time, to meet sudden orders or shortages in the UK.

Gradually sales in all products improved, as the UK came out of the 9-month recession that had started just before the takeover. Sportswear recovered most strongly in the UK, but by the end of the year fitness equipment sales there were still at their lowest level for 3 years. Tessa was pleased that the business was not reliant on UK sales for the majority of its revenue from fitness equipment. The sales in Italy and France accounted for 65% of the company's sales of fitness equipment and the T. J. Laing brand name was very strong in those two countries. Tessa's long-term strategy was to use the T. J. Laing brand name and reputation to sell its sportswear in Italy and France.

Year 2

As the business cycle moved from recession to recovery, sportswear sales grew quickly, but it took much longer for the fitness equipment sales to pick up. However, by the end of the year the growth in orders for fitness equipment was so high that Harewood was forced to subcontract manufacturing to other companies in order to keep up with demand.

In the economy, borrowing had reached record levels. A mixture of major construction projects in the public sector and high consumer spending in the private sector led to a sudden rise in inflation. Tessa was not worried overall, but did have concerns that this would have a negative effect on some products. People did not seem to be too concerned about price when buying fitness equipment and most racquets, but some of the sportswear goods were price elastic in demand. By the end of the year, the company was achieving record profits and Tessa's main problem was finding ways of meeting the huge increase in demand for fitness equipment.

Year 3

The new factory in Wolverhampton opened at the beginning of the year. Cyclical unemployment was low in the economy. However, the Midlands had been hit by high levels of structural unemployment in the metal manufacturing industry. As a consequence, it was relatively easy for Harewood Ltd to find both a suitable site and the necessary skilled labour to produce fitness equipment.

Sales (and prices) continued to grow. The announcement of a 1.5% increase in interest rates in April took Tessa by surprise. Harewood Ltd had borrowed all of the money needed to open the new factory, hoping to benefit from the low interest rates

at the time. All the same, the firm's cash flow was strong and all three product areas were producing high profits.

Tessa had expected some slowing in the rate of growth of sales, but she was shocked to see the order book at the end of June. Orders from shops for sportswear were down by 2%, racquet sales had fallen by 5%, but the biggest shock was fitness equipment — orders had decreased by 20%. Tessa wondered whether she had been too hasty in agreeing to the new factory.

The increase in interest rates also coincided with an increase in the value of the pound against other currencies. Tessa wondered whether this was good news or bad news for Harewood Ltd.

Tessa was not the only person surprised by developments. By July the economy had lurched from a strong recovery back into a downturn. In August the authorities announced a reduction of 1% in interest rates. By the end of the year, another cut (of 0.5%) had been made and the threat of a recession seemed to have disappeared.

At the end of the year, Tessa was thinking about her new year's resolutions. She decided that from now on she would seek a clearer picture of future macroeconomic changes before making any strategic decisions. On 31 December she looked at the newspapers carefully. The *Guardian* had presented a summary of the current (year 3) data, with its predictions for the next 2 years (years 4 and 5). This is shown in Table 1.

Table 1 The UK economy: current and forecast macroeconomic variables

Year	Change in GDP (%)	Unemployment (%)	Inflation (% change in CPI)	Value of the pound against other currencies (index)	Average interest rates (%)
Year 3 (actual)	+1.2	5.6	1.4	100	4.5
Year 4 (forecast)	+2.0	5.5	1.6	98	4.0
Year 5 (forecast)	+4.0	4.4	2.0	90	5.0

Questions

Total: 50 marks (60 minutes)

1 Explain why Tessa believed that inflation would not have the same effect on all of Harewood Ltd's products.

(6 marks)

2 Analyse two reasons why metal manufacturing might have suffered from an increase in structural unemployment at a time when cyclical unemployment was falling.

(8 marks)

3 Discuss the implications for Harewood Ltd of the sudden and unpredictable fluctuations of the business cycle during years 1 to 3.

(15 marks)

4 Explain one consequence for Harewood Ltd of the 1.5% increase in interest rates in April of year 3.

(6 marks)

5 To what extent will the predicted changes in the exchange rate (see Table 1) affect Harewood Ltd's ability to make profit?

(15 marks)

CHAPTER 41

UK and EU law

e **EXAMINER'S VOICE**

In this area the main focus of the AQA AS Business Studies specification is on the purpose of legislation, the impact of legislation on organisations and the overall desirability (advantages and disadvantages) of government intervention through legislation.

This chapter examines the way in which UK and EU laws influence business activity. For each of the four main categories below, key examples of legislation are described and the overall implications for businesses of the legislation are explained:

- *health and safety*
- *employment*
- *consumer protection*
- *competition*

In general, legislation is intended to protect those with weaker bargaining power: for example, individual employees working in, or individual customers purchasing from, large firms. In turn, the impact of legislation reduces the possibility of a firm exploiting its customers or its employees through unfair practices.

Some details of relevant legislation are given below, in order to provide a background understanding of the issues involved.

Health and safety legislation

The aim of health and safety legislation is to provide a safe working environment for employees. The key piece of legislation in this area is the Health and Safety at Work Act (HASAW), 1974.

Health and Safety at Work Act, 1974

This act imposes on employers a duty 'to ensure, as far as is reasonably practicable, the health, safety and welfare at work' of all staff. 'Reasonably practicable' in this context indicates that the risks must be weighed against the costs of prevention. The main provisions of the act are that employers must provide:

- all necessary safety equipment and clothing, free of charge
- a safe working environment
- safety training

In addition, all firms with five or more employees must have a written safety policy on display, and union-appointed safety representatives have the right to investigate and inspect the workplace and the causes of any accidents.

The 1974 act also set up the **Health and Safety Commission** to decide on safety policy and the **Health and Safety Executive**, which employs factory inspectors to investigate possible breaches of the act and to give advice on improving

safety practices. However, a major criticism of the act is that there are too few inspectors to have a meaningful deterrent effect on companies.

In addition to the HASAW Act of 1974, a number of European Union directives control working hours, lifting heavy weights, using computer screens and the rights of pregnant workers.

DID YOU KNOW?

European Union Directives are instructions from the EU to member countries. These usually require each country to pass legislation through its own parliament, so that there is 'harmonisation' (i.e. the same laws in each country). In practice, different countries do not always pass identical laws, as interpretation may vary.

Implications of health and safety legislation for business

The possible implications of health and safety legislation for business include the following:

- **Additional costs.** For example, the introduction of safety measures, training and the employment of safety staff will increase costs and therefore might affect profit margins and prices.
- **Influence on a firm's reputation.** For example, a lack of safety could damage sales and hence revenue and profit levels. Equally, a good safety record could have a beneficial effect on recruitment, since potential employees will want to work for a firm with a good safety record.
- **Influence on the motivation of employees.** For example, security in the work environment is recognised as one of Herzberg's hygiene factors, which are likely to prevent demotivation (see Chapter 21).

Employment legislation

This falls into two broad categories: individual employment law, which aims to ensure that employees and employers act fairly in dealing with each other; and collective labour law, which aims to control industrial relations and trade union activity.

Individual employment law

Equal Pay Act, 1970

This requires employers to provide equal pay and conditions for those doing the same jobs, or work of equivalent difficulty. This has had some effect in narrowing the pay gap between men and women, although it was not until

 EXAMINER'S VOICE

When considering the impact of specific areas of legislation or legislation in general, try to weigh up the arguments, i.e. evaluate. There will always be constraints and additional costs or administrative burdens imposed on business in complying with legislation, but there will also be benefits for individual firms and for the wider business community.

the European Union's Equal Pay Directive of 1975 that the principle of equal pay being given for work of equal value was firmly established. This regulation, for example, enabled shop workers to claim successfully that operating cash-tills (a job performed mainly by women) is as valuable and demanding as working in a warehouse (performed mainly by men). A more recent case is provided in the fact file below on the work of the Equal Opportunities Commission. Despite many successes, however, women's pay currently remains significantly below that of men.

DID YOU KNOW?

In 2003, the average full-time weekly wage for men was £514 and that for women was £383. Recent posters produced by the Equal Opportunities Commission provide the following information: 'After 30 years of equal pay law, women's wages are still 18% lower than men's' and 'Women students can expect to earn 15% less than men when they leave college'.

Sex Discrimination Act, 1975

This forbids discrimination in the workplace against either sex in relation to recruitment, terms and conditions, and access to training or promotion. Despite the existence of this act, the difficulty of obtaining legal proof of discrimination has meant that discrimination still persists. As with other issues of social responsibility, the passing of laws cannot provide a substitute for ethical behaviour.

FACT FILE

A former human resources manager for manufacturing company Barco, who claimed her job was worth the same as the male financial controllers, has received £19,000 compensation in an out-of-court settlement. Her case was supported by the Equal Opportunities Commission (EOC).

Avril Johnson, who had worked for Barco for more than 9 years, was paid £8,000 less than the financial controller. She also missed out on the annual bonus he received, was allocated fewer share options, and was the only member of the management team not to be given a mobile phone.

She resigned in August 2002 after failing to resolve her complaints with her employer. She claimed unfair dismissal, alleging that Barco had tried to demote her role to that of an HR administrator.

Julie Mellor, chair of the EOC, said:
'Employers need to be confident that there are good reasons for any differences between the pay of people in comparable jobs. The best way to make absolutely sure that your pay system is fair is to carry out an equal pay review. In some cases a review might uncover the fact that jobs usually done by women have historically been undervalued, leading to lower rates of pay than for jobs traditionally done by men. If you want to be an employer of choice, you need to be able to prove you pay fairly.'

Avril Johnson said:
'I believed that my professional responsibilities were very similar to those of the financial controller, so I was not at all happy to find I was being paid so much less. I didn't want to leave after 9 years' service, but felt I had no choice as my post was effectively being downgraded. I am relieved that we have now reached this settlement.'

Source: EOC website (www.eoc.org.uk).

The 1975 act set up the **Equal Opportunities Commission** to promote the ideas and practices required to eliminate sex discrimination in education, advertising and employment.

Sex Discrimination Act, 1986

This enables a common retirement date to be imposed on men and women. In 1993, the government stated its preference for a retirement age of 65.

Race Relations Acts, 1968 and 1976

These make it unlawful to discriminate in the workplace against any person on grounds of colour, race, ethnic or national origin. Specifically, the acts make it unlawful to refuse employment, training or promotion on these grounds, or to select someone for dismissal on grounds of race.

The **Commission for Racial Equality** (CRE) was given the responsibility to ensure the effective implementation of the Race Relations Act, 1976. Its key duties are to work towards the elimination of discrimination and to promote equality of opportunity.

Disability Discrimination Act, 1995

This forbids employers from treating those employees with disabilities less favourably than others. It requires employers to make reasonable adjustments in order to provide working conditions and an environment that helps to overcome the practical difficulties of disability.

Commission for Equality and Human Rights (CEHR)

In October 2003 the government proposed the formation of a new body — the Commission for Equality and Human Rights. Under this proposal, the work of the Disability Rights Commission, Equal Opportunities Commission and the Commission for Racial Equality will be united under this new commission.

Collective labour law

Between 1980 and 1990 Conservative governments passed a number of Employment Acts. These acts were designed to 'free up the labour market', i.e. to reduce the influence of government and especially trade unions. Their main features were:

- allowing firms to refuse to negotiate with trade unions
- limiting trade union powers to take action
- reducing employment and compensation rights for employees of small firms
- making it easier to dismiss strikers
- removing restrictions on the hours and places of work of young people and women
- removing industrial training boards, which could insist on firms paying towards training of workers

Employment Relations Act, 1999

This was the first piece of employment legislation passed by the present

Labour government. It increased employee rights in relation to union membership and claims for unfair dismissal. Among its key measures were:

- reducing the employment qualifying period for those claiming unfair dismissal from 2 years to 1 year
- requiring an employer to recognise a union if 50% or more of the workforce are members
- introducing rights to 3 months' leave for mothers and fathers when a baby is born

Employment tribunals

Employment tribunals are informal courtrooms where legal disputes between employees and employers can be settled. The main areas of dispute covered by the tribunals are: unfair dismissal; workplace discrimination on grounds of sex, race or disability; the national minimum wage; and working time. Each tribunal comprises three members — a legally trained chairperson plus one employer and one employee representative. The worker with the complaint against the employer can present his or her own case at little or no cost, but may be put at a disadvantage if the employer has hired a top lawyer.

Implications of employment legislation for business

The possible implications of employment legislation for business include the following:

- **Impact on disruption.** Fewer working days are now lost due to strikes or industrial action.
- **Additional costs.** These might be incurred in order to comply with the legislation, such as providing more rights for individual workers.
- **Influence on efficiency and productivity.** Equal opportunities legislation is likely to ensure that the 'best' candidates are recruited.
- **Influence on motivation.** Motivation will be improved if the relationship between employees and employers is clearly stated and understood by all parties.

Consumer protection legislation

This aims to safeguard consumers from exploitation or exposure to unsafe products or services. Legislation in this area is overseen by the **Office of Fair Training** (OFT).

Sale of Goods Acts, 1979 and 1994

These lay down the contract implied by the purchase of an item. They specify that goods must be of 'merchantable quality', i.e. fit for the purpose for which they were purchased, and as described.

Trade Descriptions Act, 1968

This prohibits false or misleading descriptions of a product's contents, effects or price. This affects packaging, advertising and promotional material. Advertising must be truthful and accurate.

Consumer Credit Act, 1974

This provides the regulations covering the purchase of goods on credit. It is intended to prevent consumers signing unfair contracts and to ensure that purchasers know exactly what interest rate they are to be charged for the credit they receive. The legislation limits the giving of credit to licensed brokers or organisations.

All advertising or display materials quoting credit terms must also state the annualised percentage rate (APR) of interest.

Weights and Measures Acts, 1963 and 1985

This legislation makes it illegal to sell goods below their stated weights or volume, and provides an enforcement procedure through trading standards officers and the Office of Fair Trading. The 1985 act allowed metric measures to be used.

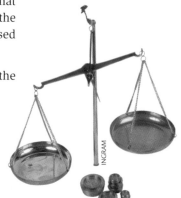

Food Safety Act, 1990

This controls the safety of food products and incorporates and strengthens the Food Act of 1984. The Food Safety Act is a wide-ranging law that brought food sources —and, by implication, farmers and growers — under food safety legislation for the first time. It made it an offence to sell food that is not of the 'nature or substance or quality' demanded by the purchaser. Other key features are that:

- premises selling food must register with the local authority
- those handling food must receive appropriate training
- enforcement officers can issue an improvement notice or, in extreme cases, an emergency prohibition notice

Implications of consumer protection legislation for business

The possible implications of consumer protection legislation for business include the following:

- **Increased costs of production.** Complying with the legislation may raise costs, which may affect price and profit margins. However, these should be balanced against the possible fines that might be incurred if an expensive legal case were successfully brought against a firm that was not complying with legislation.
- **Improved quality.** Complying with the legislation may improve the quality of a product or service, which in turn may enhance a firm's reputation and strengthen consumer loyalty.
- **Less waste.** Improved quality may also lead to potential savings in relation to rejects and returns.
- **Impact on UK competitiveness.** Higher costs of compliance need to be set against possibly higher quality of products and services.

Competition policy

Competition policy involves the use of legislation and regulation to ensure that all businesses are able to compete fairly with each other, and to limit the power of firms to take advantage of monopolies, mergers and restrictive practices. Competition should lead to better-quality, cheaper products and to increasing international competitiveness. Key legislation in this area includes the following.

Fair Trading Act, 1973

This set up the Office of Fair Trading under the leadership of the **Director-General of Fair Trading**. This is the government agency responsible for providing ministers with advice on legislation and action with regard to monopolies, mergers and restrictive practices. The office of the Director-General of Fair Trading has three main duties:

- to consider whether takeover bids should be investigated by the Competition Commission on the grounds of being against the public interest
- to investigate suspected anti-competitive practices, such as market-sharing agreements where firms agree not to compete with each other in areas of the market
- to investigate existing monopolies

Competition Act, 1998

This legislation, which came into force on 1 March 2000, reformed and strengthened UK competition law by prohibiting anti-competitive behaviour and raising substantially the fines that could be imposed on offending companies. It brought UK competition law into line with European Union law. Responsibility for applying and enforcing the act rests with the Office of Fair Trading. Key features of the act include:

- prohibiting anti-competitive agreements such as cartels
- prohibiting the abuse of a dominant market position (e.g. abuse by limiting production, by refusing supply, by restricting new technical development or by full-line forcing — forcing retailers to take the whole of a product range rather than a single item)
- allowing fines of up to 10% of UK turnover
- introducing the Competition Commission to take over the powers of the Monopolies and Mergers Commission (MMC)

The Competition Commission

This government-funded organisation oversees and enforces laws that attempt to eliminate anti-competitive business practices in the UK, oversees proposed mergers and checks that, where monopolies do exist, they are not against the public interest. Established in 1999 under the Competition Act of 1998, the Competition Commission replaced the Monopolies and Mergers Commission (MMC). To be effective, the commission must work in full cooperation with the Office of Fair Trading, the Department of Trade and Industry, and the European Commission.

Enterprise Act, 2002

The main provisions of this act, which came into force in June 2003, include:

- more transparent and accountable decision making by competition authorities
- criminal sanctions to deter cartels (agreements among companies to limit competition)
- greater opportunities for victims of anti-competitive behaviour to gain redress
- strengthening consumer protection measures

Implications of competition policy for business

The possible implications of competition policy for business include the following:

- **Lower prices.** There are likely to be lower prices for customers as a result of legislation improving the competitiveness of markets.
- **Lower profit margins.** Complying with competition laws will not usually add to business costs, but may prevent a business making the profit it could have made if it had adopted anti-competitive tactics.
- **'Fair' competition.** There will be greater incentives for firms to seek competitive advantage through 'fair' rather than 'unfair competition' (see Chapter 35).
- **Benefits to small firms.** Perhaps the main benefits of competition policy accrue to smaller firms, which will be more able to compete in the market.

PRACTICE EXERCISE 1   Total: 40 marks (35 minutes)

1 What is the general aim of health and safety at work legislation? *(3 marks)*

2 Explain one advantage and one disadvantage to a business of health and safety legislation. *(6 marks)*

3 What is the general aim of employment legislation? *(3 marks)*

4 Explain one advantage and one disadvantage to a business of employment legislation. *(6 marks)*

5 What is the general aim of consumer protection legislation? *(3 marks)*

6 Give two examples of legislation in this area and a broad outline of the specific purpose of each piece of legislation. *(6 marks)*

7 What is the general aim of competition policy? *(3 marks)*

8 Give two examples of legislation in this area and a broad outline of the specific purpose of each piece of legislation. *(6 marks)*

9 Explain the role of the Competition Commission. *(4 marks)*

Competition Commission reports

The following accounts of Competition Commission reports appeared on the Department of Industry's website. Read the articles and answer the questions that follow.

Melanie Johnson publishes Competition Commission's conclusions on the merger of Kodak and ColourCare

Melanie Johnson, minister for competition, consumers and markets, has today published the Competition Commission's (CC's) report on the proposed acquisition of ColourCare Limited (ColourCare) by Kodak Processing Companies Limited (KPCL). The report concludes that the merger is expected not to operate against the public interest.

The CC concluded that while the merger would give KPCL a 50% share of the market, the company would not be able to exploit its market position to raise prices or engage in anti-competitive practices.

The 1973 Fair Trading Act empowers the secretary of state to refer to the CC for investigation and report actual or proposed mergers which create or intensify a market share of over 25% of the supply in the UK, or a substantial part of the UK, of particular goods and services, or involve the takeover of assets exceeding £70 million.

The CC found that the merger would result in the enlarged KPCL having half the relevant market, but retailers would easily be able to shift more of their photo development and processing to mini labs in their stores or to regional wholesalers, should KPCL seek to exploit its market position. The CC found no expectation of reduction in quality of service and the likelihood of modest technological advances.

21 December 2001

Patricia Hewitt accepts Competition Commission's conclusions on Lloyds/Abbey merger

Patricia Hewitt, secretary of state for trade and industry, has decided not to permit the proposed acquisition by Lloyds TSB Group plc (Lloyds TSB) of Abbey National plc (Abbey). Ms Hewitt accepted the findings and recommendations of the Competition Commission and the advice of the Director-General of Fair Trading, both published today, that the merger may be expected to operate against the public interest.

The commission noted that personal current accounts (PCAs) were the core product in personal banking. The merger would increase the share of the PCA market held by the four leading banks (Barclays, HSBC, Lloyds TSB and RBS/NatWest — the 'big four') from 72 to 77%. Lloyds TSB, already the market leader, would increase its share from 22 to 27%. The merger would also remove one of the main sources of competition to the big four.

The commission concluded that it was important for competition that there are well-established rivals to the big four banks because:

- the entrenched position of the big four remains strong
- there is very little switching between banks by customers
- telephone and internet-based providers, as alternatives to branch-based (multi-service) providers, remain niche players only
- branch-based players entering the industry in the last 10 years have grown only slowly, despite offering better terms than the big four

The commission considered that Abbey National was an important force for competition in the PCA market, regardless of whether the proposed merger between Bank of Scotland and Halifax proceeded. It concluded that the acquisition of Abbey National by Lloyds TSB could be expected to lead to higher prices and a loss of innovation.

In banking for small and medium-sized enterprises (SMEs), the commission concluded that the market was highly concentrated, and dominated by the big four. The commission noted that Abbey National was only a recent entrant to this market, but considered that its brand name, national network of branches and presence in personal and some business markets made it one of the very few players outside the big four able to compete in the SME market.

The commission accepted that the merger would yield some efficiency savings. However, it did not consider that these would be passed on to consumers in reduced prices. It also concluded that the merger would harm consumer choice, with the possible loss of existing Abbey National products.

10 July 2001

Source: Department of Trade and Industry website (www.dti.gov.uk).

Questions

1 Read the accounts of the Competition Commission's reports on the proposed mergers of Kodak and ColourCare and of Lloyds TSB and Abbey National above. Using this information and your understanding of the government's competition policy, discuss the extent to which such intervention in business activity is likely to improve the performance of business. *(15 marks)*

2 Read the fact file on p. 356 which discusses equal opportunities at Barco. On the basis of this and your knowledge of equal opportunities in employment legislation, to what extent do businesses in general and individual employees benefit from such legislation? *(15 marks)*

3 It is often suggested that government intervention, in the form of legislation, creates a level playing field for business. Is this true and is it desirable? Justify your answer. *(You may choose to answer this question by reference to a specific area of legislation, such as health and safety, employment, consumer protection or competition, or by reference to legislation in general.)* *(15 marks)*

CHAPTER 42

Social responsibilities

Social responsibility is featuring increasingly in commentary on business activity. This chapter explains the meaning of social responsibility, studies reasons for and against firms accepting social responsibility and examines its overall importance to businesses. Specific, real-life examples of social responsibility are considered.

Business for Social Responsibility (BSR), an organisation that helps companies achieve commercial success in ways that respect ethical values, people, communities and the environment, defines corporate social responsibility as 'achieving commercial success in ways that honour ethical values and respect people, communities, and the natural environment'. It also says that corporate social responsibility means addressing the legal, ethical, commercial and other expectations that society has for business, and making decisions that balance the claims of all key stakeholders fairly.

> **KEY TERM**
>
> **social responsibility or corporate social responsibility (CSR):** the duties of an organisation towards employees, customers, society and the environment.

> **DID YOU KNOW?**
>
> There is historical evidence of firms accepting social responsibilities. For example, in the nineteenth century, religiously motivated firms such as Cadbury in Birmingham and Rowntree in York (chocolate and confectionery manufacturers, respectively) and Titus Salt, a woollen mill owner in Saltaire, Bradford, treated their workforce with respect, providing good working conditions, education, housing and a pleasant communal environment. But equally, other companies acted irresponsibly towards their employees and their local environment, making employees work in intolerable conditions and allowing their production processes to pollute the local environment.

> **e EXAMINER'S VOICE**
>
> This is an area of business studies that is value laden. People and firms have very different views of what social responsibility means and whether firms should meet their social responsibilities. Ensure that when you answer questions on this topic you provide soundly analysed and balanced arguments rather than making assertions of the 'I think...' variety.

Why should firms accept their social responsibility?

By acting in a socially responsible manner, businesses can generate benefits for society in general and for businesses more directly.

Benefits for society

There are a number of benefits for society and general arguments in favour of firms accepting their social responsibilities:

- Problems such as unemployment and pollution are likely to be reduced.
- The quality of life is likely to be improved, as decisions will be based on what is best for society rather than what is best for an individual firm.

- Society's long-term needs are likely to be considered rather than simply the short-term needs
of a business.
- Life and business activity will be easier if everyone involved is working together for the common
good, rather than if one group is trying to exploit
another for its own benefit.
- It can be argued that it is simply the right thing to
do and that firms have a duty to be concerned
with the wider impact of their activities.

Benefits for firms

In addition to the public benefits listed above, many
firms believe it is in their own best interests to
behave correctly, and that social responsibility is an important element in
business success. Some of the more tangible benefits to business of behaving
in a socially responsible manner are:

- **Improved financial performance.** A recent American study showed that
the overall financial performance of companies gaining awards in a league
table for business ethics and citizenship was significantly better than that
of other companies.
- **Reduced operating costs.** Some CSR initiatives can reduce operating costs.
For example, many initiatives aimed at improving environmental performance — such as reducing gas emissions that contribute to global warming
or reducing the use of agricultural chemicals — also lower costs. Many
recycling initiatives cut waste-disposal costs and generate income by selling
recycled materials. In the human resources area, flexible working that
results in reduced absenteeism and increased retention of employees might
save companies money through increased productivity and reduction of
recruitment, selection and training costs.
- **Enhanced brand image and reputation.** Customers are often drawn to
brands and companies with good reputations in CSR-related areas. A
company considered socially responsible can benefit both from its enhanced
reputation with the public and from its reputation within the business
community, increasing the company's ability to attract capital and trading
partners.
- **Increased sales and customer loyalty.** A number of studies have suggested
that there is a large and growing market for the products and services of
companies perceived to be socially responsible. Businesses must obviously
satisfy customers' needs in relation to price, quality, availability, safety
and convenience. However, studies also show a growing desire to buy
products from certain producers because of other criteria, such as that
they are not made in sweatshop conditions or using child labour, that they
have a lower environmental impact, and that they do not contain genetically
modified materials or ingredients.

- **Increased ability to attract and retain employees.** Companies perceived to have strong CSR commitments often find it easier to recruit and retain employees, resulting in a reduction in staff turnover and associated recruitment and training costs, because employees feel happier working in such a business.
- **Access to capital.** The growth of socially responsible or ethical investing (e.g. the Co-operative Bank) means that companies with strong CSR performance have increased access to capital that might not otherwise have been available.

> **ℰ EXAMINER'S VOICE**
>
> When answering questions on this area, always try to see the big picture. Think of this topic in relation to everything else you know about business, so that you can really consider the implications. For example, review what you know about the functional areas of the firm (marketing, finance, people and operations) and think about how acting in a socially responsible manner might affect these areas.

What are the arguments against firms accepting their social responsibilities?

A case can also be made that firms should not accept their social responsibilities:

- Efficient use of resources is likely to be reduced if businesses are restricted in how they can produce and where they can locate. This might lead to higher prices.
- Socially responsible policies can be costly to introduce. International competitiveness will be reduced if other countries do not consider externalities and social responsibility, and therefore produce more cheaply.
- Some suggest that there is one clear view of right and wrong in relation to social responsibility and firms' behaviour, but others argue that this is a subjective issue. Stakeholder groups tend to have differing objectives, as shown in Table 42.1. They are therefore unlikely to agree on what is socially responsible behaviour.
- Social responsibility is just a passing fashion. No one is sure of the value to firms of being socially responsible, even though intuitively it seems a good idea.
- If the economy is generally doing well, managers feel able to look at intangibles such as social responsibility. During a recession, however, they will look more at profits and survival, even if this means taking little or no notice of social responsibility.
- If something is important to society at large, the government should pass laws to ensure that everyone acts responsibly.
- Social responsibility is just an extension of firms being market orientated. In other words, because consumers want firms to act this way, firms

> **DID YOU KNOW?**
>
> Externalities are the effects that an organisation's decisions will have on other people and organisations. These may be negative such as pollution, or positive such as job creation.

> **DID YOU KNOW?**
>
> A 2001 survey showed that the factors most influencing public impressions of companies were social responsibility (49%) and brand quality/reputation (40%).

respond in order to maximise their profits. Firms are thus cynically using the idea of social responsibility as a method of marketing their products, and they will use the idea only for as long as it allows them to extend the product life cycle.

Stakeholders	Objectives
Employees	Secure, reasonably paid employment
Customers	Good-quality, safe products at a competitive price
Suppliers	Fair prices to be paid, regular custom and prompt payment
Owners	Good profit, leading to increases in share prices and/or dividends
Government/society	Efficient use of resources and consideration of the environment and society's needs
Local community	Employment and wealth creation without the imposition of major social costs

Table 42.1
Stakeholder objectives

DID YOU KNOW?

A key factor in any firm's attitude towards its social responsibilities is probably the time span of its objectives. For example, a get-rich-quick kitchen or window installation firm will have an approach to issues of social responsibility that is very different from an established family business that has been around for generations.

Social responsibility in practice

Examples of activities that would be viewed as socially responsible are:

- using sustainable sources of raw materials
- ensuring that suppliers operate responsibly — for example, avoiding the use of child labour
- operating an extensive health and safety policy above the legal requirements, thereby protecting the well-being of employees
- engaging in a continuous process of environmental management and monitoring the effects of production on the environment
- trading ethically and taking account of moral issues

However, discrepancies are often found between the claims of companies and their actions in practice. For example:

Barclays Bank

Claim: 'We have the skills, resources and determination to make a positive and lasting contribution to the communities in which we operate' (*Barclays Social Review*, 1999).

Action: Barclays closed 172 branches in April 2000.

Procter & Gamble

Claim: 'An employee should be able to answer "Yes" to the questions: is this the right thing to do? Will this action uphold P&G's reputation as an ethical company?' (Procter & Gamble code of conduct)

Action: Procter & Gamble continues to trade in Burma, while other companies have pulled out because of the appalling record of the Burmese government on human rights.

BAT (British American Tobacco)

Claim: its corporate social responsibility report defines targets for reducing energy use, water consumption and waste products, and describes its commitment to enlightened employment practices.

Action: it markets its tobacco products ruthlessly to young people — it was caught on television handing out packets of Benson & Hedges cigarettes to teenage volleyball players in The Gambia.

Conclusion

Although there is evidence that accepting social responsibility provides direct benefits to firms, in general the benefits tend to accrue to society as a whole or to the local community. In this sense, firms that accept their social responsibility create **external benefits** for society (or **positive externalities**). But equally, if society and/or the local community improve in terms of wealth, standard of living and quality of life, then in the longer term business will also benefit.

PRACTICE EXERCISE 1   Total: 50 marks (45 minutes)

1 Explain the term 'social responsibility'. *(3 marks)*

2 Explain two examples of a firm acting in a socially responsible manner in relation to its employees. *(6 marks)*

3 Explain two examples of a firm acting in a socially responsible manner in relation to its customers. *(6 marks)*

4 Identify three stakeholders (other than employees and customers) and for each one in turn explain a company action that could be seen as socially responsible in relation to the particular stakeholder. *(12 marks)*

5 Explain two tangible benefits to a business of accepting its social responsibility. *(6 marks)*

6 Explain two arguments against firms accepting their so-called social responsibility. *(6 marks)*

7 Why might it be difficult for a firm to act in a socially responsible way towards all its stakeholders? *(6 marks)*

8 Distinguish between negative and positive externalities. *(5 marks)*

Corporate social responsibility at Starbucks and B&Q

Read the articles on Starbucks and B&Q and answer the questions that follow.

Starbucks Coffee Co.

Starbucks defines corporate social responsibility (CSR) as conducting business in ways that produce social, environmental and economic benefits to the communities in which it operates. Starbucks has been widely recognised for its commitment to numerous stakeholders, including coffee growers, the environment, employees and communities, while simultaneously achieving rapid financial growth. The company has a senior vice president of CSR who provides strategic development of policies, strategies, processes and tools to link corporate social responsibility with business success.

Since 1998, Starbucks has supported Conservation International's (CI's) Conservation Coffee programme, which encourages sustainable agriculture practices and the protection of biodiversity through the production of shade-grown coffee and the institution of coffee-purchasing guidelines. Starbucks' work with CI won a Sustainable Development Partnership award in 2002 at the World Summit for Sustainable Development. The programme has resulted in a 60% price premium paid to farmers and a 220% increase in the coffee-growing land preserved as tropical forests. The amount of this coffee purchased by Starbucks in 2002 is estimated to be 20 times the amount it purchased in 1999.

In 1997, Starbucks formed a partnership with a division of the Environmental Defence Fund to develop environmentally friendly disposable coffee cups and promote increased use of reusable cups by customers. The company has also been praised for its generous employee benefits and its commitment, unusual in the industry, to provide full benefits for both full- and part-time employees. Starbucks also has a number of programmes to help benefit the communities in which it has stores, as well as in the developing economies where its coffee is grown, harvested and processed.

B&Q

B&Q is a do-it-yourself retailer. It operates nearly 1,400 stores in 16 countries. About 22% of B&Q's turnover is timber and timber-related products, and the company has worked to lessen its impact on forests and other environments since 1991. B&Q has monitored its suppliers' social and environmental practices, sourcing 99% of wood-based products from independently certified, well-managed forests, becoming a model to other companies and encouraging change in its business partners. B&Q also managed to reduce environmental impact at its stores by minimising packaging, increasing recycling and improving energy efficiency and waste management.

More recently, B&Q has adopted a more holistic approach to corporate social responsibility through the theme of 'being a better neighbour': 'We believe sustainable development is about improving the quality of life for all the people we touch. This can only be achieved by striving to be a better neighbour, whether it is to our store or global trading neighbourhoods.'

The company has found that close monitoring of its suppliers and their sources helps to ensure healthy working conditions, maintain good environmental practices and increase its profits through improved brand loyalty and reduced costs. B&Q is a member of a British coalition organised by the Worldwide Fund for Nature (WWF) that requires an environmental audit of all suppliers, and it won the Business in the Environment award from Business in the Community in 2000. B&Q also aims to employ people of all backgrounds, particularly older workers, and tries to meet the needs of all customers, including the disabled. B&Q has awarded almost 1,000 Better Community Grants to local store-run community projects.

Source: adapted from the Business for Social Responsibility (BSR) website (www.bsr.org).

Questions

1 Both of the businesses — Starbucks and B&Q — take their social responsibilities seriously.

   a Identify five different stakeholders mentioned in the articles. *(5 marks)*

   b Analyse how Starbucks' stakeholders benefit from Starbucks' socially responsible approach. *(10 marks)*

   c Analyse how B&Q's stakeholders benefit from B&Q's socially responsible approach. *(10 marks)*

2 To what extent might it be argued that these companies consider their approach to social responsibility as simply another strategy for increasing consumer demand and consumer loyalty? *(15 marks)*

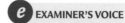

Business ethics

This chapter looks at the meaning of ethical behaviour and the types of ethical dilemmas that businesses face. Ethical codes and ethical investment are examined, leading to a summary of the main issues and problems involved in operating in a manner considered to be morally or ethically correct.

Ethics are the set of moral values held by an individual or group. An organisation may make a decision that is believed to be morally right rather than one that suits the needs of some of its stakeholders.

 TERM

ethical behaviour: actions and decisions that are seen to be morally correct (i.e. match the moral values or principles of the decision makers).

Ethical dilemmas

Firms are frequently presented with ethical dilemmas when making decisions. Typical ethical dilemmas facing businesses are as follows:

- Should an advertising agency accept a cigarette manufacturer as a client?
- Should a producer of chemicals sell to an overseas buyer that it suspects will be using the goods to produce chemical weapons?
- Should a firm relocate to a country paying lower wages?
- Should a firm release a potentially life-saving drug after only limited testing?
- Should a company practise positive discrimination in its employment and promotion policies?
- Should a company aim its advertising at children?
- Should a firm always pay suppliers on time or should it delay as long as possible in order to earn maximum interest on its savings?
- Should a manufacturer of military aircraft sell to a foreign government suspected of using force to maintain power?
- Should a firm try to minimise its production costs as much as possible in order to keep prices low, even if this means using environmentally polluting processes or less than the best quality materials?

Ethical behaviour or just responding to pressure?

Firms may reconsider the decisions they make in response to public opinion and/or media pressure. They would then appear to be acting more ethically, but this would not necessarily mean that the firm was actually becoming more ethical in its behaviour. Taking an ethical decision means doing what is morally right rather than weighing up the costs and benefits and then deciding how to proceed, or simply responding to pressure.

COREL

e **EXAMINER'S VOICE**

Don't confuse ethical behaviour with behaviour that is within the law. Behaving in an ethical way is more than behaving according to the law.

Ethical codes

ethical code: an instruction from an organisation to its employees to indicate how they should react to situations relating to moral values.

The focus of the code will depend on the business concerned. Banks may concentrate on honesty, food manufacturers on the healthiness of their products and chemical firms on pollution control. A typical ethical code might include sections on:

- personal integrity in dealing with suppliers and in handling the firm's resources
- corporate integrity, such as forbidding collusion with competitors and predatory pricing
- environmental responsibility, highlighting a duty to minimise pollution emission and maximise recycling
- social responsibility to provide products of genuine value that are promoted with honesty and dignity

Critics of ethical codes, like critics of social responsibility, believe the codes to be no more than public relations exercises rather than genuine attempts to change behaviour. The proof of their effectiveness can, of course, only be measured by how firms actually behave, not by what they write or say. Texas Instruments has a long established and well-respected ethical policy, which is summarised in the fact file.

Texas Instruments (TI) prides itself on its ethical stance and is seen as a benchmark against which other firms can measure themselves. Since 1987 it has had a specific office dealing with ethics and an ethics director. The Ethics Office has three primary functions:

- to ensure that business policies and practices are to be aligned with ethical principles
- to communicate ethical expectations clearly
- to provide opportunities for people to ask questions, voice concerns and seek resolution to ethical issues

The company's approach to ethics is clearly and simply summed up as:

know what's right   value what's right   do what's right

All employees are given a business card that carries TI's 'Ethics Quick Test':

- Is the action legal?
- Does it comply with our values?
- If you do it, will you feel bad?
- How will it look in the newspaper?
- If you know it's wrong, don't do it.
- If you're not sure, ask.
- Keep asking until you get an answer.

Source: www.texasinstruments.com.

COURTESY OF TEXAS INSTRUMENTS

Visit the Texas Instruments website to find out what an ethical policy looks like in detail. For example, TI provides its employees with guidance on the appropriate level of gift giving/receiving in different countries.

Ethical investment

 TERM

> **ethical investment:** stock market investment based on a restricted list of firms that are seen as ethically sound.

For example, the Co-operative Bank will only invest in firms that:

- do not finance weapons deals to oppressive governments
- do not make products involving tobacco, the fur trade, animal testing or exploitative factory farming
- act responsibly toward the environment
- are good employers

If most investors or purchasers of shares applied such ethical principles when deciding where to invest, responsible firms would receive a reward in the form of rising share prices or easier access to investment funds.

Reviewing a firm's ethical position

A number of elements should be considered when reviewing a company's ethical position.

DID YOU KNOW?

The arguments for and against ethical behaviour for business are similar to those for and against social responsibility (see Chapter 42, pp. 364–67).

Individuals

Each individual working in a business has his or her own set of personal standards, which is derived from their upbringing, education and background. In a business, decisions are made by individuals or by groups of individuals who inevitably bring to the decision their own ideas of what is right and wrong.

Corporate culture

Corporate culture is the set of unwritten rules that affect the attitudes and management style of a business (see Chapter 20). If, for example, managers are seen to be ruthless in their pursuit of profit, and if such behaviour helps determine who will earn promotion, then workers lower down the organisation are more likely to adopt a similar approach, even if this is against their own judgement.

Public standards

Businesses operate in an environment that affects everything they do and the results they achieve. A public outcry against a particular type of activity will force a business to look at itself and decide if it needs to change its stance. If a high-profile firm, such as Nike or Gap, is accused of using child labour, other firms that produce in similar circumstances are likely to review their own operations and perhaps change to a more acceptable method of operation. Similarly, the accounting scandals surrounding Enron and WorldCom will have caused many firms to take a closer look at their own accounting policies.

e EXAMINER'S VOICE

Because this area is value laden, ensure that you provide well argued points in your answers to questions on ethics and avoid the temptation to make value judgements and assertions that are unsupported by argument or evidence.

Competitors

Within a marketplace, businesses can attempt to create a unique selling proposition for their product by emphasising their ethical stance. A successful campaign like this can force other firms to review their operations. In the early 1980s, the Body Shop single-handedly created a market niche for environmentally friendly cosmetics that had not been tested on animals. Similarly, the Co-operative Bank has gained a reputation for its position on ethical investments.

Problems with ethical positions

A number of possible problems may arise for a firm adopting an ethical position:

- **Effect on profit.** An ethical choice can incur extra costs: for example, buying renewable resources from a less developed country or continuing extensive testing of a product before releasing it. (See the case study on pp. 376–77 for an example of an ethical choice that incurs additional costs.)

- **What is ethical?** People have different views on what is ethical and these views change over time. For example, in the past few shops opened on Sundays, since it was against many people's religious beliefs and was considered unethical. Now many firms open on Sundays and many would open for longer if legislation did not limit their opening time to 6 hours.

- **Communication of ethics within an organisation.** In large organisations, it may be difficult to inform staff of the ethical policy or ethical code and to monitor adherence to it. At Texas Instruments (TI) (see p. 372) an ethics booklet is issued to every employee. This booklet was first published in 1961 and is presently in its sixth revision. In 1961, TI's founders felt that the company was getting too large and the marketplace too complex to have ethical standards passed on simply by word of mouth, so the first version was published. This has been revised regularly to take into account expanding world markets, marketplace complexities, changing government regulations, and business growth and modifications.

- **Delegation and empowerment.** As empowered workers take more decisions, it becomes harder to maintain a consistent company policy on ethical behaviour.

AS Business Studies

GROUP EXERCISE

Discuss each of the ten actions below and rank them in order, with the most ethical behaviour first and the least ethical last. Justify your choices to the rest of the class.

A A drugs company releases a new drug before it has been thoroughly tested, in order to prevent an epidemic.

B In order to increase public awareness of child poverty, a charity publishes unpleasant images of children that upset members of the public.

C An animal rights pressure group frees animals that are being used for experiments on the effects of cosmetics.

D A recycling plant dumps toxic waste in a deep trench in the middle of the Atlantic Ocean.

E An armaments manufacturer prevents the loss of 1,000 jobs by exporting arms to North Korea.

F An animal rights pressure group frees animals that are being used for experiments that will save human lives.

G A supermarket decides that it will open as normal on Christmas Day.

H A farmer tips slurry into the river that adjoins his farm, killing all of the fish downstream for 10 kilometres.

I A sportswear business moves production of its trainers to a country that employs child labour, in order to reduce its production costs.

J A cigarette manufacturer aims its latest campaign at schoolchildren by concentrating on poster sites next to schools.

PRACTICE EXERCISE 1
Total: 50 marks (45 minutes)

1 What is meant by the term 'ethical behaviour'? *(4 marks)*

2 Explain three examples of ethical dilemmas that might occur in business. *(9 marks)*

3 Explain the purpose of an ethical code. *(4 marks)*

4 What does 'ethical investment' mean? *(3 marks)*

5 State and explain two factors that might affect the ability of a firm to adopt an ethical stance. *(6 marks)*

6 Briefly explain one marketing benefit **and** one marketing cost or problem associated with adopting an ethical stance to business decision making. *(6 marks)*

7 Briefly explain one financial/accounting benefit **and** one financial/accounting cost or problem associated with adopting an ethical stance to business decision making. *(6 marks)*

8 Briefly explain one human resource related benefit **and** one human resource related cost or problem associated with adopting an ethical stance to business decision making. *(6 marks)*

9 Briefly explain one operational management benefit **and** one operational management cost or problem associated with adopting an ethical stance to business decision making. *(6 marks)*

The Co-operative Bank plc

The Co-operative Bank has a long history as one of the UK's most innovative banks and a reputation as a leader in corporate social responsibility. The company is recognised for its strong ethical investment policy statement, its social auditing practices and its ethical marketing strategies. The bank's eight-point ethical investment policy outlines the company's position on socially responsible investing, including its decisions not to finance weapons deals to oppressive governments, and not to invest in companies involved in tobacco, the fur trade, animal testing or exploitative factory farming. According to its chief executive, the Co-operative Bank's ethical and ecological policies, which it frequently strengthens and revises based on extensive customer input, are inextricably linked to its business success; its ethical policies are the most frequently cited reason why customers choose the bank.

The company has also been a pioneer in the area of stakeholder relations and social reporting, producing a 'Partnership Report' each year since 1997 that measures the impact and identifies improvements that the company could make in social responsibility areas such as customer satisfaction, ecological sustainability, workplace practices, community involvement and ethics. The report includes the statement of an outside auditor who assessed the report. Through its ethical marketing campaign, the Co-operative Bank has contributed millions of pounds to various causes, including fair trade and living wages, environmental protection, the acceptance of diversity and bans on the financing of landmines.

The **COOPERATIVE BANK**
Customer led, ethically guided

Source: Co-operative Bank website (www.co-operativebank.co.uk).

Question

In contrast to the Co-operative Bank, some banks have continued to lend money according to customers' financial strength rather than their ethical behaviour. Some financial organisations have also transferred operations such as call centres to low-wage countries. Discuss the advantages and disadvantages to the Co-operative Bank of its approach to ethical issues, in comparison to that of other financial organisations.

CASE STUDY   Recycled Harry Potter to save muggle forests

J. K. Rowling has promised to end her part in the destruction of the world's forests by having the next Harry Potter book printed on environmentally friendly paper. The multi-millionaire author, whose novels about the teenage wizard at Hogwarts School have consumed 65 million trees so far, is one of a number of high-profile authors who have pledged their support for the environment by using recycled paper.

Ms Rowling, along with big names including Andy McNab, Philip Pullman, Ben Elton, Helen Fielding, Ian Rankin, Joanna Trollope and John O'Farrell, has signed a pledge to use 'environmentally and socially responsible sources such as those independently certified to the Forest Stewardship Council standards and/or recycled fibre made from post-consumer waste'.

She has guaranteed that her sixth Harry Potter book will be printed either on recycled or on 'ancient forest friendly' paper, which is sourced from sustainable planted forests. At present, no major publishers of fiction in the UK use 100% recycled paper. Most say they source paper from 'sustainable' forests, but research by Greenpeace showed that none could back up the claim with credible evidence. Several publishing houses are unwittingly buying paper from two of the world's ancient forest areas — Finland and Canada — while others obtain their paper from Russia, where at least half of the commercial logging is estimated to be illegal. Some forests in southeast Asia that claim to be sustainable were created by clearing areas of ancient forest and expelling indigenous peoples.

Techniques pioneered in Canada allow, for the first time, paper from waste such as office paperwork to be used to make books. Paper mills at the forefront of recycling in the UK have spent £100 million over the last 10 years on developing high-quality recycled paper, but the cost will fall as the technology becomes more commonplace. In Canada, paper made from 'post-consumer waste' is no more than 3% more expensive than conventional paper.

Despite the high cost of developing recycled paper that is strong and white enough to be used for books, there will not necessarily be a price rise in the bookshop. Instead publishers could recover their costs by using more basic book covers without embossed lettering or high-quality laminated paper, as happened in Canada.

Bloomsbury, publisher of the Harry Potter books, is expected to incur an increase of £140,000 in print costs for the UK run of the next Harry Potter book if it is printed on recycled paper. However, this is equivalent to just 4p per volume.

It has been difficult to print books on recycled paper until recently because the paper has not been strong enough to endure a lifetime of reading. However, modern methods mean that paper can be cleaned and bleached more efficiently without breaking down its fibres.

John Sauven, a director at Greenpeace, said that Canadian paper merchants guaranteed that the paper would not fade for 100 years. 'Technological breakthrough means that you can now produce paper from 100% post-consumer waste that is just as good as paper made from virgin fibre in terms of quality, colour and strength,' he said.

The Canadian edition of *Harry Potter and the Order of the Phoenix* was printed without chopping down a single tree, saving an estimated 40,000 of them. If the sixth Harry Potter book is as successful as the fifth, it could save up to 96,000 trees for the UK edition alone.

Source: adapted from an article in *The Times*, 3 October 2003.

Questions

Total: 50 marks (60 minutes)

1 The article suggests that Bloomsbury's costs could rise by £140,000 as a result of using recycled paper. Analyse the potential conflict between ethical behaviour and profits in this case. *(8 marks)*

2 Discuss why publishers such as Bloomsbury might wish to become more ethical in their approach to the environment. *(15 marks)*

3 Explain why ethical behaviour may depend on technological development. *(6 marks)*

4 Is there a difference between ethical behaviour and ethical marketing? *(6 marks)*

5 To what extent do social and ethical decisions depend on other factors such as the market and competition? *(15 marks)*

CHAPTER 44

Technological change

Technology has transformed the way we live and the ways in which organisations operate. This chapter looks at the benefits of new technology, the problems in introducing new technology and the issues that businesses need to consider when introducing new technology.

KEY TERMS

technological change: adapting new applications of practical or mechanical sciences to industry and commerce.
information technology: the creation, storing and communication of information using microelectronics, computers and telecommunications.

Technological change occurs in all sectors of business. Examples in the primary sector include: specialist machinery such as combine harvesters, mining equipment, deep-sea oil rigs and computerised fish-locating equipment; genetically modified crops, fertiliser and pesticides. Examples in the secondary sector include: production-line equipment such as robotics and computer-aided manufacture (CAM); computer-aided design (CAD); research and development; stock control; and packaging. Examples in the tertiary sector include: communications; financial records and services (e.g. automated teller machines); logistics design and transport; home shopping; and barcodes.

The innovations resulting from the use of new technology can be split into three main types:
- processes — advancements in manufacturing technology and automation
- products — new product opportunities using micro-electronic technology such as fax machines, electronic games and mobile phones
- communication links — developments in information technology

Benefits of technological change

Society, firms and consumers benefit in several ways from technological change:
- **Improved efficiency and reduced waste.** Cost-effective use of resources benefits consumers and firms, and in the long term resources last longer, thus benefiting society in general.
  - **Better products and services.** Consumers benefit from more choice, and if this leads to more demand, company profits are likely to increase.
    - **New products and materials.** Needs and wants that were previously not satisfied can be provided for, as with the invention of the dishwasher and the bread maker.
      - **Advances in communication.** Company efficiency is increased and consumer needs are met more directly.

Module 3 *External influences*

- **Improved working environment.** Employees work in safer conditions and there are a greater number of jobs that are less physically demanding and more interesting.
- **Wealth creation.** Higher living standards are achieved.

Problems in introducing new technology

Several problems are associated with the introduction of new technology:

- **Costs of keeping up to date with the latest technology.** The need to remain up to date in order to stay ahead of or level with competitors can lead to very high replacement costs that occur on a regular basis.
- **Knowing what new technology to buy and when to buy it.** In rapidly changing markets, an investment in technology that is becoming outdated can be a very expensive mistake.
- **Industrial relations between employers and employees.** As technology replaces jobs, there is a danger of resistance by workers and trade unions, and a consequent lowering of morale.
- **Personnel issues.** As technological change occurs, new skills are required and this has implications for recruitment, retention and training, and their associated costs.

A more detailed analysis

The ability of firms to benefit from new technology depends on the competition they face. The following analysis demonstrates the possible costs and benefits of new technology to business in relation to both products and processes.

New products

Price skimming can be introduced because consumers are often prepared to pay premium prices for unique products in the short term before competitors catch up. The high profits that result from such price skimming can be retained if a patent is gained that prevents competitors from copying the product. However, it is likely that copycat or 'me too' products will emerge that reduce the original uniqueness of the product. Firms might use the period before competition catches up to develop their next unique product.

In monopoly markets, a lack of competition allows companies to continue to make high profits, thus limiting the incentive for them to introduce new, improved products. In some industries, the high cost of new technology acts as a barrier to entry, allowing existing organisations to maintain high profits in the long run.

New processes

New technology can improve the efficiency of processes, which may help a company to increase its profit margins in the short term. However, in a competitive market, this advantage will soon disappear. New firms will begin to adopt these processes and prices will begin to fall, causing margins to fall.

In the longer run, if prices fall and if demand is price elastic, profits may rise as a result of greater sales volume. Labour costs can also be reduced, which may be particularly important if companies in high wage economies are to remain competitive.

Issues to consider when introducing new technology

Introducing new technology raises a number of issues for firms:

- The adoption of any new technology will be influenced by existing technology. For example, is the new technology compatible with the existing technology? Can the changeover from existing to new technology be managed effectively and efficiently?
- The reaction of the workforce to new technology is important, since their cooperation will be essential.
- In any given situation, there needs to be a reasoned judgement balancing the benefits of new technology (usually new markets and customers) against the problems created by new technology (usually personnel and operational issues).
- Potential short-term difficulties caused by the changeover must also be considered, such as possible cutbacks in production while old technology is being replaced.
- Finance is a major concern. It is likely that new technology will impose huge financial costs in the short term, but it may generate huge financial benefits in the long term.
- The reliability of forecasts and projections of costs, revenues, markets and technological developments need to be considered, since it is impossible to be totally sure of the impact of change. Firms need to be aware of, and have contingency plans for, when actual figures start to become significantly different from forecast figures.
- The use of IT within an organisation tends to reflect the prevailing management style. A supermarket chain might concentrate on its potential for collecting vast quantities of data at shop-floor level and then transmitting this to head office for analysis of the popularity of particular product lines etc. In this way, those at the top of the management hierarchy are pulling information up and then passing decisions back down to local branches. A leadership with a more democratic approach might use computer networks to allow such information to flow more freely around the branches, which might empower local branch managers with the information needed for sound decision making.

INGRAM

PRACTICE EXERCISE 1
Total: 40 marks (35 minutes)

1 Give two examples of technological change in the primary sector of industry. *(2 marks)*

2 Give two examples of technological change in the secondary sector of industry. *(2 marks)*

3 Give two examples of technological change in the tertiary sector of industry. *(2 marks)*

4 What is meant by technological change or innovation in processes? *(3 marks)*

5 What is meant by technological change or innovation in products? *(3 marks)*

6 Explain two benefits to consumers of the use of new technology. *(6 marks)*

7 Explain two benefits to firms of the use of new technology. *(6 marks)*

8 Explain two problems for business of introducing new technology. *(6 marks)*

9 Discuss the main factors that might encourage a business that makes and installs kitchens to introduce new technology. *(10 marks)*

PRACTICE EXERCISE 2
Total: 15 marks (20 minutes)

Recycled Harry Potter to save muggle forests

Read the case study in Chapter 43 (pp. 376–77) about publishing future volumes of the Harry Potter books on recycled paper.

Question

Discuss the benefits and problems for the businesses involved of technological change that allows books to be printed on recycled paper.

PRACTICE EXERCISE 3
Total: 25 marks (30 minutes)

Improving business performance with barcode technology

Analysts suggest that one of the reasons for Tesco's success has been its investment in IT and in particular in barcode technology.

Tesco's strategy is simple. It frees up shelf space in the stores by minimising the stock level of every item. This then allows it to expand its range of non-food items. Of course, minimising stock levels means it must replenish continuously. To do this Tesco must capture in-store product data. As well as scanning barcodes at checkouts, this is done by staff who monitor stock. Armed with handheld computers, they scan barcodes on the shelves at each location and check the quantity. Tesco's responsive supply chain then keeps the deliveries coming.

To add to its success, Tesco has become the world's no. 1 internet grocer. The stores themselves serve as home delivery centres. Pickers pick six orders at a time, scanning the barcode on each item with

ISBN 0-86003-376-7

9 780860 033769

a handheld reader attached to the radio-linked terminals on their trolleys.

In comparison, Sainsbury's has admitted that its supply chain puts it at a severe disadvantage compared to its main competitors, and has introduced a 3-year programme to renew its physical infrastructure, systems and processes.

Even small companies can use barcodes to cut errors and increase throughput. For example, a retailer asked its supplier of artificial flowers to put a barcode label on each bloom. The owner of the artificial flower business was loath to incur the additional cost but eventually ordered a label printer and a barcode scanner. Eighteen months later the three to five complaints the supplier used to receive almost every day (such as 'you sent five yellow and two white when I ordered two yellow and five white') had fallen to three a year – the packer scanned the barcodes before boxing the order and hence eliminated most of the errors. This simple system paid for itself in weeks by cutting the cost of errors.

Most food processors include barcodes in their pack designs. There is always a risk of loading the wrong material into the packaging machine. An in-line scanning system will detect rogue items and stop the line. A well-known jam maker uses such a system to inspect 230 jars a minute to prevent raspberry preserve going out as strawberry jam.

Barcodes are perfect for just-in-time processes, stock control and stocktaking.

A designer and manufacturer of diesel engines, with a £40 million annual turnover and a 350-strong workforce, used to check all of its stock manually. With over 25,000 stock locations, this was a tediously slow process. And even when the physical stock check had been completed, it would take up to 2 weeks for staff to input the data manually into an in-house computerised stock record. Meanwhile, stock levels would alter, making the stock take effectively out-of-date. What is more, stock auditing was a labour-intensive operation with the company having to recruit staff from other departments within the company to assist with the process. Staff hated this annual 'chore' and the company was committed to paying large sums in overtime payment.

The solution was to barcode products and locations and introduce handheld computers for counting purposes. The benefits gained through this application were impressive. Payback was immediate. Man-hours were saved, costs were reduced (the new system was able to reduce stocktaking costs by 80% of the figure normally associated with pencil-and-paper methods) and stock control procedures improved.

Source: Codeway Ltd website.

Questions

1 Using the information in the article, assess whether a small company should be as involved in technological developments as its larger rivals. *(10 marks)*

2 The article seems to suggest that there are many benefits from adopting technology such as barcodes and few, if any, costs. To what extent is this always true in relation to the introduction of new technology in business? *(15 marks)*

CASE STUDY

Social and other opportunities and constraints

The case study below covers the topics studied in Chapters 42–44. It is concerned with social responsibilities, business ethics and technological change.

CASE STUDY Smart tags

Supermarket retailers are looking at radio frequency identification (RFID) 'smart tags' as a means of managing stock control. These are tiny, ultra-thin, cheap-to-produce chips that can be incorporated into the labels of products. Items like cans of baked beans can be given unique, unalterable RFID numbers, enabling manufacturers and retailers to track individual cans from factory to shopping basket. Some supermarkets are experimenting with scanning RFID-tagged shopping in the bag, which could one day eliminate the need for checkout queues. Other retailers, such as Marks and Spencer, are considering incorporating the technology into the labels of their clothing ranges.

The smart tags, embedded in goods or built into the packaging, emit radio signals that can be read from up to 5 metres away, and unless 'killed' they remain active long after they have left the store. Unlike barcodes, the RFID labels identify individual items whose movements can be tracked by scanners connected to the internet. The microchips involved are the size of a grain of sand, and with the price falling to a few pence they can be fitted to anything from trainers to toothbrushes.

The government has been sponsoring trials of RFID tags as a means of reducing theft and counterfeiting, and the European Central Bank plans to put them in euro banknotes.

Supporters of the tags suggest that consumers would benefit from lower prices and shelves that were permanently full if companies could use a global network of scanners, connected to the internet, to track individual items wherever they were.

Pressure groups have raised concerns that this technology could mean that a retailer might be able to track customers once they have left the store. 'This technology has the potential to track people from the time they get up in the morning to the time they go to bed at night,' said Katherine Albrecht, who runs a pressure group that is campaigning to stop the introduction of these tags. She believes that the police, criminals and marketers will all be motivated to scan people's property to learn more about them from their 'electronic cloud'.

'Everything from your earrings to what's in your briefcase would be sending out information,' she said. 'My concern is this will be tied in with Britain's CCTV surveillance system, and you'll be literally under surveillance at every turn.'

Source: adapted from various articles in *Professional Manager* and *The Times*.

Questions

Total: 50 marks (60 minutes)

1 Briefly explain the possible implications for supermarket employees of the widespread introduction of smart tags by UK supermarkets. *(6 marks)*

2 Analyse **one** benefit to a retailer of introducing new technology such as smart tags into its operations. *(6 marks)*

3 The concerns raised by pressure groups suggest that firms may face resistance if they introduce smart tags. Discuss how the introduction of smart tags could be managed effectively in order to avoid such resistance. *(15 marks)*

4 Examine **two** ways in which the use of smart tags could be viewed as unethical business practice. *(8 marks)*

5 To what extent does the use of smart tag technology highlight the difficulties facing a business that tries to meet its social responsibilities? *(15 marks)*

Objectives and strategy

> "Wherever you see a successful business, someone once made a courageous decision."
>
> Peter Drucker

CHAPTER **45**

Business activity and the small firm

What exactly do we mean by business activity? Business activity can be classified according to whether organisations extract or use natural resources, manufacture goods or provide services. This chapter examines these activities and looks at the trend away from primary industry to secondary industry and then to the tertiary sector as wealth grows. The reasons for small firms and their importance to the business world are also examined.

The structure of industry

 TERMS

primary sector: those organisations involved in extracting raw materials (e.g. farming, fishing, forestry and the extractive industries such as oil exploration, mining and quarrying).

secondary (manufacturing) sector: those organisations involved in processing or refining the raw materials from the primary sector into finished or semi-finished products (e.g. paper mills, oil refineries, textile manufacturers, food processors, vehicle manufacturers and machine tools manufacturers).

tertiary sector: those organisations involved in providing services to customers and to other businesses, either in the public or the private sector (e.g. education, health, hairdressing, retailing, financial services, restaurants and leisure services).

The tertiary sector is the largest sector in terms of contribution to GDP and employment in the UK. As economies develop, the secondary sector tends to grow faster than the primary sector. However, in well-developed economies, such as the UK, the tertiary sector tends to grow faster than the secondary sector. In general, as people get wealthier, they want more manufactured products and then move on to a desire for more and more services.

Tables 45.1 and 45.2 give some indication of the relative importance of these three sectors in the UK economy, in terms of their contribution to GDP and to employment.

INGRAM

DID YOU KNOW?

GDP means gross domestic product. It is the total value of a country's output over the course of a year.

Table 45.1 The structure of UK industry (% share of GDP)

Sector	1964	1969	1973	1979	1990	1995	1999
Primary	5.7	4.5	4.2	6.7	3.9	4.2	3.0
Secondary	40.6	42.2	40.9	36.7	31.6	28.2	27.2
Tertiary	53.7	53.3	54.9	56.6	64.5	67.6	69.8

Source: adapted from ONS (2000).

Module 3 *Objectives and strategy*

Sector	1964	1969	1973	1979	1990	1995	1999
Primary	5.2	3.4	3.0	3.0	2.1	1.7	1.6
Secondary	46.9	42.3	38.5	35.5	26.6	22.7	21.9
Tertiary	47.9	54.3	58.5	61.5	71.3	75.6	76.5

Source: adapted from ONS (2000).

Table 45.2
The structure of UK industry (% of total employment)

Types of organisation

Private versus public sector organisations

It is important to recognise the distinction between private and public sector organisations.

KEY TERMS

private sector organisations: organisations owned and controlled by private individuals. They can take the form of sole trader organisations, partnerships or companies. (The legal structure and implications of these are considered in Chapter 47.) In Western economies, the private sector is the dominant sector.

public sector organisations: organisations owned and/or funded by national or local government. These include public corporations (nationalised industries), public services (such as the National Health Service and education) and municipal services (such as local council-run leisure centres).

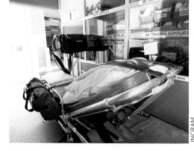

Profit-making versus non-profit making organisations

It is also important to recognise that private sector organisations may be profit making or non-profit making. For example, a charity shop and an independent school are private sector organisations that are non-profit making. In comparison, commercial organisations in the private sector, such as a vehicle manufacturer or a retail chain, are profit-making organisations. Figure 45.1 summarises the different types of organisations.

Figure 45.1
Types of organisation

Regardless of these different types of organisation, they all are involved in similar business activities. For example, they all need to market themselves, attract customers, employ staff and obtain suitable sites, equipment and finance; they all need effective management and organisation; and they all need

to produce goods or provide services. They are all affected by government policy, such as changes to taxation; by legislation, such as health and safety laws and employment laws; and by competition.

Small firms

What is a 'small firm'?

The Bolton Committee Report of 1971 originally defined a small firm as one with not more than 200 employees; however, in practice it found this definition difficult to apply to all industries. For example, the definition would allow firms that are highly automated, with substantial earnings and high market shares, to be termed 'small'. The committee therefore suggested that a new definition was needed that emphasised those characteristics of small firms that might be expected to make their performance and their problems significantly different from those of large firms. It concluded that these characteristics were as follows:

- A small firm has a relatively small share of its market and therefore little or no power over its marketplace.
- A small firm is managed by its owners or part-owners in a personalised way, and not through the medium of a formalised management structure.
- A small firm is independent, in the sense that it does not form part of a larger enterprise, so that its owner-managers are free from outside control when taking their main decisions.
- A small firm usually has limited financial resources.

According to the European Union definition, also adopted by the UK government, small firms are those with fewer than 50 employees, while very small or 'micro' firms have only 1–9 employees. Medium-sized firms have between 50 and 249 employees. **Small and medium-sized enterprises (SMEs)** are those having fewer than 250 employees.

The role of small firms in the UK economy

Table 45.3
Micro, small, medium and large enterprises (registered for VAT or PAYE) at the start of 2002

The position of SMEs in relation to the number of enterprises, the proportion of employment and the level of turnover is shown in Tables 45.3 and 45.4. Table 45.3 shows only those registered for VAT or PAYE (pay as you earn). Many firms are too small to employ staff or register for VAT (currently if their annual sales are below £56,000), and these are included in Table 45.4.

	Number of enterprises	%	Employment (000s)	%	Turnover (£m)	%
All employees	1,167,530	100.0	19,737	100.0	2,045,001	100.0
Micro (1–9 employees)	966,665	82.8	3,736	18.9	328,062	16.0
Small (10–49 employees)	167,020	14.3	3,237	16.4	330,488	16.2
Medium (50–249 employees)	27,260	2.3	2,688	13.6	330,435	16.2
Large (250+ employees)	6,585	0.6	10,076	51.1	1,056,016	51.6

Source: adapted from ONS, 2003.

	Number of enterprises	%	Employment (000s)	%	Turnover (£m)	%
All enterprises	3,797,725	100.0	22,674	100.0	2,199,923	100.0
With no employees*	2,630,195	69.3	2,937	13.0	154,922	7.0
All employees	1,167,530	30.7	19,737	87.0	2,045,001	93.0
Micro (1–9 employees)	966,660	25.4	3,737	16.4	328,062	14.9
Small (10–49 employees)	167,020	4.4	3,237	14.3	330,488	15.0
Medium (50–249 employees)	27,260	0.7	2,688	11.9	330,435	15.0
Large (250+ employees)	6,590	0.2	10,075	44.4	1,056,016	48.1

Source: adapted from ONS, 2003.

Why do small firms exist?

Small firms exist for two distinct reasons:

- The owner believes that there are benefits from being small, in comparison to other businesses.
- A business may be small because it is experiencing problems that are limiting its ability to grow into a larger business.

These are summarised in Table 45.5.

Benefits of being a small firm	Problems limiting the growth of small firms
• personal service for customers • the owner's desire for independence • the owner wishing to keep using a skill that he or she has developed • lower start-up costs (e.g. working from home) • flexibility and scope for innovation	• small market size (locally or nationally) • financial difficulties (often problems in raising additional finance) • lack of opportunities for economies of scale, limiting the firm's ability to match the prices of larger firms

Small firms: secondary or tertiary production?

Traditionally, small firms were much more likely to be found in the tertiary (service) sector than the secondary (manufacturing) sector. The reasons can be seen in Table 45.5.

Manufacturing gives opportunities for economies of scale to large firms. Consequently, small firms find it difficult to compete with larger firms if price is important. However, for individually made products there may be more emphasis on the skills of the producer, so small firms may be successful. As the economy becomes richer, people want more individual products, so opportunities for small firms increase.

In the service (tertiary) sector, small firms tend to be more significant in the provision of personal services, such as hairdressing and plumbing. Commercial services, such as insurance and banking, are more suited to large firms. In some services, such as leisure and tourism, there are opportunities for both small and large firms.

Why are small firms important?

Small and medium-sized enterprises (SMEs) contribute significantly to employment and growth in the economy. Including those without employees,

Table 45.4
Micro, small, medium and large enterprises at the start of 2002 (includes estimates of unregistered businesses and those with no employees)*

*Businesses with no employees are usually sole traders who do not employ any staff.

Table 45.5
Reasons for small firms

DID YOU KNOW?

Research has shown that the owner wanting to use a skill that he or she has developed is a major characteristic of small firms that are successful.

INGRAM

in 2000, SMEs accounted for over 99% of the UK's 3.7 million businesses, and over 50% of total UK turnover (£1 trillion).

The creation of new firms provides a significant source of job creation. New firms in the UK, especially smaller new firms, are the greatest single source of new jobs.

Entrepreneurship, in the form of small and medium-sized enterprises, boosts productivity by increasing competitive pressure within the economy. This forces existing firms to increase their efficiency in order to stay in the market. If existing firms are unable to match the productivity of new or fast-growing SMEs, either they are forced to leave the market or their market share is reduced. This then increases the productivity of the market as a whole. In addition to this, any efficiency gains can be passed on to consumers through lower prices and greater choice.

Source: adapted from *Small Firms: Big Business — A Review of Small and Medium Sized Enterprises in the UK*, Department of Trade and Industry, 2002.

> **ℯ EXAMINER'S VOICE**
>
> If your mind goes blank on a question in the exam, then leave a large space and move on. A later question may trigger your memory again. Always leave space at the end of any answer so that if there is time to go back, you can expand on your response.

PRACTICE EXERCISE 1 — Total: 40 marks (35 minutes)

1 Identify three industries in the primary sector. *(3 marks)*

2 Identify three industries in the secondary sector. *(3 marks)*

3 Identify three industries in the tertiary sector. *(3 marks)*

4 Distinguish between the primary, secondary and tertiary sectors. *(6 marks)*

5 Distinguish between private and public sector organisations. *(4 marks)*

6 Distinguish between profit-making and non-profit-making organisations. *(4 marks)*

7 Identify three similarities between public and private sector organisations. *(3 marks)*

8 Identify three similarities between profit-making and non-profit-making organisations. *(3 marks)*

9 Identify three advantages of small firms. *(3 marks)*

10 Analyse two possible reasons why small firms may be more likely to survive if they are in the tertiary sector rather than the secondary (manufacturing) sector. *(8 marks)*

PRACTICE EXERCISE 2 — Total: 30 marks (30 minutes)

1 Describe and explain the reasons for the changes that have taken place over time in the structure of UK industry, as shown in Tables 45.1 and 45.2 (see pp. 386–87). *(8 marks)*

2 Discuss the similarities and the differences in general business activity between a charity shop, a clothing manufacturer and a local comprehensive school. *(10 marks)*

3 Discuss three characteristics of small firms that mean that their problems are very different from those of large firms. *(12 marks)*

CHAPTER 46

Identifying a business opportunity

This chapter addresses four fundamental questions which are central to the establishing of a new business:

- *How do entrepreneurs identify business opportunities?*
- *How can the chances of success be assessed?*
- *What are the challenges involved in marketing a small firm with limited finance?*
- *How can a firm prevent other organisations from copying its ideas?*

People who start businesses have many different motivations. Some are motivated by a desire for independence or the attraction of high profits. If they have been made redundant and have a substantial lump-sum redundancy payment, they may see it as an opportunity to do something different. Others may be motivated by a commitment to an idea or product, or the development of a hobby or creative talent. A profitable opportunity could arise if an invention can be made into a commercial opportunity, or from the purchase of a franchise or by spotting a gap in the market. But whatever the motivation, every entrepreneurial success story starts with an idea.

Sources of business ideas

Finding a good idea that will prove to be profitable is not easy. Given that approximately one-third of all new businesses fail in their first 3 years, an entrepreneur has to think carefully about the idea for a new business and the likelihood of its success. Research suggests there are four major sources of ideas for entrepreneurs:

- **Spotting trends and anticipating their impact on people's lives.** This was the approach adopted by Innocent, the business that makes fruit juice smoothie drinks. The company, which was launched in 1998, tapped into the growing desire for healthier lifestyles.
- **Noticing something that is missing from the market or that can be improved on.** An example here is Rachel Elnaugh, who spotted a gap in the market when she could not find any interesting presents to buy for young professional people who could afford to buy most things themselves. She created Red Letter Days, a business selling extraordinary experiences, such as a champagne hot-air balloon flight, a trip in a powerboat or a session in a recording studio, as gifts.

INGRAM

- **Copying ideas from other countries.** Many entrepreneurs have found and copied successful ideas from abroad. For example, Howard Schultz of Starbucks did not invent the espresso coffee machine or the coffee bar, but he saw the coffee bar culture in Italy and thought that it could be introduced in the USA.
- **Taking a scientific approach.** Entrepreneurs sometimes work in a laboratory or university to invent original new products. An example is James Dyson and his revolutionary bagless vacuum cleaner. Inventors who start a firm on the strength of a new invention have the benefit of a short-term market niche, until the 'me-too' products start to appear.

> **ⓔ EXAMINER'S VOICE**
>
> Business ideas and opportunities come from a variety of sources, but all require lots of hard work and clear thinking. Although some look as if they were a case of having the right idea at the right time (i.e. luck), most are '5% inspiration and 95% perspiration'. When framing answers in this area, be aware of the importance of thinking through exactly what needs to be considered in assessing a business idea.

Other sources of business opportunity

In addition to developing their own business idea, people wishing to set up in business could purchase a **franchise**.

KEY TERM

franchise: when a business (the franchisor) gives the right to supply its product or service to another business (the franchisee).

This is a tried-and-tested method that limits the risk of the owner. However, it also limits profitability and the franchisee may be vulnerable if the franchisor has not researched the business carefully. Examples of franchises are Kentucky Fried Chicken, Kall Kwik, Dyno and Pizza Express.

Another source of business for small firms is **subcontracting**. Large firms give themselves more flexibility by 'buying' services such as cleaning or catering (or even manufacturing) from another firm, rather than using their own resources and employees. This often provides an opportunity for small firms, and these are sometimes run by former employees of large firms, which no longer wish to employ them directly.

Who are the entrepreneurs?

Entrepreneurs are extremely diverse in nature: men or women, young or old, those from differing ethnic, social or educational backgrounds. They engage in entrepreneurial activity for a variety of different reasons: to gain more freedom at work; to make money and aim for high growth; or to sustain a going concern (often a family concern) and provide employment for the local community. Consequently, each business founder and owner has very different needs and expectations.

DID YOU KNOW?

An entrepreneur is someone who has a business idea and develops it. He or she takes the risks and the profits that come with success, as well as the losses that inevitably come with failure. Examples include Richard Branson (Virgin), Anita Roddick (Body Shop), James Dyson (Dyson) and Martha Lane-Fox (lastminute.com).

Nevertheless, government research indicates that a typical entrepreneur in the UK is most likely to be a white man aged around 36 years, who has some form of vocational training or secondary-level qualification. He is most likely to be motivated by the freedom that running his own business offers him, or the desire to make money.

Assessing a business idea

Before proceeding, entrepreneurs need to consider a number of issues and ask themselves a number of questions relating to their business idea.

Possible issues are:
- the objectives of owners
- which product or service to provide and whether it can be produced and supplied profitably
- customers' needs and wants, and which market segment to aim at
- the possibility of competition and an appropriate pricing and selling strategy
- finance for day-to-day and longer-term operations, and the time scales between start-up and breakeven
- who will be involved, what they will be doing and what skills, expertise and experience they have
- the risks involved

Questions to consider include:
- Is there anything special, new or different about the product that would make it appeal to consumers?
- Could the product compete successfully with similar products on the market?

> **e EXAMINER'S VOICE**
>
> All business decisions include an element of risk. In your answers to questions on this area, don't assume, as many students do, that if a business venture or opportunity is risky, it should be abandoned. The most profitable opportunities are often the riskiest. Risk needs to be assessed and taken into account but, unless extreme, it should not necessarily deter action.

Market research and marketing with small budgets

A major issue for someone with a good idea for a new business is a lack of finance for market research and for marketing. However, the following options are available for individuals or businesses working to a modest budget.

Market research
- The *Yellow Pages* and local business directories will show what businesses are trading and hence which products and services are available and where.
- Market mapping of existing products and services will help to identify a gap in the market for a product or service that is not being provided at all.

- Other secondary sources of market research include census data and local government data.
- Very limited primary research could be carried out in a local area, but in addition, depending on the nature of the business, information could be gained by listening to local people and their complaints about products and services — for example, how difficult it is to clean the large council wheelie bins.

Marketing

Examples of marketing that can be carried out on a modest budget are:

- leaflet distribution done personally or through a local newspaper or distributor
- posters in shop windows
- advertisements in the local newspaper and other publications such as church or parish magazines, possibly with special offers
- local business directories and the *Yellow Pages*
- specialist magazines relevant to the product or service (these may be national — for example, small craft businesses that make handmade furniture for dolls houses advertise in specialist craft magazines with a national circulation)
- public relations (PR) — arranging events that will achieve local newspaper, radio or even television coverage
- word-of-mouth — comments from satisfied customers are a major form of marketing for a new firm

Protecting a business idea

Business ideas can be protected by using patents, trade marks and copyright.

Patents

KEY TERM

patent: an offical document granting the holder the right to be the only user or producer of a newly invented product or process for a specified period.

To register a patent the inventor must: provide full drawings of the invention for the Patent Office; demonstrate that the ideas have original features; and promise that the ideas are his or her own. The Copyright, Designs and Patents Act 1988 gives patent holders the monopoly right to use, make, license or sell the invention for up to 20 years after it has been registered.

The following issues need to be considered in relation to patenting an idea:

- Holding a patent allows the product/process to be developed further, to be positioned in the market, and to reap benefits in terms of revenue and profits.
- Having a patent means that the invention becomes the property of the inventor, which means that it can be bought, sold, rented or licensed — and can therefore be a useful bargaining tool when trying to persuade manufacturers and investors to help the business.

FACT FILE

The following account of a court case involving the inventor of the bagless vacuum cleaner, James Dyson, is adapted from an article that appeared in *The Times* in October 2000.

The inventor who sparked the vacuum cleaner wars with his revolutionary bagless machine won a multi-million-pound court battle yesterday. A High Court judge ruled that Hoover was guilty of stealing the ideas from James Dyson and had infringed the patent on bagless cleaners...In March 2000, Hoover brought out its own version, the Vortex, using a new 'triple cyclone' machine. Mr Dyson claimed it was a blatant copy of the cleaner he had spent 20 years developing... Mr Dyson... said after the hearing: 'I spent 20 years developing the technology and I am very pleased to see Hoover, who made a lot of false claims about their product, have been found guilty of patent infringement. I am also pleased on behalf of other small businesses and inventors, who should be encouraged to take out patents by the result of this case.'

- A small business with an existing patent might become an attractive proposition for a large firm to purchase, simply in order to obtain the patent.
- The cost of effectively developing and launching a product for which a patent is held may be too high for a small firm and the firm may sell the patent. Taking a patent application through can be a complex and expensive process. Although filing an initial application for a patent in the UK is free, further fees are payable at each stage of the process and amount to £200. But the biggest expense is for the services of a patent agent, whose fees can run into thousands of pounds. Moreover, if a business is planning to sell its product abroad, the cost will be much higher — the Patent Office suggests about £32,000 for patent protection across Europe.
- Although a patent grants the inventor rights that can be very valuable, there is no agency for enforcing patents. Therefore the holder has to be willing to take to court those who infringe the patent. An individual inventor is unlikely to be able to afford the legal costs and hence new patents are often sold on to larger firms.

 EXAMINER'S VOICE

Think of patents as barriers to entry and therefore a strategic tool to protect a business from competition.

Trade marks

KEY TERM

trade mark: a logo or symbol displayed on a company's products or on its advertising, which distinguishes its brands from those of its competitors.

DID YOU KNOW?

'Have a break, have a Kit Kat' was first used in a television advert in 1957. In a recent survey, when prompted with 'Have a break', 98% of Britons responded with 'Have a Kit Kat.' Despite this, Nestlé, the chocolate bar's Swiss maker, was refused a trade mark for the slogan in May 2002. The case then went to the High Court, where it was decided that the slogan was not yet implanted on the nation's consciousness and that Nestlé had not used the phrase 'Have a break' on its own enough to make it a distinctive Kit Kat slogan. The High Court therefore decided that Nestlé could not claim that it owned the phrase. This meant that Nestlé's rival, Mars, was free to begin a confectionery war by launching its own new product called 'Have a Break'. Clearly Nestlé feared that shoppers would confuse Mars's new bar with Kit Kats.

Source: adapted from an article in Metro, December 2002.

Trade marks are indicated by the symbol ®. In order to prevent rivals from copying a symbol or style of wording, the trade mark must be registered at the Patent Office. Once the trade mark has been registered, the company has exclusive rights to its use.

Copyright

KEY TERM

> **copyright:** legal protection against copying for authors, composers and artists.

Copyright is indicated by the symbol ©. It applies to printed material such as a book that cannot be copied directly without permission from the owner of the copyright. Unlike patents, there is no requirement to register an author's copyright. The law on copyright is governed by the Copyright, Designs and Patents Act, 1988.

DID YOU KNOW?

Microsoft, operator of the world's most popular free e-mail service, forgot to renew its hotmail.co.uk domain name. The company's claim on the website address lapsed on 23 October 2003. A private individual, who declined to be named, subsequently registered the domain name, but then returned it to the software group for no charge. A spokeswoman for Microsoft said: 'We have resolved the issue and we have put processes in place to ensure that this does not happen again.'

Source: adapted from an article in *The Times*, 7 November 2003.

PRACTICE EXERCISE 1 — Total: 40 marks (35 minutes)

1 State four possible ways to identify a business idea or opportunity. *(4 marks)*

2 Identify one business example to illustrate each of these four ways. *(4 marks)*

3 Explain three factors that need to be considered when assessing the likely success of a new business idea. *(9 marks)*

4 State three forms of market research that a new business with a very small budget could undertake. *(3 marks)*

5 Identify three different methods of marketing a new product/service, where the budget available is very small. *(3 marks)*

6 What is a patent? *(3 marks)*

7 Explain one benefit that a patent could provide for a business. *(3 marks)*

8 Explain why many small firms sell their patents to larger firms. *(3 marks)*

9 What is a trade mark and how might it benefit a business? *(5 marks)*

10 Explain the meaning of the term 'copyright'. *(3 marks)*

PRACTICE EXERCISE 2

Mother's nutty idea grows into a £1 million firm

A mother's struggle to find nut-free treats for her daughter, who is severely allergic to nuts, inspired her to open a small kitchen bakery that has rapidly grown into a £1 million business.

Angela Gourlay-Russell turned to home cookery last year because she was so frustrated by the lack of suitable products in supermarkets for her 13-year-old daughter, Kirsty. The venture proved such a hit that 'It's Nut Free', which became a limited company in March 2003, moved out of the kitchen at her home in Harrogate, North Yorkshire, and now operates from a purpose-built factory near Ripon.

Mrs Gourlay-Russell's biscuits, muffins, flapjacks and cakes, already on the menu at every school in the Harrogate area, are drawing enquiries from distributors in Europe, America and Australia. Contracts have been signed to supply Morrisons and Asda, and the company is holding discussions with a leading restaurant chain to supply nut-free hot meals and puddings.

The venture's success has depended on strictly observing the need for every stage of the production process to be entirely free of any trace of nuts.

Mrs Gourlay-Russell and her husband initially invested £5,000 to ensure that their kitchen met health and safety regulations, but then invested £100,000 in the new premises. All the equipment has been manufactured in a nut-free environment, which includes ensuring that none of the cleaning products contains nut oil, and staff must shower before entering the kitchen to prevent contamination.

Source: adapted from an article in *The Times*, 5 September 2003.

Question

Taking into account the inspiration for the business 'It's Nut Free', and what you know of other sources of ideas for new businesses, to what extent is it luck or judgement that determines whether a new idea becomes a successful business?

PRACTICE EXERCISE 3

Take a chance on a bright idea: the patent

Mandy Haberman, entrepreneur and inventor of the Anywayup Cup, has spent hundreds of thousands of pounds protecting her product. The non-spill baby cup that she launched in 1996 has been a huge commercial success, with annual sales of 10 million units. But taking out patents to deter others from copying the cup — and defending her rights when others have tried to infringe them — has eaten into her profits. 'I had no idea it would cost so much, but if you are serious about your product, you have to regard intellectual property rights as a necessary business expense,' she says.

Her view is an isolated view. A new survey, conducted by the Survey Shop, has confirmed what has long been suspected — UK businesses are not doing enough to protect their good ideas or monitor and exploit their intangible assets. Less than a fifth of companies surveyed had funds devoted to protecting their ideas and products. More than half said that they had no process for dealing with their intellectual property.

While individual business owners stand to lose out if they fail to pay attention to intellectual property, the government is concerned about wider implications. A report produced last year by Michael Porter of Harvard Business School, at the request of the Department of Trade and Industry, found that the UK economy was losing out through low levels of innovation and a reluctance by company owners to protect their ideas.

Ramin Pirzad was certain he had hit on a winning product when he launched ActivAllergy Mite-Alert. The product, which he spent 2 years developing, enables allergy sufferers to test whether dust mites inhabit the immediate vicinity. It can then pinpoint the areas and finish off the microscopic pests. It will, he hopes, be a big commercial success, helping to relieve the suffering of hundreds of thousands of sufferers of asthma, eczema and other allergies. His intellectual property, he says, will play a big part in that success.

'If there is no intellectual property, there is no barrier for entry to a market. If people were given a chance, they would copy this product and reduce my profit,' he explains. 'At the moment, competition is not stiff. But as soon as a product is successful, others are quick to imitate it.'

The cost of developing intellectual property rights has been significant for his company, Acaris. Pirzad, who is managing director, has spent more than £50,000 on two patents and those costs will increase as he extends the protection to other parts of the world. Furthermore, in an effort to protect himself against significant legal costs if his rights are infringed, he pays £5,000 a year for patent insurance.

Many owners of small companies spend money on patents but then make the mistake of failing to exploit their intellectual property. Pirzad says, 'Once you have paid for a patent, you have to market the product in every way you can, let people know about it and about your brand. Otherwise you have wasted your money.'

Source: adapted from an article in *The Times*, 9 September 2003.

Questions

1 To what extent is a very small budget for market research and marketing likely to affect adversely the possibility of success for a small business idea? *(15 marks)*

2 Based on the two inventions in the article, discuss the extent to which a patent increases a firm's chances of success. *(15 marks)*

Legal structure

This chapter examines the various legal structures that businesses in the private sector can adopt. It investigates their characteristics and the pros and cons of each type of legal structure. Unlimited and limited liability are compared and the significance of limited liability is discussed. The meaning, causes and implications of the divorce between ownership and control are also studied.

The range of legal structures in the private sector is illustrated in Figure 47.1.

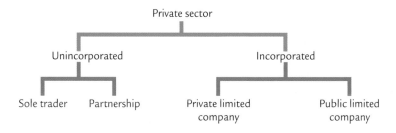

Figure 47.1
Legal structures of business

Unincorporated and incorporated businesses

KEY TERMS

unincorporated business: there is no distinction in law between the individual owner of the business and the business itself. The identity of the business and the owner is the same. Such businesses tend to be sole traders or partnerships.

incorporated business: this has a legal identity that is separate from the individual owners. As a result, these organisations can own assets, owe money and enter into contracts in their own right. Such businesses include private limited companies and public limited companies.

The distinction between unincorporated and incorporated businesses can be illustrated as follows. If you have a part-time job with Tesco plc, your employer, with whom you have a contract of employment, is Tesco and not the shareholders (owners) of Tesco. If, however, you have a part-time job with the local newsagents, known (say) as Robinson's, which happens to be run as a sole trader by the owner, Mary Robinson, then your employer is the individual who owns the business, Mary Robinson. Similarly, if you had an accident on the premises of Tesco and were advised to sue, then you would sue Tesco plc, not the shareholders (owners) of Tesco. If, however, you had an accident on the premises of Robinson's newsagent, you would sue Mary Robinson, the owner.

Limited and unlimited liability

KEY TERMS

unlimited liability: a situation in which the owners of a business are liable for all the debts that the business may incur.

limited liability: a situation in which the liability of the owners of a business is limited to the fully paid-up value of the share capital.

Unlimited liability is a characteristic of businesses that are unincorporated, meaning that there is no distinction in law between the owners and the business. If the debts of the business are greater than the personal assets of the owners, they may be forced into bankruptcy. The main types of business with unlimited liability are sole traders and partnerships.

In contrast, if a business with **limited liability** goes into liquidation because it cannot pay its debts, the shareholders (owners) have no responsibility for further payments as long as they have paid in full for the shares they have purchased; their personal assets cannot be used to pay the debts of the business. Legally, such a business has 'died' and so its debts 'die' with it. Limited liability is a feature of incorporated businesses, where the identity of the owners and the business are separate in law. The main types of business with limited liability are private limited companies and public limited companies. Limiting the amount of shareholders' liability is an important factor in encouraging people to invest, as they will be aware of the level of risk that they face.

EXAMINER'S VOICE

Ensure that you are absolutely clear about the distinction between limited liability and unlimited liability, so that you do not confuse the two in your answers.

DID YOU KNOW?

Insolvency occurs when the liabilities of a business are greater than its assets and it is unable to meet its financial obligations. Where this happens, it is likely that the business will go into **liquidation** — that is, it will turn its assets into cash, for example by selling the firm or its assets, in order to pay creditors. The terms insolvency and liquidation are applied to incorporated businesses with limited liability. For individuals and for unincorporated businesses, with unlimited liability, the situation when liabilities cannot be paid in full is called **bankruptcy**.

Types of business unit

Sole trader

KEY TERM

sole trader: a business owned by one person. The owner may operate on his or her own or may employ other people.

Sole traders usually have little capital for expansion and are heavily reliant on their own personal commitment to make their business a success. If the business is unsuccessful, there is no protection from limited liability as a sole trader is unincorporated, i.e. the firm's finances are inseparable from the owner's. Sole traders are most commonly found in the provision of local services.

INGRAM

Partnership

A partnership is a form of business in which two or more people operate for the common goal of making a profit. Partners normally have unlimited liability, which means that each partner is liable for the debts of the other partners. Because this requires a high degree of trust, partnerships are most common in the professions, such as medicine and the law. A partnership allows more capital to be used in the business than is the case with a sole trader and enables the pressures of running the business to be shared. It also gives partners more personal freedom to take holidays etc. However, unlike private or public limited companies, partners retain major responsibilities for the success of the organisation, and their ability to raise finance remains rather limited.

Private limited company

KEY TERM

> **private limited company:** a small to medium-sized business that is usually run by the family or the small group of individuals who own it.

A private limited company can keep its affairs reasonably private and thus the owners can determine their own objectives without the pressure to achieve short-term profit that is so common for public limited companies. Private companies are funded by shares that cannot be sold without the agreement of the other shareholders, which means that their shares cannot be traded on the Stock Exchange. In addition, the share capital of private companies may be less than £50,000. As a result of both of these factors, private limited companies generally tend to be limited in size. A private limited company must have 'Ltd' after the company name to warn people that its owners (shareholders) have limited liability.

EXAMINER'S VOICE

No understanding of partnerships is needed for the AQA Business Studies course, but some brief references and descriptions are included in this chapter for the sake of completeness.

FACT FILE

The Stock Exchange is a market where second-hand shares (i.e. shares that have already been issued by public limited companies) can be bought and sold. When a public limited company wishes to raise finance, it does this by issuing (selling) shares to the public. Once these have been issued, the owners can sell them on the Stock Exchange. The Stock Exchange assists companies in raising finance, since people would be more reluctant to buy shares if they could not easily offload them when required.

Public limited company

KEY TERM

> **public limited company:** a business with limited liability, a share capital of over £50,000 and, usually, a wide spread of shareholders.

The shares of public limited companies are traded on the Stock Exchange, which enables these businesses to raise finance more easily. An important issue in changing from a private limited company to a public limited company

is that the business is moving away from the control and support of a family or close-knit group of individuals towards a focus on achieving short-term profits for its shareholders, including institutional investors, and having its performance scrutinised constantly by the financial press. Public limited companies must have 'plc' after the company name.

> **DID YOU KNOW?**
>
> Institutional investors are pension funds, insurance companies and other financial organisations that invest huge sums of money in the shares of public limited companies quoted on the Stock Exchange. They are by far the largest group of investors in company shares and therefore have huge influence on companies. Critics suggest that it is pressure from institutional investors, which are seeking to maximise their funds and profits, that forces businesses to focus on short-term profits (known as **short-termism**) rather than on long-term performance.

The move from a private to a public limited company is an important step for any business. The motive is usually to obtain extra funds for growth, but disadvantages do arise, including loss of control, continual scrutiny, short-termism regarding share prices and possibly takeover pressure, all of which detract from long-term decision making. These disadvantages are such that a number of large, successful private limited companies resist becoming public limited companies, while other successful public limited companies revert back to private limited company status. Examples include Virgin and The Body Shop, both of which went from private to public and back again to private limited status because of the issues mentioned, and Timpson, which chooses to remain a private limited company (see practice exercise 2 on p. 406).

The advantages and disadvantages of each type of organisation considered here are summarised in Table 47.1.

THE BODY SHOP

TOPFOTO

The divorce of ownership and control

Traditionally, entrepreneurs have two functions: **ownership** and **control**.

> **KEY TERMS**
>
> **ownership:** providing finance and therefore taking risks.
> **control:** managing the organisation and making decisions.

In a sole trader business, the owner and manager are likely to be the same person, so these functions remain with that one person, the entrepreneur. However, in public limited companies, the owners (shareholders) vote for a board of directors, who in turn appoint managers to control and manage the business. In this case, the two functions of ownership and control are separated or divorced.

The functions have been separated for a number of reasons. In order to raise finance for further growth, many private limited companies become public limited companies. In turn, large public limited companies attract shareholders,

EXAMINER'S VOICE

As both private limited companies and public limited companies are incorporated businesses and have limited liability, ensure that you are clear on the distinction between them and don't confuse them in your answers.

	Advantages	Disadvantages
Sole trader	• easy and cheap to set up • few legal formalities • able to respond quickly to changes in circumstances • owner takes all of the profit and hence there is good motivation • independence • more privacy than other legal structures, as financial details do not have to be published	• unlimited liability • limited collateral to support applications for loans • limited capital for investment and expansion • difficulties when the owner wishes to go on holiday or is ill • limited skills as the owner needs to be a 'jack of all trades'
Partnership	• between them, partners may have a wide range of skills and knowledge • partners are able to raise greater amounts of capital than sole traders • the pressure on owners is reduced, as cover is available for holidays and decisions are made jointly	• control is shared among the partners • arguments are common among partners • there is still an absolute shortage of capital — even 20 people can only raise so much • unlimited liability
Private limited company	• limited liability and the business has a separate legal identity • access to more capital than unincorporated businesses • more privacy than a plc, as it is only required to divulge a limited amount of financial information • more flexible than a plc	• shares are less attractive, as they cannot be traded on the Stock Exchange and hence could be difficult to sell • less flexible if expansion needs finance, which is more difficult to raise than for a plc • there are more legal formalities than for an unincorporated business
Public limited company	• limited liability and the business has a separate legal identity • easier to raise finance as a result of its Stock Exchange listing • greater scope for new investment • can gain positive publicity as a result of trading on the Stock Exchange • suppliers tend to be more willing to offer credit to public limited companies	• must publish a great deal of financial information about its performance • greater scrutiny of activities • significant administrative expenses • founders of the firm may lose control if their shareholding falls below 51% • a stock exchange listing means emphasis may be placed on short-term financial results, not long-term performance

Table 47.1
The advantages and disadvantages of different legal structures

who may only be interested in the dividends they can earn on their shares or in the capital gain they can make from buying and selling shares. They often have little or no real interest in the management of the company or its long-term performance.

The fact that managers and shareholders become more separated as the company grows can mean that shareholders find it difficult to access the information needed to challenge or judge the quality of managers' decisions. The more autonomy managers have, the more likely they are to pursue objectives that benefit themselves rather than shareholders, such as furthering their own careers or increasing their job satisfaction.

A more positive view of the divorce of ownership and control is that shareholders have too narrow a focus on short-term finance and also have less

EXAMINER'S VOICE

Ensure that you
understand the effect
that becoming a public
limited company with a
quotation on the Stock
Exchange can have on a
company, as this is a
crucial factor for a
company that wants
to grow.

understanding than management of the needs of the other stakeholders.
Figure 47.2 illustrates this issue.

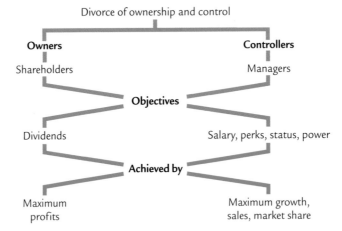

Figure 47.2
The divorce of ownership
and control

Corporate governance

Recently, attention has been directed to issues of **corporate governance**. This
refers to the systems and mechanisms established by a firm to protect the
interests of its owners (shareholders). In theory, the board of directors is
elected to represent shareholder interests, determine strategy and ensure that
the firm acts legally. But how do shareholders make sure that the directors
actually do a good job? Most of the information they receive will be from the
directors themselves, so how can investors make sure that the directors are
not being negligent or that they are not being misled?

The delicate relationship between shareholders, directors and managers has
been reviewed in the UK several times at the request of the government. The
Cadbury Report (1992), the Hampel Report (1998) and the Higgs Report
(2003) have made numerous recommendations for UK companies, mainly
focusing on the need for public limited companies to have more **non-executive
directors**, i.e. directors who do not have a full-time job within the business.
The argument is that these non-executive directors will be more independent
and provide a better check on managers' behaviour than executive directors,
who are in effect checking on themselves. Allowing managers to police
themselves might mean that issues are not examined from enough perspectives — the right questions don't get asked, so the right solutions are not
found.

The challenge of making sure that companies are run in the best interests of
their owners is a complex one. Shareholders do not want to know everything
that happens within the business — this would simply lead to an information
overload and the directors must be given some freedom to do their job. On the
other hand, the shareholders do own the company and so should be kept
informed of relevant issues — but how do they know this is happening and

that the directors are presenting the information truthfully? While there is no doubt that an independent, questioning approach is desirable to keep a check on a firm's actions, there is also the need for strong leadership and good-quality directors who have a deep inside knowledge of the business. So what is the right mix?

In the UK, and more recently in the USA, much greater pressure is now being put on directors to be more accountable to their shareholders and to make greater use of non-executive directors. However, investors still cannot be sure that their money is being used in the way they want or that power is not being abused.

Conclusion

A number of factors affect the choice of legal structure. These include: the need for finance in order to expand; the size of the business, and the level and type of investment required; the need for limited liability; the degree of control desired by the original owners; the nature of the business (e.g. limited liability is not available to professions such as solicitors); and the level of risk involved.

For example, a manufacturing business requiring heavy investment in plant and equipment before anything can be sold may need limited liability in order to raise sufficient funds. On the other hand, a business that requires much less investment and therefore very little borrowing will involve relatively little financial risk, and there may be no need for limited liability. In other cases, image might be vitally important and the word 'Ltd' after a name may add status, and 'plc' even more so.

PRACTICE EXERCISE 1 — Total: 45 marks (40 minutes)

1 What is meant by the term 'incorporated business'? *(3 marks)*

2 What is meant by the term 'unincorporated business'? *(3 marks)*

3 Explain the implications of a business having unlimited liability. *(4 marks)*

4 Explain the implications of a business having limited liability. *(4 marks)*

5 Distinguish between a private limited company and a public limited company. *(6 marks)*

6 Describe two advantages and two disadvantages of a business trading as a sole trader. *(8 marks)*

7 Identify two advantages of a private limited company over a public limited company. *(2 marks)*

8 Identify two disadvantages of a private limited company as compared to a public limited company. *(2 marks)*

9 Explain the term 'divorce of ownership and control' in relation to public limited companies. *(4 marks)*

10 State and explain three factors that are likely to influence the choice of legal structure. *(9 marks)*

Staying private

A number of large, high-profile, public limited companies have made the decision to revert back to private limited company status in order to reduce media scrutiny and pressure with its emphasis on short-termism. Other expanding companies have made the decision to remain as private limited companies. In 2003, the family-owned shoe repairer, Timpson, bought Minit UK, which owns Sketchley cleaners, Supasnaps and Mister Minit.

Timpson now controls more than 1,000 retail outlets nationwide. John Timpson, the group's chairman, said at the time of the purchase that he was in the process of integrating the various divisions, but he added: 'We only have one firm plan, which is that we will not float the business. We think staying private is the best way to run the business.'

Source: adapted from an article in the *Financial Times*, May 2003.

Questions

1 Examine two advantages and two disadvantages to a firm such as Timpson of deciding not to float the company on the Stock Exchange.   *(12 marks)*

2 Identify and explain one implication of limited liability in comparison to unlimited liability for a business from the following points of view:
   a the firm's customers   *(3 marks)*
   b the firm's suppliers   *(3 marks)*
   c its workforce   *(3 marks)*
   d its shareholders   *(3 marks)*

3 To what extent do the problems of the divorce of ownership and control in a public limited company depend on the degree of effective corporate governance in the company?   *(16 marks)*

CHAPTER 48

Practical problems of start-ups

Setting up a new business is not easy. The practical problems of starting a new business are scrutinised in this chapter, which focuses specifically on the following areas of difficulty:
- *raising finance*
- *controlling cash flow*
- *finding a good location*
- *building a customer base*
- *business planning*

One way to look at the problems facing new businesses is to consider the main reasons for business failure: poor cash-flow management; lack of effective market research; lack of skills needed to run a business; failure to turn what looks like a good idea into a profitable business; lack of finance to fund the business; difficulties in developing a solid customer base; and difficulties in acquiring affordable premises. These reasons for business failure clearly translate into potential problems that business start-ups might encounter. For example:

INGRAM

- **finance** — raising funds, problems of cash flow, uncertainty about profitability
- **marketing** — deciding on the product, forecasting sales, deciding on the target market, conducting market research, deciding on a competitive price and the most appropriate form of advertising and promotion
- **operations** — finding suitable premises, deciding on location and the most appropriate production methods, identifying the sources of supply, new technology
- **personnel and the organisation** — deciding on recruitment and selection strategies, organising appropriate training, deciding on the most effective organisational structure
- **external factors** — complying with regulations, the impact of macro-economic policies including interest rates and taxation
- **personal problems** — suitability for self-employment, how the owner will provide cover for illness, what the opportunity cost of this business start-up is for the owner

Table 48.1 (see p. 408) shows the results of a government survey about the main barriers to small business success. The top four concerns of business owners and sole traders that prevent them from running their business to its

Sole traders	Business owners
Cash flow and finance	Regulations
Sales and marketing	Cash flow and finance
Regulations	Taxation
Taxation	Sales and marketing
Economic environment	Economic environment
Staff-related issues	Staff-related issues
Finding suitable premises	Finding suitable premises
New technology	New technology

Source: Small Business Service, Omnibus Survey, November 2001 (www.sbs.gov.uk/research).

Table 48.1
Key obstacles to success, identified by small business owners and sole traders (in order of importance)

full potential include: regulation; cash flow and difficulty obtaining finance; sales and marketing; and taxation. Those businesses surveyed generally felt that regulations, although necessary, can be complex, and that they spend a disproportionate amount of time and resources in complying with changing regulations. The main worries in relation to taxation centred on the administrative time taken to pay taxes. Sales and marketing obstacles related to the problems of limited budgets for market research and for marketing products and services. Problems related to finance and cash flow are considered in more detail below.

Finance

Raising sufficient finance to get started is a major concern for most small businesses. As a new business has no 'track record' or past success upon which lenders can judge its future potential, it is seen as much more of a risk than an established business. This is likely to lead to difficulties in finding suitable sources of finance. In addition, the finance that is available is likely to be expensive, with high interest rates being charged in order to balance the risk to the lender. This is why many small businesses are funded by their owners and by their relatives and friends, with owners often remortgaging their homes (using their homes as **security** for a loan) in order to raise funds, or using lump-sum retirement or redundancy payments.

Banks provide a majority of the external funds for small business start-ups, mainly in the form of loans and overdrafts. They will, however, want **collateral** or security, i.e. they will want the owners to put up personal guarantees for any loans, offering their own assets, such as their homes or their business premises, as guarantees in case of default on the loan. In other words, if the borrower is unable to repay the loan, the lender will take the property (collateral or security) instead. Thus the owner is taking the risk rather than the lender, which should ensure that the owner is highly motivated and works hard to make the business succeed. (See Chapter 14 for more detail on sources of finance for business.)

Finance to cover two types of expense needs to be obtained: finance for equipment and premises (i.e. fixed capital) and finance to cover day-to-day expenses including workers' wages, suppliers etc. (i.e. working capital). Fixed capital costs are reasonably straightforward to estimate, but estimating working capital needs is much more complex. For this reason, cash-flow forecasting is essential for a business start-up in order to ensure that it has sufficient working capital to cover its trading needs.

Over 20% of small business owners said they experienced difficulty in obtaining the finance they needed, and that this consequently slowed the growth or even threatened the survival of their business. A higher proportion

FACT FILE

Smaller firms rely on personal savings at the start-up stage, but then obtain about 60% of external finance from banks, although very small firms also use hire purchase and leasing arrangements. Many surveys suggest that the real problem in relation to financial support for small firms is not necessarily the availability of finance but its cost. The rate of interest for the smallest firms is often between 3% and 5% above base rates and this may be doubled if their overdraft is exceeded.

In the past, UK banks were accused of using a very narrow range of financial information for assessing whether to offer loans to small businesses compared to banks in other European countries. The Bank of England, however, notes some 'improvement' in this

area, in that banks now appear to be taking lending decisions based less on security and more on cash flow and business plans.

Approximately 70% of all external funding for UK businesses comes from overdraft finance compared to an EU average of 53%. The major disadvantage of overdrafts is that they are payable on demand and therefore restrict the ability of smaller firms to take a long-term view. However, although UK banks have been criticised for 'short-termism' — that is, lending for only short periods of time — this is changing. Only 9% of UK loans are for less than 3 years compared to an EU average of 14%, and 20% of UK loans are for more than 5 years compared to an EU average of only 17%.

Source: *Applied Economics*, A. Griffiths and S. Wall, 10th edn 2004, Pearson Education.

of sole traders (27%) had problems raising finance. Table 48.2 provides more detail on the possible effects on small businesses of difficulties in raising finance.

Cash flow

Even firms that are profitable sometimes find it impossible to continue trading because they are unable to meet their current debts. Often cash is tied up in stock that cannot be used immediately to pay bills, or creditors are slow to pay their debts. It is absolutely essential, even for a very profitable business that has full order books and is working at full capacity, to ensure that it has enough cash available for its working capital needs. In order to do this, it is usual for business start-ups to prepare a cash-flow forecast as part of their business plan. This shows the expected variation in working capital needs over a period of time and should indicate when overdraft facilities will be needed to cover any shortfalls. (For a more detailed analysis of cash flow, see Chapter 13.)

Location

In order to break even as soon as possible, a business needs to keep down its costs, particularly its fixed costs. Premises are a major cost that needs to be minimised. Many new small businesses operate from the owner's home at first (see practice exercise 2 on It's Nuts Free in Chapter 46, p. 397). This keeps costs down but can create its own pressures by affecting family life — for many people, the working day never ends and there is no clear distinction between work and home.

Effect	% of respondents
Can't grow as fast	38
Threatens survival	23
Affects productivity	20
Affects investment	19
Takes up management time	10
Pushes up costs	9

Source: Small Business Service, Omnibus Survey, November 2001 (www.sbs.gov.uk/research).

Table 48.2 The effect of difficulties in raising finance

DID YOU KNOW?

Research suggests that 70% of business failure can be put down to poor cash-flow management.

The actual location of the business and the significance of location will depend on the nature of the business and on the rate at which it grows. Clearly, in It's Nut Free, the business could not remain in the owner's home as the scale of operations increased, hence more suitable premises had to be found. For a retail or service business that deals directly with customers, the actual location in relation to customers is crucial. For example, a new gift shop or restaurant would need to have a prime location in order to attract customers, rather than being tucked away on a housing estate. However, such prime locations are likely to be much more expensive than other sites.

Location is dealt with in more detail in the A2 course.

Building a customer base

The success of a business start-up will be determined by its ability to attract and retain its customers. Satisfied customers are likely to recommend the business to others, and such recommendation is the most effective but least expensive form of advertising. In order to attract customers, the business will have to engage in some form of advertising, as discussed in Chapters 8 and 46. However, customers will return to do business on a regular basis only if they are satisfied with the goods and the service they are offered.

Factors to consider when trying to encourage customer loyalty include:
- Providing customers with service that is efficient and meets their expectations. For example, products must be available in the quantities and the range intended by the business and expected by customers. A shop that is constantly out of stock of essential or popular items is unlikely to retain customers, who are more likely to go elsewhere.
- Providing a good after-sales service and dealing effectively and positively with customer complaints. For example, a restaurant that does not use customer complaints or comments as an opportunity to improve its provision is unlikely to encourage customers to return on a regular basis.
- Understanding customers' buying habits and ensuring that stock and staff availability is in tune with this. For example, hairdressers need to recognise which days of the week and times of the day are busy and which are slack in order to have sufficient staff available to meet demand. They can thereby ensure that people are not sitting around waiting for the stylist or colourist to finish with another client.
- Ensuring that contact between customers and staff is always friendly and efficient. Customers will remember this and be encouraged to continue to do business with the firm.

Business plan

KEY TERM

business plan: a report describing the marketing strategy, operational issues and financial implications of a business start-up.

An initial business plan is useful in helping entrepreneurs to clarify their objectives and to consider their business idea thoroughly from every perspective, which should improve the likelihood of its success. This kind of business plan is drawn up principally to persuade lenders to invest capital in the business by demonstrating why it is likely to succeed. Banks insist on seeing such a plan before granting loans or overdrafts.

Subsequent business plans are also useful as an ongoing means of monitoring progress — for example, by checking the performance of the business against its objectives and forecasts, and investigating the reasons for variations.

The main sections of a business plan are as follows:

- Details about the business, its name, address, form and type, and personal information about the owner, including a CV and an account of their business experience and financial commitments.
- The objectives of the firm or what it is aiming to achieve, stated as quantifiable or SMART targets.
- A marketing plan showing the gap in the market that the business start-up is intended to fill, product positioning, type, size and location of the market, description of potential customers, comparison of the firm's products/services with those of its competitors, promotion and selling techniques to be used.
- A production plan detailing how goods and services will be created, the day-to-day practical details of the activities involved, including the materials needed, staff and equipment needed, and capacity.
- Details of fixed and other assets, including those needed for immediate plans and how these are to be financed.
- Details of key staff and staffing requirements.
- A cash-flow forecast and a projected **profit and loss account** and **balance sheet** for the end of the first year, together with details of pricing and breakeven level. (The profit and loss account and balance sheet are dealt with in detail in the A2 course.)
- Details of the finance needed from the lender or investor and the forecast speed of repayment or rate of return on the investor's capital.
- The collateral to be offered. Most business start-ups are likely to rent premises or work from home, rather than own their own business premises. In this case, the owner would have to offer his or her own personal assets (usually their home) as security.
- A brief account of the long-term forecasts and plans of the business.

> **DID YOU KNOW?**
>
> SMART targets or objectives are those that are specific, measurable, agreed, realistic and time-bound.

> ### EXAMINER'S VOICE
>
> Most of the issues considered in this chapter are covered in more detail elsewhere in the AS course. This highlights the importance of taking an integrated view of business studies and thinking broadly about issues such as small business start-ups. To quote from the specification, 'This module section draws together all the other modules, and…should be seen as integrating themes which emphasise the interactive nature of the business world.'

1 List three major reasons for business failure. *(3 marks)*

2 Explain two reasons why raising finance for a new business start-up can be difficult. *(6 marks)*

3 Which two main types of finance do banks provide? *(2 marks)*

4 Why are banks likely to ask for collateral or security before offering finance? *(4 marks)*

5 Identify the two main examples of finance that a new business start-up needs to consider. *(2 marks)*

6 Explain how a business can fail despite being profitable. *(3 marks)*

7 Why might location be a significant issue for a business start-up? *(4 marks)*

8 Identify and explain one factor that is vital in building a solid customer base for a new business. *(3 marks)*

9 What is the purpose of a business plan? *(4 marks)*

10 Identify and explain the importance of three sections that are likely to appear in a business plan. *(9 marks)*

CASE STUDY Business start-ups

Read the following articles and answer the questions that follow.

Cobra Beers

The owner of Cobra Beers, Karan Bilimoria, describes his best decision and his worst decision.

HIS BEST...The idea of Cobra beer, like many of the best business ideas, was born out of consumer frustration. When he came to the UK as a student, Karan found that most lagers were too harsh and gassy to go with hot spicy food. He wanted to produce a lager from India that was less gassy and extra-smooth. His aim was to brew the finest Indian beer and to make it a world brand. That was in 1989. Today, Cobra has an annual turnover of £50 million.

HIS WORST...He and his business partner decided on the name of Panther. They did all the artwork for the Panther brand and took it to India. At that point, one of their distributors decided to do some consumer testing. They discovered that the Panther brand was not going down well with consumers. They switched to their second choice brand – Cobra. The consumer response was great. Karan suggests that this experience 'taught me that you've got to test your ideas with consumers and listen to what they say. Never make a decision without checking with the consumer. Panther was not a very expensive mistake, but it could have been.'

Source: adapted from an article in *Management Today*, October 2003.

Babel Media

Algy Williams launched his first and only computer game in time for Christmas 1996. Critics loved it but within weeks it had disappeared from the shelves. His publisher, the Time Warner subsidiary Inscape, unexpectedly closed down. The media giant had, apparently, taken fright at the amount of cash it was pouring into the games market without adequate return.

Williams was devastated. 'It would have been the beginning of a whole series of games,' he said.

His game — *Drowned Gods* — failed not only because of a lack of marketing and sales support, but because it had been rushed to hit the Christmas market and was full of bugs that made it irritating or difficult to play. At the time, 'the quality of computer games was dreadful', Williams recalls, suggesting that this issue and his experience with it 'fundamentally shaped what we are doing now' and laid the foundations for his latest venture, Babel Media.

His business, Babel Media, is a new kind of creature in the video games sector. It neither writes nor publishes games, but provides a broad range of production services to games developers and publishers. These include testing games to ensure that they work in the way their authors intended, developing and testing the instruction manuals, designing and constructing related websites and converting games to run on the multiplicity of devices available today: consoles, PCs, personal digital assistants and mobile phones. Most significantly, it checks that games written for one national market have been successfully converted for another — a process known as 'localisation testing'. This avoids the notorious gems of translated English, such as the Italian helpline that threatened: 'Tell us your problem and someone will call you back between 9 a.m. and 5 p.m. every day, Monday to Friday.' Thus, Babel Media has expanded its range of services to 'occupy the whole niche' and, as a result, the company is a full-service provider for games companies, which gives it a useful edge over other European companies in its sphere.

In a sense, Williams discovered the business niche that his company now occupies by accident. Since then Babel Media has grown by identifying an industry that is going to require an increasing number of outsourced services as it expands and matures. 'I think it is terribly important that we do not offer any service which cannot be integrated with the others,' he says. 'We started with one service line and now we provide a whole suite. We have to make sure our clients use our multiple service lines. If you do the whole process, you get greater efficiencies.' 'Find a niche, the larger the better, and stick to it,' he recommends. 'Interactive entertainment is a huge market — a huge niche — and it will keep me busy for many years to come.'

Source: adapted from an article in the *Financial Times*, 18 November 2003.

Questions

Total: 50 marks (60 minutes)

1 Briefly explain two factors that have helped Babel Media to succeed. *(6 marks)*

2 Explain the importance of market research to Cobra Beers. *(6 marks)*

3 The owners of both Cobra Beers and Babel Media encountered problems in the initial start-up period. To what extent could you argue that the skills of the individual owners were the main factors leading to the later success of both businesses? *(15 marks)*

4 Using the data in this chapter and elsewhere, analyse the reasons why approximately one-third of new businesses are likely to fail within 3 years of start-up. *(8 marks)*

5 Both Cobra Beers and Babel Media spotted a gap in their respective markets. Evaluate the importance of spotting a gap for the success of a small business. *(15 marks)*

CHAPTER 49

Corporate aims and objectives

Aims and objectives underpin all business activity. This chapter scrutinises how objectives are set; the qualities needed for an objective to be helpful to a firm; and the types of aims and objectives. Short-term and long-term objectives are contrasted.

Corporate aims

KEY TERM

▌ **corporate aims:** the long-term intentions of a business.

Corporate aims are often provided in the form of a mission statement and give a general focus from which more specific objectives can be set. Aims determine the way in which an organisation will develop. They provide a common purpose for everyone to identify with and work towards, and a collective view that helps to build team spirit and encourage commitment. They are not usually stated in numerical terms.

Example: the mission, aims and objectives of Tesco plc

Mission statement
'Tesco is one of Britain's leading food retailers. The company owes its success to its emphasis on meeting changing customer needs through service and innovation, while maintaining its commitment to value and quality.'

Aim
'To increase value for customers continually and to earn their lifetime loyalty.'

Objectives
1 'To understand our customers better than any of our competitors do.'
2 'To earn the respect of our staff for these values and to appreciate their contribution to achieving them.'
3 'To be energetic and innovative and to take risks in making life better for our customers.'
4 'To recognise that we have brilliant people working for us and to use this strength to make our customers' shopping enjoyable in a way that no competitor can.'
5 'To use intelligence, scale and technology to deliver unbeatable value to customers in everything we do.'
Source: Tesco plc website (www.tesco.com).

DID YOU KNOW?

A **mission statement** is a qualitative statement of an organisation's aims. It uses language intended to motivate employees and convince customers, suppliers and those outside the firm of its sincerity and commitment.

Each of these five objectives is then broken down into more specific targets. For example, objective 1 includes 'To reduce customer complaints by 5% over a 3-year period'; objective 4 includes 'To increase the return to staff from profit-sharing on a year by year basis' and 'To ensure that all staff are involved in on-going training and development with a view to increasing their professional competence levels'.

Corporate goals and objectives

 **KEY TERM**

corporate objectives: targets that must be achieved in order to realise the stated aims of the business.

Corporate goals or objectives are medium- to long-term targets that give a sense of direction to a manager, department or whole organisation. They act as a focus for decision making and effort, and as a yardstick against which success or failure can be measured. If a team can be given a sense of common purpose, it becomes much easier to coordinate actions and to create a team spirit, which in turn is likely to lead to improvements in efficiency and a more productive and motivated staff. Corporate objectives govern the targets for each division or department of the business.

Figure 49.1 illustrates the hierarchy of objective setting within an organisation.

> **ⓔ EXAMINER'S VOICE**
>
> Try to remember this hierarchy of objective setting when considering case study situations. Clearly, departmental objectives must be related to corporate objectives, which must in turn be related to corporate aims. Where this is not the case, the business is likely to encounter problems.

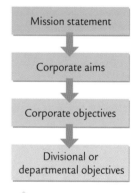

Figure 49.1
The hierarchy of objectives

SMART objectives

For maximum effect, objectives should be SMART: that is, specific, measurable, agreed, realistic and time-bound. This is the case with Tesco's objective 1: 'To reduce customer complaints by 5% over a 3 year period'. Objectives should be specific, measurable and timed so that it is possible to assess the extent to which they have been achieved and to ensure that people are clear about what it is they are trying to achieve. An objective that is vague

> **DID YOU KNOW?**
>
> Objectives form the basis for decisions on **strategy**. Strategy is the medium- to long-term plans through which an organisation aims to attain its objectives. The plans include not only what is to be done, but also the financial, production and personnel resources required. Therefore decisions about business strategy should not be considered until the company's objectives have been agreed.

EXAMINER'S VOICE

When assessing the effectiveness of objectives, always try to use the SMART criteria.

and difficult to measure will serve no purpose and provide no direction. In addition, objectives must also be realistic, otherwise they can be demotivating and counterproductive. Objectives that are agreed by the whole workforce are much more likely to be pursued and therefore achieved than those that are imposed.

Possible aims and objectives for firms

Aims and objectives vary from firm to firm, depending on the size of the business and the legal structure. For example, a corner shop may simply aim to survive, whereas a multinational organisation may be more interested in its corporate image and the possibility of diversifying. Aims and objectives can be concerned with any of the following:

- **Survival.** This is a key objective for most small or new firms, especially if they are operating in highly competitive markets, and it is an even more significant objective during periods of uncertainty and recession.
- **Profit.** Profit maximisation is often cited as the most important objective, but in practice firms are more likely to aim for a satisfactory level of profit. Financial objectives will always be influenced by the business environment. For example, the level of competition, the existence of spare capacity, the stage of the business cycle and the demand for the product will all affect the chances of making a profit.
- **Growth.** This could relate to increasing market share, turnover, number of outlets or number of business areas, and can be achieved by growth of the existing business or by takeovers of other businesses. Growth is less likely to be an important objective for small businesses that value their independence. External factors are also likely to influence the attainment of objectives related to growth.
- **Diversification.** A firm might wish to diversify in order to spread risk by reducing its dependency on a single market or product.
- **Market standing.** Depending on the organisation, this might involve being seen as the most innovative and progressive organisation or the leader in technology or the best retailer. It is linked to corporate image and an organisation's reputation. Achieving an appropriate corporate image is likely to assist with the achievement of other objectives, such as growth and profit. The nature of this objective will vary according to the target market. For example, a different corporate image will benefit the company if the target market requires products that are 'cheap and cheerful' than if the target market is influenced by an exclusive image and high prices.
- **Meeting the needs of other stakeholders.** To an extent, the above objectives benefit owners or shareholders. However, organisations also place a high value on considering the needs of other stakeholder groups, such as customers, workers and the local community, which in turn will enhance the company's reputation. For example, Tesco's aims and objectives (see p. 414) are clearly related to satisfying customer and staff needs.

Other areas for aims and objectives include: maximising shareholder wealth; maximising sales revenue; focusing on the firm's core capabilities rather than venturing into risky diversification; social and environmental responsibility; adding value; and enhancing reputation through continuous technological innovation.

 YOU KNOW?

Small businesses are unlikely to write down their aims and objectives, or even consider them formally, although they are likely to be tacitly understood. Even if aims and objectives are not written down, it is still important for employees to know what the business is striving to achieve and to share the vision.

Long-term and short-term objectives

Decisions about objectives need to be made in the context of a firm's overall aims. In practice, however, objectives are constantly modified in response to changes in the market and the external environment, and in relation to present levels of achievement and future opportunities. Thus, short-term objectives may vary from the longer-term objectives and aims for a number of reasons. For example:

- A financial crisis is likely to encourage a firm to focus on short-term survival rather than, say, growth or market share. This does not mean that its long-term aims and objectives in relation to growth or market share have changed, but clearly in the very short term, contingency plans and alternative strategies may be required.
- A firm may have a long-term objective of improving profitability, but in the short term profitability might be sacrificed in order to try to eliminate a competitor. For example, in the short term, a firm might use destroyer or predatory pricing in order to force a competitor from the market. This might mean losses being sustained in the short term in order to pursue growth and increase market share, which in turn should improve long-term profitability.
- In a recession, emphasis is likely to be placed on survival, whereas over the longer term and in a boom, the potential for high profits may encourage other objectives, such as helping the environment or local community, or diversification.
- Changes in government policy may force a company to adopt different short-term priorities. For example, the increase in national insurance contributions introduced by the government in 2002 led to a substantial increase in costs for organisations. This in turn caused them to focus more attention on efficiency and cost-cutting goals in the short term.
- Negative publicity — for example, from a faulty product or an environmental disaster — will cause a firm to focus on improving its image in the short term in order to re-establish itself in the market, regardless of its longer-term objectives.

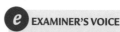 **EXAMINER'S VOICE**

Remember that external factors can provide benefits as well as problems. For example, the law banning hand-held mobile phones in cars has provided a business opportunity for makers of hands-free kits.

There is no single corporate aim or objective that every firm should aspire to or that guarantees success. However, as long as clear objectives are derived from sound aims, and as long as these objectives are pursued with realistic and well-resourced strategies, business success is much more likely.

PRACTICE EXERCISE   Total: 40 marks (35 minutes)

1 Distinguish between corporate aims and corporate objectives.   *(4 marks)*

2 Give two examples of corporate aims.   *(2 marks)*

3 Explain the hierarchy of objective setting in an organisation.   *(4 marks)*

4 What are the benefits to a business of having stated aims and objectives?   *(4 marks)*

5 What are SMART objectives?   *(5 marks)*

6 'To brew the finest Indian beer and to make it a world brand.' Explain whether this is an aim or an objective.   *(3 marks)*

7 Write a corporate objective that meets the SMART criteria.   *(5 marks)*

8 'To improve our company's performance by 10% in the future.' Consider whether this objective is SMART.   *(4 marks)*

9 Identify three areas about which companies are likely to have aims and objectives.   *(3 marks)*

10 Explain two reasons why short-term objectives are likely to differ from longer-term objectives.   *(6 marks)*

CASE STUDY   **Tesco plc**

Read the information below and use it, together with the other information about Tesco in this chapter (see p. 414), to answer the questions that follow.

Tesco is the UK's biggest supermarket retailer, but how has it grown? Because its profits were almost entirely dependent on the food market in the UK, it had to pursue a policy of diversification in order to grow and in order to spread its risks.

The market for supermarkets in this country is close to saturation and Tesco probably has almost as many stores as it wants in the UK. If it simply opened more stores, it would be in danger of cannibalising the sales of its existing stores. So in order to continue to grow, it needed to expand overseas and/or into other markets in the UK. It has done both. It has expanded abroad by opening stores in mainland

Europe and more recently in Thailand. In addition to this, it has moved into faster-growing domestic markets. In November 2003, it reported a 34% increase in the sales of its clothing lines, with clothes sales growing at more than six times the market rate. It also claims that it sells more CDs than HMV, the music store, and more toiletries than Boots, the health and beauty retailer.

Questions

Total: 50 marks (60 minutes)

1 Rewrite two of Tesco's five objectives (p. 414) so that they meet the SMART criteria. *(6 marks)*

2 What are the likely benefits to a company such as Tesco of having detailed aims and objectives? *(8 marks)*

3 To what extent is it clear that Tesco's objectives are based on its corporate aims? *(15 marks)*

4 One way that Tesco has grown is by diversifying abroad. Briefly explain how this might have affected Tesco's short-term objectives. *(6 marks)*

5 Discuss whether the information provided indicates that Tesco is successfully pursuing its broad aim: 'To increase value for customers continually and to earn their lifetime loyalty'. *(15 marks)*

CHAPTER 50

Conflicting and common aims of stakeholders

All business organisations, regardless of their size and ownership status, are subject to the influence of stakeholders. Stakeholders are people or groups with an interest in an organisation, such as owners, workers and customers. In this chapter, the aims of each group of stakeholders are considered and the extent of agreement and/or conflict between different stakeholders is discussed.

KEY TERM

stakeholder: an individual or group with a direct interest in the activities and performance of an organisation.

The main stakeholders in a business are its shareholders, its staff, its customers, its suppliers, the financiers, the local community and the government. Figure 50.1 illustrates the stakeholder groups that might have an interest in a football club such as Manchester United.

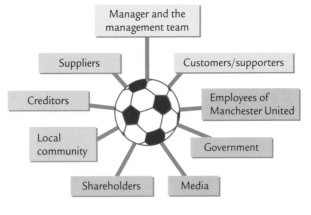

Figure 50.1
Manchester United: its stakeholder groups

Shareholder versus stakeholder approaches

The traditional view: the shareholder approach

Traditionally, firms were established by their owners to meet the needs of those owners. Business aims and objectives were therefore dominated by the needs of the shareholders (the owners). Today this view assumes that

> **EXAMINER'S VOICE**
>
> Make sure that you understand the difference between stakeholders and shareholders. Shareholders are those people who provide a share of the capital needed to run a business in exchange for part-ownership; thus shareholders are stakeholders in the business. However, there are a lot of other stakeholder groups with an interest in the business apart from shareholders.

management is responsible solely to the owners of the organisation (i.e. the shareholders), who employ the managers to run the company on their behalf. Thus everything managers do should be in the direct interest of shareholders, and their aim should be to maximise shareholder value by striving for short-term rewards, such as profit and dividends.

The alternative view: the stakeholder approach

Over time, a number of organisations have taken a different view by giving prominence to the needs of other groups of stakeholders. For example, the John Lewis Partnership meets the needs of employees and the Cooperative Society aims to satisfy the needs of its customers. Firms have also been encouraged by government and pressure groups to meet the wider needs of society by taking into account the **externalities** arising from their decisions. This approach emphasises the need to meet, or at least to consider, the objectives of wider groups of individuals who have an interest in the business. It takes the view that firms benefit from cooperation with their stakeholder groups and from incorporating their needs into the decision-making process.

'Win–lose' or 'win–win'

Because a firm may not be able to meet the needs of all stakeholder groups, it has to set priorities and is therefore likely to encounter conflict. For example, if it helps the local community, fewer funds will be available for shareholders. Conversely, if more rewards are directed towards the owners (shareholders), less are available for employees. This analysis takes a 'win–lose' approach to the situation: that is, it views the company as having a fixed pot of benefits to share out among all groups; if one group gains more, another gains less.

An alternative approach is that of 'win–win'. According to this analysis, a firm can, by its actions, cause the pot of benefits to grow and thus all groups to gain more. For example, better conditions and rewards for employees, although reducing rewards for shareholders in the short run, may increase them in the long run. This occurs because increased staff loyalty and motivation result in better-quality work, which in turn increases consumer loyalty and enhances the firm's reputation. This in turn leads to less marketing expenditure in order to achieve the same level of sales and/or an increase in sales, and therefore profit. Social responsibility might therefore make good business sense.

What stakeholders want

The things that stakeholders may look for from an organisation are called **stakeholder expectations**. As an organisation's survival depends, to a great extent, on support from its stakeholders, how and to what extent it can

DID YOU KNOW?

Externalities are those costs and benefits that occur as a result of a firm's activities, but which are not taken into account in its profit and loss account. For example, pollution and congestion may be caused by a firm's activities, but the costs are borne by the local community and not by the firm.

EXAMINER'S VOICE

Remember that limited resources and opportunity costs are fundamental issues to consider when discussing the stake-holder and shareholder approaches.

satisfy their demands is crucial. What makes the task difficult to accomplish is the fact that, on some occasions, different groups of stakeholders share common interests, while on other occasions their interests conflict.

Common interests

All stakeholders in an organisation, except its direct competitors, have much to gain from a prosperous business. Some stakeholders, such as shareholders and employees, have a vested interest in the business, while others, such as suppliers and buyers, have their own business interests tied to that particular organisation. The closure of a car manufacturing firm affects not only the employees of that firm but also the dealers and small servicing outlets specialising in the cars made in that factory.

The shareholders who have invested money in the business naturally expect a good return on their investment in both the short and the long term. If the business fails, they stand to lose some or all of their money.

The directors and managers may lose the privileges associated with their present position if the business fails, and may be forced to look for alternative employment. Moreover, with a change of job come the problems and costs associated with having to relocate their homes and families.

The desire to see the business prosper is also likely to be strong among the other employees, whose job security and livelihood are dependent on the success of the organisation. The closure of a large factory can often be detrimental to the families affected and the local economy.

Conflicting interests

In the business world, however, there are many situations where conflicts of interest can arise. For instance, the directors of a public limited company are appointed to manage, coordinate and make profit. If they fail at any of these, they may be voted out by the shareholders at the next annual general meeting. The nature of their job requires them to adopt a view on what is going on both inside and outside the organisation.

Unlike the managers, most employees of the firm are there to carry out specific tasks. It is often difficult for them to see things from the management's point of view. This does not mean that management is always right and the employees are always wrong, but it does present a potential source of conflict.

Even within a particular stakeholder group there may be conflicting aims. For example, some customers will favour low prices, while others will favour quality.

Table 50.1 summarises the possible aims of each stakeholder group in relation to the activities of the firm. All stakeholders are concerned that the firm they are associated with has a good corporate image. However, the table illustrates the possibilities for conflict between the aims of different groups of stakeholders.

DID YOU KNOW?

If a business is failing, short-term profits and survival are likely to become the most important objectives regardless of its obligations to other stakeholder groups.

Stakeholder group	Aims
Shareholders	Shareholders may want the firm to achieve high profit levels either by keeping costs low or by charging high prices. High profits will in turn allow high dividends to be paid. Shareholders may also wish the firm to achieve a positive corporate image and long-term growth in order to create favourable conditions that will encourage share prices to rise.
Employees	Staff may want job security, good working conditions, high levels of pay, promotional opportunities and job enrichment.
Customers	Customers may want the firm to provide high-quality products and services at low prices, and to offer a good service and a wide choice.
Suppliers	Suppliers may want the firm to provide regular orders, prompt payment and steady growth, leading to more orders in the future.
Local community	The local community may want the firm to provide local employment opportunities and to behave in a socially responsible manner, safe-guarding the environment and accepting the full **social costs** associated with its activities.
Government	The government may want the firm to make efficient use of its resources, to provide employment and training, and to comply with legislation on consumer protection, competition policy, employment, and health and safety.

Table 50.1
The aims of different groups of stakeholders

DID YOU KNOW?

Social costs are the internal or financial costs plus the external costs of an activity. For example, the costs of operating a particular plant include not only the financial or internal costs involved but the costs of pollution and congestion that might be imposed on the local environment as a result of its activities.

Conclusion

A stakeholder can be defined as any person, organisation, interest group or other body that has an interest in the business of an organisation. Stakeholders may be either internal or external to the organisation. On certain issues, stakeholders may share common concerns, while on others they may not. Stakeholders exert their influence over the organisation through the position they hold and the means available to them. Successful modern businesses must prove as effective at managing their stakeholders as they are at managing their market or financial position.

e EXAMINER'S VOICE

Depending on their relationship with the organisation, stakeholders can be divided into two categories:

■ internal stakeholders — owners, shareholders, employees, managers etc.
■ external stakeholders — customers, competitors, suppliers, central and local government agencies, pressure groups, bankers, trade associations etc.

Think about the implications of this division when analysing stakeholder issues.

PRACTICE EXERCISE | Total: 45 marks (45 minutes)

1 Distinguish between the terms 'shareholder' and 'stakeholder'. *(5 marks)*

2 Explain the traditional shareholder approach in relation to the objectives of a business. *(4 marks)*

3 Explain the alternative stakeholder approach in relation to the objectives of a business. *(4 marks)*

4 What are externalities? *(4 marks)*

5 What is meant by the 'win–lose' approach to meeting stakeholder needs? *(3 marks)*

6 How can a 'win–win' approach be applied to meeting stakeholder needs? *(3 marks)*

7 Consider the extent to which different stakeholder groups have aims in common. *(9 marks)*

8 Identify and explain two examples of conflicting stakeholder aims. *(6 marks)*

9 Identify three examples of internal stakeholders and four examples of external stakeholders. *(7 marks)*

CASE STUDY Mr Big the Baker heats up a warmer vision of growth

Ian Gregg lacks both the rotund rosiness of Mr Bunn the Baker in the Happy Families card game and the hard-nosed appearance that might be expected in a businessman who has transformed a single Newcastle bake shop into the UK's largest bakery chain. Gregg, aged 62, is this year expected to quit the board of Greggs — now a company with more than 1,100 outlets and sales of more than £375 million last year — after 40 years at the helm.

The development of Greggs has been characterised by a number of pivotal moments. The first of these was expanding beyond his home territory of Newcastle once he had opened about 20 shops there. According to Gregg, 'The real point of the decision was to move out of having just one bakery, one business site in Tyneside. It was a difficult decision. It would have had its attractions to stay in one area and build up a business focused on excellence.'

The second pivotal moment was floating the company in 1984 to fund long-term expansion. Along with the change to plc status came the appointment of Mike Darrington as managing director. Darrington took the company into the fast-growing market for takeaway sandwiches and savouries such as sausage rolls and pasties that have driven the group's performance against a declining bakery market.

With a new non-executive chairman, Derek Netherton, having taken over from Ian Gregg, Gregg will become a mere shareholder — albeit one of the largest. In this role, he will be better placed to defend what some see as the group's cavalier attitude towards investors, in a strategy that puts shareholders third in line behind employees and customers.

Gregg is unapologetic about this stance, which he says reflects the values and sense of responsibility that underpins the business. 'We will not seek to maximise shareholder value in the short term. We take a lot of flak about it, but if the profit of the

business is the last thing on the page, we try to get the focus on the lines higher up. If you get these right then everyone benefits.'

He is also clear that shareholders have had little cause to complain about the group's financial performance — or its future plans. The business has ambitious expansion plans, with a target of 2,000 shops in the UK and annual sales of £1 billion by the year 2010.

Source: adapted from an article in the *Financial Times*, 4 January 2003.

Questions

Total: 50 marks (60 minutes)

1 Greggs appears to take a stakeholder rather than a shareholder approach to the business. Distinguish between these two approaches and explain what evidence there is to support this view. *(10 marks)*

2 Assess the possible long-term benefits to Greggs of a 'strategy that puts shareholders third in line behind employees and customers'. *(10 marks)*

3 Discuss the aspects of the business in which there is likely to be conflict between the aims of different stakeholders in Greggs? *(15 marks)*

4 To what extent are there likely to be common aims among the different stakeholders in Greggs? *(15 marks)*

CHAPTER 51

SWOT analysis

*To achieve its corporate goal, a company needs a strategy or a plan of action. To produce the plan, it needs to gather information about the business and its market. Such information looks at both internal and external aspects of the business. An **internal audit** assesses the strengths and weaknesses of the firm, and an **external audit** assesses the opportunities and threats present in the environment within which the firm operates. Analysing these **strengths**, **weaknesses**, **opportunities** and **threats** is called **SWOT analysis**. This chapter explains how it is done and assesses its usefulness as a technique.*

Internal audit

KEY TERM

internal audit: assessment of the strengths and weaknesses of a firm in relation to its competitors.

An internal audit involves looking at current resources, how well they are managed and how well they match up to the demands of the market and to competition. It needs to range across all aspects of each of the functional areas. For example:

- **Finance and accounting** — production costs, fixed assets, profitability and liquidity, analysing sales and cost variances, assessing the profitability of past capital investments etc.
- **Marketing** — sales trends for each product, advertising spend per product, size and skills of sales staff, brand loyalty, product pricing, product portfolio, corporate image and reputation etc.
- **Operations management** — trends in production quality, productivity, lead times, stock turnover, levels of innovation, research and development, the appropriateness of location etc.
- **Human resources** — employee motivation, absenteeism, recruitment, selection and training, company structure and organisation etc.

External audit

KEY TERM

external audit: assessment of the opportunities for, and threats to, a firm in the general business environment, i.e. the factors that have the potential to benefit the organisation and the factors that have the potential to cause problems for the organisation.

An external audit involves looking at the possibilities for development in different directions in the future. One method of analysing these external factors is to categorise them according to a **PEST analysis** (see Chapter 35).

> **DID YOU KNOW?**
>
> Remember, PEST stands for political, economic, social, technological. Alternatives to this include STEEP and PESTLE, where 'environmental' or 'legal' and 'environmental' factors are added.

SWOT analysis

> **KEY TERM**
>
> **SWOT analysis:** a technique that allows an organisation to assess its overall position, or the position of one of its divisions, products or activities. The internal audit of the company represents the present position of the product or company (its **strengths** and **weaknesses**), whereas the external audit represents the future potential of the company (its **opportunities** and **threats**).

Once the internal and external audits have been carried out, all of the information obtained is presented in such a way as to assist decision making, usually in the form of a **SWOT analysis**. An example of SWOT analysis is shown in Table 51.1 (see p. 428).

Advantages of SWOT analysis

- It highlights current and potential changes in the market and encourages an outward-looking approach.
- It assists an asset-led approach to marketing by encouraging firms to develop and build upon existing strengths.
- It relates the present position and future potential of a business to the market in which it operates and the competitive forces within it, and is thus an excellent basis on which to make decisions.
- By determining the organisation's position, it influences the strategy that will be employed in order to achieve the organisation's aims and objectives.

> **EXAMINER'S VOICE**
>
> Avoid using bullet points in the examination. You should concentrate on discussing a few points in detail rather than covering a lot of ideas briefly.

Disadvantages of SWOT analysis

A SWOT analysis can be time consuming and the situation — especially the external factors — may change rapidly. Thus organisations must use the results of a SWOT analysis with caution, as a strength may become a weakness or a threat become an opportunity.

> **EXAMINER'S VOICE**
>
> Opportunities and threats are about the future. This fact introduces the issue of uncertainty into any analysis. Remember, therefore, that when considering external factors in a SWOT analysis, the future is uncertain.

INTERNAL FACTORS	
Strengths	**Weaknesses**
• excellent reputation for high-quality products	• reputation as a poor employer
• seen as innovative	• product portfolio has too many products in decline and growth stages, with a shortage of products in maturity
• highly skilled staff, selected through a well-organised recruitment and selection process	• expertise in a limited range of market segments
• sound investment in fixed assets and modern equipment and methods	• limited provision of training for office staff and production-line workers
• an international leader in research and development in its field	• high levels of staff turnover and absenteeism
• an efficient, delayered company structure	• poor accessibility to location of main headquarters
• very profitable in comparison to similar organisations	• communication difficulties between different divisions and subsidiaries
	• low level of liquidity; cash-flow problems in recent years

EXTERNAL FACTORS	
Opportunities	**Threats**
• change in social attitudes towards environmental protection (e.g. green consumers)	• downturn predicted in the business cycle
• low wages and high unemployment levels among local people with appropriate skills	• high levels of competition within the market
• main competitor experiencing financial difficulties	• many new products are being released by new entrants into the market
• government economic policy encouraging more spending	• technological changes mean that recent capital purchases will soon become obsolete
• recent legislation requires many companies to buy one of the firm's pieces of equipment	• an ageing population will mean fewer sales of certain products
• increase in skills-based training schemes	• pressure group activity against the opening of a new factory
• a fall in the exchange rate, helping exporters	• windfall tax on certain companies
• new markets opening up in other parts of the world	increase in interest rates
• social trends will encourage families to purchase more of certain products	

Table 51.1
SWOT analysis

Conclusion

All firms, whether large or small, will do something similar to a SWOT analysis, even if it is not as formalised as discussed here. A large firm will use a formal approach to establish and maintain competitive advantage. It needs the discipline of this approach in order to coordinate action and provide a focus for strategic analysis. A small firm, on the other hand, is likely to conduct a SWOT analysis in a much less formal and much more intuitive way.

 EXAMINER'S VOICE

Always do a SWOT analysis of your pre-issued case study. It will assist you in getting to know the case, in recognising the important issues involved, and in considering the possible strategies and future direction that might be taken.

PRACTICE EXERCISE
Total: 30 marks (25 minutes)

1 What does SWOT stand for? *(4 marks)*

2 Which parts of a SWOT analysis does an internal audit involve? *(2 marks)*

3 Give two examples of possible strengths a business might have in relation to:
  a marketing *(2 marks)*
  b operations management *(2 marks)*

4 Give two examples of possible weaknesses a business might have in relation to:
  a finance and accounting *(2 marks)*
  b people management *(2 marks)*

5 Give two examples of opportunities in the external environment that might be available to a firm. *(2 marks)*

6 Give two examples of threats in the external environment that might confront a firm. *(2 marks)*

7 Which aspects of a SWOT analysis relate to:
  a the present? *(2 marks)*
  b the future? *(2 marks)*

8 Why might issues about uncertainty and time be important considerations in relation to a SWOT analysis? *(4 marks)*

9 Explain one advantage to a business of undertaking a SWOT analysis. *(4 marks)*

GROUP EXERCISE 1
Time allowed: 50 minutes

1 Complete a SWOT analysis of your school/college. In doing so, consider how your school/college can attempt to:
  a minimise the effect of the threats facing it
  b take advantage of the opportunities available to it
  c build on its strengths
  d overcome its weaknesses

2 On the basis of your SWOT analysis, discuss the possible strategies open to your school/college.

GROUP EXERCISE 2
Time allowed: 60 minutes each

Produce a SWOT analysis for each of the two exemplars of pre-released (pre-issued) case studies provided in this book.

The first pre-released case study (Ethel the Pork Pie) is on pp. 302–06 (after Chapter 34).

The second pre-released case study (Cutting Edge) is on pp. 430–34 (immediately after this chapter).

Units 2 and 3

CASE STUDY Cutting Edge

A. 1995 — Strands

Jeannie O'Connor watched as her customer paid and left the salon. She'd been watching for 2 years now — 4 years if she counted her training. It wasn't that the owner of Strands, Simon Parker, didn't pay her well. He did — and well above the minimum wage, but at the same time he was making about five times as much as she was, and yet it was Jeannie who was booked solid 4 weeks in advance!

She had thought about asking him if he had ever considered taking on a partner. She was sure there was potential to expand — open another salon and offer more than just haircuts. She could see the posters...'Get your nails done while your colour takes'...But when she thought about it, she knew that if she went into partnership with Simon, he would be the boss. It was time she took charge of herself. 'The time is definitely right,' she thought to herself. Time to tell Simon she was setting up on her own. She had worked it all out and she was sure that she could cover her costs and make enough to pay herself a decent wage.

'Your next victim's in,' whispered Lily, the receptionist, in her ear, waking her up out of her daydream. Lily was a bit cheeky, but great with the customers and really keen to learn. 'She'd be someone I'd need to take with me,' thought Jeannie as the plan in her head continued to take shape. Of course, Simon would be really fed up if she took his best staff and some of his best customers, but...

B. 2000 — Cutting Edge

Five years later, Jeannie had a large salon in Stafford called Cutting Edge. She knew she was successful because she gave her customers what they wanted. It wasn't just a haircut people came for. It was good coffee, a therapeutic chat, a head massage and a manicure.

Jeannie put her pen down and relaxed back in her chair. She had just finished going through the 1999 figures with her accountant. 'Things are looking OK, aren't they?' she said. 'They certainly are,' said Nigel. 'And you could do more if you had more space and access to more finance. You could consider opening a new salon on the other side of town. You have a great reputation and no one, except Simon Parker at Strands, is a threat.'

Jeannie knew there were new opportunities she should consider. She had been toying with an idea of her own for a few weeks now. One or two things had happened recently that were beginning to worry her a little and she knew she needed to take action.

Lily had left her to go back to Simon. It wasn't the end of the world, but this was the third member of staff whom she had lost in the same way in the last year. And she just couldn't afford to keep losing her best people, especially not when she had spent so much time and effort developing them. It was a shame she didn't have enough jobs to promote everyone. But Lily had never really made it beyond being a fabulous receptionist. Jeannie wondered just how much extra Simon was paying. There was no doubt that Strands was her major competitor and was thriving. Although he didn't offer his customers quite the same level of service (he didn't do nails and his coffee was instant), he gave great haircuts and his prices were just a tiny bit cheaper than hers were.

The details of the new unit available in the brand new shopping mall were just too good to ignore. The mall was a conversion of a huge Victorian warehouse, right by the river in *the* up-and-coming part of town. Fantastic shops and restaurants were being built and lots of trendy businesses were moving in. The trouble was: where would she find the energy, never mind the funds, to open another salon? That was where Simon came in.

Maybe now was the right time to talk to him seriously. They had always stayed on reasonably good terms. He said at the time that he wasn't surprised she was leaving because he had soon spotted her ambition and talent. Wouldn't they be better off working together? After all, she had definitely proved herself now, and there could be no doubt that she was his equal.

C. 2001 — Simon and Jeannie

'Let's keep the name as Cutting Edge. It's better than Strands and suggests that we're innovative and brave,' Simon had said. He and Jeannie had agreed to work together, setting up their new business as a private limited company and renaming his salon as Cutting Edge. Their accountant had suggested becoming a limited company because this might make future expansion easier and allow them some protection from the risks they might encounter.

Jeannie had made the first move, approaching Simon with the idea of opening a salon together in the new shopping mall and with an eye on further openings around the county. They both had a reputation for quality, fashion and innovation, so it seemed a great idea to join forces. Simon had organised some small-scale market research inside the mall, which established that in the 18–35 age range, very few of those interviewed were customers of Cutting Edge or Strands (which were at opposite ends of town), but many had heard of both of them and would consider using a salon that either of them opened here.

So here they were, putting the finishing touches to their new salon.

Because of their individual earlier success, they had no problems in obtaining finance for the new salon and decided to go to town on its interior design work, with up-to-the-minute furnishings, hi-tech equipment, non-stop music and videos, comfortable seating areas and great coffee. Their accountant had helped them with the business plan needed to persuade the bank to lend them finance. They both recognised that this was all so much easier this time around, compared to

when they both started out on their own. For a start, they both had their existing salons to offer as collateral, a track record of running a sound business plus a growing reputation that would reasonably guarantee a sound customer base.

D. 2002 — going regional

Simon and Jeannie worked well together and the new Cutting Edge business was a real success. However, it was restricted to the Stafford area. Jeannie suggested that they should think of expanding by opening salons in other towns in Staffordshire. Although there was plenty of competition, there was no 'name' out there and she felt sure they could establish themselves. The economic conditions were right, interest rates were low and predicted to fall further, and inflation and unemployment were also low (see Table 1). Hairdressing was a highly income-elastic business and so should benefit from this.

Table 1 Selected UK economic indicators, 1999–2003

	1999	2000	2001	2002	2003*
Inflation (%)	1.5	3.0	1.8	1.7	3.0
Unemployment (%)	6.1	5.7	4.9	5.2	5.1
Economic growth (%)	2.4	3.1	2.1	1.9	1.9
Interest rates (%)	5.50	6.00	4.00	4.00	3.75

*Figures are for the first 6 months.

They identified two locations with excellent available premises — in Stoke-on-Trent and in Burton-on-Trent. While Simon concentrated on getting the salons ready, Jeannie worked on recruiting staff — stylists and colourist, trainees and salon managers. It was often a case of attracting or poaching good stylists from other salons. Jeannie knew this was unfair, but it was a characteristic of the industry. She reflected that they ought to have some way of training more of their own staff. At present, as in most small hairdressing businesses, training was on-the-job and a lengthy process — usually at least 2 years.

The two salons quickly built a solid customer base. However, recruitment and training continued to be an issue. Then Jeannie came up with the idea of an academy — that is, a training school for their own trainees. It would mean a consistent and high-quality

training programme for every trainee plus regular updating and professional development for experienced staff. Simon and Jeannie and some of the very experienced managers would do the teaching. Simon was very enthusiastic about Jeannie's idea and thought it would be a great way of providing the business with a good source of trained staff, at the same time as improving skills and motivation and assisting them in their workforce planning.

E. 2003 — A-level business studies and the Mailbox

Jeannie's niece, Amy, who worked as a trainee on Saturdays and sometimes on late-night openings, was at college studying for A-levels. One day she asked Jeannie if she could use the chain of salons as a base for her business studies coursework. She wanted to do a project on motivation and leadership. Jeannie talked to Simon and they both agreed that Amy could go ahead as long as she shared her findings with them. This was timely, as recently they had begun to have slight concerns about some of the salons, but as takings were not down, they had not pursued these. The findings from the project might highlight some important issues that they were unaware of.

The business prospered and Martin, one of their top stylists, won the Hairdresser of the Year Award. He had come in the top ten in each of the last 2 years, but his top position this year was a real coup for him and possibly for Cutting Edge if he stayed with them. The problem was: would Martin be poached or be looking to leave? Cutting Edge couldn't offer him promotion, as he was already their top stylist.

They organised a coach to take all the staff from the salons down to London for the award. Jeannie sat next to Martin on the way home from London. It turned out that his aim was to manage his own salon. When he said this, Jeannie's heart sank — what a competitor he would be! But Martin went on to say that he didn't want his own business; he just wanted to manage a top-class salon. He had apparently spotted a fantastic site in the Mailbox, the exclusive shopping centre in the centre of Birmingham, which included Harvey Nichols and other designer shops. Jeannie's mind raced on.

Simon agreed that it was a fantastic idea. They had the funds to rent and refurbish the unit to the high standard it would require. Martin was thrilled; Cutting Edge opened its sixth, but most exclusive, salon in the Mailbox shopping centre. With Martin's personal status as Hairdresser of the Year and the fact that Cutting Edge already had a good reputation, it went with a bang. Martin was an excellent manager as well as a top-class stylist. The only thing was that he made absolutely clear to Simon and Jeannie that he did not want them interfering. They were a little surprised that he raised this, as they hadn't thought of themselves as interfering but, given his status and their need to keep him in the business, they made sure they didn't interfere at all.

Amy's coursework project was nearly complete and a meeting was arranged for them to discuss her findings. These came as quite a shock to Simon and Jeannie. According to her findings, in most of the salons, junior staff appeared really to enjoy their jobs — they thought their pay and conditions were great and they realised that the training they received was excellent. However, for senior staff and managers there was a different story — pay and conditions were fine, but they felt that they had little freedom to make decisions and many of them would leave if an opportunity arose.

Simon and Jeannie were surprised and queried the findings, but Amy said, 'I'm sorry, Jeannie, but you know that you and Simon make all the decisions and get quite shirty if anyone tries to use their initiative or authority. Quite often when I've been working on a Saturday and something comes up for the manager to decide, she says, "I'd better check it out with the top — you know what they're like if we don't consult them about everything."' Simon said, 'Do you think everyone thinks like this?' 'Yes,' said Amy quietly. 'Why do you think Martin was so adamant that you shouldn't interfere?' Jeannie admitted, 'I suppose they're right — I hadn't thought about other people's needs. I just thought that if all our staff were paid well and had good conditions, they'd be happy. How stupid of me. That was exactly why I left you and Strands in the first place! We must change our management approach if we are going to keep our staff and keep them happy.'

F. 2003 — going national and formalising the organisation

Simon and Jeannie met with their accountant, Nigel, to discuss the performance of Cutting Edge, its future and the bombshell Amy had dropped. Nigel was great — a skilled accountant but also a great business adviser, who had encouraged Jeannie from the start. He suggested they consider opening salons in Bristol and Leeds and then eventually in London, in order to build on their high profile and to establish a national rather than just a regional reputation. If the right properties and locations could be found, the business was bound to follow. Funding was not an issue. However, before they considered this, he suggested that they needed to review the organisation of the business.

To date, Simon and Jeannie had done everything themselves with varying levels of success. They had no organisational chart and no management structure as such. They were the two owners who did all the centralised tasks and generally ran the whole show, although each salon did have its own manager. Nigel suggested an organisational structure similar to that in Figure 1. Simon and Jeannie said they needed to think about this. It looked as if it took a lot of power and control away from them and, in addition, they were concerned about the fact that external appointments might need to be made for some staff. Since introducing the academy, they had always promoted internally to fill senior appointments.

Nigel also suggested that, as the business had grown so much and still had the potential to grow further, they should formalise their aims and objectives. He had mentioned this before to them, and Simon and Jeannie had been thinking about it and had already arranged a general meeting of all staff — salon managers, stylists, colourists and trainees — to discuss the aim they had come up with:

'To remain at the cutting edge of hair styling and colouring for all our customers.'

They hoped to get all staff to agree to this and then to agree objectives for the business as a whole for the next 5 years and also for each salon. They wondered if they should allow each salon to set its own objectives or whether they should impose general objectives on all salons.

G. 2004 — the future

The business was nationally recognised, but Nigel, their accountant, suggested an urgent meeting next week. He outlined the problems briefly on the phone. Some of their salons had suffered quite poor performance last year. Capacity utilisation at the Stafford salon was down. A closer look at demand at these salons showed staff being under-utilised as client appointments had fallen. Identifying the reason was easy: a major chain from London — Macey and Josh — had been expanding throughout the country. The problem was that it was very good and did excellent marketing in the national press and occasionally on television. This was worrying and needed serious consideration. Hairdressing was a very competitive business — salons appeared and disappeared regularly. Despite this, there were only one or two big, national players who posed a threat, and Macey and Josh was one of them.

Figure 1 *Cutting Edge: proposed organisational structure*

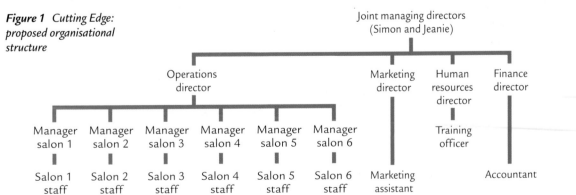

Macey and Josh was renowned for the quality of its approach, its adherence to all sorts of standards and legal requirements, particularly in the areas of health and safety and employment, and it was certainly the organisation against which others in the industry would benchmark their actions. Cutting Edge had never paid such close attention to quality. Good staff had been rewarded financially and those who provided a poor quality of customer service had received less money. This approach seemed to have worked, as the less efficient staff had found employment elsewhere.

Compared to Cutting Edge, Macey and Josh was also highly innovative and had patented a speedy and effective computerised imaging process that was available in each of its salons. This involved clients being photographed and then being able to play about with the computerised image, changing their hairstyles and colours. There had been an article in *Hairdressing Monthly* about it, not only explaining how it worked but also identifying the issues that people were concerned about or encouraged by. For example, some wondered whether it would reduce the need for advice from stylists and colourists (a part of the job that good staff took very seriously and felt highlighted their skill and creativity), while others suggested that it would enhance this aspect of their job.

At the same time as Macey and Josh was setting up salons in the regions, adverse publicity hit Cutting Edge. It resulted from an incident in Stafford concerning one of their salons. The colour applied to a number of clients' hair had caused a rash that appeared to be due to the dye rather than to an allergic reaction on the part of the clients. The story ran for days in the local press and damaged the firm's reputation for some time. As a result, they reviewed the contract they had with their supplier and the products they were actually using. The supplier was a large national wholesaler that they had chosen because it was cheap, as were the products they purchased.

It was impossible to prove that the supplier was at fault and Cutting Edge suffered from a high level of stock wastage as a result.

They decided to change to a smaller manufacturer of quality hair care products that was prepared to deliver throughout the country. The products were significantly more expensive, but they decided that this was a price they needed to pay in order to re-establish their reputation and ensure that no conflict between ethical behaviour and profitable behaviour ever occurred again.

Because the products they began to use had a reputation for quality, they tied this change in with another business development that was aimed at improving their marketing and pushing their national reputation further — the introduction of their own branded hair care products: Cutting Edge shampoo, conditioner and other hair care products. This meant they could purchase the stocks for use in the salons and for sale to clients, leading to economies in buying. They kept the same manufacturer, who was very pleased with the contract and was prepared to be quite flexible, producing the products they wanted on a batch basis in order to meet their needs. Because the salons did not have much storage space, the supplier also agreed to a just-in-time delivery system for its products. The salons would ring the supplier with their needs at the end of every day and have them delivered very early the following day.

Despite the setbacks, Simon and Jeannie were convinced that Cutting Edge was a match for Macey and Josh if they began to advertise more extensively and publicise their own strengths. The meeting next week would need to consider all of these issues and their overall competitive position in the market in order to decide the way forward.

Source: Sections A and B of this case study were written by Jenny Hendon who teaches business studies at Walton High School in Stafford.

Unit 2: People in Organisations and Operations Management

PAPER A

Questions

Total: 50 marks (60 minutes)

1 Briefly explain how an organisational structure such as that provided in Figure 1 would improve the effectiveness of management at Cutting Edge. *(Section F)* *(6 marks)*

2 Examine whether economies of scale could contribute significantly to the success of a business such as Cutting Edge. *(8 marks)*

3 With reference to theories of motivation, discuss the possible reasons why the senior staff and management at Cutting Edge are not motivated. *(15 marks)*

4 Explain whether Cutting Edge has been affected by market failure in relation to staff recruitment. *(6 marks)*

5 To what extent can just-in-time production be usefully applied to a service business such as Cutting Edge? *(15 marks)*

PAPER B

Questions

Total: 50 marks (60 minutes)

1 Explain how benchmarking against Macey and Josh might improve the performance of Cutting Edge. *(6 marks)*

2 Analyse the implications of a reduction in capacity utilisation for Cutting Edge. *(Section G)* *(8 marks)*

3 To what extent has a centralised approach to the management structure of Cutting Edge been effective? *(15 marks)*

4 Explain how workforce planning might help to improve the effectiveness of Cutting Edge. *(6 marks)*

5 Discuss the benefits and problems of introducing a system of 'quality assurance' at Cutting Edge. *(15 marks)*

Unit 3: External Influences and Objectives and Strategy

PAPER A

Questions
Total: 50 marks (60 minutes)

1 Briefly explain how the degree of competition in the hairdressing industry has affected Cutting Edge. *(6 marks)*

2 Explain why it might be important for Cutting Edge to agree formal aims and objectives with all staff. *(8 marks)*

3 Discuss how successful Simon and Jeannie have been in identifying profitable opportunities and in building a customer base. *(15 marks)*

4 Explain the effect on the staff of Cutting Edge if the business decides to introduce the new technology that is currently used by Macey and Josh. *(Section G)* *(6 marks)*

5 Evaluate the possible conflict between ethical behaviour and profitable behaviour for a business such as Cutting Edge. *(15 marks)*

PAPER B

Questions
Total: 50 marks (60 minutes)

1 Why might becoming a private limited company have made 'future expansion easier' for Cutting Edge? *(6 marks)*

2 To what extent have low interest rates assisted the development and success of Cutting Edge? *(15 marks)*

3 Explain why consumer protection legislation might be considered a threat to Cutting Edge. *(8 marks)*

4 With reference to Macey and Josh's computerised imaging process, explain the benefits of patenting a business idea. *(6 marks)*

5 To what extent might there be a conflict between the aims of the various stakeholders in Cutting Edge? *(15 marks)*

Index

Index

Index